BRITAIN'S KOREAN WAR

Manchester University Press

# Britain's Korean War

Cold War diplomacy, strategy and security
1950–53

*Thomas Hennessey*

Manchester University Press

Copyright © Thomas Hennessey 2013

The right of Thomas Hennessey to be identified as the author of this work has been asserted by him in accordance with the Copyright, Designs and Patents Act 1988.

Published by Manchester University Press
Altrincham Street, Manchester M1 7JA, UK
www.manchesteruniversitypress.co.uk

*British Library Cataloguing-in-Publication Data is available*

*Library of Congress Cataloging-in-Publication Data is available*

ISBN 978 0 7190 9738 6 *paperback*

First published by Manchester University Press in hardback 2013

This paperback edition first published 2015

The publisher has no responsibility for the persistence or accuracy of URLs for any external or third-party internet websites referred to in this book, and does not guarantee that any content on such websites is, or will remain, accurate or appropriate.

Printed by Lightning Source

For Sean Greenwood

# Contents

| | |
|---|---|
| Abbreviations | viii |
| Introduction | 1 |
| 1  Invasion | 6 |
| 2  To cross or not to cross: the 38th parallel | 47 |
| 3  Enter the dragon: China's first intervention | 75 |
| 4  Attlee in Washington | 108 |
| 5  Divisions: January 1951 | 135 |
| 6  MacArthur goes | 169 |
| 7  The long war | 204 |
| 8  Breakthrough | 227 |
| 9  Manchurian candidates | 242 |
| Epilogue: Bermuda | 262 |
| Conclusion | 279 |
| Bibliography | 284 |
| Index | 291 |

# Abbreviations

| | |
|---|---|
| BJSM | British Joint Services Mission |
| BRPWIU | British Repatriated Prisoner of War Interrogation Unit |
| CAS | Chief of the Air Staff |
| CIGS | Chief of the Imperial General Staff |
| CMC | Collective Measures Committee |
| CPG | Chinese Peoples' Government |
| DBOP | *Documents on British Overseas Policy* |
| FRUS | *Foreign Relations of the United States* |
| GA | General Assembly |
| HMG | His/Her Majesty's Government |
| IRD | Information Research Department |
| JCS | Joint Chiefs of Staff |
| JIC | Joint Intelligence Committee |
| MI5 | Security Service |
| NATO | North Atlantic Treaty Organisation |
| NCO | Non-commissioned officer |
| NSC | National Security Council |
| POW | Prisoner of War |
| PRC | Peoples' Republic of China |
| RAF | Royal Air Force |
| RNVR | Royal Navy Volunteer Reserve |
| ROK | Republic of Korea |
| UNO | United Nations Organisation |
| UNSC | United Nations Security Council |

# Introduction

This book is a study of Britain's diplomatic, military and security policy during the Korean War as seen from the perspective of the British Government. This subject has attracted a limited, albeit, significant interest, among historians in contrast to what may be regarded as the defining event of the 1950s UK–US 'special relationship': the Suez crisis of 1956. Essentially, at various times, critics have argued that, in Danchev's description, the 'special relationship is not what it was, nor what its fervent believers would like it to be. The party is over, but the guests linger, reluctant to separate, spellbound by the storied past'.[1] But, despite its often predicted demise, Marsh and Baylis have termed this 'special relationship' the 'Lazarus' of international relations. They argue that its survival owes much to four principal continuities in the post-Second World War approach of British foreign policy-making: a determination that Britain remain a global actor; the continuing reality of US power; an enduring calculation that a position closely related to, but independent of, the United States has best served UK interests since the Second World War; and a persistent assumption that 'a combination of consanguinity and superior British diplomatic wisdom that allows British policy-makers to guide the naïve American giant'. A series of other continuities, suggest Marsh and Baylis, have flowed directly from the last of these to underpin Anglo-American cooperation, irrespective of periodic differences and international systemic change. The first of these is the continuing importance of the symbols, memories and practices to Anglo-American 'specialness'. The second is a consistent willingness of British policy-makers to 'pay the price' of making the 'special relationship' forward-looking and relevant to the United States. And, thirdly, UK policy-makers have employed a number of strategies designed to reinforce the Anglo-American relationship and guard against American 'desertion'.² In the context of the early Cold War an assessment of Anglo-American interaction in diplomacy has to take into account how, in Warner's description, the disparity of power and influence between the UK and United States, during 1950, 'clearly show the dangers inherent in such a "special" relationship'.³

Why Britain was even involved in the Korean War is important as the origins of the conflict are of academic controversy themselves. Cummings advanced the 'civil war' thesis as a conflict emerging from a series of border clashes along the 38th parallel; this is his 'second mosaic' argument: that South Korea provoked the war by its actions on the Ongjin peninsula and the North's counter-attack; the 'first mosaic' thesis is the view that the Soviet Union and North Korea launched a surprise attack on the South; the 'third mosaic' thesis is the claim that the South launched a planned attack on the North. Youngho Kim's view, however, maintains that Soviet documents reveal the border conflicts were the 'focal point around which the strategic calculations' of Stalin and North Korea were made.⁴ The evidence provided for this interpretation appears convincing.

In the main British participation in the Korean conflict has been the preserve of a number of pioneering articles and chapters. At the centre of such works continues to be an attempt to understand the dynamics of the Anglo-American relationship, articulating differing degrees of British influence on American policy, during the war. MacDonald, on the other hand, has argued that: 'There is no evidence that British pressure prevented the Americans from adopting any course which they might otherwise have taken in the Far East.' It was London and not Washington which made compromises for the sake of the 'special relationship'. Korea exposed British illusions about guiding the American colossus and revealed, well before Suez in 1956, the shift towards US hegemony within the Atlantic alliance.⁵ Lowe, agrees, concluding that the significance of the war, for Anglo-American relations, was that 'it demonstrated beyond doubt how dependent Britain was upon the United States and that no special relationship existed'.⁶ However, Lowe also appears to contradict himself, elsewhere, suggesting that President Truman's dismissal of the commander of United Nation (UN) forces, General MacArthur, in April 1951, was an example where 'British protests propelled Truman towards the point of decision'.⁷ Belmonte, though, disagrees with this and, convincingly, demonstrates that 'British pressure was less significant than the internal strategic and political calculations bearing on Washington's decision-making. The Truman administration did something the British wanted, but for its own reasons and to suit its own perceived interests.'⁸ That there was, certainly, a British belief that they could influence the Americans is the argument put forward by Ruane and Ellison: in 1952, the Foreign Secretary, Anthony Eden, raised the concept of 'power-by-proxy' from a desire to a need, given a recurrence of Britain's balance of payments crisis with the goal of maintaining the UK's position as a world power.[9] As Dockrill has pointed out, the Foreign Office and its political masters regarded the United States as 'relatively inexperienced in world affairs' and so 'would be willing to listen to the sage advice of a more mature' United Kingdom. For: 'British diplomats regarded the Americans as mercurial people who could not be relied on to follow a consistent course'; and so 'only continuing British moderating pressure would keep the US administration on the right lines'.[10]

Greenwood highlights the limits of British influence in Washington, pointing out that British success in moderating Truman's rhetoric in condemning world communism only succeeded in 'fostering the illusion that the Americans would be susceptible to more general counsels of moderation from London'.[11] He argues that Bevin should have been able to see that, to Washington, Britain 'was not especially special'[12] and contends there was never any serious question of breaking with the Americans, quoting Aneurin Bevan's comment to Kenneth Younger that 'if the clash came, we could do nothing but support the Americans. "When you are in a world-wide alliance, you cannot retreat from it on a single issue"'.[13] But this was uttered by Bevan in August 1950, not in January 1951, when a majority of the Cabinet took the view that supporting the Americans in a condemnatory resolution of Communist China, in the United Nations, was likely to begin a process leading to extending the Korean War into World War III. Nevertheless, Greenwood concludes that the United Kingdom had 'welded themselves to a demanding and difficult partner who proved essentially impervious to the British point of view no matter how politely presented'.[14] But, equally, Yasamee's suggestion that the British came close to severing the 'special relationship' with Washington in January 1951[15] amplifies diplomatic differences over one issue within a wider complex series of other issues that bound British and American concerns into a strategic community of interest. The Americans were, of course, influenced by events on the ground. Foot points out that the military setbacks following Communist China's entry into the war, in November 1950, made Washington 'more receptive' to other Powers' opinions with the result that 'British intervention at a time when a loss of [US] confidence and international criticism were at their height reinforced still further US doubts about entering into a new and more dangerous phase of the conflict in which America would stand virtually alone.'[16]

This study argues that the British did have – albeit a limited – influence over American decision-making during the Korean War. While Lowe is correct to state it 'is a myth that Attlee's famous visit to Washington in December 1951 saved the world from a wider war' and that British diplomacy was frustrated by the realities of power,[17] it is argued in this book that comments such as this deal in absolutes and misunderstand the complexities of coalition politics in war, however great the might of the dominant power in the alliance. The study also takes issue with Lowe's assertion that Eisenhower, President from 1953, showed a 'balanced, sensible approach and normally concluded his assessments by rejecting dangerous courses of action.' Lowe argues that the United States was closer to using the bomb in November–December 1950, under Truman, than in 1953[18] whereas the work of Foot illustrates how real was Eisenhower's claim that he was prepared to use atomic weapons. Eisenhower was prepared was use atomic weapons on strategic targets in North Korea, Manchuria and on the Chinese coast.[19] Instead, it is argued that Eisenhower's acceptance of the legitimacy of atomic weapons in general warfare spurred the British on to, in Ruane's phrase, 'contain' the United States.[20] It was the British experience in the Korean War that led them to this conclusion.

## Notes

1. Alex Danchev, 'The Cold War "Special relationship" Revisited', *Diplomacy & Statecraft*, 17 (2006), p. 579. Please note that where multiple quotations are taken from a single source, the source is indicated by a note on the final quotation
2. Steve Marsh and John Baylis, 'The Anglo-American "Special Relationship": The Lazarus of International Relations', *Diplomacy & Statecraft*, 17 (2006), p. 174
3. Geoffrey Warner, 'Anglo-American Relations and the Cold War in 1950', *Diplomacy & Statecraft,* 22:1 (2011), p. 58
4. Youngho Kim, 'The Origins of the Korean War: Civil War of Stalin's Rollback', *Diplomacy & Statecraft*, 10:1 (1999), pp. 187–189
5. Callum MacDonald, *Britain and the Korean War* (Oxford: Blackwell, 1990), pp. 95–96
6. Peter Lowe, 'The Significance of the Korean War in Anglo-American Relations 1950–53', in Michael Dockrill and John W. Young (eds), *British Foreign Policy 1945–51* (London: Macmillan, 1989), p. 145
7. Peter Lowe, 'An Ally and a Reluctant General: Great Britain, Douglas MacArthur and the Korean War 1950–51', *English Historical Review*, 105:416 (1990), p. 652
8. Laura Belmonte, 'Anglo-American Relations and the Dismissal of MacArthur', *Diplomatic History*, 19:4 (1995), pp. 641–667

9 Kevin Ruane and James Ellison, 'Managing the Americans: Anthony Eden, Harold Macmillan and the Pursuit of "Power-Proxy" in the 1950s', *Contemporary British History*, 18:3 (2004), p. 148
10 Michael Dockrill, 'The Foreign Office, Anglo-American Relations and the Korean War, June 1950–June 1951', *International Affairs*, 62:3 (1986), pp. 474–475
11 Sean Greenwood, '"A War We Don't Want": Another Look at the British Labour Government's Commitment in Korea, 1950–51', *Contemporary British History*, 17:4 (2003), p. 5
12 *Ibid.*, p. 9
13 *Ibid.*, p. 19
14 *Ibid.*, p. 20. Interestingly his undergraduate student, Claire Thomas, argued the opposite in her dissertation on Attlee's visit to Washington in December 1950 – and which her supervisor – Sean Greenwood – conceded that he agreed with her and had to modify his views!
15 Heather Yasamee, 'Britain, Korea and the Politics of Power by Proxy', Foreign and Commonwealth Office Historical Branch Occasional Papers, No. 5, *Korea*, April 1992, p. 18
16 R.J. Foot, 'Anglo-American Relations in the Korean Crisis: The British Effort to Avert an Expanded War December 1950–January 1951', *Diplomatic History*, 10 (1986), p. 57; see also J.Y. Ra, 'Special Relationship at War: The Anglo-American Relationship during the Korean War', *Journal of Strategic Studies*, 7:3 (1984), pp. 301–317; Roger Dingman, 'Truman, Attlee and the Korean War Crisis', in Ian Nish (ed.), *The East Asian Crisis: The Problem of China, Korea and Japan* (London: London School of Economics and Political Science, 1982), pp. 1–42; William Stueck, 'The Limits of Influence: British Policy and American Expansion of the War in Korea', *Pacific Historical Review*, 55 (1986), pp. 65–95
17 MacDonald, *Britain and the Korean War*, p. 95
18 Peter Lowe, *Containing the Cold War in East Asia: British Policies Towards Japan, China and Korea 1948–53* (Manchester: Manchester University Press, 1997), pp. 256–257
19 R.J. Foot, *The Wrong War: American Policy and the Dimensions of the Korean Conflict, 1950–1953* (Ithaca: Cornell University Press, 1985), p. 205
20 Kevin Ruane, '"Containing America": Aspects of British Foreign Policy and the Cold War in South-East Asia 1951–54', *Diplomacy & Statecraft*, 7:1 (1996), pp. 141–174

# 1

# Invasion

By mid-1950 the Grand Alliance of Great Britain, the United States and the Soviet Union, that had defeated the Third Reich in 1945 had collapsed into two armed camps of East and West. On the one side stood the democracies of Britain and the United States, defending the recovering countries of Western Europe; and, on the other, stood the Soviet dominated states of Eastern Europe. As Winston Churchill had expressed it, an Iron Curtain had fallen across the continent. Of the Big Three wartime leaders who had been in office when their country had embarked upon war with Germany, only Generalissimo Joseph Stalin survived in power. As Soviet Russia feared the West, so the British and Americans feared the East. It appeared to the British that Stalin sought to supplement Communist dominance in Central and Eastern Europe with forays elsewhere in the world. The British were fighting Communist insurgents in Malaya while the French were fighting against similar foes in Indo-China. When Nationalist China fell to the Communists in 1949 the number of the world's population under Marxist-Leninism doubled at a stroke. But it was in Europe that Britain's fears of Soviet moves were focused the most. And the task of devising the strategy of defending the United Kingdom fell to the Chiefs of G Staff: the Chief of the Imperial General Staff (CIGS), Field Marshall Sir William Slim, representing the British Army; the First Sea Lord, Lord Fraser representing the Royal Navy; and Chief of the Air Staff (CAS), Sir John Slessor, representing the Royal Air Force (RAF).

These were the men who had to assess the strategic threat to the United Kingdom and its worldwide interests. On 7 June 1950, in their 'Allied defence Policy and Global Strategy' paper, the Chiefs set out, as the 'first essential' to define clearly the political and military aim – of Britain and her Allies – in the struggle against Russian Communism. They concluded that the 'enemy's aim is quite clear – it is a communist world dominated by Moscow'. They were worried that Allied defence policy had been confused by the lack of a clear definition 'of what we are fighting for and by a failure to recognise that our aim in this struggle, in its present "cold" phase as well as in a possible "hot" phase, must be consistent'. The Chiefs concluded that Allied defence policy 'cannot be divided into water-tight compartments of "cold" and "hot" strategy'. The former was largely conditioned by the ability, in the last resort, to defend Allied interests against armed aggression; while Allied readiness to fight defensively was inevitably affected by the demands of the Cold War: 'Our aim must be to reduce to the minimum the extent to which it is so affected, but not to the fatal compromise of our ability to win the cold war which is rightly our first defence priority.'

The aim in the Cold War, 'which must be achieved if possible without real hostilities', involved 'first a stabilisation of the anti-communist front in the present free world' and then, as the Western powers became militarily less weak, the intensification of 'cold' offensive measures aimed at weakening the Russian grip on the satellite states and ultimately achieving their complete independence of Russian control. The aim in a Hot War, if real hostilities were forced upon the Western Allies, would remain broadly the same: 'Our first preoccupation must be to ensure survival in the face of the initial onslaught. Our ultimate military aim must be to bring the war to the speediest possible conclusion, without Western Europe being overrun, by bringing about the destruction of Russian military power and the collapse of the present regime.'

The Chiefs had concluded that Russian policy was 'fundamentally opportunist and the Soviet will always exploit any weaknesses – especially the weakness inherent in a lack of unified policy on the part of the Western democracies'. But historically, also, the Russians, whilst always aggressively expansionist in policy, 'do draw back when faced with determined opposition, a characteristic which communist Russia appears to share with imperial Russian policy – the tactical withdrawal when conditions are unfavourable'. The Chiefs, therefore, cautioned that the West should not be unduly impressed by the 'war of nerves' which would undoubtedly continue with varying intensity over the coming years: 'The war of nerves by Hitler from 1933 to 1939 was in many ways similar to the present cold war, and the history of that period is eloquent proof of what happens if foreign policy and military preparedness do not march closely in step.' The Chiefs recommended that: 'We should bear always in mind that half of the Russian "split mind" is traditionally defensive and – however unreasonably today – genuinely apprehensive of attack by the Western Powers; we should, therefore, give the Russians no ground for a degree of apprehension that might drive them to a preventive war.' Short of that, however, the Chiefs were of the opinion that:

> we should not be unduly anxious about provoking the Russians. If it suited them to embark on armed aggression they would do so without waiting for provocation; they have no public opinion capable of rushing their government into hostilities against their better judgment; and their acceptance of our moral victory in the Berlin airlift (when, if ever, they were in a position to defeat us if they had chosen to resort to force) shows that their historic tendency to hold back in the face of determined opposition still holds good.

The Chiefs described the current phase of East–West relations as the 'deterrent phase'. Western military weakness as a whole was now such that, from the purely military point of view, 'Russia could march to the Atlantic at any moment.' That she had not done so, 'and in our view is unlikely to do so', was due to her realisation that a certain consequence of aggression would be war with the United States involving 'immediate retribution in the form of the atomic weapon'. Russia was not prepared for a long-drawn-out struggle with the prospect of ultimate defeat in face of the superior war-making capacity of the United States and the British Commonwealth. The '"Pax Atlantica" rests to-day on the atomic weapon as the Pax Britannica rested in the 19th century on the British Fleet'.

The Chiefs then identified the three main theatres in which Allied interests were threatened: Western Europe, the Middle East and East Asia. The Chiefs were of the opinion that: 'European civilisation could not survive a Russian occupation of a Western Europe.' It would only be with the utmost difficulty and sacrifice that Britain could survive, 'as she did last time', an enemy occupation of Channel and Atlantic coasts. In the long run 'the rest of the free world could not survive the submergence of Europe and Britain'. It was clear, therefore, that the defence of Western Europe, initially at least as far as East of the Rhine, was absolutely vital. Militarily, this meant that the defence of Europe – including the United Kingdom – 'must have top priority. The primary offensive weapon in hot war must remain the atomic bomb'.

The second most important theatre was the defence of the Middle East which had 'always been one of the three pillars of British defence policy and it is of equally critical importance in Allied strategy'. It was the land bridge between Europe, Asia and Africa and a most important link in the Commonwealth system of sea and air communications. Its oil supplies were of very great importance, and, if it fell under Russian influence, 'the repercussions on the whole Moslem world from French North Africa through Pakistan to South East Asia would be critically serious'. There could be no doubt that to retain the countries of the Middle East within the Western orbit was 'a vital cold war measure, and we must be prepared to make military sacrifices to that end'.

The Chiefs considered the key to the Cold War problem in the Far East to be China. Allied policy in that direction, 'while inflexibly anti-communist, should not be anti-Chinese'. It was important that 'we should not drive China irrevocably into the arms of Russia'. The Chiefs accepted that there was room for doubt whether the inherent xenophobia of the Chinese would submit to Russian any more than to any other foreign intervention. The problem of the 'unassimilated' Chinese and 'hence our internal security difficulties' in British and French dependent territories could only be aggravated by the permanent hostility of the new China. This should involve no policy of appeasement. Unlike the Americans the British had, in recognising the Communist Chinese People's Republic, taken the line that their system of government was a matter for the Chinese themselves. The aim with Chinese Communism, however, 'must be the same as that with Russia – to confine it within the borders of China'; and the Allies should react firmly and vigorously 'to any threat of its extension'. Therefore:

> The front line of the cold war in Asia lies in Indo-China. If that front gives way it is only a matter of time before Siam and Burma fall under communist influence. In that event our difficulties in Malaya would become almost insuperable and ultimately communism would probably prevail throughout Malaya and the Archipelago. Nothing is more important than to make sure that the French restore order and establish a stable and ultimately independent friendly government in Indo-China.

The history of the previous three years left no room for doubt, in the Chiefs' minds, that from a military point of view the most important object of British foreign policy in the Far East should be to achieve a firm unity of policy between the British Commonwealth, the United States and France. 'Nothing could suit our enemies better than for the Western Powers to pursue divergent objectives in the Far East and South-East Asia' considered the Chiefs. The aim of a unified policy should be to resist the encroachments of communism beyond the borders of China and thus enable the French, and to a lesser extent the British, to reduce their garrisons and devote resources now tied up in the jungles of Indo-China and Malaya to the 'really vital' end – the defence of Western Europe.[1] There was no mention of Korea in all of this. It just was not a strategic concern in the British view of Cold War priorities. The very idea that Korea would be the principal theatre in which East and West turned the Cold War into a Hot War seemed absurd at the beginning of June 1950. That view changed a few days later.

Politically, Korea was a divided nation by 1950. Its population had suffered terribly under a three-decade occupation by the Japanese Empire. During the Second World War, at the Cairo Conference, in 1943, Franklin Roosevelt, Winston Churchill and Chang Kai-shek, of China, met to decide what should become of Japan's colonies after the war. They decided that 'all the territories Japan has stolen from the Chinese, such as Manchuria, Formosa and the Pescadores, shall be restored to the Republic of China … in due course Korea shall become free and independent'. Following the surrender of Japan, in 1945, the United States and the Soviet Union agreed to temporarily occupy Korea between them using the 38th parallel as the dividing line between the two. The Americans occupied the territory south of the parallel while the Russians took the area north of it. The Americans were only interested in Korea – if Communists came to power there – as a potential threat to Japan. In 1947, the fledgeling United Nations Organisation (UNO) passed a resolution announcing that free elections should be held across Korea. It also declared that foreign troops should withdraw, and created a UN Commission to oversee progress. The Soviets boycotted the vote and claimed that the resolution was invalid as a result. The man the United States picked to be their agent in securing South Korea from Communisation was the fervent nationalist, Syngman Rhee, who returned from a long exile in America. He was committed to the reunification of the Korean peninsula by either peaceful or violent means. The South held elections in 1947; in 1948, Rhee became the first president of South Korea. The same year most US forces left the new country. As they did so, Rhee crushed leftist opponents in the South. In the North, meanwhile, the Soviets established a puppet regime, the North Korean Provisional People's Committee, under the leadership of Kim Il-Sung, a former guerrilla leader who had fought against the Japanese occupation. Kim was also committed to the unification of Korea.

Before Kim could fulfil his ambition to unite Korea under his rule he had to get the consent of Moscow. This meant the go ahead from Joseph Stalin. Kim first requested Stalin's permission to invade South Korea, while on a visit to Moscow, in March 1947. Stalin was reluctant. He pointed out to Kim that the United States might interfere; instead Stalin offered the prospect of a South Korean attack on the North – which would result in Soviet support to repel it. Given the dire state of the North Korean forces,

Kim could not instigate a war without Stalin's support. But then Stalin suddenly gave Kim his support for an attack. Kim had kept pushing to be given the green light from Moscow. There were already fierce clashes occurring between Northern and Southern factions on the 38th parallel. And Kim had thousands of Communist guerrillas operating in South Korean territory. But what seems to have changed Stalin's mind was the dramatic change in the Chinese civil war during 1949.[2]

In China, bordering both the Soviet Union and North Korea, Mao Zedong had finally driven Chang Kai-shek's Kuomintang forces off the mainland to the island of Formosa (Taiwan). Mao established the People's Republic of China. While the British recognised Communist China as the *de facto* Chinese Government, the United States, with a strong pro-Chang Kai-sheik lobby in Congress, refused; instead the Americans supported the retention of the Nationalist Chinese Government in exile on Formosa as one of the permanent members of the UN Security Council. Mao and Stalin rejected this. Unsurprisingly, on 30 June 1949, Mao issued his 'lean-one-side' statement – that was to ally Communist China 'with the Soviet Union, with the People's Democratic countries, and with the proletariat and the broad masses of the people in all other countries, and form a united front ... We must lean to one side'.[3] While Mao was keen to finish the job and invade Formosa, Stalin encouraged Peking (Beijing) to support Kim's ambitions in Korea instead. Stalin, though, put the onus on Kim to gain Mao's acceptance for the attack. He also emphasised to Kim that, if things went wrong, the North Koreans would have to look to the Chinese not the Soviets for help – Stalin still feared American intervention. But the job had to be done quickly. Kim assured Comrade Stalin that North Korea would be victorious in three days. After Kim approached Mao, the latter cast doubt on the operation. Stalin, however, informed Mao he agreed with Kim's proposal – but the final decision had to be made jointly by 'Chinese and Korean comrades'. Mao agreed albeit reluctantly.[4] Stalin's position might, he thought, have removed Moscow from the scene of the crime but, without his permission, there would have been no invasion of South Korea.

At 0400 hrs on 25 June 1950, North Korean Forces launched attacks across the 38th parallel followed, at 1100 hrs, by a declaration of war by North Korea against the Republic of (South) Korea (ROK).[5] The first news received in Britain of the invasion of South Korea came via the United States the UN and the press. A telegram, sent to the Foreign Office by Captain Vyvian Holt, His Majesty's Minister in Seoul, on 25 June, gave no indications of any forthcoming conflict. Captain Holt was soon to have more pressing concerns however, as he was to be captured shortly afterwards by the advancing North Koreans.⁶ The same day, at No. 10 Downing Street, in London, D.H. Rickett, Principal Private Secretary to Clement Attlee, the Prime Minister, passed the premier the following note: 'The Foreign Office thought that you should know that a state of war has been declared between Northern and Southern Korea. The United States Government are calling an emergency meeting of the Security Council.'⁷ It was just the latest in a series of East–West crises that the Prime Minister had had to face in the evolving 'Cold War' with Marshall Stalin's Soviet Union. Korea, although it was not immediately apparent, threatened to develop into World War III. While Attlee was the Prime Minister he was content, as far as possible, to rely upon the judgement of his Foreign Secretary the extraordinary – a term somewhat overused to describe statesmen but in this case fully justified – Ernest Bevin. For Bevin and Attlee the cornerstone of British foreign policy was the 'special relationship' with the United States. And, in 1950 the President of the United States was Harry S. Truman. Truman was a President under severe domestic criticism. The administration had suffered huge domestic criticism for effectively 'losing' China to Communism the previous year. Britain, recognising the importance of maintaining economic interests in China and also in view of its Hong Kong colony, had on 6 January 1950 officially recognised the Communist regime, to the fury of the Truman administration.

But, on 25 June 1950, His Majesty's Government (HMG) and the United States Government were agreed that the invasion of South Korea by North Korea should not go unpunished. The Security Council adopted a resolution recognising South Korea as 'a lawfully established government' and condemned the 'armed attack' from North Korea. The Council called for an immediate cessation of hostilities and for the North Koreans to withdraw their forces to the 38th parallel. Finally, the Resolution called upon all Member States 'to render every assistance to the United Nations in the execution of this resolution and to refrain from giving assistance to the North Korean authorities'.⁸ On the UN Security Council each of the permanent members (the United Kingdom, United States, the Soviet Union, France and Nationalist (Kuomintang) China, possessed a veto over Council decisions – but the Soviets had been absent from the UN since 13 January in protest at Nationalist China's continued representation there and the exclusion of Communist China. Despite the passing of the Resolution on 25 June there was ongoing uncertainty as to whether, in the absence of the Soviets, the Security Council was entitled, legally, to pass it in the first place.

From an Anglo-American point of view it was important to establish the principle that the Soviet absence did not invalidate the 25 June Resolution.

# Invasion

In London, the Foreign Office considered the courses of action open under the UN Charter and the course the British delegation to the UNO, in New York, might follow. 'Academically' it acknowledged that the competence of the Security Council to take action in the Korean dispute in the absence of a permanent member was still debatable, 'but in practice we could not of course admit that the Council was prevented from taking any action by the Soviet absence'. London's position was the same as when this question was examined, previously, in connection with the Kashmir dispute during which the Soviets had also walked-out:

> The Council must be able to function continuously and the voluntary absence of a permanent member should be regarded as an abstention rather than as a 'blanket veto'. It is now a fairly well established practice that the Council can take decisions even if substantive in the face of an abstention by a permanent member. In any case the Council has already adopted one substantive resolution about Korea despite the Soviet absence. On the assumption that it is competent the Council may under Article 39 determine the existence of a breach of the peace (already done) and decide what measures shall be taken in accordance with Articles 41 and 42 to maintain or restore international peace and security.

Under Article 40 the Council could call upon the parties concerned in the Korean dispute to comply with the provisional measures deemed necessary or desirable. This had also been done. Also under Article 40 'the Security Council shall duly take account of failure to comply with such provisional measures'. Once it was clear that there had been a failure to comply with the provisional measures consideration of possible further action, under Articles 41 and 42, would be appropriate. Meanwhile the South Koreans were entitled to continue to defend themselves. American military aid to Southern Korea appeared to be covered (as a measure of collective self-defence) so long as it was immediately reported to the Council and ceased once the Council had restored the situation. The Russians, however, could not legally claim a similar right to assist the Northern Koreans since the latter have already been designated the aggressors.

The Foreign Office pointed out that if the aggressor – in this case North Korea – failed to comply with the provisional measures enacted, the Council might decide, under Article 41, what measures not involving the use of armed force were to be employed to give effect to its decisions and might call upon members to apply such measures – although the measures specified under this article were unlikely to be of any practical use in the present situation. If the Council considered that such measures were inadequate it might, under Article 41, take such action by air, sea or land forces as might be necessary to maintain or restore international peace and security. These might include demonstrations, blockades and other operations by air, sea or land forces of members of the United Nations. The Council could not in these circumstances compel any member to provide armed forces, 'but it certainly need not refuse an offer of help voluntarily proffered by, for example, the United States. In short it can ask for offers of help, but cannot demand such help. Nor is it bound to accept any offer of help which it might consider would serve no useful purpose (eg an offer by the Soviet Union)'. If acceptable offers of help were forthcoming the Foreign Office considered that the Council could avail itself of them under Article 42.[9] The Security Council duly recommended that Member States 'furnish such assistance to the Republic of Korea as may be necessary to repel the armed attack and to restore international peace and security in the area.'[10]

In Washington, the British Joint Services Mission (BJSM), a relic of Anglo-American cooperation from the Second World War whose influence had steadily declined in US strategic thinking, acted as a forum for UK military conversations with the Joint Chiefs of Staff (JCS), the American equivalent of the Chiefs of Staff. Lord Tedder, Marshall of the Royal Air Force, was the head of the BJSM, and, on 26 June, he telegraphed to the British Chiefs in London what he had been told by General Omer Bradley, Chairman of the US Joint Chiefs of Staff, immediately after the latter's meeting with his colleagues: 'He tells me that Southern Korean resistance appears to have virtually collapsed. The Southern Korean handicap of having only light field artillery and armoured cars faced by tanks and heavy artillery has proved too severe. Latest report was that Northern Korean troops were South of the capital and threatening port and evacuation of American dependants was becoming difficult.' Bradley's personal view was that, had it been possible to give a free hand to American air power, which included three fighter groups, the attack might have been held; but he concluded that, under present conditions, no useful military action could be taken to prevent collapse. American air assets had the authority to take any action found necessary to cover the evacuation of American dependants. Detailed evidence regarding operations, reported Tedder, was 'naturally very limited but of course Northern Koreans are Russian trained and no doubt Russian instructors are with Northern Korean forces as American instructors have been with Southern Korean forces'.

On the subject of Formosa, Tedder thought it was clear that the United States had not formulated any definite military policy in this respect.

Bradley's personal view was that Formosa should be held against any attack from the mainland China but this 'presupposes sensible agreement' with Chiang Kai-shek regarding his ongoing air attacks on mainland. Tedder concluded that the Americans 'evidently have formed no ideas regarding possible UNO action in Korea. Bradley's concern regarding Korea was rather as [a] further step in Soviet world policy than as a specific additional threat to Japan'. This view tallied with similar views expressed to Tedder by General Douglas MacArthur, the Supreme Commander of Allied Powers in Japan – and that country's virtual dictator – some three years ago. Bradley suspected that the next Soviet move might well be in the oil rich Middle East – particularly Iran – and that the sooner the British and US Governments decided what action they would take in such circumstances the better: 'The lesson of Korea was that action against aggression must be immediate.'[11]

In Whitehall, Air Marshall Sir William Elliot had reached similar conclusions as he conducted a quick military appreciation of the situation in Korea as it affected the United Kingdom. Elliot was the link between the Chiefs of Staff and their civilian masters at the Ministry of Defence as Chief Staff Officer to the Minister of Defence, Emanuel Shinwell, and Deputy Secretary (Military) to the Cabinet. Now, in the immediate aftermath of the North Korean invasion, Elliot suggested to the Government that the Communist attack must have received the approval of the Russians 'and is therefore almost certainly another move in the cold war in South East Asia'. He warned that if Southern Korea was defeated by North Korea 'this will mean that the whole of Korea will come under Communist influence. Militarily it will give the Russians a second base area from which they could easily launch an attack against Japan in any future war'.[12]

Kenneth Younger, Minister of State, was in charge of the Foreign Office during the absence of Bevin, who was admitted to the London Clinic on 30 May, but was kept informed of important developments and regularly consulted until his return to duty on 27 July. So it was on Younger's watch that the US Embassy in London passed on the substance of a resolution that the Americans wanted to submit to the UN. The essence of the message accused the Soviet Union of arming the North Korean invaders with planes and tanks; and: 'Attack makes amply clear centrally directed Commie imperialism has passed beyond subversion in seeking conquer independent nations and now resorting to armed aggression and war. It has defied UNSC [United Nations Security Council]. In circumstances Commie occupation of Formosa would directly threaten security of Pacific area and United States forces performing necessary and legitimate functions that area.'[13] Younger, after consulting with his hospitalised Foreign

Secretary, telegraphed to the Washington Embassy the fundamentals of British policy in connection with the Korean conflict:

> It must be a major and indeed the primary objective of our policy to contain situations such as the Korean [conflict] and to prevent a world war. For this purpose it seems to us essential to give Russians an opportunity of beating a retreat when confronted with this welcome manifestation of American power and determination. Russians have so far made no statement of policy and have most carefully avoided identifying themselves with North Koreans.
>
> We therefore most strongly urge that the statement be so worded as to omit any reference to Soviet responsibility for the attack which however obvious is not susceptible of proof. We further strongly urge that no challenge should be thrown which Russians might feel bound to take up. It would in our view be more effective if steps which the President has ordered in connexion with Formosa, Philippines and Indo-China should be allowed to speak for themselves. Specifically we suggest that statement should omit any reference to the situation in terms of 'Centrally directed Communist imperialism'.[14]

The Americans accepted the British changes. But the opinion that London was most anxious to receive was that from the State Department in Washington. Despite the fact the British Government were not consulted by the United States for the first 36 hours of the conflict, the Anglo-American relationship remained central to London's strategic thinking. Crucial in all this was Britain's man in Washington: Sir Oliver Franks. He was appointed as Ambassador to the United States in 1948. A rapport was built up with Dean Acheson, Truman's Secretary of State. On 27 June, when Franks was called, along with other the Ambassadors of the North Atlantic Powers by the State Department, to hear the United States Government's decision on Korea, George Kennan and George Perkins, from the State Department, were 'at pains' to tell Franks 'how much they regretted their inability to consult with us during the last thirty-six hours. They ought to have done so and would like to have done so but the rapidity of developments in Korea and the difficulty of bringing the cumbrous machinery of the American Government' together, not excluding General MacArthur, the Supreme Allied Commander in the Pacific, based in Japan, 'had been such that they could not do so as they would have wished'.[15] The North Atlantic Pact Ambassadors was chosen as the best medium for disclosure of the American plan. Perkins read the text of the President's imminent statement, to the gathering, ordering the 7th Fleet to prevent any attack on Formosa.[16] Kennan then explained that, in attempting to analyse Soviet motives for the Korean operation, the President's advisers had come to conclusion that the Russians considered:

(a) North Korean forces had completed their training.
(b) They could not now have any association with Japanese peace treaty arrangements.

Nevertheless the President's advisers did not consider that the Soviets were preparing to enter the war. There were signs that they had intended to leave themselves a way out and it was a reasonable assumption, therefore, that the Russians were merely making an important probing. Kennan added that the United States did not attach overwhelming importance to strategic position of South Korea. The symbolic significance of preservation of the Republic was, however, 'tremendous, for if the world should notice weakness in the handling of this problem the repercussions would be great, first in Japan and then all over the orient'. Developing the argument Kennan pointed out that, if Korea went, Formosa would be next on the list. The Philippines were, of course, sensitive to anything that might happen in Formosa and there was a chain of reactions which, if it revealed weakness in the attitude of the Western powers, would cause discouragement that would most likely spread to Europe after doing its damage in Japan.[17] Later that day, the Security Council adopted a resolution recommending that the members of the United Nations furnish such assistance to South Korea 'as may be necessary to repel the armed attack and to restore international peace and security in the area'.[18] With the situation critical, President Truman announced that General MacArthur had been authorised to deploy US ground troops in Korea.[19] The United States was now committed to a full-scale confrontation with Communist forces; and the man given the task of repelling them was the most famous general – possibly even more so than Eisenhower – in the entire US Army.

When George Perkins asked Sir Oliver Franks to see him on the morning of 28 June the State Department official had been instructed to put a number of points to His Majesty's Ambassador. The most important was whether Britain would give military assistance under the United Nations resolutions, in the Korea situation. Perkins, Franks informed London, expressed a strong hope that 'we should be willing to do so and that it might be possible for us to decide quickly'. He gave two reasons. The first 'and much the more important' was the effect in all Asia 'of us all acting together and demonstrating our unity of view'. The second, of less importance, but real, was the major effect it would have on American public opinion. Franks reported to London: 'I do not think he had in mind that we could do a very great deal though the substance of whatever we could do would be greatly appreciated. His chief emphasis was on the symbolic value of any contribution we might make.' Perkins added that other countries were also being approached. He named Australia, New Zealand, France and Holland.[20]

This put the British on the spot. The Chiefs of Staff had to decide what, in their view, was the military contribution the British could make to the defence of Korea – and, just as importantly, what was in the best strategic interests of Britain. Lieutenant-General Brownjohn, the Vice Chief of the Imperial General Staff, summed up the view of the Chiefs in a telegram to Lord Tedder in Washington. The Chiefs believed that it would be 'unacceptable' to move any land forces from Malaya or Hong Kong. In Hong Kong the British Garrison had already been reduced below the strength that the Chiefs considered necessary to meet external aggression; and in view of the increased threat likely to result, on account of the release of the Communist armies from the commitment to invade Formosa, it would be quite wrong to reduce it still further. Apart from this, there was the effect on the morale of the population in Hong Kong to consider, and the Governor had recently stated that any further withdrawal of British forces would have 'most unfortunate results'. In Malaya, British forces were already fully committed in the anti-Communist campaign. As for the Middle East, British forces there had already been seriously reduced. 'We must be on our guard against further Russian diversions' Littlebrown explained and emphasised that, should the Russians stage an incident in, say, Persia, there were no Allied forces other than British military assets available in the area to deal with it: 'We could in fact be said to be holding the ring for the Americans in the Middle East just as we had been doing for some time past in South East Asia.'

As for the Army's strategic reserve in the UK, it would, admittedly, be possible by transferring men from one unit to another to get together a token force. The difficulty, of course, was to find men with the right terms of service for despatch to the Far East. A token force would have to be sent out, if it was to get there in time, by air at very short notice and there would be no time to give it the necessary specialist training. To send such a force from the United Kingdom 'would be fundamentally unsound and would be playing into Russian hands by dispersing our resources'. The Chiefs realised that, from the political standpoint, a token force was desirable but considered that if such a force was provided it should be a British Commonwealth force rather than a United Kingdom force. The

Chiefs were quite clear that it would be 'fundamentally unsound on military grounds to send land or air forces to Korea'. It seemed certain that the aggression by North Korea was a deliberate move in the Cold War by the Russians who intended to face the Allies with the alternative of either allowing the forces of South Korea to be overrun – with the disastrous loss of prestige involved – 'or of diverting our own resources from the more important theatres'.[21] The Chiefs could not have been any more plain in their opposition to military participation in the conflict.

So what, if anything, would Britain contribute to the defence of South Korea? The answer the Chiefs came up with was that 'by far' the most important contribution which Britain could make in support of the United States would be a 'demonstration of solidarity, making clear to the Russians and the Eastern peoples our firm support for the resolution by the United Nations Security Council and the action being taken by the United States to implement it' – i.e. moral support. The extent of the armed support that Britain could make available would be small. Nevertheless, they believed that if 'token forces' only were sent in support of the United States, this 'should adequately demonstrate our solidarity of purpose and consequently enhance greatly the moral effect'. The Chiefs noted that action intended by the United States was at present – 27 June – limited to Naval and Air Forces 'but we doubt whether the advance of the North Koreans can be stemmed and their forces compelled to withdraw to the frontier without some intervention'.

As for British Commonwealth forces available, the Naval Commander-in-Chief, Far East Station, had already deployed one aircraft carrier, two cruisers and a small number of destroyers in Japanese waters to await further instructions. The Chiefs recommend that these should be placed at the disposal of the United States Naval Commander-in-Chief. There were, however, no United Kingdom Land or Air Forces which could quickly be deployed in Korea and the Chiefs did not feel justified in recommending the transfer of any forces from either Malaya or Hong Kong until a careful study had been made of the implications of the present situation in Korea on the overall situation in the Far East and South-East Asia. The best they could do was to 'use our influence with the other members of the British Commonwealth to persuade them to make similar token contributions.' With France facing what appeared to be similar Communist aggression in Indo-China (Vietnam), the Chiefs recommended that Britain should meet French requests for military equipment in that theatre, by making available any equipment 'which is surplus to our own requirements free of charge, and, at the minimum replacement value, any taken from our own war reserves'.[22] This was the advice the Chiefs presented to Ministers, including the Prime Minister.[23] The most the RAF, when pushed, could spare for Korea was a Flying Boat Squadron.[24] As Sir William Elliot put it to Manny Shinwell: 'We have numerous commitments in different parts of the World and are already fully extended to meet them. It would therefore, be extremely difficult if not impossible, to find the forces. There is always the possibility that the Russians will create a diversion elsewhere; and we must be ready for this.'[25] Later that day – 28 June – Attlee announced Britain's Naval contribution in the House of Commons. The Americans were delighted and George Perkins immediately telephoned Oliver Franks to say that news of the Prime Minister's announcement had been received with much gratification. The President was 'anxious to make some appreciative statement as soon as possible'.[26]

There was, however, one thing lingering in the back of the British bureaucratic mind –the Americans might suggest to the British that, in the event of US forces being insufficient to restore the situation in Korea, an Atomic Bomb should be dropped in North Korea. The Chiefs were united in their – understated – response to this: the dropping of an Atomic Bomb in North Korea would be 'unsound'. The effects of such action would be worldwide and might well be 'very damaging' – politically that was. Moreover it would probably provoke a global war. Although it did not appear that the military situation in Korea could be restored unless American ground troops were deployed against the North Korean forces the Chiefs considered it would be 'unwise to advise' the dropping of an Atomic Bomb in order to restore the situation.[27]

In his Weekly Political Summary to London, covering the period 24–30 June, Franks observed how the United Kingdom offer of assistance and the subsequent Australian, New Zealand and Dutch offers and the Canadian expression of willingness to help, had been gratefully received and had a good effect. 'Publicity for the promptness and magnitude of our commitment (there are said to be more British than American naval vessels immediately available in the area) was greatly enhanced by the fact that at the moment our decision was being announced in London, Senator Wherry, the Republican floor leader, was caustically implying on the floor of the Senate that we would probably hang back.' Friendly commentators seemed to take great delight in reporting the two items in juxtaposition. The step was welcomed, 'not only because we will thus share the military burden, but because it confirms our reliability as America's principal ally and because it underlines the fact, which Mr Truman and Mr Acheson have been at pains to emphasize, that the operation is not an American act of war but a police action under the aegis of the UN. There is some speculation about how we will square our participation in the Korean affair with our recognition of the Chinese Communist regime and it is hoped that we may now revise our divergent and unpopular policy'.[28]

On the propaganda front, with the Americans committed to military intervention it was imperative, thought the British, to win the battle for world opinion. It had been claimed, notably by the Soviet Government and the North Korean authorities, that the hostilities in Korea constituted a civil war and as such were domestic matters with which the United Nations should not interfere under Article 2 (7) of the Charter. In the view of His Majesty's Government this was a misrepresentation of the true state of affairs. A full reply to these arguments was given by Attlee in the House of Commons debate of 5 July where he pointed out that, on the one hand the Government of South Korea had been recognised by the United Nations in the General Assembly Resolution of 12 December, 1948, as 'a lawful government ... having effective control and jurisdiction over that part of Korea where the temporary commission was able to observe and consult', that was, in the area south of the 38th parallel. The North Korean Government, on the other hand, was a body, set up by 'procedures of doubtful legality', which had defied the authority of the United Nations, and had forbidden their officers to enter the territory under its control. It had, however, been considered to be the *de facto* Government of a *de facto* State, exercising control over the area of Korea north of the 38th parallel. Attlee pointed out that a civil war took place when there had been one Government over the whole of one State and as a result of internal conflict two Governments competing for the control of this State engaged in hostilities with each other. In the case under review the South Korean Government had never had jurisdiction over North Korea or the North Korean Government any jurisdiction over South Korea. There had been no split in an entity which had been duly constituted as a single independent state, because owing to circumstances beyond the control of the United Nations and against its wishes, it had never been possible to constitute Korea as a single State with one Government.[29]

The Foreign Office was 'reluctant to expose ourselves to accusation that at time like this we have made no attempt to establish direct contact with Soviet Government'. On 29 June the United Kingdom Ambassador in Moscow was, therefore, instructed to seek an urgent interview with the highest available Soviet official and urge the Soviet Government in general terms to cooperate in effecting a peaceful settlement of Korean conflict.[30] Thus the British, keeping Washington informed at all times, sent the first, tentative, peace feelers out to Moscow. His Majesty's Ambassador in Moscow was Sir David Kelly, who offered his own appreciation, 'however speculative', of Soviet tactics and intentions. He cautioned: 'We have little to go on and I submit following observations with all reserve.' The main elements in the situation seemed, to Kelly, to be as follows:

(a) Attack was certainly launched with Soviet knowledge and almost certainly at Soviet instigation;
(b) Campaign began well and Soviet Government probably hoped for a walk-over;
(c) Security Council acted with unexpected speed, and prompt United States reaction had not been foreseen;
(d) To judge from press presentation and comment, Soviet Government although happy to exploit 'evidence' of United States aggressiveness, is in no hurry to commit itself to North Korean cause;
(e) Official statements ... although uncompromising, have not so far been provocative from Soviet standards.

I think we can conclude that

(a) North Korean attack was intended to exploit a favourable *local* situation, not to provoke a general conflict;
(b) Successful outcome would represent shattering blow to Western prestige, thus justifying taking of certain risks. But as precautionary measure, and to avoid prejudice to peace campaign Soviet Government kept itself well in background, hoping that swift Northern victory would make effective United Nations action impossible while keeping its own line of retreat open if unexpectedly things went badly;
(c) Military intervention by United States was not expected and Soviet Government either has no policy ready to deal with this new situation or has decided to sit on the fence until military situation is clearer.

'More tentative still', Kelly judged that the Soviet Government were extremely anxious not to find themselves engaged directly in a military confrontation with the United States. This meant that, 'if [the] fence on which they are now sitting becomes untenable', the following three courses of action would be open to them:

(a) Climb down, and console themselves for diplomatic feat by exploiting, on ideological front, claim that at least they have not compromised with aggressors, who have now unmasked themselves completely;

(b) Intervene *indirectly*, either by involving Communist China in Korean fighting or by staging major incident elsewhere (eg Berlin, Yugoslavia or Persia) where risk of direct armed clash with United States would be less likely;
(c) Agree to call North Koreans to order on condition that United States Government first makes Soviet return to United Nations possible. I would hesitate at this stage to put these three possibilities in order of probability.

Kelly noted that a new factor in this 'highly speculative picture' was the spectacular campaign for signatures to the Stockholm Peace Manifesto that had suddenly been launched in the Soviet Union. One object of it was 'certainly' to contrast the 'Soviet love of peace' and the United States 'aggressiveness'.[31]

It took a week before the Soviets made a substantive response. Andrei Gromyko, from the Soviet Foreign Ministry, asked Kelly to call upon him at 2 pm on 6 July whereupon the British Ambassador urged the Soviet Government to cooperate in effecting a peaceful settlement. Gromyko replied that the Soviet Government wished for a peaceful settlement and he asked Kelly if he had any specific propositions to make. Kelly answered that the sense of his instructions, from London, was that 'we hoped Soviet Government would use their influence with North Korean Government to stop bloodshed. Pressed to be more explicit I said we obviously wished to restore the status quo'. A United Nations Commission had been working in South Korea to promote the peaceful union of the two halves, continued Kelly, 'and we wished to return to the status quo and to stop the war. He nodded assent.' Kelly asked if he could report Gromyko as meaning that despite his own recent statement that the Soviet policy was one of non-interference Moscow would be willing to act 'if they found suitable means'. 'He said I knew the position of the Soviet Government from the documents which have been published but the Soviet Government wished for peaceful settlement and therefore he had asked me if I had any proposals. I said that all I asked was for the use of their influence with the North Korean Government, that I would report at once what he had said and that I would ask to see him again if I received a further communication for him.'[32]

When Attlee and Bevin discussed their response to the Soviets it was not lost upon them that the only reason that the Security Council was able to act with such speed 'in connexion with the naked aggression by Northern Korean forces' was because the Soviets were not present at the meetings of the Security Council and therefore 'did not indulge in its ordinary frustrating and obstructionist tactics'. Among the questions that

Bevin now had to face, after all his and the Government's championing of Communist China's entry into the UN, were:

> Would not the Soviet return to the Security Council now, particularly after having exacted through the exercise of coercion upon us a blackmail price, merely place her in a position where she could obstruct and frustrate in the event that she had any further moves in mind either in Asia or Europe?

Attlee and Bevin, of course, did not wish the USSR to leave the United Nations: they understood the changes in the character of the United Nations which would follow upon such a move. 'But', considered Bevin, 'it is one thing to pay an extorted price for their return to their appropriate place in the United Nations so that they can sabotage the fundamental purposes of this great organisation at this critical time, and it is another thing for them to return to the United Nations with the full knowledge that aggression is not a profitable undertaking'.[33] As for the tentative British moves, in Moscow, Dean Acheson had given his cautious blessing[34] for their continuation. This was the response London had hoped for. Attlee and Bevin discussed the Kelly telegram, from Moscow, on the morning of 8 July with US Ambassador Douglas. Attlee told Douglas that he intended to authorise Kelly to inform Gromyko unobtrusively that his conversation of 6 July was being studied. The Prime Minister explained that, without wishing to appease the Russians, 'we thought it would be as well to let them realise that their response was not being neglected'. Attlee emphasised that while the British Government was in general agreement with Acheson's position: 'We should, however, prefer to put the matter in our own way and in particular we should wish to emphasise that, while His Majesty's Government could only speak in this matter as a member of the United Nations, equally they could not make bargains or constitute themselves the spokesman of the United Nations.' Douglas did not dissent from this and asked whether he was right in supposing that the UK's object would be to draw out the Russians, while not betraying over-anxiety. Attlee confirmed that this was 'our view; certainly we should in no way imply that we were afraid of the Russians'. Douglas, speaking off the record, anticipated that a price that the Soviet Government might ask in return for their assistance in ending the Korean fighting, would be connected with China. They might well demand that the Peking government should take its place at the Security Council and other organs of the United Nations. If this happened, the United States might find itself forced by the 'over-whelming opinion of the rest of the world to agree that the Peking Government should hold the seat at the United Nations'. The Peking Government would then have a claim that might prove irresistible to the reversion of Formosa to mainland control. In other words the United States might be faced by a 'horse-trade' involving the surrender of Formosa to the Communists in return for a cessation of the fighting in Korea. Douglas 'did not seem to think that such a bargain would be attractive to the United States'. Attlee, in turn, laid stress on the importance of the attitude of India in this question and urged that the United States 'should not get into a position where whites could be represented as contending against coloured races'.[35] It was becoming clearer that while London and Washington agreed in fundamentals there were underlying differences between the capitals on what was essential for a settlement in Korea involving the Soviets.

Kelly was instructed by Bevin in the line of the oral reply which he wished the Ambassador to make to Gromyko. This was intended as a first step, which, if the Soviet Union were now genuinely anxious to find a way out of the Korean conflict, might, Bevin hoped, encourage them to show their hand a little further. But Bevin was clear that: 'You should not (repeat not) however seek an interview with Mr Gromyko until you receive further instructions from me … Do your best to keep the door open after your next talk with Gromyko however unresponsive or annoying he may be.'[36] Regarding Gromyko's question as to whether London had any specific proposals to make, Bevin told Kelly that he was well aware of the precise and concrete sense attached by the Soviet Government to the word 'proposals': '(The Russians read into the word "proposals" far more than we do and are apt to regard them as something by which the proposal is irrevocably bound, just as they regard a "basis of discussion" as something which is firmly agreed. Hence my use of the phrase "preliminary suggestion" in this telegram.)' So it would be difficult for His Majesty's Government, as a member of the United Nations, to come forward with proposals in this sense. Britain could not properly do so unless it had assured themselves that what it proposed carried with it the assent of the other members of the United Nations chiefly concerned. In view of its collective responsibility as a member of the United Nations, London could not, as an individual government, run so far ahead as this. 'We therefore think it best to make a preliminary suggestion.'

The Soviet Government might well make the comment that 'they saw nothing new in the preliminary step which we propose'. But, Bevin emphasised, any step was tremendously important if it led to a cessation of hostilities and the clearing up of difficulties among members of the United Nations. It, therefore, seemed to Bevin that the 'influences making for peace' ought to join together in order to bring about a cessation of hostilities, without concerning themselves for the moment with other causes of difference which had arisen in the 'more distant or more recent past' in connexion with the Korean question: 'I want you therefore to emphasise to Mr Gromyko that, irrespective of any other consideration', the plain fact was that the hostilities in Korea had arisen from the movement over the 38th parallel by the forces of North Korea. It followed that the best suggestion which His Majesty's Government, as a member of the United Nations, were in a position to put forward was to urge the Soviet Government – who HMG were glad to note had expressed their desire for a peaceful settlement – to add their efforts to those of other members of the United Nations by using their influence, as a member of the UNO, with the North Korean authorities, to bring them to cease hostilities and to withdraw their forces to the 38th parallel.

Bevin then told Kelly: 'What you are now concerned to do is to suggest a step whereby, in the view of His Majesty's Government, the way might be paved for an ultimate solution. If Mr Gromyko, for his part, has any suggestions to make, you should of course say that you would be very glad to convey them to me.' Gromyko might also raise other questions such as Chinese representation in the United Nations or Formosa. Bevin suspected that he might also be angling for an opening to suggest a meeting of the Council of Foreign Ministers of the Four Powers (the United States, UK, France and the USSR). This would give the advantage to Gromyko, since it would arise out of a Far Eastern issue, of opening the way for the Soviet Government to bring the question of the Japanese Peace Treaty – still to be concluded five years after the end of the war – into this forum, which they had ('unjustifiably in our view') always wanted to do – for the Americans, in particular, were anxious to keep the Soviets out of Japanese affairs. Bevin made it clear to Kelly:

> You will have to avoid such traps. Your best line would, I think, be to say that, without prejudice to other questions which remain to be settled, the cause of peace is of such over-riding importance that we feel entitled to call upon the Soviet Government to lend their assistance. What do they think? Have they any suggestion to make? They and we have an equal interest in bringing hostilities to a close. You are not speaking for any other government or organisation but for His Majesty's Government who feel deeply about the dangers of the present situation and make an earnest appeal to the Soviet Government to join their efforts to these of other members of the United Nations and to use their influence in the interest of peace. I want you to drive home the thought

that it is essential to stop the fighting in Korea, to get back to methods of peaceful settlement and to promote the restoration of peace.[37]

With London very much at the heart of the diplomatic moves on Korea, Bevin seized the opportunity to push for the British to brought into the heart of American strategic thinking. He cabled Acheson and told the Secretary that he had been giving a lot of thought to the problems which they were likely to face as the situation in Korea developed. The problems facing the West were, of course, primarily military 'but they were likely to have increasingly wide political implications'. As he informed Acheson the implications 'will concern not only the way in which we should like to see the situation in Korea develop but also the likely reactions of the Russians as it develops. Russian reactions may be expected not only in the Far East; we have been giving some thought to other parts of the world where the Soviet Government may cause trouble for us'. A particular aspect of the situation in Korea 'which is causing us concern is that the Russians have involved the Western powers in a heavy commitment without themselves playing an overt part, and there are other areas in the Far East where the same tactics are open to them. You have already made known your concern with Indo-China and Formosa. There is some reason to think that Communist-inspired activities in Malaya have already been stepped up in tune with the Korean affair. And we can not ignore the possibility of a Chinese attack on Hong Kong'. But further, 'we can not be sure that these activities on the part of Russia will be confined to East Asia. I understand your military advisers have already expressed the view that Persia may again become a danger spot. We should consider whether the opportunity may not be taken of relighting the fire in Greece. And there may be other areas of potential trouble'.

Bevin told Acheson that, while no one could attempt to provide precisely in advance for every eventuality, 'I hope you will agree with me that we should look as far as we can and reach some agreement as to our common policy in these areas in the event of further outbreaks.' Bevin proposed, therefore, that representatives of both Governments should meet to consider what courses of action were most likely to be adopted by the Soviet Government and should have an exploratory discussion of the plans they should adopt to meet them. Plans had already been concerted between them over a wide field but Bevin thought that the time might have come for extending the area to which their detailed plans should apply. Other Governments, in particular the French, might be concerned 'but it will suffice if they are informed as and when the situation demands'. Bevin suggested Acheson should authorise the appropriate United States authorities to discuss these problems with Lord Tedder.³⁸ The Foreign Secretary was clearly attempting to use the Korean crisis in an attempt revive British influence.

Kelly, meantime, called on Gromyko at 4 pm on 11 July. As he reported to Bevin: 'I told him you were glad to note the Soviet Government's wish for peaceful settlement which was also the earnest wish of His Majesty's Government. I said that by specific proposals he no doubt meant offers binding if accepted.' Kelly then spoke along the lines instructed by Bevin and ended by saying he would be glad to pass on any suggestions which Gromyko had to make. With the 'expressed object of elucidation' Gromyko tried to formulate essential points in a rapid exchange of dialogue, while Kelly impressed that 'we were making [the] preliminary proposal that the Soviet Government should use its influence with the North Korean government to procure cessation of hostilities and withdrawal of their forces beyond 38th parallel'. As Gromyko asked about the phrase that the Soviet Government should use its influence, Kelly replied that the Soviet Government naturally had 'special influence' with the North Korean Government, and 'we were appealing to them' as a member of United Nations to use it. Gromyko said 'interrogatively "you say you do not wish to run too far ahead with the proposals with regard to the United Nations" and I repeated that we were making a preliminary proposal to get matters back to the field of peaceful negotiation'. Gromyko then said the Soviet Government would be informed of His Majesty's Government's proposal, but that the hostilities had been 'provoked' by South Korea; Kelly continued:

> To my comment that I knew there was a difference of opinion, he said it was a difference of nature not of opinion. I pointed out that anyhow the North Koreans were fighting far south of their frontier. As he repeated that he had no other comments to offer, I concluded by saying that His Majesty's Government felt that the cause of peace was of such importance that they felt entitled to approach the Soviet Government as a member of the United Nations with an appeal to help to stop hostilities without prejudice to other questions which remained to be settled, and that we put forward our suggestion as a step to pave the way to an ultimate solution. He repeated that he would inform his Government. I was accompanied by a member of the Russian Secretariat, but the conversation was conducted in English. Mr Gromyko was polite throughout.³⁹

Although Gromyko gave no positive indications of the way the Soviet mind was working, Kelly thought, on reflection to Bevin, that his conduct of the interview and fact that it had not yet been mentioned in the Soviet press justified certain inferences. With the exception of his reference ('made with a possibly cynical smile') to South Korean provocation, Gromyko 'showed real interest in getting full and exact report of your message'. Kelly felt this was at any rate consistent with the possibility that 'they are looking for some peaceful solution and also with the possibility that they have not in fact made up their own minds. This latter possibility is quite likely in view of the fact that they are now for the first time working with a partner namely the Chinese whom they cannot treat as they would a European satellite and who have probably strong views of their own'. Kelly warned that on either of these suppositions there would be a grave danger of a complete stiffening of their attitude if they came to the conclusion that 'our real object was to secure a major prestige victory at their expense and that our approaches were for propaganda motives'.[40]

In the meantime a minor crisis appeared to develop in Anglo-American relations for Bevin had despatched a telegram to Acheson highlighting his concerns at the price the Soviets might try and extract for a peaceful resolution of the Korean conflict. Bevin pointed out that, if the Soviet Government did show a readiness to cooperate in re-establishing the status quo in Korea, they would almost certainly raise the question of Formosa. It also seemed to Bevin that the question of Chinese representation in the United Nations would be raised and become acute, the Russians arguing that they could not play their part in the Security Council with China not represented. So, Bevin thought that Acheson and the United States Government should appreciate, 'and I put it to them very frankly, the way I see the situation, which is as follows':

> Whereas the United States have the whole-hearted backing of world opinion in the courageous initiative they took to deal with the aggression in Korea, I do not believe they could rely on the same support for their declared policy in connexion with Formosa. Not only would many Powers, particularly Asian Powers, dislike the prospect of an extension of the dispute which might follow if the Central People's Government were to attempt an attack on Formosa, but some undoubtedly feel that, now that the Central People's Government are in control of all Chinese territory, it would not be justifiable, in view of the pledge under the Cairo Declaration, to take steps which might prejudice the ultimate handing over of the territory to China … In general, I think that the United States Government would be wise in their public statements to concentrate on the Korean issue and play down the other parts of the President's statement of 27th June, otherwise there may

be a risk of a breach in the international solidarity happily achieved over Korea.

Thus the latest Soviet move has forced us to ask ourselves the question what the attitude of the United States would be if the Russians agreed to help in restoring the status quo in Korea in return for United States readiness to reconsider their present declared attitude in regard to Formosa.

Finally I want Mr Acheson to know that I am keenly alive to the possibility, and even likelihood, that this Soviet move has a sinister significance. For example, the Russians, knowing there is a divergence of policy between Great Britain and the United States in regard to China, may well calculate that their move may increase the divergence. We must both be on our guard against this … Mr. Acheson will understand my feeling that this is a time for us to be frank with each other. I know he will answer me with equal frankness.[41]

Acheson, in turn, instructed Douglas to emphasise to Bevin that his reply had been approved at the 'highest levels represents both my own strong personal views and has fullest concurrence of all official quarters here.' He considered that the Ambassador might also remind Bevin, orally, of the grave doubts the Foreign Secretary had personally expressed in private conversation with Acheson in London: 'I want you to leave him in no doubt of seriousness with which I views implications of his message and their possible effect on our future relationship.' Acheson told Bevin his message would 'contribute to a full understanding between us if I am equally frank'. Acheson rejected any notion of negotiation with the Communists over Korea:

This is sheer unadulterated blackmail on their part which has no support in the Charter or in reason or conscience. I am certain we both agree that we cannot repeatedly pay appeasement prices to get the Sov[iet] Union to take their seats in the UN nor permit them to establish by indirection.

The United States was aware of the commitments of Cairo and Potsdam concerning Farmosa but 'existing conditions were clearly not envisaged at the time they were made'. Commitments made with the Soviets in connection with Cario and Potsdam – the independence of Korea and support of the Nationalist Government of China – had been flouted. It was one thing to turn Formosa over to the then Republic of China and quite another to turn it over to the Soviet Union or to a Chinese regime 'which at the least is encouraging aggression against its neighbours in open cooperation with Moscow'. Acheson concluded by looking to an early and complete a liquidation of the Korean aggression as was militarily possible and in any case without concessions which would whet Soviet appetites and bring on other aggressions elsewhere. The issue of China's 'seating problem' should be considered by the UN on its merits 'and out from under the duress and blackmail now being employed' while the peaceful resolution of the Formosa problem should form part of a Japanese peace settlement without the employment of force. Acheson was glad to have Bevin's further views 'at your earliest convenience'.[42]

When Douglas saw Bevin to deliver the telegram from Acheson, the Foreign Secretary was once more in a hospital bed. The message did not improve Bevin's health. The resulting conversation, noted the Ambassador, was long 'and somewhat rambling'. Douglas began by pointing out to Bevin that, in his previous conversation with Attlee, the latter had said that the position of HMG was that the Korean problem and the question of seating Communist China in the UN, Formosa and other matters were unrelated. Bevin agreed but seemed 'somewhat surprised and taken aback' by Acheson's response. Douglas thought him 'rather defensive' in explaining the British position which was that he felt that it was well worth exploring in advance what the position of the United States would be in the event that the Soviets should respond with proposals which might, on the surface, appear to be honest and inviting. Bevin said he wanted to provoke the question in order that the British and Americans might have consultations in anticipation of a Soviet question or proposal. But Douglas considered Bevin 'indefinite' to his frank question as to what possible practical advantages he saw in getting Communist China in the Security Council and the return of the Russians to it. Bevin merely said that he would have to consider the matter carefully. In passing Bevin commented that he had never doubted the wisdom or justice of Britain's decision to recognise Communist China but had expressed doubts to Acheson as to a satisfactory outcome. Douglas had the impression, he reported to Acheson, that Bevin 'had not quite appreciated the significance of his message to you and it may well be that some of his subordinates with less fortitude than he persuaded him to despatch his telegram to you without explaining its implications'. As a caveat Bevin stressed that the UK's position with regard to Korea was not to be construed as a commitment that the same position was taken with regard to Formosa as that of the United States. The UK was willing to consult with the United States, the Commonwealth – especially India – and others with respect to Formosa, but great care must be taken not to weaken UK–Commonwealth relations particularly with India and Pakistan. India, Bevin emphasised, was an important influence in the

Orient. Bevin concluded by saying that he could not make a final comment on Acheson's message as it would require careful study – but he would reply in a few days time.⁴³

What had disturbed Bevin the most was that Douglas had used the phrase 'serious consequences' in his presentation of the message. In Washington, Sir Oliver Franks was ordered to convene an urgent meeting with Acheson and put the Foreign Secretary's concerns directly to him.⁴⁴ Bevin wrote to Acheson to 'remove any misapprehension about the purpose of the message which I sent to you'. It was never in Bevin's mind, when he asked what the United States view would be in the event of the Soviet Union asking a price in return for using their influence with the North Koreans, to suggest that a bargain was desirable: 'We are just as determined not to submit to Soviet blackmail as you are. I want to make it quite clear that we could not agree with you more whole-heartedly when you say that you have faced squarely a calculated act of aggression. We ourselves, and I think the whole right-thinking world, appreciate to the full the stand which the United States Government have taken in Korea on behalf of us all.' Bevin thought it essential to remove any misunderstanding before 'we discuss, as I hope we can dispassionately, the two questions of Formosa and our attitude towards China where clearly there has been a difference in our thinking. I know that I can explain without troubling our relationship exactly why we have been very seriously worried here about the implications of the President's declaration about Formosa.'

Britain was, 'as you know', continued Bevin, in a very vulnerable position in Hong Kong, 'and we have vast Chinese communities in Malaya where we have a long drawn campaign on our hands. You know our views on China and that our aim remains that China should not go irrevocably into the Soviet camp and be lost permanently to the Western world.' The President's declaration on Formosa evidently had an impact on all these situations, and it therefore could not be said to affect the United States alone. As Bevin saw it the possibilities of the Formosa situation were as follows. If the Chinese Peoples' Government (CPG) took heed of the President's declaration and abandoned any attempt to invade Formosa and thus avoided an armed clash with the United States forces, no very serious consequences might ensure.

But the Chinese Peoples' Government had addressed a communication to the Security Council stating their intention to 'liberate' Formosa whatever the United States might do, and though this might only be bravado, it might be unwise to assume that no attempt to stage an invasion would be made. If an attempt was made, 'we must', in view of the position taken by the President in his statement of the 27 June, expect hostilities between the forces of the United States and those of the Central People's Government: 'We consider that the consequences of such a clash would be very grave. They might lead to an extension of the conflict' warned Bevin. Even if that did not happen it was not improbable that Russia would appeal to the Security Council and accuse the United States of aggression. 'While no doubt you have considered this, and would have a good case, I am concerned lest the solidarity of the support you now have should not be maintained in these circumstances. The Russians will of course be out to make mischief.' Bevin recognised that Acheson attached great strategic importance to Formosa:

> What I am anxious to avoid is that we should give the Russians a chance to divide Asia from the West on an Asian problem. I really think there has been some misinterpretation of what the President said about Formosa and of course the Russians are doing their best to encourage this. Maybe the President in his own inimitable way could say something to remove any misapprehension by making it clear that the final disposal of Formosa is an open question which should be settled on its merits when the time comes, and that nothing which has been said or done implied any decision to go back on the position as set out in the Cairo Declaration. I realise the delicacy of this matter.

Acheson's communication to Bevin had dealt in some detail with the question of Chinese (and Russian) representation in the United Nations. Bevin only raised this question in his message to Acheson because of the likelihood that the Russians would put it forward as part of a bargain, 'and I am in entire agreement with you that we cannot bargain on the Korean issue. We should refuse to discuss with the Soviet Union the question of Chinese representation in the United Nations and, in order to give a sense of security to the world, must renounce the practice by which one nation can claim to prevent the United Nations from working'. The question of Chinese representation did not, therefore, seem to Bevin to arise at this present stage. He continued:

> You have elaborated to me at length the attitude of the United States Government towards China, and their reasons for that attitude. I do not think that we should necessarily find ourselves in full agreement with all your statements, but that is not the point which I want to make. You know our policy towards China, and I think it is the right policy. On the question of recognition you and we have differed, but I did think that ... we were agreed that we did not want to see China irrevocably alienated

from the West. What I am afraid of is that the present situation will, if we are not careful, push China further and further in the direction of the Soviet Union. On our information China, though reacting violently to your declaration on Formosa, has committed herself no more than Russia has over Korea, and I should doubt if she wishes to become involved in that conflict. I should also doubt whether, for the present, she would embark on adventures further afield apart from Formosa, although we cannot afford to disregard that possibility. But I think we must be careful not to accuse China of what she has not yet done, or to give her the impression that she is already so much beyond the pale that she has no hope of re-establishing her position with the West. Once she becomes convinced that the Western powers will have nothing to do with her, she will turn even more to the Soviet Union, who will be out to exploit such a tendency to our detriment and we may find that we have aligned against us a Power whose influence in Asia, for good or evil, is bound to have a profound effect upon the course of events. This is a question of vital concern to us because of our position in Hong Kong and Malaya. It is also of vital concern to all Asian countries, who are very conscious of it. Therefore I say that we must be very careful not to add China to our enemies by any actions or attitudes of ours. If China eventually demonstrates by practical evidence that she will in no circumstances cooperate with the free world; if she takes her seat in the United Nations and behaves in precisely the same way as the Soviet Union has in the past, then at any rate it will be clear to Asian as well as to other nations what she is and where she stands. I do think it is important that we should not put ourselves in a position where it can be alleged that, but for some action of ours, China could not have gone irrevocably into the Soviet Communist camp.

I will now try to summarise my views.

I think that the governing factor in our politico-strategic policy should be to localise the Korean conflict and attempt to prevent it from spreading. I think that this objective would be helped by some public clarification regarding Formosa and by adoption of policy towards China which would not press her to the point where still closer association with the Soviet Union would appear to her to be her only course.

If you agree with this I should hope that we could find common ground on the following points.

The first is that the aggression in Korea must be repelled and North Korean troops must go back to the 38th parallel.

The second is that there can be no submitting to Soviet blackmail, but that Russia's right course is, as said above, to come back and take her place in the United Nations, having renounced the practice of holding up the work of the United Nations by the action of one nation.

Thirdly the question of Chinese representation in the United Nations should be considered in the United Nations and not in relation to any possible Soviet blackmail connected with Korea. In any case as a matter of practice I cannot believe that the necessary majority for the change-over at the United Nations could be secured so long as the Korean conflict lasts, even if any Power were to attempt to push it at the United Nations.

If our policies are somewhat divergent in the meanwhile, I think it very important that the United States and Britain should do their best not to take opposing lines in any statements we have to make to third Powers or publicly, and that we should make sure that these divergences do not prejudice the future.[45]

On 15 July, Franks saw Acheson and handed over a copy of the report of the Moscow meeting with Gromyko who read, with approval, Kelly's language in his talk with Gromyko. Franks then told Acheson that Bevin did not intend any further action in Moscow but would leave it to the Russians to make the next move. If they did Bevin would immediately consult the United States Government. When Franks delivered Bevin's message and told Acheson that the Foreign Secretary was surprised by the last sentence in Douglas's letter, Acheson made it clear that he was 'distressed'.[46] Acheson was at pains to tell 'Sir Oliver that what we intended to convey was that we regarded most seriously the possibilities of our policies drifting apart, and that there was no other meaning intended'. Franks said that he was sure of this but that he wanted to reassure Bevin who was 'apparently disturbed'.[47] Acheson was anxious that Franks relay to Bevin how: 'He very much hopes you will continue to feel free to state your views with full frankness and receive his own expressed in the same way.'[48]

Washington took on board London's concerns over Formosa. On 19 July, President Truman sent to Congress a special message on Korea during which he made special mention of the island. In it he stated that the United States had no territorial ambitions whatever concerning the island and 'nor do we seek for ourselves any special position or privilege on Formosa'. The present military neutralisation of the island was without prejudice to political considerations affecting it: 'Our desire is that Formosa not become embroiled in hostilities disturbing to the peace of the Pacific and that all questions affecting Formosa be settled by peaceful means as envisaged in the Charter of the United Nations.'[49] The same day Acheson met with Franks. The Secretary asked him what he thought the reaction would be to the President's message. Franks replied that he thought it would be taken 'the way we would like it to be taken'. He also indicated that he sensed a 'growing feeling of realism' in the messages that were coming through from London although there was nothing tangible that he felt he could point to.[50]

As for the approach to Moscow, HMG was facing a delicate balancing act not merely between London and Washington but with the emerging power within the Commonwealth that highlighted the UK's global interests. On 10 July, Pandit Jawaharlal Nehru, the Prime Minister of India, had sent a personal message to Attlee, after having just seen a summary of Kelly's conversation with Gromyko and the Ambassador's comment on what Gromyko said. Nehru believed a strong argument now existed for HMG pressing upon the United States the solution 'for which we have been working' – the admission of the 'New China' to the UNSC. This, and the return of the USSR to it, could be secured without the United States either recognising the Peking Government or voting for its admission to the Council; no surrender by America would be involved in Peking's admission. The United States might be afraid that the entry of China into the Security Council and the return of USSR might, through adopting an unreasonable attitude by one or both, or by the exercise of the veto, impede rather than accelerate the settlement of the Korean dispute. Unless the USSR desired an extension of conflict, which seemed unlikely to Nehru on present evidence, the resort to such obstructive tactics was 'hardly probably'. World opinion would react unfavourably to both the Soviet and the People's Government of China if they utilised their presence in the Council to defeat progress toward a settlement. In the Indian view, the end of the present deadlock in the Council would be a step forward. It could not make the present situation worse, it might well improve it.[51]

Nehru had, by now, began a parallel correspondence with Stalin. Sir Girija Shankar Bajpai, Nehru's principal foreign adviser, showed the UK's Acting UK High Commissioner in New Delhi, Stalin's reply to the Indian Prime Minister as well as the latter's subsequent messages to Attlee and Acheson on Korea. In the course of a 'general and rather personal' conversation Bajpai was 'most emphatic that India was not repeat not anxious to play a leading role in this crisis.' The Indian Minister of External Affairs and Nehru himself realised only too well how inexperienced India's diplomacy was after only three years of independence and they were very conscious of the many pitfalls in a crisis of such magnitude (Bajpai said, in strict confidence, that Nehru had recently instructed the Indian Ambassador in Moscow to be most careful not to go beyond his instructions in any way and that India's UN delegate had been discouraged from trying to form a special ad hoc committee of the six non permanent members of the Security Council). The Acting UK High Commissioner felt, however, that owing to their position in Asia and to their special relationship with China, it was India's clear duty to do all in their power to prevent the Korean crisis dragging on and possibly spreading. When he reminded Bajpai of the obvious difficulties about trying to seat the Peking Government in the Security Council while the North Korean forces were continuing their aggression beyond the 38th parallel, the Indian replied that he quite understood the difficulties this would create for the United States, but that he could see no other way in which the present deadlock could be broken.[52]

Nehru now told Attlee he considered Stalin's reply 'most encouraging ... My honest belief is that Moscow is seeking a way out of present tangle without loss of prestige and that there is real chance of solving [the] Korean problem peacefully by enabling Peking Government to enter and Soviet to resume its place in Security Council without insistence on conditions. This may be an act of faith but the gravity of alternatives seems to justify it. In view of urgency of matter I shall be grateful for earliest possible answer'.[53] Before Attlee responded, Bevin rejected Nehru's optimism and commented that he thought Stalin's reply showed that the Russian attitude had hardened in that they were now trying to make it a condition that the five Great Powers (including Communist China) should meet before any action could be taken to settle the Korean question. The reply did not contain a word about the aggression of North Korea. The Foreign Secretary thought the Russian tactics were reminiscent of those adopted by Stalin and Molotov during the Berlin crisis. Stalin was in effect asking other people to surrender their positions. Bevin could not imagine that the US government would fall for this proposal, and he did 'not think we could possibly press them to do so'. If the United States were to accept such an arrangement, the Security Council would meet and everything which was not a Soviet proposal would be vetoed. Bevin was sure that Molotov was proceeding on the assumption that the United States would get pushed out of Korea, and that they would then 'give up the struggle'.[54]

As Bevin informed Franks: 'There can I am afraid be no doubt that Nehru's intervention in Moscow has placed all of us in an extremely awkward position although without any doubt it was made with the best possible intentions and in a genuine desire to try to bring about a peaceful settlement.' The principal danger was that, 'if we are not very careful, we shall bring about a cleavage between Asia and the West on the issue of Chinese representation in the United Nations'. It was quite clear that India did not consider the admission of China as representing any bargain with the Soviet Union, and in view of the stand she had taken there was no reason why she should. While on the one hand India should realise that the United States was in a different position, Bevin thought it was equally necessary for the United States to take India's position into account if 'we are to avoid a serious clash of opinion'. It was true that of Asian nations Siam and the Philippines had not recognised the Chinese Peoples' Government. But in general the rest of Asia looked to India for a lead, 'and what we for our part want to avoid is the situation where the Western nations take one attitude on a primarily Asian question, while Asian countries take the other'. The Foreign Secretary did not know 'whether we can now avoid this question being raised in the Security Council, though you will see from the Prime Minister's message to Pandit Nehru that we have done our best to dissuade him from pursuing the matter. What we are anxious to do is to try to avoid a situation where there is a head on collision between the United States and India in the Security Council'. Quite apart from the awkward situation in which this would place the United Kingdom it might result in the rift in East–West relations to which Bevin referred. The result in the Security Council might be inconclusive but the damage would have been done. Apart from the East–West relationship, 'we in the United Kingdom have to consider what the impact would be on the Commonwealth of such a situation'.

So Bevin wanted Franks to discuss the position which had been created by Stalin's reply to Nehru with Acheson and to put to him 'very frankly our fears as to what may happen if there is an open conflict between the United States and India. I do not expect the United States to give way on their point of principle, but I do ask that they should in handling the situation, avoid arousing Indian sentiment, and to try to stifle as far as possible any adverse comment on India's action in the United States'. Perhaps the best thing that could happen was that nothing should come of Nehru's proposal. But if it became a live issue 'I think very close consultation will be necessary if we are to get out of the very awkward predicament in which we shall find ourselves.'[55]

Attention, then, once more shifted to the British overtures in Moscow as, on 17 July, Gromyko had carried the exploratory discussions about Korea a stage further by handing to Sir David Kelly a message to the effect that the Soviet Government considered the best approach towards a peaceful settlement of the Korean question was the convening of the Security Council, with the participation of representatives of the People's Government of China 'as an indispensable condition' and that 'representatives of the Korean people' should be heard by the Council. Attlee informed the Cabinet that a message in similar terms had been sent to Nehru. The Indian Government had already voted for the admission of the People's Government of China to the Security Council, and the British Government had indicated that they would accept a majority vote on this issue. Attlee was, of course, worried that if the Soviet Government and the People's Government of China took part in the deliberations of the Security Council, 'one or other might veto any measures proposed by the other members in respect of Korea, and the action of the United Nations in dealing with a flagrant act of aggression would be completely nullified'. Attlee realised that there was no prospect that the United States would be willing to entertain the Soviet proposal in the absence of any indication that the North Koreans were to be asked to stop fighting and withdraw to the 38th parallel.

The Cabinet agreed when Attlee put these concerns to them. The Prime Minister was of the opinion that the discussions with the Soviet Government should be continued, since it was possible that the Soviets might be feeling their way towards a settlement. There was no reason to suppose that Stalin's reply represented the final attitude of the Soviet Government. The Prime Minister thought protracted negotiations which had led to the raising of the Berlin blockade might be analogous; in the course of those negotiations the Soviets had eventually taken up a position which had afforded a real basis for a solution. At present there was no basis for negotiation, 'but we should leave the door open for a further Soviet proposal which might enable the Soviet Government to save face and which was nevertheless not irreconcilable with the withdrawal of the North Korean forces'.[56]

Before Sir David Kelly delivered Attlee's response the Soviets, on 18 July, published the texts of the exchanges between Nehru and Stalin. In Moscow, Kelly found that the reply given to him by Gromyko the previous night was the same as Stalin's message of 15 July to Nehru. 'This was of course only to be expected, particularly in view of Nehru's encouraging response' commented Kelly although he considered it noteworthy that no publicity had been given to his last interview with Gromyko, any more than to the earlier ones. Kelly imagined that the explanation for the differing publicity treatment was the obvious one; namely, that the Soviet Government realised from the moment of the first Indian approach on 1 July that exchanges with India offered much better prospects than did HMG's approach, of eliciting proposals which they could accept or exploit, and thus of strengthening their propaganda position, and perhaps even splitting the non-Communist powers. This would suggest that the Soviet Government were trying to 'keep a number of irons in the fire while maintaining their pose as defenders of peace, rather than in seeking a way out'. The Ambassador wondered whether the insistence on Communist Chinese representation at United Nations might indicate not merely a desire to turn the Korean war to their advantage by scoring an extraneous point (or by proving that aggression pays) but rather a need to give some satisfaction to Mao in compensation for the check to his plans for Formosa; or that the Soviet Government 'may have felt it necessary to keep us in play in order not to present us with a propaganda point, even in case it became necessary to disengage themselves from the Korean adventure'. Whatever part these and other considerations played in Soviet reasoning, Kelly thought the following conclusions emerged:

(A) Soviets cannot now be talked into calling off North Koreans without *quid pro quo*;
(B) We cannot offer any *quid pro quo*;
(C) Unless or until military situation is reversed, Soviets have no motive for departing from the Stalin Nehru line;
(D) Any further approach by us to Russians in present circumstances would play into their hands.

It looked therefore as if the Indian manoeuvres, and Soviet action in publishing the Nehru–Stalin exchanges, had (for the present at least) ended all hopes of any solution other than a military one. Kelly believed that the only non-military steps now open to the West were:

(A) To make known story of our approaches to Soviet Government before latter do so, and (B) to explore all possible means of driving a wedge between Chinese and Russians.

As regarded (A) it was quite on the cards that the Russians would publish details in the next few days. They would almost certainly do so if HMG announced that the Nehru–Stalin line was unacceptable: 'We should therefore lose no time in getting our account across, stressing particularly Soviet evasion of our main point, and their blatant attempt to turn our appeal to political advantage by introducing issue of Chinese representation' recommended Kelly. As for (B), the fundamental Sino-Soviet contradiction at the moment was that Soviet action in Korea had frustrated Chinese action against Formosa. Kelly thought that this theme could usefully be exploited without any change in the line the Foreign Office had taken on Formosa with Acheson.[57]

When Kelly did, finally, deliver Attlee's rejection of the Soviet conditions, the Ambassador, on reflection, was inclined to think that Gromyko showed 'faint signs of disappointment when I had finished reading the

Aide-Memoire' although he accepted it 'would be rash to build anything on such an impression'. Kelly felt the Soviet Government 'can certainly not have expected us to accept their "solution", but it is not impossible (despite publication of Nehru–Stalin exchanges) that they hoped we would come forward with a compromise (which they would accept or exploit according to circumstances) or at least that we would keep the door open'. As it was, the Soviets were bound to conclude from Kelly's demarche that 'we have abandoned hope of a peaceful settlement and resigned ourselves to inevitability of a preliminary military solution. They may also have been confirmed in their suspicion that our object all along has been to improve our propaganda position at their expense'. Despite this, Kelly saw no reason to modify his views that any further approach to the Russians at the present stage would play into their hands. This would not necessarily be true of a further public statement indicating that 'we had not closed the door to a settlement by agreement. Plain fact is, however, that ... insistence on withdrawal to 38th parallel without any *quid pro quo* or face-saving device for Russians makes such a settlement inconceivable'.

Kelly then, without in 'any way advocating a weakening' of the present Anglo-American attitude, 'with which I am in full agreement', informed Bevin: 'it seems to me that we ought at least to have a really new approach which could be tried at a propitious moment. Only possibility which occurs to me', having regard to United States attitude, 'is that we (and necessary minimum of other Security Council members) let it be known that we would vote' for admission of Chinese Communists to United Nations as soon as (a) the Soviets resumed their seat on Security Council; and (b) the North Koreans had withdrawn to 38th parallel and ceased fighting: 'I am conscious of objections to *form* of bargain, and I would not rate chances of Soviet acceptance of this one very high. If however a non-military solution is still hoped for I can think of no other possible one. If Americans could be induced to accept or at least not oppose it, it would further strengthen our moral position, even if the Russians rejected it. It might also help in the field of Anglo-Chinese relations and, if rejected by Russians, contribute to wedge-driving process'.[58]

Thus ended the approach to Moscow. But the Indian exchanges illustrated the dangers the British felt the Korean conflict posed to Western interests. On 21 July, Nehru ventured to write to Attlee and in this message articulated the core of British fears which they, with their colonial past, felt the Americans could not comprehend. The Indian Prime Minister had written to his British counterpart, 'because I am greatly distressed at the turn events are taking'. It seemed to Nehru that there had not been any clear realisation of the position in Asia by the countries of the West. An attempt was no doubt made to understand the new forces at work in Asia, but the process of adaptation lagged behind and events occurred, which continually took people by surprise and upset preconceived plans: 'We never seem to catch up with events. You will forgive me, I hope, if I say that there has been a consistent record of failure in the policies adopted in the Far East and in parts of South East Asia by Western Powers' Nehru complained. That failure was due, he thought, to a complete lack of understanding of the vast dynamic forces that were at work in Asia. To a small extent, 'we in India are in a somewhat better position to judge of these forces. We are more directly and closely affected by them and so we have given a great deal of thought to them'. The first fact to be borne in mind was that Asia was undergoing vast revolutionary changes. Those changes, before they appeared on the surface, had already taken place in the minds of millions of people. These people were not Communist. But they sought social change, more especially in the agrarian sphere, and they were not prepared to put up with existing conditions. In particular, they were intensely opposed to any form of colonial control. If a choice was to be made by them, they preferred Communism to colonial control warned Nehru. To talk to them of the dangers of Communism did not frighten them at all. Any help or encouragement given to a colonial or a socially reactionary regime immediately produced a powerful reaction in them against the country that gave that help. 'I am merely stating facts, not expressing an opinion' wrote Nehru.

If this was the state of mass opinion in most of the countries of Asia, it had to be dealt with in some other way than a rather naïve condemnation of Communism argued Nehru. 'As we have seen in China, military strength and money cannot win in the end, if they are opposed to these basic urges of the people.' Again in Indo-China, a curious situation had existed for some time. The more help that was given to the French there, the more the people became hostile to the French and their supporters. There might be ultimately a French military victory in Indo-China: 'But it will be at the cost of a hostile population. How long can that victory endure? Step by step, we are getting entangled and there is no clear way out even by victory in war.' This, believed Nehru, was the position in a great part of Asia. The approach of the Western powers made no appeal to a great majority of people in Asia because it lacked understanding of what those people desired and there was a general impression that the Western powers supported reaction. The Soviet Government and its allies generally appeared to support what might be called the progressive forces in most countries: 'I know very well that the Soviet Government is probably playing its own expansionist game and that it would be a disaster if it succeeded in that.' Nevertheless, the fact remained that the Western powers, by their policies in Asia, indirectly helped the Soviets in Asia. The continued exclusion of the New China from the UN helped to increase sympathy for the People's Government in Peking among vast numbers of Asian peoples and distrust of the policies of Western powers.

Nehru had little doubt that the North Koreans would be driven out of South Korea in the end. But what would happen then he asked Attlee. The moment foreign troops were withdrawn, the same position would arise again or perhaps a worse one. The alternatives would be: armies of occupation and full control on colonial lines of these countries or leaving them to drift inevitably to Communism. The former alternative appeared to Nehru out of the question for any length of time and the longer it endured, 'the more we strengthen communism there'. Could the Western powers lead world opinion to a solution which was satisfactory to them and, no less importantly conducive to world peace? In a sense this argument might apply to Japan also, thought Nehru.

There was another aspect to the general world situation to which, Nehru thought, he should make at least passing reference. It was conceivable that, in the event of the military campaign in Korea being prolonged, the Western powers might get involved in deeper commitments along the periphery of the Soviet Union. The Soviet Union might not be directly engaged in these conflicts and its striking power would thus not be affected. In this way also a world war might be brought nearer. If there was world war, that would be a disaster for everyone. But apart from the disaster, what would even victory in it lead to? War, of course, could not be avoided, if there was aggression and there was no other way out. But war was meant to help in achieving a certain objective. That objective was not merely the defeat of the enemy but something more positive. If that positive objective disappeared, then the sole redeeming feature of a war also disappeared 'and we have not only the disaster of a war but also complete failure afterwards, in spite of military victory'. Nehru conceded to Attlee these were 'rather trite and obvious remarks and you will forgive me for making them. But I do feel that we are drifting fast in a wrong direction, which can only lead to evil results'.[59]

After reading through Nehru's letter, Hugh Gaitskell, the Chancellor of the Exchequer, in effect summarised the fears of the Government when he wrote to Attlee: 'I agree very much with practically all that he says.' The key to the present difficulties was the attitude of the United States and the Western powers toward the nationalist upsurge in Asia: 'We recognised this even before the war and we took action upon it immediately after the war' to reflect this, said the Chancellor; but now he feared: 'We shall inevitably lose all influence in the Far East and SE Asia to the Soviet.'[60]

## Notes

1. *Documents on British Overseas Policy* (DBOP): Korea, June 1950–April 1951 Series 2, Defence Policy and Global Strategy Report by the Chiefs of Staff, 7 June 1950
2. William Stueck, *Rethinking the Korean War: A New Diplomatic and Strategic History* (Princeton: Princeton University Press, 2002), pp. 71–72
3. Chen Jian, 'The Sino-Soviet Alliance and China's Entry into the Korean War Cold War', *International History Project*, Working Paper No. 1, June 1992, p. 1
4. Stueck, *Rethinking the Korean War*, pp. 72–75
5. TNA WO 308/56, *The History of the Commonwealth Division in Korea 1950–1956*, by Lieutenant Colonel H.F. Joslen
6. Heather Yasamee, 'Britain, Korea and the Politics of Power by Proxy', Foreign and Commonwealth Office Occasional Paper No. 5, *Korea,* April 1992, p. 8
7. DBOP: Korea Minute from Mr Rickcett to Mr Attlee 10 Downing Street, 25 June 1950
8. Foreign Relations of the United States (FRUS) 1950, Volume VII (Korea). Resolution Adopted by the United Nations Security Council, 25 June 1950
9. TNA DEFE 11/193 Addressed to United Kingdom Delegation New York Telegram No. 703 of 26 June 1950
10. FRUS 1950, Volume VII (Korea) Resolution Adopted by the United Nations Security Council, 27 June 1950
11. TNA DEFE 11/193 BJSM Washington to Ministry of Defence, London. For Chiefs of Staff from Lord Tedder, 26 June 1950
12. TNA DEFE 11/193 Air Marshall Elliot: Situation in Korea, 26 June 1950
13. TNA DEFE 11/193 Outward Telegram from Commonwealth Relations Office, 27 June 1950
14. TNA DEFE 11/193 Outward Telegram from Commonwealth Relations Office 17.10 hours, 27 June 1950
15. TNA DEFE 11/193 Washington to Foreign Office Telegram No. 1775, 27 June 1950
16. *Ibid.*
17. TNA DEFE 11/193 Washington to Foreign Office Telegram No. 1772, 27 June 1950
18. TNA DEFE 11/193 New York (Lake Success) to Foreign Office from Secretary-General UN Telegram No. 24, 27 June 1950
19. FRUS 1950, Volume VII (Korea) Editorial Note p. 257

20 TNA DEFE 11/193 Washington to Foreign Office Telegram No. 1789, 28 June 1950
21 TNA DEFE 11/193 Ministry of Defence to BJSM, British Land and Air Force Contribution
22 TNA DEFE 11/1 DO (50)48 28 June 1950 Defence Committee: Situation in Korea. Memorandum by the Chiefs of Staff
23 TNA DEFE 11/1 Cabinet Defence Committee. Minutes of a Meeting held in the Prime Minister's Room, House of Commons, SW1, on Wednesday 28 June 1950 at 4 pm
24 TNA DEFE 11/193 Chiefs of Staff Committee Confidential Annex to COS (50) 97th Meeting; held on Wednesday, 28 June 1950
25 TNA DEFE 11/194 Situation in Korea, 3 July 1950
26 TNA DEFE 11/193 Washington to Foreign Office Telegram No. 1792, 28 June 1950
27 TNA DEFE 11/193 Chiefs of Staff Committee Confidential Annex to COS (50) 97th Meeting; held on Wednesday, 28 June 1950
28 TNA DEFE 11/194 United States: Weekly Political Summary Period 24–30 June 1950, from Washington to Foreign Office
29 *Summary of Events Relating to Korea 1950*, Cmd 8078 (London: HMSO, 1950)
30 TNA DEFE 11/194 Far Eastern Department Cypher, 29 June 1950
31 TNA DEFE 11/194 Moscow to Foreign Office No. 543, 30 June 1950
32 TNA DEFE 11/195 Moscow to Foreign Office Telegram No. 567, 6 July 1950
33 TNA DEFE 11/196 Foreign Office to Washington Telegram No. 3159, 12 July 1950
34 TNA DEFE 11/195 Washington to Foreign Office Telegram No. 1881, 7 July 1950
35 TNA DEFE 11/195 Foreign Office to Washington Telegram No. 3105, 8 July 1950
36 TNA DEFE 11/195 Foreign Office to Moscow Telegram No. 569, 9 July 1950
37 TNA DEFE 11/195 Foreign Office to Moscow Telegram No. 570, 9 July 1950
38 TNA DEFE 11/195 Foreign Office to Washington Telegram No. 3070, 6 July 1950
39 TNA DEFE 11/195 Moscow to Foreign Office Telegram No. 597, 11 July 1950
40 TNA DEFE 11/196 Foreign Office to Moscow Telegram No. 607, 13 July 1950
41 DBOP: Korea Foreign Office to Washington, 8 July 1950
42 FRUS 1950, Volume VII (Korea). Secretary of State to the Embassy in the United Kingdom, 10 July 1950

43 FRUS 1950, Volume VII (Korea). Douglas to Acheson, 11 July 1950
44 FRUS 1950, Volume VII (Korea). Memorandum of Conversation by the Secretary of State, 13 July 1950
45 TNA DEFE 11/196 Foreign Office to Washington Telegram No. 3186, 14 July 1950
46 TNA DEFE 11/196 Washington to Foreign Office Telegram No. 1946, 13 July 1950
47 FRUS 1950, Volume VII (Korea). Memorandum of Conversation by the Secretary of State, 13 July 1950
48 TNA DEFE 11/196 Washington to Foreign Office Telegram No. 1946, 13 July 1950
49 FRUS 1950, Volume VII (Korea). Editorial Note p. 430
50 FRUS 1950, Volume VII (Korea). Memorandum of Conversation by the Secretary of State, 19 July 1950
51 TNA PREM 8/1409 Prime Minister's Personal Telegram Serial No. T57/50 Pandit Jawaharlal Nehru to the Rt Hon CR Attlee, 10 July 1950
52 TNA PREM 8/1409 Inward Telegram to Commonwealth Relations Office from Acting UK High Commissioner in India
53 TNA PREM 8/1409 Prime Minister's Personal Telegram Serial No. T62/50 Message from Pandit Jawaharlal Nehru to the Rt Hon CR Attlee, MP, 16 July 1950
54 TNA PREM 8/1409 Barclay to DHF Rickett
55 TNA PREM 8/1409 Foreign Office to Washington Telegram No. 3243, 18 July 1950
56 TNA CAB 128/18 Cabinet 47 (50) Conclusions of a Meeting of the Cabinet held at 10 Downing Street SW1 on Tuesday, 18 July 1950 at 11.30 am
57 TNA PREM 8/1409 Moscow to Foreign Office Telegram No. 626, 18 July 1950
58 TNA DEFE 11/197 Moscow to Foreign Office Telegram No. 646, 22 July 1950
59 TNA PREM 8/1409 Jawaharlal Nehru to Attlee, 21 July 1950
60 TNA PREM 8/149 Gaitskell to Attlee, 30 July 1950

# 2

## To cross or not to cross

### The 38th parallel

In Korea the initial deployment of under-trained US forces led to serious military setbacks for the UN. Very quickly it seemed as if the American ground commitment was going to be driven out of Korea and into the sea. On 17 July the Chiefs of Staff in London reported the grim news from Korea to their political masters. The best that the Americans could now hope to achieve was to hold a bridgehead around Pusan until they were reinforced. But some weeks must elapse before reinforcements could arrive; and this would undoubtedly be a critical period. The naval situation was considerably better, although the Chiefs reported that there were signs of increased activity by Soviet submarines in the Far East. A suggestion had been made that British troops might be sent from Hong Kong to Korea, on the understanding that they would be replaced by the early despatch of United States troops to Hong Kong; but the Cabinet thought that any such suggestion should be discouraged: there would be political disadvantages in associating the United States with the defence of Hong Kong[1] (Bevin, who had been too ill to attend the meeting, was pleased to see the Cabinet's reluctance in the minutes; he feared that bringing US troops to Hong Kong would be merely inviting the Chinese to attack the colony.)[2] Clearly, the Cabinet were agreed that no British ground troops should be sent to Korea. But there was now a problem in holding this position when the UN Secretary-General formally made a request to Member States for ground forces for use in Korea. The Cabinet felt that this might prove embarrassing, in view of the publicity which had been given to it. Secretary General Trygve Lie had, however, made it clear that his request had been made after consultation with United States authorities and the Cabinet was aware it might be that, on political grounds, the

United States Government had preferred that such a request should be made through United Nations channels. The Cabinet agreed that it would be impossible to form a final view on Lie's request, or to frame an answer to it, until more was known about the American position.[3]

This was clearly a holding operation. Lie's request had altered the entire political complexion of the war. The pressure for British ground troops to be committed to Korea was clear given that the UK remained a Power with a global reach – however stretched it was. The Chiefs came up with an alternative suggestion that they fired off to Lord Tedder, in Washington, on 20 July. They pointed out that, whether the Americans succeed in keeping a foothold in South Korea or had to go back again after an evacuation from the mainland, the subsequent campaign, if conducted on 'ordinary' lines, 'cannot fail to be long, arduous and expensive in human life and material'. It was bound to take time to mount and conduct an offensive campaign up through Korea on the lines of the Italian campaign, in the Second World War, from a bridgehead in the South; while to mount a combined army-naval-air operation to get back on to Korean soil might well take 6 to 9 months. Meanwhile the Communists would be consolidating their hold on the country and the UN might well be faced with the situation that the Koreans as a whole would urge it not to return. In any event the people who could mainly suffer from any kind of normal campaign of 'quote liberation unquote' would be the South Koreans, whose villages, roads and railways would be destroyed and their country turned into the 'usual squalid battlefield'. Therefore, argued the Chiefs, it would surely be worth examining whether the objective of the United Nations, namely the withdrawal of North Korea forces behind the 38th parallel and subsequent occupation of South Korea by United Nations forces, might not be achieved at much less cost by the use of air power on the following lines: 'We should not play the enemy's game and lock up great resources there which we may need elsewhere.' The North Koreans should be informed that, instead, 'we propose progressively to destroy by precision bombing, and after due warning to avoid loss of civilian life', everything of value in North Korea – factories, oil refineries, hydro-electric plant, railways, docks and so on. This process would continue until the order was issued for North Korean troops to withdraw behind the 38th parallel. As soon as that order became effective, the bombing would stop, and United Nations troops would re-occupy South Korea up to 38th parallel. If these forces met with any opposition, bombing would be resumed until opposition ceased.[4]

The Foreign Office, however, were not so sure that this might be the right time to advocate such a policy. Sir Pierson Dixon wondered, in a letter to the Chiefs, whether such instructions to Tedder 'might not convey the wrong impression? I do not presume to discuss the merits of strategic bombing, but I am inclined to think that at this moment it might have a bad effect on our relations with the Americans if we broached with them a plan based on the assumption that they would be driven out of Korea. We do not want to seen defeatist, nor to interfere with MacArthur; nor of course would we like it if the Americans thought we were seeking an excuse not to make a contribution on the ground'.[5] The Americans were, thus, not informed of the Chief's view – which was, essentially, a way of trying to avoid the commitment of British ground forces to the campaign.

What led to British troops being committed arose from discussions, held between 20 and 24 July, between US and UK representatives in Washington on the 'Present World Situation'. The Americans were represented by General Omar Bradley and Ambassador Jessup and the British by Sir Oliver Franks and Lord Tedder. The meetings were to alter fundamentally the British part in the Korean War. At the first meeting, on 20 July, the question of UN land forces in Korea was raised by Bradley. He emphasised that such reinforcements were of utmost importance from a military as well as a political aspect. He stressed the need for considerable forces, not only to secure rapid and decisive results when an advance became possible, but also to keep secure very lengthy lines of communication which would be subject to and vulnerable to guerrilla attacks. Any units of battalion strength upwards would be of genuine assistance. Tedder explained the British position and commitments and emphasised that it would be most undesirable for any UK land forces to be taken from Hong Kong or Malaya: 'I also explained that we had had to draw from [the] Middle East, and from our meagre reserves in the UK to meet the situation in Malaya and Hong Kong. I said however, that we had not till now appreciated that even very small reinforcement[s] would be of definite military, repeat military value in Korea, or that the time factor for its arrival in Korea was not an urgent matter.'[6]

It was now clear that the Americans were preparing for a campaign that would last for months and that it was important that, when the counteroffensive was undertaken, it be carried out with strong enough forces that the North Korean Army be 'destroyed to the maximum extent' before UN forces reached the 38th parallel. Franks and Tedder declared that in the light of what they had just heard they would represent the points made to London.[7] While Tedder reported back to the Chiefs, Franks informed Bevin how the talks were 'conducted in an open and cordial atmosphere'; but he also added that it was quite clear that the question of United Nations forces for Korea was foremost in the American mind 'and I would judge that as a result of the representations made to us we shall now be expected to respond with at any rate a token force. There was no doubt in our minds that what was said to us had been carefully thought out beforehand and had the highest authority. We therefore now have a clear indication of United States thinking on the subject'.[8] Meanwhile, the US Ambassador, in London, urged Acheson to allow him to sound Attlee out informally on the question of British ground troops. Ambassador Douglas feared the reactions of certain parts of the Labour Party to an *aide-mémoire* from Washington: it would be better if the British made an offer of ground troops on their own initiative because the existence of an *aide-mémoire* could probably not be withheld from the House of Commons and could be interpreted as the United States pressing the issue.[9]

But Attlee did not need prodding. Both he and Bevin were aware that if they did not unilaterally offer ground forces they were likely to be formally asked by the Americans. On 21 July, the Foreign Office informed the Chiefs that their understanding was that there would be a specific request for the armoured regiment at present in Hong Kong to be sent to Korea. Obviously no answer could be given until an official request was received, but the Foreign Office considered that the Chiefs of Staff should know of this approach. As part of their reply, General Brownjohn, standing in for Slim, warned that while the armoured regiment at present in Hong Kong, equipped with Comet tanks, could be moved to South Korea in about 10 days or 2 weeks, there would, however, be serious logistic difficulties encountered in operating British tanks in South Korea. Furthermore, the move of the armoured regiment would be contrary to the views which the Chiefs had previously expressed that it would be militarily unsound to take forces from Hong Kong or Malaya. If the armoured regiment was sent to Korea, it would take 'many months to replace it'.[10] The situation, then, was that the Chiefs still regarded it as militarily unsound to despatch ground forces.

But the emphasis had shifted away from military advice to trans-Atlantic policy. Franks despatched a telegram to London putting the case for the offer of British ground forces in Korea. The Ambassador's telegram changed British policy. While Franks had not consulted the Americans: 'I am sure that United States Administration attaches great importance to a British offer of ground troops for Korea ... I was present at the meeting when General Bradley made his statement. It was clear that his statement was very carefully prepared and that it represented not his personal views nor the view of the Joint Chiefs of Staff only but the views of the United States Administration.' On the political side, pointed out Franks, the administration attached importance to Britain making this offer in his view mainly for the following reasons: they regarded the United Nations character of the Korean operations as fundamental. This flowed from their 'constitutional habits which leads them to require and insist upon full legal documentation for their actions. It also flows from their general policy springing equally idealistic and practical motives to maintain and strengthen the United Nations organisation. It flows also in the Korean case from the view that the United Nations character of American action is essential to their relations with the new nations of Asia and as a refutation of imperialism'. This last consideration did not conflict in the American mind as yet with the action taken on Formosa, 'because they are only now perceiving and setting themselves to minimise the political consequences of that action'. The Truman administration believed it essential for the United Nations character of the Korean operations that they should not be carried out solely by United States forces. 'They foresee a long and difficult ground campaign and therefore, despite the high appreciation with which sea and air assistance is regarded, apply this belief to those most closely engaged in the battle. They know that many nations will follow the British decision on this matter. They see us as the key to the situation and hence await our decision as more important to them and their purposes than any other.'

There were further reasons, argued Franks, which moved the administration 'partly because those reasons count heavily with the American people and partly because the Administration as Americans share the views of the American people'. Firstly, underneath the thoughts and emotions engendered at times by 'difficulties and disagreements between us and them there is a steady and unquestioned assumption that we are the only dependable ally and partner. This derives from our position in the world over past decades, our partnership with them in two world wars and their judgement of the British character. The Americans in Korea will be in a tough spot for a long time. They look round for their partner'. The administration knew that Britain's economy was only just recovering to sustain its commitments. 'They know we have these commitments all over the world. They know that in many of them, especially in the Far East, we are taking a heavy lead in the same struggle. Nevertheless, the United States administration faces and shares the expectation of the American people that we shall show we are with them on the ground in Korea.'

The second reason was that despite the power and position of the United States, the American people were 'not happy if they feel alone. This feeling is paradoxical but it is real and a reality in the Korean situation. The American people will not understand it if they are alone on the ground in Korea. They will think it shows coolness to them or even disapproval of what they are doing'. The administration was aware of this feeling and its vigour. It therefore moved the administration to look for assistance on the ground and once again they turned to Britain as the key. It was also true that the Americans who composed the administration shared this feeling. For these reasons Franks expected the reaction of the United States administration to a negative decision by Britain to be deep and prolonged. The Ambassador was not thinking primarily of the effects that it would have on relatively short-term matters however important, such as additional appropriations for European defence. The important consideration was the effect such a decision would have on the basic relationship of the two countries: 'I believe that because of the rational and irrational elements in the American mind about this for them unparalleled undertaking to act as a policeman in the world, a negative decision would seriously impair the long term relationship. This is so partly because of the significance our decision would acquire as giving a lead, which they expect to be followed by other countries.'[11]

On 24 July, the Defence Committee met and, having taken everything into account, the Prime Minister informed the Chiefs of his decision. Attlee said that, though he fully understood there were strong military reasons for not sending land forces to Korea, 'there were now strong psychological reasons for reviewing the situation'. The Secretary General of the United Nations had invited member nations to offer combat forces and the United States authorities had hinted very strongly that even small land forces would be very acceptable. Franks' telegram from Washington was the key in that he thought that the moral effect of providing this force would be considerable and that it was in fact now essential for a British token force to be provided. The question for decision was the size of this force and how soon it could be sent.

With this decision by their civilian master, the First Sea Lord, on behalf of the Chiefs, replied that they had not had time to consider the views contained in Franks' telegram. They had previously been opposed to the provision of a UK contribution to the land forces in Korea 'but the view expressed in this telegram appeared to alter the situation completely'. Field Marshall Slim added that, although in the Chief's view it was still militarily unsound, they recognised the strong political arguments in its favour. In their view it would be wrong to send less than a Brigade Group. Nothing less would achieve the political objective. They were examining in greater detail how to find this Brigade Group and how to constitute it. It should be a mixed force – perhaps an Armoured Regiment equipped with the new Centurion tanks, an Anti-Tank Regiment equipped with 17-pounders, a Field Regiment and three Infantry Battalions. There would be at least some military advantages in sending this force: it would be an exercise in finding the strategic reserve which the War Office were always trying to constitute, and it would provide a practical test for certain weapons, especially the Centurion tanks. Slim warned that the force could not be constituted in a day and it might be necessary to call up, perhaps, some 2,000 reservists, especially signallers, of which the Army was very short. The American Command, under which the British Brigade Group would come, would probably not want reinforcements until the battle was stabilised and they were in a position to counter-attack. The despatch of the Brigade Group was not therefore urgent which would allow Britain at least two months in which to make the necessary preparations. Crucially, the Committee decided that the Brigade Group should not be formed at the expense of the Hong Kong Garrison. In the meantime the decision should be made known to Lord Tedder and also to the United States Ambassador who would be asked to keep the matter secret until after a defence debate in Parliament. Commonwealth Prime Ministers were to be informed of the action to be taken.[12]

The Prime Ministers of Canada, Australia, New Zealand and South Africa – the Old ('White') Dominions – were duly informed by Attlee who telegraphed the decision to them. He emphasised the importance of Franks' views in the decision (and attached a copy of the Ambassador's views) and pointed out how: 'From the military point of view it is, of course extremely hard for us to provide even a token force, but having regard to the wider political considerations, we have come to the conclusion that it would be desirable for us to make an offer of ground forces. I should like to emphasise that we have received no repeat no request from the United States Administration and that our position is that we propose to make a spontaneous offer in accordance with our obligations under the Security Council resolution.'[13]

On 26 July, Emanuel Shinwell announced the decision to the House of Commons. On the same date the Australian and New Zealand Governments also announced their intention to provide an Infantry force and an Artillery formation respectively. The Chiefs of Staff with the concurrence of the US Joint Chiefs and General MacArthur appointed Air Vice-Marshal C.H. Bouchier as their representative on MacArthur's Headquarters staff. He would be the eyes and ears of the British Chiefs inside the Supreme Commander's camp. Bouchier was issued with a directive, on 1 August from the Chiefs, outlining his responsibilities and duties:

> You are appointed to General MacArthur's Headquarters as Senior British Military Liaison Officer between him in his capacity as

Commander-in-Chief of the United Nations forces operating in support of South Korea, and the British Chiefs of Staff.

Sir A. Gascoigne, the Head of the United Kingdom Liaison Mission in Japan, is the Senior British representative in Japan. You will therefore act in close co-operation with him and his staff and keep him generally informed of your work.

You will be responsible for:–
(a) The despatch of periodical reports on the battle situation.
(b) The despatch of periodical appreciations of the general situation as seen by the Commander-in-Chief himself.

On 2 August the War Office issued a formal executive order for the mobilisation of 29 Infantry Brigade Group for service in Korea, and to be ready to sail, from the UK, on 1 November. This was to be the British military contribution to the campaign. This commitment would soon escalate. On 7 August, Bouchier reported to General MacArthur at his Headquarters. On the same date the Canadian Prime Minister, L.S. St. Laurent, had announced that the Canadian Government would recruit a new formation of Brigade strength and make it available for carrying out Canada's obligations under the Charter of the United Nations. Then, on 10 August, Bouchier, in a telegram, to the Chiefs of Staff reporting his interview with MacArthur, stated that the General required, 'urgently now', and in the immediate future, more infantry in Korea. The US Divisions were at present under-manned and reinforcements were being flown in daily. The General added 'that a little got in fast was better than a lot later on'; he was prepared to provide American rations and hospitalisation and handle all base supplies except ammunition for two additional British battalions now. On 16 August as a result of representations from MacArthur through the US Joint Chiefs the date of sailing from the United Kingdom for Korea of 29 Infantry Brigade Group was put forward to 1 October from November; and after considerable discussions between the War Office and General Sir John Harding, the Commander-in-Chief Far East Land Forces, the Chiefs of Staff, on 17 August, agreed to the despatch from Hong Kong – despite the weakening of the colony's defences – to Korea of two infantry battalions and the necessary headquarters with Cabinet approval.[14]

And, by the end of August 1950, Ernest Bevin could be satisfied that he had reasserted British influence in Washington. The Foreign Secretary, of course, was realistic about the limitations of this influence; but he was concerned that, unless British influence was maintained, the trend of American policy in its absence would have serious and negative consequences for the West in the Cold War struggle with Communism. But

Bevin not only had to carry the Americans but his Cabinet colleagues too. So, Bevin explained his strategy for Anglo-American relations, in detail, to the Cabinet on 30 August. He began by outlining how, since the end of the war, the policy of His Majesty's Government in South and South-East Asia 'has been to encourage the legitimate aspirations of the peoples of that area for independence'. As Bevin identified it, the problem before London was to seek, at a time when the general atmosphere in the United States was least favourable for such a course, to persuade the United States administration not to adopt policies in relation to the Far East which would fail to command general support amongst friendly nations and which would antagonise Asia. Despite this somewhat gloomy interpretation, Bevin pointed out: 'The position is by no means hopeless. For the first time since the war the United States administration have shown a desire to consult with us on Far Eastern affairs and to give consideration to the views which we express, and they are also showing signs of appreciating the importance of Asian (and particularly Indian) opinion in dealing with these matters.' Though Bevin was clear that the United States administration would not change its policies in response to purely British suggestion, it might be willing to modify those policies in response to a majority view in the United Nations Assembly, provided an agreed view emerged as a result of debate and consultations. Bevin had it in mind, therefore, to try to get the Americans to agree to consult with other Powers, in particular with Commonwealth countries, with France and possibly with some other European countries. If the support of these could be secured, the next step would be to try to get the broad agreement of other friendly members of the United Nations, and thus build up a common front against any manoeuvres of the Soviet Union, whose main purpose was to create a split:

> The task will obviously be a difficult one, but it offers the best hope for reconciling United States and Asian opinion and of enabling the Commonwealth to keep in line with the United States. Only by pursuing this course can we hope to avoid open divergence with the United States on China and the related question of Formosa, and the unfortunate consequences which might ensue in the present highly-charged atmosphere in the United States.[15]

One example of the Americans new willingness to listen to the British had occurred, on 26 August, when President Truman ordered the withdrawal of a message from General MacArthur to the Chicago Convention of Veterans of Foreign Wars which had been given press circulation in advance of its release date of 28 August. In this message MacArthur emphasised the strategic importance to the United States of Formosa in the Pacific island defence line: 'If we hold this line we may have peace – lose it and war is inevitable'. When reports of MacArthur's message were received in the Foreign Office on 25 August, Bevin despatched instructions that evening to Sir Oliver Franks to inform Acheson: 'I do hope, therefore, that General MacArthur can be restrained from making any statement on Formosa at this extremely delicate moment.' Franks replied that he had acted immediately and had been informed that the President had ordered the statement's withdrawal.[16]

The strategic position of UN forces in Korea, meanwhile, was about to be changed utterly by MacArthur's inspired landings at Inchon. As early as 16 September, in a letter to the Chiefs of Staff, Air Vice Marshal Bouchier reported that, assuming the complete defeat of the North Korean Army, 'the feeling in Tokio [sic] was that our forces would not stop at the 38th parallel but would continue Northwards short of the Manchurian border.' And China. This might be done either after obtaining United Nations authority or else by 'unilateral military action' for reasons of military security and relying on the subsequent endorsement of the United Nations for this action. The British military leadership felt uneasy about this. Upon receiving this information, Lord Tedder was concerned that the result would be to leave Korea in a state of chaos and practically all the industrial resources of North Korea destroyed. However, Tedder considered a crossing of the parallel acceptable, if the United Nations were to take the line with the Koreans that they did not wish to leave the country in the state of waste in which it would be at the end of hostilities, thought they might be able to revive the whole of Korea as a single entity. Field Marshall Slim's initial response was against United Nations forces crossing into North Korea: South Korean forces plus a small United Nations force could hold the 38th parallel. He thought the United Nations should take the line, with the North Koreans, that if they were willing to accept a United Nations mission they would be given assistance in re-establishing their country. There was general agreement, among the Chiefs, that the problem was mainly political but the military aim should be to get as many British troops out of Korea as early as possible leaving behind the minimum commitment for the minimum time. There was a shared concern that unless instructions were issued to General MacArthur there was a grave danger of forces being moved forward into North Korea without the implications of such action having been fully studied. One result of such action might be to provoke the Russians or Chinese Communists to invade North Korea.[17]

The most concerned of the Chiefs was clearly the Chief of the Air Staff, Sir John Slessor. He told his fellow Chiefs that Bouchier's letter 'has strengthened a feeling I have had for some time that the Americans have not even yet cleared their minds on what is the object of the exercise in KOREA: and that, if we are not careful, a victory in South Korea, instead of enabling us to reduce our commitments there and concentrate our resources on the really important things – particularly securing the European front – may let us in for extended and indefinite commitments and even, in the worst case, involve serious risks of a clash with Russia and Communist China. I … am not sure that we ourselves have really thought this out carefully enough'. 'What' he asked 'is the object of this exercise? I think the Americans would agree with us that we have really no strategic interest in KOREA whatever. Politically I know our object is to see an independent, unified and democratic Korea as a result of free elections under U.N.O. auspices – we can keep our tongues in our cheeks as to the extent to which any Korean regime would in fact ever be democratic or, for that matter, independent with Communist China and Russia just across the Yalu' river. But the West certainly did not want to be 'let in' for a very big and prolonged commitment to maintain forces throughout Korea maintaining law and order. On the broad strategic view the more and the sooner they could reduce their forces in Korea and have them available either to deal with further Russian 'proxy' wars on the Korean model elsewhere, or to strengthen the European front, 'the happier we shall be. We shall no doubt have to maintain some forces in South Korea for a long time to come, to ensure that Russia or China does not immediately nullify all we have fought for there'. That did not mean maintaining forces in Korea strong enough to withstand a Russian or Chinese attack, but only enough to ensure

(a) that such an attack, or 'liberation' at the behest of local Communists, can't happen without forcing a major war, (i.e. a deterrent) and
(b) that we are no *worse* off than before the North Korean invasion – that, having had a great moral victory in getting overwhelming U.N. support and standing up to Communist aggression, and a great physical victory by destroying the North Korean invaders, we don't have a disastrous moral and political set-back by losing South Korea in the next few years to the form of attack which the Russians would have adopted this time if they had had any sense, the political conquest on the Czecho-Slovak model, which the United Nations could have done nothing about.

That being so, what was the object of the UN sending any forces – except perhaps South Korean forces – north of the 38th parallel at all, asked

Slessor? 'If we assume the N.K. Army is destroyed south of the 38th parallel as the result of present operations, what is the military advantage to be gained by occupying North Korea? True, it would ensure more certainly that anything else could that North Korea does not repeat her invasion of South Korea in a few months or years time. But after having had her Army destroyed and all her industries knocked flat, I find it difficult to envisage North Korea, even with Russian assistance, becoming a menace again for a long time to come.' Anyway was that risk worth the cost of

   (a) doing something which is at least questionably justified from the legal U.N. stand point and would certainly be unpopular with some Asiatic Powers, such as India;
   (b) letting ourselves in for an enormously increased commitment in the shape of forces for internal security and law and order throughout North as well as South Korea;
   (c) running a pretty serious risk of clashes with Russia and Communist China: I'd have thought from that point of view there was a lot to be said for having a couple of hundred miles between American/British troops and the Yalu.

The argument for crossing the 38th parallel would be, Slessor had no doubt, that if there were to be an independent, unified, democratic Korea there must be properly supervised elections and these must see that Communist fifth columns in North Korea after the elections did not organise local insurrections leading ultimately to the fall of the new unified Government, 'and so on'; and that this could not be done that unless there were UN Forces in North Korea: 'I'm not at all sure that argument holds water. Should we not consider something on the following lines' he asked:

   (a) As soon as we have completed the reconquest of South Korea, we (U.S. or ourselves or both) should put a resolution to the General Assembly to the effect that there should now be national elections throughout all Korea under U.N. auspices, with the object of establishing an independent, unified, democratic State.
   (the necessary steps dropping pamphlets, broadcasting etc. to be taken to make sure that everyone in North Korea is fully informed about this at all stages).
   (b) The North Koreans should be instructed
      (i) to send representatives to meet the Truce Commission ... for preliminary discussions on the political future of the country in accordance with the U.N. resolution.

(ii) that in due course the representatives of the new U.N. Commission charged with the supervision of the elections ... will enter North Korea to get on with their work. It may be necessary that they should have escorts of South Korean troops.

(iii) that no other U.N. troops will enter North Korea.

(c) If the N.K. Government has not disintegrated and refuses to accept these terms, we should make it clear that we are not interested in forcing upon them an independent, unified, democratic State at the point of U.N. Bayonets, and if they prefer to remain a Russian satellite, that is their affair.

But we intend to go ahead in re-establishing S. Korea as an independent State, with all the advantages of American ... aid, etc., and to take the necessary steps including the retention of some U.N. forces as long as S. Korea needs them, to ensure against a repetition of the first invasion.

(d) It will then be up to us to see that S. Korea really does become a better, more prosperous, better governed and more properly democratic State than N. Korea. Synghman Rhee and co. must not have a free hand to misgovern the place as they did before; land reforms etc. should be enforced and the U.N. Commission will have to remain in S. Korea for a long time.

If 6(c) eventuated, then it would be a pity – it would mean in effect the *status quo ante*, 'and I dare say it will be difficult to induce America to accept that'. From a political point of view it would not be so good as to get a Unified Korea under UN auspices; but it would be much better than it was before in relation to US and British and UN prestige in Asia – 'we shall have inflicted a great defeat on aggressive Communism and re-established the legal U.N. position, and that will serve as a warning to others. It would have some added advantage that the free countries could not be accused of achieving any gains at the expense of the Communist Powers'. And, from a military point of view, it would mean a much less onerous commitment than any occupation of North Korea.[18]

In fact, everyone was wondering what the Soviets would do as the UN advanced north. In Washington, following the Inchon landings, Dean Rusk, Assistant Secretary of State for Far Eastern Affairs, mentioned to Sir Oliver Franks, on 18 September, that the Americans were very much on the alert for any Russian reaction – however slight – to the latest military development in Korea. Rusk wondered whether the British had noticed any odd remarks by Malik, the Soviet representative who had retaken his seat on the Security Council, or others, or anything which could be construed as the first step in an approach over the Korean situation. Rusk made it clear that the State Department would much appreciate London's views on how the Russians were likely to act, in view of the apparently 'firm lodgement' that the United Nations forces secured at Inchon. Franks reported to London that, whilst realising that 'we probably have little local intelligence on which to base an assessment Rusk said it would very very helpful if we could attempt an estimate of the Soviet reaction on these recent developments'.[19]

In Moscow, the United States Embassy agreed with the British view that there had been no indications of any official Soviet reaction to the turn of the military tide in Korea. Thus, in the absence of any firm evidence, Sir David Kelly was forced into personal speculations on the way the Kremlin might be thinking. He considered the possibility that the Soviet Government might regard the occupation of North Korea by United Nations forces as a *casus belli*. If the Soviets realised that the prospect of tangible gain from the North Korean aggression had now evaporated, their leaders must seek to minimise the Communist setback and its potential consequences. And, thought Kelly, if there were any chance of a settlement on the basis of a North Korean withdrawal beyond the 38th parallel and a so-called restoration of the *status quo* as was originally proposed to Gromyko, 'they would presumably now welcome it'. The Kremlin must, however, be contemplating the 'obnoxious' possibility that United Nations forces would occupy North Korea and must be considering ways of either (1) forestalling that eventuality; or, failing that, (2) neutralising the danger it would constitute. On either count, 'I imagine that the Russians themselves will be somewhat inhibited from putting forward a detailed proposal which would not be *prima facie* absurd, by the fact that this would either link them with a lost cause or entail a too obvious disavowal of their Communist protégés' concluded the Ambassador.[20]

Meanwhile the long-term political settlement in the Korea matter was discussed, on 21 September, when Attlee telegraphed to Bevin, who was in New York: 'The reports from Korea seem to me to indicate the possibility of the collapse of the North Korean forces operating in South Korea.' This made the consideration of what was to happen next 'a matter of urgency … It is, I think, important that the United Nations Organisation should be considered the deliverer, not the destroyer of Korea'. Attlee thought there was much to be said for some kind of declaration that the United Nations Organisation would take the responsibility for the rehabilitation of the whole country. 'Otherwise the Russians might step in with a view to appearing as the benevolent restorer of what the United Nations

Organisation has destroyed.' The Prime Minister imagined that 'China would not be sorry if Russian influence were eliminated from Korea provided that the new regime was a real United Nations Organisation trusteeship for the eventual freeing of the Koreans.' Attlee wished 'to know how your mind is moving on this matter'.[21] Bevin replied: 'The really tricky thing is whether the United Nations forces are to go north of the 38th parallel. Clearly they must do so if the unification of Korea is to be achieved.' The Foreign Office had prepared a UN resolution that sought to cover this contingency, 'though admittedly in veiled terms'.[22] The question was: how to get the UN to adopt it given the return of the Soviets to the Security Council where they now could exercise their veto on any attempt to pass such a resolution?

At the House of Commons, on 19 September, the Attorney and Solicitor-General, together with Kenneth Younger, agreed it might be possible for the UN *Assembly* as opposed to the UN *Security Council* to grant UN forces in Korea an air of legitimacy in crossing the 38th parallel and unifying Korea. When this question had come before the Cabinet there had been a discussion as to whether Korea could or should be put on the agenda of the General Assembly – where a vote in favour of a resolution was merely an expression of a majority of Member States' views and did not carry the legal force of a Security Council approved resolution – but could be interpreted as reflecting the will of the vast majority of the UNO representatives. The problem was that, having regard to the fact that under Article 12(i) of the UN Charter, the General Assembly was *not* to make recommendations on a dispute or situation that was *already* on the agenda of the Security Council unless the Security Council so requested – and of course it would not thanks to the Soviet veto there. The Law Officers concluded:

(i) It is clear under Article 12(i) that the General Assembly could not make recommendations on a question if that same question was still on the agenda of the Security Council.
(ii) Because of the obvious dangers of this course Korea should in no event be taken off the agenda of the Security Council merely for the purpose of facilitating discussion in the Assembly.
(iii) Theoretically it was possible to divide the Korean question into two parts, (A) 'the restoration of peace and security', and (B) 'the future of Korea' assuming that peace and security had been restored; and therefore it might be held that it was possible without a breach of Article 12(i) for the Assembly to make recommendations on question (B) while question (A) remained the affair of the Security Council.

The distinction in paragraph 3(iii) above was 'easier to make in theory than to maintain in practice', e.g. the question whether the United Nations Forces should go north of the 38th parallel might well appertain to both A and B. On the other hand, it was agreed that an overwhelming majority of the members of the Assembly would certainly want to express their views on Korea and propose recommendations. Further, 'there are obvious political reasons why it is desirable that the Assembly should discuss Korea, freed from the shadow of Russian vetoes'.[23] In this way the British came up with a mechanism to get the UN General Assembly to authorise the unification of Korea without having to disturb the Security Council. Its legal basis was dubious but the UNO was the court of world political opinion not a court of international law. When the Cabinet came to make a decision on the issue, the Attorney-General explained that, 'in strict law', the General Assembly was 'probably not entitled' to make recommendations about Korea while the matter was still in the hands of the Security Council. He recognised, however, that this was an occasion on which the action of the Assembly should be guided by the wishes of the great majority of the Member States. The Cabinet approved a revised draft resolution and recommendations to be put before the General Assembly subject to amendments.[24]

There was still time, on the morning of the 24th, for Sir William Elliot to inform Bevin in New York of the anxiety felt by the Chiefs concerning the need to give explicit instructions to MacArthur in view of the rapidly approaching likelihood of the military collapse of North Korea. Bevin was 'fully seized' of the urgency of the need to formulate some definite plan to meet the situation, if the surrender of North Korea came quickly – 'as may well happen'.[25] But while the Chiefs were inclined to prevent MacArthur crossing the 38th parallel, Bevin was more disposed to agreeing with the Americans a framework for unifying a non-Communist Korea. Once again the question was: how would the Soviets react? For advice Bevin turned to the Joint Intelligence Committee (JIC); but even the JIC, the apex of the British intelligence community, found it difficult to forecast Soviet intentions – 'in the present case we have exceptionally little to go on' – although it considered there to be three courses open to the Soviet Government:

(a) military occupation of North Korea (presumably by invitation of the North Korean People's Government) before United Nations forces reach the 38th parallel;
(b) political effort in the United Nations and elsewhere to bring about a compromise that would leave intact Soviet influence over North Korea and offer a chance of extending it later over all Korea;

(c) the strengthening of Soviet military dispositions on the Manchurian/Korean border without military or political intervention in Korea.

Course (a) appeared advantageous to Russia, if carried out quickly enough. The United Nations forces were likely to make contact with Sino-Soviet forces in the end anyhow, and the Russians might prefer a meeting on the 38th parallel to one on the Manchurian/Korean border. After a preventive occupation of North Korea the Soviet Union could negotiate from a situation of strength in order to obtain a political compromise solution as in course (b). Course (a) did, however, involve risk of a direct Soviet–American clash leading to general war, 'which we think the Soviet Government is still anxious to avoid … though risk might be reduced if the Soviet forces could be sure of reaching the 38th parallel before the United Nations forces'; the Soviet Government might reckon that United Nations forces would not cross 38th parallel to attack Russian forces already holding it. A meeting at some indeterminate point in North Korea would be much more risky, and if the Soviet Government did not reoccupy North Korea in time to forestall the United Nations forces at the 38th parallel, 'then they probably will not send forces into North Korea at all. Time is getting short, and the absence of any intelligence indications of Soviet forces in North Korea tells against course (a)' warned the JIC.

As for course (b), Bevin agreed with the British Embassy in Moscow that the Soviet Government 'would jump at any well-intentioned but naive compromise' proposal put forward at Lake Success; but unless Soviet troops were already in possession of North Korea the Soviet bargaining position would be 'weak with the United Nations majority in their present mood'. If course (c) were followed and the United Nations forces occupied North Korea, Soviet prestige would suffer a blow which, though domestically unimportant, might have repercussions in China and elsewhere abroad. But the Soviets might feel able adequately to counter this by a heightened propaganda campaign including accusations of aggression, illegality, etc. Course (c) would, moreover, leave the United Nations (and primarily the United States) with the incubus of a largely devastated Korea and with a problem offering endless opportunities of offending Asiatic opinion. The Soviets, freed from responsibility, could stand back and do its best to make mischief.

There was, lastly, the question as to whether the Soviets might regard the invasion of North Korea by United Nations forces as a *casus belli* for a general war. On this Bevin agreed again with the Moscow Embassy that the Soviet Government might regard the American threat to Vladivostok and the Trans-Siberian Railway to be such as to warrant sending Soviet troops in from the North whatever the risk of a military clash; 'but if, as we believe, Soviet policy is to avoid a general war, United Nations occupation of North Korea would not (repeat not) in our view be a grave enough threat to make the Soviet Government abandon that policy.' As Bevin put it in a message to Franks in Washington:

> To sum up. The crossing of the 38th parallel by United Nations forces must involve an increased danger of a head-on clash with the Soviet Union. But we do not (repeat not) consider that the Soviet leaders would risk provoking a general war on this issue. They might seek to forestall such an eventuality and at the same time to strengthen their bargaining position by themselves reoccupying North Korea (either alone or under Chinese cover) at the invitation of the North Korean People's Government. But such indications as there are suggest that they may well decide to cut their losses, take no (repeat no) military or political initiative themselves, and leave the whole responsibility for clearing up the mess with the United Nations.[26]

Bevin's assessment of Soviet reactions was also sent to the UK High Commission in New Delhi for transmission to Prime Minister Nehru alongside the text of the UK draft resolution on Korea. Speaking personally to Sir Archibald Nye, the UK High Commissioner, Bajpai, Nehru's principal adviser, said that he thought that there had been a complete change of outlook in China during the past fortnight or so, which suggested that they 'can no longer look to the United Nations Organisation for fair treatment, that they cannot tolerate the frequent violations of Manchurian territory by American aircraft, that the presence of a hostile force on their flank can no longer be permitted and that they have no alternative but to take military action'. Nye reported to London that K.M. Pannikar, the Indian Ambassador to China, seemed to accept these statements by the Chinese as *bona fide* and 'clearly regards the situation as very grave. He has suggested that Nehru should send a personal message to the Chinese Government and Bajpai has prepared a draft which has not yet been seen by the Prime Minister'. Whilst Bajpai agreed that Pannikar was a 'somewhat volatile person' he felt, nevertheless, 'that there is no alternative but to accept the views of the man on the spot who is in close touch with the Chinese authorities'. Bajpai also felt that it was of extreme importance that 'we should know of this development before we table our proposed resolution to the Assembly because he considers that the proposed action north of the 38th parallel may either (a) confirm the proposed action of the Chinese Government if they have not in fact already decided to take action, or (b) if they have already made their decision, give them a good excuse for intervening in the Korean war'.²⁷

So concerned were the Indians by developments in China that they once again took the relatively unusual decision to pass on the telegrams from the Indian Ambassador in Peking to the British. On the evening of 26 September, General Nieh Jung-Chen, the Chief of Staff in overall charge of Chinese military planning, had dined with Pannikar who reported that the military man was 'emphatic that [the] Chinese Government will not take lying down continuous provocation of Americans meaning violations of Manchurian territory by aeroplanes. They consider they have no option but to resist if America does not stop this'. In the second telegram shown to the British, from Pannikar to Nehru, the Ambassador warned:

> There was one sentence in Chou En Lai's talk with me on 21st to which I did not then attach much importance. He said 'since United Nations claim to have no obligations towards us we also have none to them'.²⁸

On 28 September, the day after the High Commissioner's telegrams were received in London, the Cabinet made the crucial decision to support the American forward policy in Korea. There was general agreement that the policy of the United Kingdom Government towards the Korean problem should stand. At the same time, it was deemed 'desirable', to allay Communist Chinese fears, that the United States Government should be pressed to agree that representatives of the People's Government be invited to take part in discussions in the United Nations on some of the outstanding questions, such as Formosa, and should also endeavour to placate the Chinese Government in regard to the flights of United States military aircraft over Manchuria and the alleged bombing of places in Manchuria.²⁹ Despite the unsettling news, from New Delhi, the British Government did not judge Chinese intervention as imminent. And so, the text of a draft resolution was submitted on 30 September by the United Kingdom delegation to the Political Committee of the General Assembly of the United Nations with the co-sponsorship of the Australian, Brazilian, Cuban, Netherlands, Norwegian, Pakistani and Philippine delegations. The resolution had been drafted in full consultation with Commonwealth and other friendly delegations and with the approval of the United States Government. The latter were, however, anxious not to appear as co-sponsors. The main objectives of the resolution were:-

(a) To lay the foundations of a *unified* Korea under a democratically elected Government.

(b) To provide for the rehabilitation of Korea under the aegis of the United Nations and to prevent the U.S.S.R. stepping in with proposals which would make her appear as the benevolent restorer of what the United Nations had destroyed.
(c) To allay the suspicions of the U.S.S.R. and the Chinese People's Government regarding the intentions of the United Nations' forces should they be obliged to cross the 38th parallel and to deter these Governments from intervening in the conflict.

It was important that the resolution should be so worded as to secure Asian and in particular Indian public and Governmental support and to eradicate suspicions of 'United States imperialist designs' from the minds of friendly Governments in Asia; to this end a number of personal messages were exchanged between the Foreign Secretary and Pandit Nehru. The resolution was, however, designed to implement the 1948 UN resolution concerning the unification of Korea. Nehru made it clear that he was not opposed in principle to the introduction of a resolution declaring the objectives of the United Nations to be the creation of an independent and united Korea by means of free elections, under United Nations supervision; but he was opposed to any mention of the intention of the United Nations' forces to cross the 38th parallel. In deference to his views the final draft of the resolution omitted any specific reference to the 38th parallel and it was hoped that the Indian Government would agree to act as co-sponsors. In the event, however, their delegation did not receive instructions to do so.[30] The resolution was passed by the General Assembly.

While His Majesty's Government was fully behind the US strategy at this point, it nevertheless remained unclear to the British as to *who* was driving American strategy in Korea. Was it President Truman and the State Department; the Joint Chiefs of Staff; or General MacArthur in Tokyo? Assessments of what was going on in the mind of the Supreme Commander were priceless for policy-makers in London – even if they did not result in any clearer understanding. Sir Avery 'Joe' Gascogine, the British High Representative in Japan, met with him in late September: 'I had not seen General MacArthur since the 15 June; I found him in good spirits and in excellent physical condition; he has lost a little weight, but he seems to have weathered the storm of these past three months extraordinarily well for a man of 70.6 years of age.' He was 'evidently seriously preoccupied' by the problem of the parallel, and the amount of resistance which was still being shown to the United Nations forces in Seoul, which he said must spell casualties for the Americans. As regarded the Korean war, *per se*, 'he evidently was supremely pleased with himself, and rightly so', with the results of the amphibious landings at Inchon, and the fact that they had been carried out against the advice of his principals. Afterwards Gascogine reflected:

> I left MacArthur with mixed feelings – on the one hand intense admiration of his handling of the military situation in Korea and in particular of course of the lone hand which he had played so successfully over Inchon, and on the other anxiety regarding his future conduct of the occupation of Japan. In his present state of over-confidence which has quite naturally been induced by his overwhelming success in Korea, he will be likely to become more of a dictator than ever, and we may have considerable trouble with him in the future. He is annoyed with his leaders at Washington, from Truman downwards, because of what he conceives to be their unwarranted interference in the conduct of the war. He is also, evidently, still smarting under the President's rebuke which he suffered at the time of his Formosan message to the Chicago veterans. He seems now to be playing to the Republican gallery whence he evidently secures considerable support (vide Formosa). If we do not wish him to take further headstrong action as he did on Formosa, it seems obvious that he must, henceforth, be ridden by Truman on a very severe curb. He must, and will, submit to the President's direct orders, but I doubt whether he will obey anybody else. He is flushed with success and is convinced that he, and he alone, knows best, not only about military matters but also about the tangled skein of international relations which we now have to unravel in the Far East.
>
> So highly confident is he in his own powers, and so ambitious for the future, that I wonder whether he may not harbour renewed designs on the presidency of the United States, standing for the Republican cause. At any rate he seems now to be well favoured by the Republicans and to be out of tune with the Democrats; it is possible that he hopes to use the increased prestige and influence which he has gained on the Korean battlefield to bolster his candidature for the presidential elections to be held in 1953.[31]

It was only a day after Gascogine's unnerving report from Tokyo that another, far more alarming, message arrived from Japan. Bouchier informed the Chiefs of Staff that heavy bombers were scheduled to put a 'maximum effort' on Pyongyang, the second largest city in North Korea, on 1 October. Bouchier reported that: 'Some opinion here has always wanted a maximum incendiary attack to be made against Pyongyang to burn the city off the map after due warning to the local population to get out. Americans have flinched however against attacking towns with incendiary bombs. One object of such attack is obviously to provide Communist Chinese and Russians across the border with a visible object lesson and to serve as a warning.'[32]

Everyone in Whitehall, with an interest in Korea, seemed agreed that 'any such attack at this particular time would be most unwise and dangerous' and in particular the reactions of Chinese and Indian opinion to such an attack 'would almost certainly be adverse to our cause and the interests of the United Nations. Apart from these arguments and the economic and psychological unwisdom of such a course when every emphasis is being laid on the need for United Nations rehabilitation of Korea, such an attack would provide the Communists generally with a bull point for propaganda exploitation'.[33] In Washington, Lord Tedder sought out an urgent meeting with the Joint Chiefs. Both Bradley and General Norstad agreed 'that in the present circumstances' the air action proposed was 'untimely'. It turned out that both Bradley and Norstad were ignorant of any proposal for such an attack but, in view of the possibility that MacArthur might have such action in mind, instructions were sent to the Supreme Commander that: 'If for any reasons attack on Pyongyang is still being considered full details of proposals are to be submitted to Washington for clearance by higher authority before any such attack is launched.'[34] The British intervention had thwarted MacArthur – this time. But as events on the ground in Korea continued to tilt in favour of the UN Command the Supreme Commander's confidence in his judgement – and his destiny – had far extended beyond egotism to megalomania. By the end of September, Seoul was once again in South Korean hands.[35]

With the recapture of Seoul the moment of decision with regard to the 38th parallel was almost upon the UN Command. The Chief of the Air Staff, in London, was more worried than ever about what would ensue as a result of its crossing. He told his fellow Chiefs that the latest developments in connection with the Chinese attitude to the possibility of UN Forces going North of the 38th parallel 'all strengthen my view that the risks involved and the inevitable military commitment – even in the absence of overt Chinese participation – more than outweigh the political advantages to be obtained'. Slessor added: 'I find it hard to understand Mr Bevin's view that if we stop at the 38th parallel and leave N Korea as an entity Russia will virtually have triumphed and the whole U.N. effort will have been in vain. I should have thought that the complete defeat of this obviously Soviet-inspired Communist aggression, the destruction of the whole North Korean industry and the elimination of the Communist Army represents a triumph for the U.N. on any count.' Slessor thought that any boost to UN prestige in Asia resulting from successful UN operations in North Korea would be more than offset by the strong nationalist feeling throughout Asia against Western intervention north of the parallel. 'The Asiatic Powers backed us in resisting the aggression against S Korea; it is already clear that we should not have their backing for an occupation of North Korea.' While the unification of all Korea under UN 'is no doubt desirable, the one *essential* is that the U.N. position in Korea must be no worse than if the invasion had never happened. As long as Communism makes no gains to offset the calamitous losses it has now suffered, we should only seek to extend those losses if we are sure that the cost of doing so is commensurate with the advantages to be gained. Surely the Russians have already been made to realize that "they are up against it"'.

The latest information the Chiefs had received suggested that the Americans proposed to remain approximately south of the 40th parallel. This took them to the Chinese border on the western side of Korea, and, pointed out Slessor, involved the occupation of territory not much smaller than South Korea. It avoided contact with the Russian border, 'but apart from that why does it make sense to have to cross one arbitrary line on the map and stop short of another? If the N.K. "Peoples' Republic" does not collapse as a result of the operations South of the 38th parallel, I see no reason to imagine it will be allowed by the Russians to do so as a result of operations south of the 40th. There will still be a N.K. "Peoples' Republic" North of the 40th parallel which will be a harbour and base for Russian and Chinese backed N.K. guerrillas, who will be just as much a curse to the U.N. occupying forces South of 40° North as those in the present N.K. will be to U.N. occupying forces South of 38° North'. The UN forces necessary to protect the imaginary line of the 40th parallel would have to be stronger (it was longer and, if anything, less naturally defensible than the 38th). And the forces required to maintain law and order, suppress guerrillas, etc. would be much larger. Slessor concluded: 'We are probably in for something like another Malaya even in South Korea. By going North, we merely increase that commitment by about 100%.' Finally it was clear that by operating North of the 38th parallel 'we run really serious risks of extending the war by the intervention of Communist China – and possibly also Russia. Even if China does not overtly intervene, it seems clear ... that they will give every sort of covert support to the North Koreans, and thus enormously increase our military commitment there'.[36]

The same day that Slessor submitted his concerns – 2 October – Ambassador Pannikar was summoned by the Chinese premier. The resulting telegram from Peking was immediately passed on to the British High Commissioner who, in turn, despatched it to London. Chou En Lai warned if the American army crossed 38th parallel China would be 'forced to take immediate steps'. Chou thought it was obvious America no longer attached value to the decision not to cross 38th parallel and the United Nations might find itself faced with a *fait accompli* dictated by MacArthur. That Chou, said, 'will mean definitely enlargement of the war'.[37]

On 3 October, the day the despatch from New Delhi arrived in London, the Foreign Office convened an urgent meeting with the Chiefs of Staff. Representing the Foreign Office, Robert Scott wondered if Chou's warning 'might be a bluff on the part of the Chinese' although it could not be ignored. Slim responded by suggesting that there were two courses open. Either the United Nations forces should stop on the 38th parallel or they should go forward up to the borders of Manchuria and risk a clash either with the Russians or with the Chinese. From a military point of view, in his opinion, the eventual military commitment would be greater if the United Nations forces remained south of the 38th parallel than if they were to go forward and occupy the area north of the 38th parallel. If it was decided to occupy the whole of Korea 'then we should only need to maintain sufficient forces to control guerrilla operations in the whole area. On the other hand, if the United Nations forces were confined to the area south of the 38th parallel, not only should we have to maintain forces to deal with guerrillas in South Korea but we should have to maintain sufficient forces to stop large scale incursion from the North'. Lord Fraser agreed with Slim that, in his view, the United Nations forces should go as far North as was necessary in order to prevent the North Koreans from building up for a major attack. Slessor, on the other hand, again said that he could not agree, even on military grounds, that it would be better to occupy North Korea.[38]

Following the news from India an anxious Bevin urged Sir Oliver Franks to 'very urgently' contact the State Department warning: 'If the Chinese should in the event intervene, it would seem very difficult to localise the conflict.' At the same time, after consultation with Lord Tedder, Bevin wanted Franks to obtain urgent clarification from the United States Government of the following points:

> whether (i) South Korean forces have actually crossed the 38th parallel as reported in the Press and if so whether on their own initiative or on instructions from the United Nations Command;
> whether (ii) United Nations forces other than South Korean have in fact already crossed the Parallel.

Bevin had discovered, after referring to the conclusions of a series of Tripartite US–Franco-British meetings (at the official level) in September, (and which 'appeared' to have been approved by Ministers such as himself) that they showed ambiguity on the point as to whether the United Nations forces might cross the parallel without United Nations direction. The subsequent United States view was that United Nations forces had already adequate cover for crossing the 38th parallel under the terms of the Security Council Resolution of 27 June. But what was the present United States view on this and had any instructions been issued to MacArthur regarding this or were any contemplated? London noted that MacArthur told Joe Gascoigne that he had received the most definite instructions from the President himself that he was not to send United Nations forces across the parallel without explicit instructions to do so. For London it was 'difficult for us to formulate views until we have the answers to the questions listed above'. In general however, the British objectives were still to localise the conflict and to bring the Korean affair to an end as soon as possible, including the withdrawal of United Nations Forces, so that they might be ready to deal with the possibility of more serious trouble elsewhere. 'At the same time we cannot risk a repetition of aggression from North Korea. If North Korean military machine has already been so damaged as no longer to constitute a serious threat then, as we see it, (and pending clarification of points enumerated above) there is everything to be said for settling the Korean question by political rather than military means.'[39] Uncertainty had clearly crept into Bevin's mind about Chinese intervention and the wisdom of MacArthur's advance north – which he had supported.

After consulting Lord Tedder, Franks put these questions to Rusk. It was Rusk's understanding of the conclusions of the Tripartite meeting that it had been generally agreed that whereas the existing United Nations resolutions would permit 'swirling' across the 38th parallel operations of a politico-military nature would require further United Nations consideration. The present United States view on this was that there was, indeed, adequate cover in the United Nations resolution of 27 June for the tactical crossing of the parallel for military reasons but that for the wider politico-military purposes (e.g. occupation) it would be necessary to have further United Nations endorsement. In so far as MacArthur was concerned, his present directions applied only to present events and Rusk said that the position was that MacArthur had received a general policy directive setting forth the policy of military operations across the 38th parallel provided that there was at the appropriate moment no active intervention by the Russians or Chinese on any major scale or any real threat of such intervention. But under this directive he was required to send his plan of operation to Washington so that the United States Government could review the situation in the light of developments in United Nations and elsewhere. This plan had in fact been sent to Washington and had received general approval but Rusk did not know whether any further specific approval was required before implementation.[40] Unknown to the British and Americans, Communist China had already decided its response to the UN military advance. Mao's decision was for war with the West.

## Notes

1. TNA DEFE 11/196 Extract from CM (BO) 46 conclusions held on 17 July 1950
2. TNA DEFE 11/196 Barclay to Elliot, 19 July 1950
3. TNA DEFE 11/196 Extract from CM (BO) 46 conclusions held on 17 July 1950
4. TNA DEFE 11/196 Chiefs of Staff to Lord Tedder, 20 July 1950
5. TNA DEFE 11/196 Copy of a letter dated 21 July 1950, from the Foreign Office to the Secretary, Chiefs of Staff Committee
6. TNA DEFE 11/196 BJSM Washington to Ministry of Defence, London, 20 July 1950. For Chiefs of Staff from Lord Tedder
7. FRUS 1950, Volume VII (Korea) Agreed Memorandum, Summary of United States–United Kingdom Discussions on the Present World Situation, 20–24 July 1950
8. TNA DEFE 11/196 Telegram No. 2022 Washington to Foreign Office, 21 July 1950
9. FRUS 1950, Volume VII (Korea) The Ambassador in the United Kingdom to the Secretary of State, 22 July 1950
10. TNA DEFE 11/196 Chiefs of Staff Committee Confidential Annex to COS (50) 115th Meeting Held on Friday, 21 July 1950
11. TNA DEFE 11/197 Outward Telegram from Commonwealth Relations Office, 25 July 1950 from Prime Minister to Commonwealth Prime Ministers
12. TNA DEFE 11/197 Cabinet Defence Committee Extract From DO (50) 15th Meeting held on 24 July 1950
13. TNA DEFE 11/197 Outward Telegram from Commonwealth Relations Office: Korea
14. TNA WO 308/56 *The History of the Commonwealth Division in Korea 1950–1956* by Lieutenant Colonel H.F. Joslen
15. DBOP: Korea Memorandum by Bevin, 30 August 1950
16. DBOP: Korea note 6, pp. 122–123
17. TNA DEFE 11/201 Chiefs Of Staff Committee Confidential Annex to C.O.S. (50) 152nd Meeting Held on Wednesday, 20 September 1950
18. TNA DEFE 11/201 Top Secret Appendix Policy Following on Enemy Defeat in S. Korea. Note by the Chief of the Air Staff, 14 September 1950

19 TNA DEFE 11/201 Washington to Foreign Office Sir O. Franks No. 2499, 18 September 1950
20 TNA DEFE 11/201 Moscow to Foreign Office Sir D. Kelly No. 849, 21 September 1950
21 TNA DEFE 11/201 C.P. (50) 215, 25 September 1950; Cabinet: Future Political Settlement in Korea Note by the Prime Minister; Annex from Foreign Office to New York (to United Kingdom Delegation to United Nations) Telegram No. 1357, 21 September 1950. Following from Prime Minister for Secretary of State
22 TNA DEFE 11/201 From New York to Foreign Office (from United Nations Delegation to United Kingdom) Telegram No. 1156, 22 September 1950. Following for Prime Minister from Secretary of State
23 TNA DEFE 11/201 Foreign Office to New York (to United Kingdom Delegation to United Nations) Telegram No. 1401, 23 September 1950. Following for Secretary of State from Makins. Long-term political settlement in Korea
24 TNA DEFE 11/201 Cabinet Extract from C.M. (50) 61st Conclusions held on 26 September 1950
25 TNA DEFE 11/201 U.K. Delegation, New York to Foreign Office, 24 September 1950. For Price from Elliott for Chiefs of Staff
26 TNA DEFE 11/201 Foreign Office to Washington Telegram No. 4313, 28 September 1950
27 TNA DEFE 11/201 1st Inward Telegram to Commonwealth Relations Office From: UK High Commissioner in India, 27 September 1950
28 TNA DEFE 11/201 2nd Inward Telegram to Commonwealth Relations Office From: UK High Commissioner in India, 27 September 1950
29 TNA DEFE 11/201 Cabinet: Extract from C.M. (50) 62nd Conclusions held on 28 September 1950
30 TNA DEFE 11/201 Outward Saving Telegram from Commonwealth Relations Office (dated 2 October 1950) United Nations Assembly Resolution on the future of Korea
31 TNA DEFE 11/201 United Kingdom Liaison Mission in Japan, British Embassy Tokyo, 28 September 1950
32 TNA DEFE 11/201 UKDEL, New York (for Minister of State), 29 September 1950
33 TNA DEFE 11/201 Washington telegram repeated for information on to UKDEL, New York (for Minister of State)
34 TNA DEFE 11/201 Ministry of Defence, London to British Embassy, Tokyo, 2 October 1950. For Bouchier from Chiefs of Staff
35 TNA DEFE 11/201 Telegram No. 98 Korea to Foreign Office, 1 October 1950
36 TNA DEFE 11/201 Policy Following the Enemy Defeat in South Korea (COS (50) 152nd Minutes. Appendix Note by CAS), 2 October 1950

37 TNA DEFE 11/201 Inward Telegram to Commonwealth Relations UK High Commissioner in India, 3 October 1950
38 TNA DEFE 11/201 Chiefs of Staff Committee Extract from COS (50) 160th Meeting held on 3 October 1950
39 TNA DEFE 11/201 Foreign Office to Washington Telegram No. 4396, 3 October 1950
40 TNA DEFE 11/201 Washington to Foreign Office Telegram No. 2662, 3 October 1950

# 3

## Enter the dragon

### China's first intervention

The same day as the Franks-Rusk meeting, news was received in London that the South Korean 3rd and Capitol Divisions had crossed the 38th parallel near the coast, that they had now advanced 30 miles to Kansong against only slight resistance, and that it was believed the North Koreans would not offer strong opposition before the important centre and port of Wonsan was reached. Wonsan was 80 miles further north, and was east of the Northern capital of Pyongyang.[1] As this information was being digested, London's man on the spot in Peking remained sanguine about events in Korea; John Hutchinson thought that Chou's comments to Pannikar 'do not seem to me to amount to a categorical statement that if American forces cross the 38th parallel China is quite determined to intervene in the war in Korea, though that is certainly what I understood Mr. Panikkar to say that Chou had told him.'[2] However, any optimism generated by Hutchinson's views were soon dispelled and the tension raised further when Bajpai sent for the UK High Commissioner, on 4 October, and handed him the following message which had been received from Panniker in Peking.

BEGINS
Chou en Lai's conversation only confirmed previous impressions. There is no doubt that whatever the consequences Chinese Government will resist by arms movement into North Korea of foreign forces as distinct from South Korean units.

If as seems inevitable American forces cross 38th parallel and conflict follows it may still be possible to limit operations to Korea and not extend them to Manchuria or the mainland. The impression here is that attack on Manchuria will immediately bring Soviet into war with unforeseeable consequences.[3]

It coincided with the alarming intelligence from Tokyo that MacArthur proposed to carry out an amphibious operation for the invasion of Northern Korea on 10 October. Sir William Elliot was ordered, by Manny Shinwell, to convene an urgent meeting of the Chiefs. This meeting was held with the First Sea Lord in the Chair; only Slessor was absent. Faced with the news of a possible amphibious landing and the evident concern of Ministers, the Chiefs of Staff adopted a less bellicose tone than the day before and, in effect, produced a radical shift in the Chiefs' position. Lord Fraser was now of the opinion that if the United Nations forces crossed the 38th parallel, 'we should be accused of aggression.' In fact there now did not appear to be any military necessity for taking this step as it would probably take the North Koreans at least 3 or 4 months in which to re-equip. Indeed, if the United Nations forces did cross the 38th parallel 'it was almost certain that the conflict in Korea would spread. Furthermore, we should lose the co-operation of India and other South East Asian countries'.

Slim also altered his previous position and agreed with the First Sea Lord: there was a distinct possibility that the Chinese might be so frightened of American intentions that once US troops had crossed into North Korean territory the Chinese would immediately come down into North Korea; but Slim could not quite abandon his prior, bellicose, position: 'On the other hand', he added, 'we should not allow ourselves to be intimidated by Chinese threats. There was no reason why the South Koreans should not be allowed to advance into North Korean territory'. So, the qualification was that while the UN – the Americans and British in particular – should not advance across the parallel, it would all right for the South Koreans to do so. With Slessor absent, Elliott provided the RAF view – and he felt that the only competent person to judge whether it was militarily necessary to cross the 38th parallel was General MacArthur who was the Commander on the spot. It seemed important, therefore, to give him military freedom in order to restore law and order.[4] It was highly unlikely that Slessor would have come to anything like a similar view as Elliot; so, in the former's absence, the Chiefs were able to agree the following position:

(ii) Any crossing of the 38th parallel by United Nations troops will clearly risk an extension and aggravation of the war.
(iii) The military situation may, however, be such as to necessitate a crossing of the 38th parallel in due course, but the Chiefs of Staff

are of the opinion that there is no *immediate* military need for such a crossing.
(iv) They therefore advocate that General MacArthur should be instructed to pause on the 38th parallel for a limited time – say 7 to 14 days – and that this pause should coincide with an immediate announcement to the North Koreans to surrender within that period.
(v) The announcement will continue to say that if the North Koreans fail to surrender within the stipulated period, the United Nations forces will then cross the 38th parallel in order to affect their surrender by force.
(vi) Whilst the United Nations forces under General MacArthur pause on the 38th parallel, South Korean forces should be allowed to continue their advance and tactical air action against military targets should also be permitted.[5]

This was a half-way house position between what Fraser and Slim had argued beforehand and the new concern regarding China's intentions. But it still did not address the key point: the danger of Chinese intervention after the end of any UN 'pause' and subsequent advance into North Korea.

Added to this was the confusing news from Washington. Rusk had promised Franks that he would try to show the British a paper giving the background directive upon which MacArthur was acting. It was arranged for a member of Frank's staff to see the paper. But, contrary to the impression received from Rusk, it did not contain any clear indication of what MacArthur was authorised to do without further United Nations action or further instructions from the President. It consisted largely of a description of surrender terms to be announced to the North Koreans. The rest of the paper was a programme for occupation and post-hostilities political action that was to be the basis of discussion with friendly United Nations powers.[6]

From Japan, Bouchier, reported how MacArthur now claimed 'the enemy was already licked but that they refused to admit it'. He had called upon the North Korean Commander-in-Chief to surrender in terms worded so that he could accept and in so doing save as much face as possible. The Supreme Commander did not think the Russians would intervene 'nor did I gather that he was worried about Chinese intervention in the conflict though the latter may threaten to do so'.[7] The following day, 7 October, Bouchier was granted the unusual privilege of another meeting with MacArthur, this time in the presence of Admiral Brind of the Royal Navy, where the Supreme Commander declared that 'the war would be over in a month'.[8]

In London, Bevin was probably glad to receive word from the High Commissioner in New Delhi that Bajpai had told the British representative that a message had been sent from Nehru, to the Chinese Prime Minister, conveying an appeal for him to 'hold his hand for the present'. Chou En Lai's reply to this message, however, would have removed any temporary relief that Bevin had: whilst the Chinese Government had no intention of taking any action provided American forces did not cross the 38th parallel they were nevertheless still determined to do so should American troops move into North Korea.[9] The best that the Foreign Secretary could do to reassure the Cabinet was to tell his colleagues that, as far as he knew, United Nations forces had not yet crossed the 38th parallel 'in strength', and he was suggesting that the President of the United Nations Assembly might issue a further appeal to the North Koreans to abandon active resistance.[10] As he did so, MacArthur issued his final surrender appeal to Kim Il Sung.[11]

In the aftermath of the General's declaration, Truman's dramatic visit, on 15 October, to see MacArthur, on Wake Island, led to Franks scurrying around Washington to learn what he could of the meeting between the two. The Ambassador reported to Bevin that, on 19 October, he was able to have a word with Dean Rusk about the talks 'and it was arranged that we should be given a sight of the confidential record of the official portion of the conference. This is a privilege which is not being extended to any other nation but Rusk was anxious that I should let you know, for very restricted use, what had passed between the President and the Supreme Commander'. Rusk commented that the meeting was a very successful one. The atmosphere was said to have been cordial all the way through and MacArthur was reported as having cooperated fully: 'There is no doubt that a little Missouri political strategy entered into the whole business but the benefits resulting from a meeting between these two important men far outweigh, I think, anything of a more trivial nature' reported Franks. Most of the time was spent on Korea. MacArthur intended to finish the military part of the campaign by about the end of November. He then wanted to withdraw American troops as quickly as possible and he thought this could be done after all-Korean elections had been held, say early in 1951. In the interval he hoped to set up the South Korean army in good shape and to hand over the main responsibility of government to Korean organs. MacArthur was most anxious to get his best troops back to Japan – not for occupational purposes but to keep them in good training for transfer to another theatre when required.

The available information about Formosa was 'unfortunately very scanty. All we know is that the President said "General MacArthur and I

## Enter the dragon: China's first intervention

have talked fully. We are in complete agreement'" Franks told Bevin. Rusk did not know how the private talk went on this subject but he believed that MacArthur 'fell into line'. If so it meant that the naval screen between Formosa and the mainland would be withdrawn at the close of the Korean campaign, but it would obviously be possible to reach a broad area of agreement without either party surrendering his main points: 'I do not therefore place too much reliance on the sentence "We are in complete agreement" and I should not be surprised if the Formosan problem remains with us for some time, the temperature of the subject rising or falling according to developments within that area of the Pacific' concluded Franks.[12] Franks later learned, from Rusk, that the subject of Formosa, was not discussed in any detail and that the President's advisers had not wished, at this conference, to bring the problem too much into the open. It seemed likely, therefore, that Truman's statement – 'General MacArthur and I have talked fully. We are in complete agreement' – must be interpreted in the very broadest sense. It was 'a permissible guess (but only a guess)' that the President referred to the exclusive responsibility of the United States Government in matters of high policy, such as that affecting Formosa, and that MacArthur expressed complete agreement with that remark. 'I can only infer that we must expect the persistence of differences of opinion over the role Formosa is to play in the military strategy applicable to the Far East' the Ambassador warned Bevin.[13]

The North Koreans, in any case, did not surrender. And UN forces – both British and American – advanced, steadily, northwards – across the 38th parallel. On 23 October, Bouchier reported, triumphantly, from Tokyo that the: 'Over-all picture is one of North Korean Army completely destroyed.'[14] A few days later, however, a Reuter's report from Tokyo, dated 27 October, quoted 'unconfirmed reports that 40,000 Chinese troops have been thrown into North Korea to prevent United Nations troops getting control of Yalu power plants feeding Manchuria's war industries'. The report went on to quote a South Korean Major General as saying that Chinese troops were committed at Unsan, 45 miles south east of the Yalu River frontier. The identification of Chinese regiments was given.[15] Bouchier dismissed this report and others like it, reassuring the Chiefs in London: 'There is no (repeat no) evidence whatever that any Chinese Communist troops have crossed over South of Yalu River and are in conflict with our forces advancing Northwards to Manchurian border. I make this positive and authoritative statement to negative any exaggeration and alarmist reports which may appear at any time now in your home press as a result of irresponsible reports made here by some newspaper men. Such reports are generally based upon a single unconfirmed statement made by a single enemy prisoner of war who does not know what he is talking about. Moreover because intervention now by the Chinese would be a sensational world news item the more irresponsible newspaper men here tend to magnify ten times such totally unconfirmed reports'.[16] But, by 31 October, Bouchier was eating – a small portion of – humble pie as he now reported to the Chiefs accounts from prisoners of war suggesting a distinct possibility that two Chinese divisions 'might' have crossed the Yalu River and moved south to the Onjong area.[17] From Washington, Franks was reporting that, before the 31st only three Chinese prisoners had been identified. But the reports received on 31 October had caused the State Department to review the situation. They found that 48 Chinese Communist prisoners had, in fact, been captured and the US 10 Corps tentatively accepted the presence of the 370th Regiment (probably 2,500 strong) of the 124th Communist Chinese Division. This division's strength and commander were unknown. The prisoners recently taken belonged to the Chinese Nationalist army from 1947 to 1949, when units were integrated into the Communist army. One prisoner, whose information was unconfirmed, said that 5,000 men crossed with him, from China, over a railway bridge leading to Sinuiju.[18]

On 6 November, the Cabinet held a preliminary discussion about the possible consequences of Chinese intervention in Korea. They were informed that the United States was thinking of moving a resolution in the Security Council calling on all Member States to refrain from assisting the North Koreans. Bevin was anxious to avoid any extension of the area of hostilities, such as might follow from the application of United Nations sanctions against China. Meanwhile the aggressive intent of the Chinese was being demonstrated elsewhere – via their invasion of Tibet, with the High Commissioner for India calling on Bevin later in the day to update him on events there.[19] The same day the Chiefs of Staff telegraphed Tedder: 'You will understand that we are anxious about the Korean situation and we should be grateful if you could discover from Bradley what are the US intentions in respect of an advance to the Manchurian and Russian frontiers of Korea when it becomes possible. We should like to know under what directive MacArthur is operating or whether he is deciding his own policy in this respect.' The Chiefs originally understood that it was the intention that only South Korean forces should advance north of a line approximately Chonju/Wonsan: 'We were thus assured only about a fortnight ago by US Chiefs of Staff that MacArthur had orders that anyway US and British troops should not go nearer than 30 miles of Northern Frontier. We are not clear whether in fact they have done so, but Bouchier repeatedly refers to "our advance to the Manchurian border".

Does this mean US or British troops as well as South Koreans? ... it looks as though it does.'[20]

Tedder discussed Korea with Bradley, on 8 November. The intention to avoid direct conflict with China was more firm than ever, he reported back to the Chiefs. As Bradley had said 'What we want is to be able to get together with these people and talk things over – if it is the power station and dam on the Yalu they are worried about we could come to an arrangement.' Bradley did not speak of Chinese divisions but there was plenty of evidence of continual and very heavy movement down the Yalu eastward. In view of this, after consultation with the State Department, MacArthur had that day been authorised to attack the eastern end of the main bridges across the Yalu with orders to avoid flying over the border. In the course of another three or four weeks the Yalu would probably be frozen over and bridges would no longer be essential for any crossing from China.

But, since the heavy reinforcement of North Korea forces had developed, it was clear that the original endeavour to differentiate between the South Korean forces and the UNO forces was no longer possible and the idea of the South Koreans alone dealing with the final stage had become academic. As Bradley put it, the problem in Korea now was not one of holding this or that terrain, but of destroying the armed forces in North Korea. MacArthur still thought 'we can do this'. In conclusion it was clear that Bradley and the US Chiefs were as concerned about the dangers of the present situation 'as we are and for much the same reason'.[21] With MacArthur no doubt in mind, the Chiefs reminded Bouchier, as 'our representative', that he 'should continue as far as possible to exercise a moderating influence whenever this is necessary with a view to localising the conflict and avoiding a general conflagration in the Far East. Korea is only one facet of the world struggle against the forces of Communism'.[22]

Back in the Cabinet, Bevin, with some understatement, said that Chinese intervention, the extent of which was still uncertain, had led to 'great difficulties affecting our attitude' towards the People's Government of China. The People's Government had now been invited to state their case in the Security Council, 'and we could do no more at present than await the outcome'. The situation was an 'ugly one', and Bevin was concerned lest the results of the upcoming US Congressional elections (in which the Republicans would make significant gains) might unfavourably affect its handling by the United States Government, but he did not feel that either China or Russia was at present working deliberately to spread the conflict.[23]

As HMG attempted to understand what was happening, on the ground in Korea, on 7 November the Foreign Office received a despatch from its

Mission in Peking informing it that members of John Hutchinson's staff were told, on 4 November, by a 'well informed' Chinese (the Dean of Studies of Peking National University) that large numbers of Chinese were already in Korea. The source did not think their presence would be officially announced by the Chinese Government. Hutchinson suggested the Foreign Office would have seen the joint declaration, issued 4 November, by the 'Chinese democratic parties' (including the Communist party) 'pledging' that they would 'support all the Chinese people who voluntarily undertake the sacred task of resisting America, aiding Korea, protecting their homes and defending their country'. The association of the Communist Party with this declaration was deemed 'noteworthy and perhaps supports the view that the Chinese Government will not issue any official statement'. It might well be that the next development would be an announcement by that Chinese volunteers were fighting in Korea. As long as this remained the line, noted Hutchinson, the Chinese Government could claim that they were not themselves responsible for hostile actions by Chinese nationals against the United Nations forces, but that they saw no reason to restrain their 'just demands' to volunteer for the purposes in the last sentence of the declaration. On this basis it might be easier for them to disentangle themselves if the whole operation proved a failure, speculated Hutchinson.[24]

Attention shifted to the UN where the Americans informed Sir Gladwyn Jebb, head of the UK Mission at the UNO, on 8 November, that they intended to add an additional paragraph to a draft resolution, authorised by the President, which would affirm the intention of the United Nations forces to hold the Chinese frontier in Korea inviolate and to protect 'legitimate' Chinese interests in the frontier if the Chinese withdrew and refrained from intervention.[25] Bevin brought forth his own plans for the UN too. As he told the Cabinet: the 'present situation was critical; and the peace of the Far East turned largely on the handling of the discussions in the Security Council over the next few days'. In the light of experience he felt no confidence in India's influence as a mediator with China. The Cabinet were also updated on the military situation by Sir John Slessor who reported that the Chinese, though they had large forces in Manchuria, had not yet deployed very substantial numbers of troops in Korea. Elements of five Chinese armies had been identified in Korea; and the United States authorities estimated that about 35,000 Chinese troops were operating there. With this in view the Chiefs of Staff Committee favoured the withdrawal of United Nations forces to a shorter line across the neck of the country, running from Chongju to Tokchon, roughly along the 40th Parallel. In addition to being a much shorter line to defend, this would have the great advantage of leaving a buffer area to the north, on the Korean side of the Manchurian frontier, in which military targets could be attacked from the air without the grave international risks involved in making air attacks on targets within Manchuria. It might be possible to declare this buffer area to be a demilitarised zone, with the reservation that any offensive concentration of Chinese or North Korean troops within that area would be liable to air attack. A cease-fire might be arranged on the basis of that line, pending the result of discussions in the Security Council. Meanwhile, United Nations forces would be free to clear up the guerrilla activities to the south.

Bevin added that this proposal, which was put forward by the Chiefs of Staff on military grounds, was in accord with his political objectives. He was anxious to prevent the United States Government from being led by their military advisers into policies which would provoke further intervention by China. He was also anxious to do everything he could to allay the reasonable fears of the Chinese lest the Western powers should occupy large areas of Asian territory under a plea of military necessity. It would be reassuring to public opinion throughout Asia if it could be made clear that United Nations forces were not offering any threat to China. The moment was ripe for putting forward in the Security Council a comprehensive solution of the Korean problem; and he would like to have the Cabinet's authority to seek agreement on the basis of a buffer area on the lines suggested by the Chiefs of Staff Committee. It would help him in securing such an agreement if he could take a rather more forthcoming attitude towards the amount of the contribution to be made by the United Kingdom towards the fund for reconstruction in Korea. The Cabinet approved Bevin's request.[26] Bevin then telegraphed Franks: 'we should endeavour to find a solution to the Korean problem which will not result in the hostilities dragging on in Korea with the ever growing risk of extension beyond Korea'. What the Foreign Office had in mind was a fresh approach to the problem which might be embodied in a resolution in the Security Council on the following general lines:

The resolution
(a) would recall previous resolutions and declare that with the destruction of the great bulk of the North Korean armed forces and the extinction of any threat from the North Korean authorities the military campaign may in fact be regarded as at an end and that there need now be no delay in proceeding with the urgent task of political and economic rehabilitation;
(b) would propose the establishment of a demilitarised area from

which all foreign forces and combatants would be withdrawn. This area would extend from a United Nations line (running roughly from Hungnam in the East to Chongju in the West) to the existing Manchurian–Siberian–Korean frontier;

(c) would declare that this demilitarised area is only to be set up for a temporary period pending the unification of the whole of Korea;

(d) would reaffirm the objectives of the United Nations already declared in relevant United Nations resolutions and reassure the Central People's Government of China that there is no intention to damage their interests.

The resolution would also have to provide for the assumption by an appropriate United Nations body of responsibilities in connection with the demilitarised area and define those responsibilities. It would, in addition, provide for appropriate association of the Central People's Government of China with this United Nations machinery. One problem of particular difficulty would be the disposal of the North Korean Government and the remnants of the North Korean forces in the proposed demilitarised area. The best solution would be for the North Korean armed forces to lay down their arms and for a suitable *de facto* temporary administration of the area to be set up under the aegis of the United Nations, though admittedly this solution might be difficult to achieve.

From the political point of view the suggestions outlined above 'may afford us a means not only of terminating the whole Korean campaign earlier and thus liquidating a costly military commitment in an area of little strategic importance, but also of satisfying the Chinese that the United Nations have no aggressive intent against Manchuria'. The most important difference between Bevin's proposals and a suggestion made by Franks was that 'we omit' any reference to territory lying north of the Yalu. To include any such reference would, in Bevin's view, 'defeat the whole object we have in mind as it would be inevitably rejected by the Chinese'. It could be argued, continued Bevin, that these proposals involve a unilateral concession on the part of the United Nations. This was, however, not the case. They would also mean that the Chinese themselves would have to withdraw their considerable forces already disposed in the proposed demilitarised area, thus giving up positions of considerable military advantage to them: 'I feel that this aspect of the problem, together with the grave risks inherent in the present situation of an extension of hostilities beyond Korea, needs special emphasis with the Americans.' If the State Department were receptive to these suggestions, they should work out a draft resolution on the basis of the thoughts explained above, so that the two drafts could be compared. If the United States Government liked the proposal of a demilitarised area, it was important that there should be no further general advance by United Nations forces beyond their present positions. Bevin asked Franks to consult Acheson and telegraph his reply urgently: 'It is easy to see many objections to the course which we are proposing and no doubt detailed working out of the proposals may present difficulties. Moreover, it is possible that the Chinese would reject any such proposal. If they do so, their rejection can only mean that they are bent on making mischief.'[27]

From New York, Jebb commented that, broadly speaking, Bevin's proposed new line offered much the best chance of some eventual solution. On the other hand, 'and with great deference', to the Foreign Secretary, he felt that this solution was unlikely to be achieved by the tabling in the Security Council of some new resolution on the lines now proposed. His reasons were as follows:

(a) The achievement of any demilitarised area in the north of Korea must, as I see it, be a result of a *negotiation*. It is most unlikely to come about as a result of some unilateral declaration. Since the Peking Government have refused to attend meetings of the Security Council at which this question is discussed, any resolution we put forward would almost certainly be vetoed by the Soviets and rejected by them.

(b) Withdrawal of draft resolution altogether at this stage and its replacement by one which is clearly much milder from the Chinese point of view, would no doubt have an effect on United States opinion which can only be assessed by the Embassy.

(c) The existing resolution as modified will of course probably be vetoed if it is put to the vote next week, but this really in itself does not matter very much, since the representatives of Peking will not be present in the Security Council during its discussion. In any case a vote on the resolution in the Council would not in our view prejudice subsequent negotiations for the sort of settlement which you contemplate.

(d) Unless we are to maintain completely rigid attitude and thus run a considerable danger of ending up in a world war, we must at some stage be prepared to negotiate with somebody. This would either be of course with the representatives of Peking or with the Russians or indeed with both, though I imagine that you will not wish any approach to be made to the Russians (whose general objective would seem to be to maintain the tension rather than diminish it) except in some specific point affecting their interests in the frontier zone. If, however, such negotiations are to have any prospect of success, the solution (which may not be completely in accordance with our present ideas and objectives) should be allowed to emerge from the negotiations themselves and cannot so to speak be laid down in advance before the negotiations start.[28]

As there appeared to be still several days before the resolution had to be voted on, and in view of Jebb's comments to Bevin, Franks decided to await the Foreign Secretary's further views before speaking to Acheson. At first sight, Franks cabled Bevin, there was attraction in Jebb's suggestion that the achievement of a demilitarised area in the North of Korea should result from a negotiation and that it was unlikely to come about as a result of a unilateral declaration: 'If we exclude (as I agree with you that we must) the possibility of getting the Chinese to agree to a demilitarised zone north of the Yalu we are depending on what might appear, especially to the [American] Middle West, to be a unilateral concession.' Franks thought it be extremely difficult for Acheson, at this stage, to accept the proposal. It was relevant to the foregoing that United Nations forces were shortly to resume their offensive, which, if successful, should in a short time give them possession of most of the ground south of the Yalu.[29]

Bevin accepted that it might be that a demilitarised area in Korea could be achieved only as a result of negotiation. Nevertheless, he was most anxious to know Acheson's views on the proposals. This was all the more urgent in view of the démarche made the day before, 14 November, by the United States Ambassador to the Foreign Secretary on the subject of permission for United Nations aircraft to cross the Manchurian border: 'Unless we have a full exchange of views at the earliest possible moment there is a danger of divergence between the lines on which we and the Americans are thinking and this I am of course anxious to prevent' Bevin told Franks.[30]

Bevin, meanwhile, asked that the views of the Chiefs of Staff should be obtained as a matter of urgency on the US *aide mémoire*.[31] The memorandum stated that, with the use of Manchuria by the enemy as a privileged sanctuary, from which attacks were being launched on the United Nations forces in Korea, the United Nations Command were confronted with a grave problem. Ground forces opposing the United Nations army in Korea were enabled, after moving into Korea from Manchuria, to use lines of communication and supply bases protected from attack in large part by the immunity of Manchuria. In addition, enemy aircraft operating from Manchurian airfields were able to lunge into Korea to attack United

Nations ground or air units, and return within a very few minutes to the safety of Manchuria. The *aide mémoire* referred to the statement made by Austin, the head of the US UN delegation, on 10 November in the Security Council, in which he reported that two B–29 bombers of the United Nations forces in Korea had been damaged in combat over the Korean city of Sinuiju by Russian-type aircraft coming across the border from Manchuria; this indicated the serious nature of those attacks. By the use of Manchuria, the enemy could easily impose an intolerable burden on the United Nations forces. For these reasons, the United States Government had concluded that 'it may soon become necessary to permit the limited application of the doctrine of hot pursuit, to the extent that United Nations aircraft would be permitted to defend themselves in the airspace over the Yalu river by pursuing attacking enemy aircraft into Manchuria, up to two or three minutes flying time'. It was contemplated that the United Nations aircraft would be limited in this regard to driving off enemy aircraft conducting offensive missions into Korea.[32]

The Chiefs of Staff discussed the *aide mémoire* on 15 November. There was general agreement that it was 'just the sort of problem' which they had in mind as being bound to arise if the United Nations forces were to be permitted to move up to the Yalu River. The strength of the argument put forward by the Americans could be recognised only if it were possible to consider in isolation the action required to support UN operations in Northern Korea. There was, therefore, general agreement that if United Nations aircraft were authorised in any way to fly over Manchurian territory this would inevitably result in incidents; moreover, such limited authorisation would assuredly become the thin end of the wedge towards the bombing later on of objectives on Manchurian soil. In view, therefore, of the wider strategic importance of confining the present conflict to Korea, there was general agreement that 'we must reluctantly accept the present situation whereby aircraft were not permitted to infringe the Manchurian frontier, even if this should mean that we would thereby be unable to bomb targets as close to the Manchurian frontier as we would wish'. The proposal should be opposed and 'we should stress to the United States our contention that the establishment of a demilitarised zone south of the Yalu River provided the best solution to this difficult problem'.[33] Far from agreeing to extend the rules of engagement, Sir William Elliot went on to say that immediate action was required to delay the impending UN offensive, since if it took place it would subsequently be extremely difficult to put into effect HMG's proposals to set up a demilitarised zone in North Korea. The Chiefs argued that, for the reasons put forward by Elliot, it was most important that Franks should, without delay, put to Acheson the demilitarised zone proposals with a view to early instructions being sent to MacArthur. Tedder would speak on similar lines to Bradley.[34]

So, Bevin's reply to the aide memoire was to tell Acheson: 'I have now considered the memorandum fully and regret that I cannot endorse the United States suggestion that violation of the Manchurian border may be necessary. To my mind this is a most dangerous proposal and likely to result in the very thing which we want to avoid, namely spreading of the conflict. For your information, the Chiefs of Staff have also drawn my attention to the warning given by the Soviet Embassy in Peking that United States bombing of Manchuria would bring Soviet aircraft into action.'[35] And, on 15 November, Franks finally put Bevin's ideas to Acheson who was in 'complete agreement' with the general view of the situation from which the Foreign Secretary's proposals sprang. Acheson therefore regarded the proposals with sympathy. His great difficulty was to find out and assess Chinese intentions. If they intended to hold and dominate part of Northern Korea or even to push back United Nations forces to the south then an approach such as the one Bevin had in mind could effect nothing. If, on the other hand, Chinese intentions were limited and they were preoccupied with worries about Manchuria and their legitimate interest in the supply of power to Manchuria from the power plants on the Korean side of the Yalu River, then the kind of approach Bevin had in mind was constructive and helpful. Since at present it was not possible to find out about Chinese intentions by talking to them, the only way open to the UN was military probing. For this and other reasons Acheson did not feel that the course of operations in North Korea could be suspended or interrupted at this stage. Such a course would involve MacArthur in grave risks if the Chinese used any time given to them to build up their offensive power. Franks thought it was noteworthy that Acheson and his associates at no point raised the issue of getting the Chinese to agree to a parallel demilitarised zone north of the Yalu as the Ambassador thought they would do. From this and from the general tenor of the talk it seemed clear to Franks that they were very deeply troubled about the present situation and its possibilities.[36]

Bevin, as he told Franks, regarded Acheson's response as encouraging. But since the Chiefs of Staff continued, in the meantime, to press for MacArthur's impending offensive to be held up pressing for this through their own channels: 'I endorse their views.' Nevertheless, if the Americans felt that it was too late to call a halt now, 'I would still consider it essential to secure the demilitarisation of the area by the eventual withdrawal from it of United Nations and other foreign forces.'[37] Bevin also informed Franks that he proposed making a statement in the House of Commons designed to secure publicity in China. In it he would try to convince the Chinese that the objectives of the United Nations in Korea were those publicly stated, 'that we have no ulterior designs and no intentions to violate Chinese territorial integrity, that the implications of Chinese action in Korea are extremely grave, and that while it is our earnest desire to prevent any extension of the conflict, the decision and the responsibility will lie with them'. But the situation was so serious that Bevin thought 'we ought to go further than making governmental declarations and attempt to bring our intentions home to the Chinese through any other available channels. I think it is also important from the point of view of public opinion in our countries that we can be shown to have tried all possible means to make our position clear'. Though Hutchison, in Peking, had no right of access to the Chinese Government on matters of general policy, Bevin proposed to instruct him to try to see Chou En Lai (even at the risk of inviting a snub), or at any rate the highest available responsible official, to convey a statement on the general lines above: 'I do not propose to convey to the Chinese Government an indication of our proposals and ideas for a demilitarised area.' If, however, the Chinese should give any opening to Hutchison in the course of conversation about future possibilities in the frontier area, 'I would ask him to enquire from them (as being an enquiry from him personally) whether they had ever given any thought to the idea of a demilitarised area in North Korea and if so, whether they would like him to convey any suggestions regarding this to me.' Bevin also proposed to inform Pandit Nehru of the approach which Hutchison would be making to the Chinese Government and to ask him to consider sending instructions to the Indian Ambassador in Peking to make a parallel approach. Finally, Bevin proposed to instruct His Majesty's Ambassador in Moscow to inform the Soviet Government, in view of their declared interest in the maintenance of peace, of the views of HMG on the gravity of the situation in the Far East. Sir David Kelly, though, would *not* raise the question of a demilitarised zone.[38]

It was as Franks and Acheson were discussing Bevin's proposals that it emerged the latter expected the general offensive of United Nations forces in Korea to commence about 22 to 24 November. Franks put it to Acheson that this meant he was asking Bevin to postpone his approaches to the Chinese and Moscow until very near the time of the start of the offensive. Acheson explained that he, Lovett (Deputy Secretary of Defense), General Bradley and Bedell-Smith (Director of the Central Intelligence Agency) had gone over the intelligence situation in the last two days. Bedell-Smith thought the only useful question to ask was what MacArthur should do. There were three possibilities: he could stay where he was, go forward or move backwards. American military opinion was that the decision between these possibilities could not be made 7,000 miles away from the scene of operations. The position had to be left to the General Commanding in the light of his general directives.

Acheson then went on to say that he was seriously concerned about the situation and that his mind moved along parallel lines to that of Bevin. He did not think the Joint Chiefs of Staff would take it on themselves to try to tell MacArthur what to do in a military way – they were too far off and too ignorant of the ground and the general possibilities. Acheson himself was therefore working at a political directive which he opted to complete and clear with the Defense Department and the Joint Chiefs by 20 November at the latest which would not make the conquest or occupation of the rest of North Korea a requirement on the Commanding General. He would be required, as before, to unify the large part of Korea which he had occupied and to hold elections and equip a Korean Army of 10 or 12 divisions as rapidly as he could. The political directive could not, however, specify what from a military point of view the Commanding General should or should not do in the unoccupied part of North Korea in order to fulfil his mission. Franks formed the clear impression that Acheson was very troubled about the timing of the planned offensive. It might coincide almost exactly with the arrival of a Chinese delegation in New York and would thus form an unhappy prologue to whatever talks might develop. Franks also formed the clear impression that Acheson was not in a position and was not willing to attempt to overcome the strong objections of the Joint Chiefs to telling MacArthur in Korea how to conduct his military operations there.[39]

At the Chiefs of Staff Committee, on 20 November, Slim said that he was very concerned about the present situation in Korea. It seemed that the war there was largely regarded in the United States as a domestic affair, and that decisions on the conduct of operations were coloured by the internal political situation in the United States. Although there was general agreement on all sides that it was desirable to avoid a clash with Communist China, the American authorities did not seem able to give practical effect to this policy on account of their internal politics and the personalities involved. He felt strongly, however, that the United Kingdom Government must enforce its right to exercise some control over the purposes for which British troops were used. With the arrival in Korea of the 29th Brigade, there would be two British brigades in action, together with their supporting units, and this amounted to quite a substantial force. There might well be heavy casualties, which it would be necessary subsequently to justify to Parliament and public opinion. Slim was convinced of the importance of restraining MacArthur temporarily in his offensive towards the Yalu River.

Also attending the Committee was Robert Scott who stated that the Foreign Office were already preparing a telegram from Bevin to Acheson which was designed to clarify MacArthur's status; but this telegram did not attempt to deal with the specific issue of the immediate military situation. Scott was in sympathy with the line proposed by Slim, and he believed that the Foreign Secretary would also support it. As regarded the method of approach to the Americans, he suggested that there might be a general message from the Prime Minister to the President simultaneously with a message from the Minister of Defence to General Marshall the US Secretary of Defense. It seemed that the President and Marshall were in the best position to influence MacArthur, and that an approach to them would be more profitable than to Acheson.[40]

From the information gathered in Washington, Elliot informed Attlee that, at present, the State Department and Joint Chiefs 'agree with us in principle that it is important to avoid a clash with China; but it seems that for political reasons and on account of the personalities involved, the Americans are not able to give practical effect to this policy. Thus the point of view of His Majesty's Government does not seem to have prevailed in Washington'. The Chiefs of Staff considered, therefore, that the time had, therefore, come to 'represent our views to the Americans in the most forcible and unequivocal terms'. Indeed there was, in the opinion of the Chiefs, a fallacy in the conception of advancing to a military objective in the form of a line on the map, since, in the process, the combat zone must inevitably spill over that line. The Chiefs recognised that a halt to the United Nations offensive might be represented as a success for the Chinese. They felt, however, that this was a small disadvantage when weighed against the risks of promoting general war by continuing the offensive. The urgent requirement now was to provide, militarily, a breathing space during which the negotiations could be given a chance to succeed; all other considerations must be secondary. In advocating this policy, the Chiefs were not recommending that the United Nations offensive should be postponed indefinitely. They merely asked that it should be halted for at least a week; after which, depending upon the success of negotiations, it might be necessary to order its resumption in the clear acceptance of the risks entailed.[41]

The Chiefs' views were discussed at a meeting Shinwell had with Attlee and Bevin on 21 November. It was agreed that Bevin should send a telegram to Washington conveying the views of the Chiefs and that a copy of the signal should be sent to Tedder.[42] In his message to Washington,

Bevin stressed that he hoped it would have been possible for the offensive in North Korea to be delayed 'until my suggestions could have been put forward in the Security Council and subsequently discussed with the Chinese. I again urge this course of action upon the United States Administration'.[43]

On 22 November, John Hutchinson renewed his request, of 20 November, for an interview and was granted a meeting with the Vice Minister for Foreign Affairs, Chang Han Fu, that afternoon. Hutchinson handed Chang a message, from Bevin, emphasising its urgency and expressing the hope that Chou En Lai would be able to give it very early consideration. In order to obviate the possibility of a controversial discussion Hutchison then proceeded immediately to speak as follows:

> May I now have Your Excellency's permission to say a few words personally?
>
> The dangerous international potentialities of the situation in Korea are only too obvious to all of us.
>
> It seems clear that one principal motive actuating the Chinese fighting in Korea is to prevent an attack which they anticipate may be made on north-east China.
>
> I am most anxious to make to my Government some practical suggestion for action which would immediately make it clear that any such anticipation is in fact entirely unwarranted and which would at the same time relax the tenseness of the international situation.
>
> It has occurred to me personally that one means by which these objectives could be attained (pending the establishment of a free united and independent Korea and the withdrawal of all foreign forces from the country) would be the setting up of a demilitarised zone on the Korean side of the frontier.
>
> I do not wish to submit suggestion to my Government for action from which satisfactory results could not be reasonably expected, and I should be grateful for Your Excellency's opinion as to whether the establishment of such a demilitarised zone would be likely to have the desired effect.
>
> If Your Excellency does not feel that a proposal for a demilitarised area would be fruitful, I should be grateful if Your Excellency could suggest other means by which Chinese interests in the frontier area could best be safeguarded.

Chang listened with 'grave attention' and asked whether this was Hutchison's own suggestion or whether he was putting it forward as a suggestion made by His Majesty's Government. Hutchison repeated that he was putting it forward tentatively as his own suggestion. Chang then asked what Hutchison meant by a de-militarised zone: 'I said I had in mind a sort of cushion on the Korean side of the border in which fighting would cease and from which military units would be withdrawn.' Finally Chang enquired who would keep order in such a de-militarised zone. Hutchison replied that he had only so far thought of the possibility of such a zone in a general way and had not considered it in detail, but that he would suppose that the local North Korean authorities would be responsible for keeping law and order in the Zone: 'I fancy that he had thought I might suggest that the United Nations authority should administer the demilitarised Zone' reflected Hutchison who considered that the pertinence of Chang's question suggested that the idea was not new to him, and the impression was that the Chinese were already considering some such possibility. 'I feel sure they realise in spite of my denial that you have instructed me to raise the question in this way' Hutchison telegraphed Bevin. While Chang made no suggestion of any other way in which Chinese interests in the frontier area could best be safeguarded, he said that he would convey to Chou En Lai both Bevin's message and also the substance of what Hutchison had personally said. Hutchison felt sure that Chang fully appreciated the urgency of the matter; he insisted more than once that the Chinese translation of Bevin's message should be delivered that night. This was being done.[44]

Bevin, meanwhile, still had it in mind to make a statement in the House of Commons on the course of policy which he had followed in relation to Korea.[45] On 22 November, he telegraphed Franks: 'There is general anxiety on all sides in the House of Commons lest General MacArthur should commit the United Nations forces in Korea to large scale hostilities with the Chinese. I shall have to deal with this, possibly quite soon, and in any case during the debate on foreign affairs due to take place next week.' Whilst he had certain indications of the nature of the instructions issued to MacArthur, e.g. in regard to civil affairs, even these had been communicated to Bevin for his secret information only. 'This places me in a most difficult and embarrassing position.' There was a campaign going on in Korea in which British forces were engaged; the command of the forces was ultimately subject to the United Nations through the agency of the United States Government and the objectives of the Commander must be those set out in United Nations resolutions. Despite this the United Nations had no real say in the instructions issued to the Commander, 'and I am not at liberty to disclose such information as I have'. Parliament and the British public were entitled to expect that the objectives of the United

Nations Commander in the field were no more and no less than the stated objectives of the United Nations as expressed in its resolutions. Bevin was aware that, under the American military system, it was customary to leave more latitude to the Commander in the field than under the British system. But the same principles applied whether the Commander was acting on his own initiative or under instructions:

> I can reasonably claim that it is not in the public interest to disclose the precise nature of the instructions issued to him. I must, however, be careful not to leave the impression that the reasons why the instructions are not made public is either because these give General MacArthur more latitude than a strict fulfilment of the United Nations Resolutions would justify or that quite simply we have no knowledge of their contents.
>
> I recognise that General MacArthur must be given discretion (within the broad limits outlined above) to conduct the campaign on the lines he thinks best. I recognise also that in view of military requirements and with the Russians back in the Security Council there can be no question of the latter issuing detailed military instructions or of his being required to seek such instructions from the Council through the representative of the United States.
>
> All this, however, does not meet my particular difficulties. I should therefore like you to explain these urgently to Mr Acheson and ask him how we can best overcome them. Public opinion here is getting restive and it is of very great importance that I should be able to assure the House *first* that the objectives of General MacArthur are no more and no less than the objectives of the United Nations, *second* that proper consultation is taking place and *third* that General MacArthur through the United States Government is in fact as well as in name the agent of the United Nations.

There should not be much difficulty in giving the first and third assurances, thought Bevin. The main problem arose over consultation. The Commander's view of military necessity might prompt him to action going beyond his mandate without the United Nations being given the opportunity to consider its political implications. As regarded this, Bevin felt that the UK should press the United States Government to agree:

> (i) to consult confidentially at least those member States of the Security Council who are providing forces in Korea on any contemplated action of this character and

(ii) not to issue instructions to the Commander to proceed unless those States consulted express their agreement to what is proposed.

If we get an assurance on these lines (which I feel is our due) I shall, during the course of the Debate, be able to tell the House that there is a satisfactory arrangement in force regarding consultation, though of course I would not propose to divulge any details. I would consult as to the words to be used.[46]

With Acheson not being available, on 23 November, Franks arranged for Bevin's message to be given to Rusk who said he was sure Acheson would be very grateful for the friendly tone of the communication. Rusk went on to say that MacArthur's offensive was due to start in the early hours of 24 November (Japan time) and hoped to eliminate all opposition within a very short time (possibly a matter of days). This would not mean that United Nations troops would thereupon line the Chinese frontier. They would, in fact, be disposed in a manner guaranteeing control of the frontier, but not its continuous oversight. The present American approach to this solution did, however, disclose a difference over the nature of the zone which, in Bevin's proposals had been referred to as a 'demilitarised area', and in the American considerations as a 'band of non-belligerency'. There had clearly been very recent discussions with the military as a result of which American views had become more definite. Rusk said that the constitution of a demilitarised zone in the strict sense of the phrase would be difficult for the Unified Command to agree to.

It was possible at this point in the conversation for Franks to probe this matter. Rusk did not agree that the military command necessarily intended to withdraw all United Nations troops, other than South Korean troops, from a strip south of the Yalu. The strip would in fact, be lightly patrolled, so that, if there should be a re-incursion of Chinese troops or if North Koreans resumed military activity, United Nations forces would immediately re-enter the zone in force. It would in fact be a lightly patrolled security zone, a *de facto* buffer, but not an agreed area of demilitarisation in which United Nations forces would be debarred from ensuring an adequate control. What the Unified Command now had in mind was an area of manoeuvre, dominated by themselves, so that, in chasing away marauders, United Nations forces would not have to operate close to, or over, prohibited country.[47]

On 24 November, Acheson received word from the US Embassy that Bevin had agreed not to present the proposal at the UN for a demilitarised zone before the arrival in New York of the Chinese Communist delegation. Since the delegation was due to arrive on 25 November, and since there would probably be a meeting of the Security Council early the next week, Acheson wished to lay before Bevin in more detail 'why I have the gravest apprehensions regarding the presentation of any such proposal, pending such clarification and reconsideration of the situation following General MacArthur's offensive'. Acheson's reasons were as follows: firstly, 'Your proposal contemplates the creation of a very considerable demilitarised zone in Northern Korea. Your message ... suggested that it would include an area running roughly from Hungnam to Chongju in the west.' MacArthur's forces in the west were taking off from positions which at many points were already north of this line in an endeavour to defeat the enemy and drive them from the proposed demilitarised area in the west. In the east, a substantial part of his forces were already considerably to the north of this line both along the coast and inland. Therefore, to make such a proposal at any time in the near future in the United Nations, would be suggesting that 'we abandon considerable areas and population in the east which had already been brought within United Nations protection, and in the west that we should abandon positions which may be of very considerable military importance to secure, and for which General MacArthur's forces would at the very moment be putting forth a great effort under adverse circumstances and undoubtedly heavy losses.' The effect of such a proposal on the conduct of military operations, upon the morale of the troops, upon the morale of the Koreans and upon public opinion in the United States, which had furnished the great bulk of the troops, would, 'in my opinion, be disastrous. I do not think that it is possible to fight a war or to maintain the support of the population in Korea under these circumstances'.

Furthermore, Acheson did not think that it was possible at this time to say that the proposal if adopted would have the benefits claimed for it. The idea of a demilitarised zone was to remove contending forces from it and interpose a buffer between them. It seemed to Acheson that the effect of the proposal at this time and of this nature upon the Communist delegation and its Government would be unfortunate. Acheson believed it would be taken by them as a starting point for negotiations to obtain something much more favourable to them and 'as an indication of the greatest weakness on our part. I think that we will hurt rather than advance the prospect of aiding the situation by negotiation if at this time and in this way we put forward the proposal you suggest'.

Under these circumstances, it seemed to Acheson of the greatest importance that MacArthur's operation be given every support by the United Nations and by the countries contributing forces. The results of his operation would make much more clear many matters which were now obscure, the strength and effectiveness of the Chinese forces, and the intention and capacity of the Communist authorities to support and reinforce them. If these matters became clearer, a number of alternatives would emerge, 'among which we would now not wish finally to choose'. By taking present military requirements as a starting point, 'we may be able to stabilise the political situation by proposals which originate from a position of strength and which will help to end the fighting and achieve the results of the United Nations on a more permanent basis'. Acheson finished by telling Bevin: 'I do not think I need to dwell upon the possible divisive effects of making such a proposal under the circumstances, as outlined above. I think it is an understatement to say that the reaction to it in this country at the moment that our troops are making a great effort would be most violent. I think we are all trying to do the same thing' – that was, to devise ways in which political action and negotiation helped in the most effective way to bring about the end of the fighting and the unification of Korea, under circumstances which would amply assure its neighbours that neither the United Nations nor any of its members had the faintest hostile intention toward them. 'We are, as you know, working on possible measures which would keep Western forces away from direct contact with Chinese or Russian forces at the Korean frontier and which would clearly demonstrate that United Nations forces in Korea have no purposes beyond those set by the United Nations. I do believe most strongly, however, that the putting forward of any proposal at this particular time would do the greatest damage. I have given you all my thoughts on this subject because I am deeply conscious of the gravity of the ensuing days and of the far-reaching consequences of any misstep.'[48]

On 25 November the Chiefs of Staff warned Tedder that the present situation in Korea seemed, almost inevitably, bound to lead to a demand by MacArthur to be allowed to bomb targets in Manchuria: 'We remain firmly opposed to any such thing.' From the local military point of view this may be illogical, but they concluded, that one view of the reasons for the present 'unpleasant' situation was that the local military point of view in relation to Korea, in isolation from the major strategic issues, had been given far too free a rein: 'We are not being wise after the event. We have always foreseen the possibility of the present situation arising, and have never shared MacArthur's optimism about Chinese intervention, and for that reason have always been opposed to pushing on to the frontier.' At the same time there was a good local military reason for confining air action to North Korea: 'We have had a warning, through the same channel that accurately predicted Chinese intervention if we went North of the 38th parallel, that to bomb targets in Manchuria would bring the Soviet air force into action.' If this happened it would 'largely nullify our great military advantage in this war, namely our complete air superiority and the ability of the USAF to concentrate on support of the Army'. Its still wider implication in extending the conflict, possibly even to the point of general war, must be obvious.

The Chiefs understood the difficulties of any attempt to exercise a moderating influence in the present political atmosphere in the United States, 'and the strength of that school of thought to which, as the "Times" said today "any attempt to avoid a large scale war seems to be appeasement". We know the State Department and Chiefs of Staff are as anxious as we are to avoid war with China'. But, again apart from the possible worldwide implications, 'we feel strongly that it is not sufficiently appreciated that the extent of our right to a say in Korean policy is not limited to the proportion of our military contribution actually in Korea. We need not tell you of the repercussions of Korean affairs on our difficult campaign in Malaya, or on our position in Hong Kong'.[49]

The stakes were dramatically raised when MacArthur's offensive was met, head on, by a massive Chinese offensive of their own. With UN forces having been split in two, previously by MacArthur, one of his armies was virtually surrounded in the coming days and had to fight its way back down south in a general retreat – termed the 'Great Bug Out'. Slim, on 27 November, wondered if the Chiefs would now be wise to examine the problems they would face if the Korean campaign should develop into a war with China, 'with a view to clearing our minds as to the general policy to be accepted and the immediate action to be taken.' In such an examination, there were a number of factors to be taken into account, amongst them:

(a) In view of the vast size of China, it is most improbable that she could be defeated by conventional land campaigns.
(b) In fighting China, we do not hit Soviet war potential; and, in deploying our forces against her, would be playing the Soviet game.
(c) Russia, while giving covert help to the Chinese, would probably not take part openly; but the possibility of a war with Russia would be brought a great deal closer.
(d) In a global war the Far East must be treated as a defensive theatre.

The aim, considered Slim, must clearly be to localise the war with China as far as possible, to resist the diversion of forces to the Far East, and to accelerate the build-up of forces in the West against the possibility of global war. 'We need to consider how best to achieve that aim' concluded Slim.[50]

Franks flashed the news to London, on 28 November, that the United States considered the position disclosed by the Chinese offensive in Korea as serious, relatively so in regard to the present military situation, but particularly so in respect of the general intentions which the Chinese action appeared to indicate. United States military authorities were confident that:

(a) Chinese offensive was not in response to the drive launched by United Nations forces on 24th November. There is already ample proof that Chinese attack was mounted some time ago and it was coincidental that offensives met head on.
(b) Chinese are not merely protecting power installations and the frontier zone. Nature of their attack suggests a major move to destroy United Nations forces.

The following identifications had been made in the enemy battle order: the 38th, 39th, 40th, 42nd, 66th, 50th and 20th Chinese Communist armies plus six additional but unattached divisions. This gave a strength of at least 200,000 men. They had practically no air cover but were operating with a small amount of spearhead tank support and were moving artillery forward. Horse cavalry units were assisting the advance. The central position was at the moment insecure and British and Turkish brigades were being moved eastwards to restore the line. A withdrawal of units within the north eastern finger (reaching to Chongjin) to a point below Hamhung was now being considered.[51]

The Chiefs' fears regarding US demands to bomb Chinese territory now proved prophetic: Rusk told Franks, on 29 November, for his 'most confidential information' that some two hundred twin-engined bombers had been brought on to the airfields of Manchuria. Should they be used to attack United Nations forces in the near future, and more particularly United Nations airfields where aircraft were massed tip to tip, the effects would be very serious. An immediate decision would have to be taken in order to deal with this attack if it occurred. Rusk said the Americans were turning over in their minds the advisability of giving the Chinese a solemn warning through the United Nations against taking such action. This would make it clear on whom responsibility rested for expansion of the area of hostilities in terms of retaliation from the air which might be forced upon MacArthur.[52]

Tedder saw Bradley and thought it advisable to show him the Chiefs' message. Bradley reiterated US determination to avoid extension of conflict. This had been discussed at length and emphasised in the JCS meeting and the National Security Council (NSC). MacArthur's directives left no ambiguity on the subject of not taking action across the Yalu. They were worried at the potential air threat. Recent intelligence showed some two hundred medium or light bombers. The previous night, 28 November, an air attack on an airfield at Pyonyang did considerable damage. Bradley said that the only consideration which could make air attack on air bases in Manchuria thinkable, would be if Communist air attack seriously endangered the security of UN Forces and in such case it would only be done to cover a withdrawal. Tedder pointed out that such action, by bringing in the Russian Air Force openly, would 'probably' make the situation both in the air and on ground worse than ever. 'The point was taken.' Tedder also pointed out, and Bradley agreed, that this would possibly if not probably lead directly to world war. Tedder emphasised that a decision with such possible implications was one which must call for full consideration with other Governments and presumably with the UNO. Bradley 'registered and agreed'. Tedder's impression at his end was that political or party considerations were not playing a large part in US views regarding military action in Korea. It was purely military considerations that had weighed in the past and still were the decisive ones.[53]

On 28 November, MacArthur confirmed to the United Nations that organised Chinese forces of an aggregate strength of over 200,000 men were arrayed against the United Nations forces in Korea, which 'now faced an entirely new war'. This situation, he added, posed issues which were beyond the authority of his military command and called for a political solution. In the Security Council the United States representative, Austin, denounced the Chinese action as open aggression; and the representative of the Chinese Peoples' Government (CPG), attending the General Assembly (GA), replied with an intransigent attack upon American imperialism. Bevin informed the Cabinet that the Chinese offensive went beyond anything necessary for the limited purpose of protecting the hydro-electric installations or the frontier zone. It seemed clear that the Chinese aimed at destroying the United Nations forces in Korea. Franks, in Washington, was reporting that the State Department were of opinion that a charge of aggression must now be brought, in the Security Council, against the Chinese Communist Government. Upon receipt of these reports, Bevin had at once communicated with the United States Government. He had been apprehensive that American military opinion might favour some precipitate action: in particular, he had been concerned lest MacArthur should press his previous request for authority to launch air attacks on military targets beyond the Manchurian frontier.[54]

Bevin also called on Holmes, the US chargé d'affaires, to complain that he had just read MacArthur's communiqué and, in view of his anticipated difficulties in Parliament the following day, and his desire to say nothing that would 'upset [the] applecart' the Foreign Secretary wanted Holmes to ask Acheson personally for an 'appreciation of the situation' which would assist him in the debate. Bevin's mood was 'friendly and understanding but he anticipates he will face questions tomorrow along line of "is MacArthur getting us into full-scale war with China" and naturally wanted as much ammunition as possible to use in his reply.[55] Bevin received a personal message from Acheson containing assurances which were satisfactory 'so far as they went'.[56] Crucially, for Bevin's purposes, Acheson reassured him that, in 'arriving at our position, we will continue to consult closely with the UK and bear in mind the special interest of those nations represented by combat forces in Korea'.[57] Acheson also said that the United States intended to handle the situation through the United Nations and not unilaterally. Their purpose would remain the same, namely, to resist aggression, to localise the area of hostilities and to settle the Korean problem on a satisfactory United Nations basis in such a way as to avoid committing large United Nations forces indefinitely in these operations. Bevin endorsed these purposes but strongly deprecated any move to carry hostilities into Manchuria: 'If we had to fight the Chinese, it was much better, from both the political and the military point of view, that we should do so in North Korea' he told the Cabinet.

The Foreign Secretary's conclusion was that, although the situation was serious, it was not out of hand. But these developments in Korea called for even greater vigilance in Europe; and the Cabinet should be alive to the risk that Allied preoccupation with the Far East might provide opportunities for those who were anxious to make trouble in Austria and Berlin. Attlee agreed and pointed out that it was of the first importance that the United Nations should not be trapped into diverting a disproportionate effort to the Far East. Their operations in Korea had been important as a symbol of their resistance to aggression; but Korea was not in itself of any strategic importance to the democracies and it must not be allowed to draw more of their military resources away from Europe and the Middle East. MacArthur had been 'over-optimistic' about the course of the campaign; and the check which he had suffered might lead him to exaggerate the strength of this Chinese attack. It was therefore the more important that Governments should avoid any precipitate action at the present stage.[58]

From the UN, Jebb informed Bevin: 'You may care to know of the impression which I have gained as a result of a large number of conversations with leading delegates in the last 48 hours.' There was a great deal of pessimism about the outcome of events in Korea and almost everyone blamed the recent turn of events to some extent upon MacArthur. The most serious feature was perhaps a total lack of confidence in any information emanating from him whether contained in an official report or not: 'I have had this today from ... leading people ... Almost everyone one talks to believes him capable of even cooking intelligence reports for his own personal or political ends.' Jebb had told Gross, Acheson's Ambassador at Large, this confidentially and urged upon him the need for the United States Government to do something to restore confidence. Among Jebb's conversations was one with Michalowsky the Polish Ambassador in London who took advantage of the loss of confidence in MacArthur 'to urge upon me that the situation must not be left in military hands a day longer and that either we or the Indian delegation should attempt to bring the matter back on to the diplomatic plane before military events drag us into wider hostilities'. Michalowsky insisted that his suggestion was purely personal but it was noticeable that he spent much of the afternoon in a 'conspicuous situation' talking to members of the UK delegation: 'I think one must assume that he was acting on instructions unless as I have sometimes suspected he is in process of working his passage into the Western camp. I am not of course subscribing to any of the opinions referred to but I think they are typical even among people well disposed to the United States.'[59]

Jebb had, by now, received instructions from Bevin to seek postponement of any vote on Chinese intervention. What worried Bevin was that the Americans would introduce a charge of aggression, in the UN, against the Chinese – which would lead to full-scale war with the Communists. The basis of his instruction was so that, in 2 or 3 days, the situation might be clarified sufficiently so that Jebb could make a statement which would include a 'last call for the use of reason'. Jebb, in conversation with Austin, summarised the attitude of the UK Government in the following manner: the UN Charter was not considered at San Francisco to be an instrument suited to handling the problem of war among major powers. Irrespective of who recognised what government in China, *de facto* the situation which confronted the world was the prospect of precisely the kind of war with which the UN was neither competent nor capable to deal. Regarding Korea itself no one knew on June 25 whether victorious UN forces would proceed north of the 38th parallel. In fact, the original purpose and mission of the UN action had been accomplished with the restoration of the *status quo* and the restoring to power, in South Korea, of Syngman Rhee.

Jebb added that for all practical purposes the Republic of Korea really meant South Korea. A resolution which included a finding of aggression constituted an undertaking to commit the already inadequate defence forces of the free world to a campaign of reconquest and liberation of areas seized by the Chinese Communists. This would be taking place at a time before the 'constitution of sufficient strength' by Western Europe 'to make at least a pretence of defending itself against a Russian attack'. A basic understanding of the UK had been that such forces would be created in Western Europe and that had not yet been accomplished. 'Launching a quite obvious barb at France', Jebb added that the slowness of developments in Western Europe along these lines had not been the fault of the British Government or people. In any event, Jebb continued, he was certain from his discussions with other Western European delegations that they shared with the UK the tremendous apprehension that the US was committing Western Europe to conduct a war in the Far East at an impossible time and under the most difficult possible strategic conditions. Jebb mentioned, specifically, discussions he had held with the Belgian, Dutch and Norwegian representatives in New York. He strongly favoured a two-step process, involving the tabling of a resolution in the GA along the lines of the pending Security Council resolution and subsequently, if necessary, the introduction of a stronger resolution of the sort the Americans seemed to be considering. In this connection, Jebb said he was bound to make clear that the UK Government had not yet decided that the matter should be taken into the GA at this stage and Jebb was awaiting instructions on this point. The two-phased procedure he described as his personal view[60] – it was certainly further than the Foreign Secretary had instructed him to go. Bevin was no doubt relieved to receive a cable, from Franks, that he had been to the State Department and the Americans were not planning to introduce a charge of aggression against the Chinese in the UN.[61]

In a despatch to the Foreign Office, Jebb felt that, during the next few days, the military developments in Korea would be all important. Anything that was done or not done at Lake Success was subsidiary he concluded. Jebb feared that Austin 'seems to have adopted a rather irresponsible attitude'. In his present mood Austin 'seems almost inclined to welcome a war with China but he has obviously not considered the consequences of such a development or the support which such a move would get in the United Nations'. An issue which Jebb thought might arise at any time was the question of whether MacArthur should be given authority to undertake tactical bombing of airfields, communications, troop concentrations etc. in Manchuria. Jebb hoped this issue would not present itself but if it did and if MacArthur reported that such authority was essential to safeguard United Nations forces in Korea, Jebb personally did not see how it could be withheld even though the crossing of the Manchurian frontier in this way would obviously carry with it the risk of extending the conflict and prejudicing the chance of a peaceful settlement: 'I feel that we should try to deal with this question as a military issue and try to keep it separate from action we take in the diplomatic field either here or in Washington. We may have to exercise great restraint on the United States Administration and on the United States Delegation to the United Nations but I hope that we would not put ourselves in a position where we could reasonably be accused of sacrificing the lives of United States (and indeed British) troops. This would I am sure provoke very serious resentment throughout this country.' Jebb also mentioned that there was 'much loose talk here about atom bombing Chinese towns from Formosa; but I have no reason as yet to think that this is a serious possibility'.[62]

Jebb's final sentence must have seemed ironic to him given that, the following day, in the course of questioning on the Korean crisis, the following exchange occurred between President Truman and the press:

> The President: We will take whatever steps are necessary to meet the military situation, just as we always have ... Q. Will that include the atomic bomb? The President: That includes every weapon that we have. Q. Mr. President, you said 'every weapon that we have.' Does that mean that there is active consideration of the use of the atomic bomb? The President: There has always been active consideration of its use. I don't want to see it used. It is a terrible weapon, and it should not be used on innocent men, women, and children who have nothing whatever to do with this military aggression. That happens when it is used.[63]

## Notes

1 TNA DEFE 11/201 Situation Report No. 58: Korea Situation as Known at 0900, 3 October 1950
2 TNA DEFE 11/201 Peking to Foreign Office Telegram No. 1554, October 1950
3 TNA DEFE 11/201 Inward Telegram to Commonwealth Relations UK High Commissioner in India, 4 October 1950
4 TNA DEFE 11/201 Chiefs of Staff Committee Confidential Annex to COS (50) 161st Meeting held on Wednesday, 4 October 1950
5 TNA DEFE 11/201 Elliot to Minister, 4 October 1950
6 TNA DEFE 11/201 Washington to Foreign Office Telegram No. 2679, 4 October 1950

7 TNA DEFE 11/202 British Embassy Tokyo to Ministry of Defence, London: CAB 72. For Chiefs of Staff from Bouchier, 6 October 1950
8 TNA DEFE 11/202 British Embassy Tokyo to Ministry of Defence, London: CAB 72. For Chiefs of Staff from Bouchier, 8 October 1950
9 TNA DEFE 11/202 Inward Telegram to Commonwealth Relations UK High Commissioner In India, 7 October 1950
10 TNA DEFE 11/202 Cabinet Extract from C.M. (50) 63rd Conclusions held on 9 October 1950
11 TNA DEFE 11/202 British Embassy Tokyo to Ministry of Defence, London CAB 75, 9 October 1950. For Chiefs of Staff from Bouchier
12 TNA FO 800/517 Franks to Bevin 20 October 1951
13 TNA FO 800/517 Franks to Bevin 31 October 1951
14 TNA DEFE 11/202 British Embassy Tokyo to Ministry Of Defence, London CAB 86, 23 October 1950. For Chiefs of Staff from Bouchier
15 TNA DEFE 11/202 Foreign Office to Peking Telegram No. 1669, 27 October 1950
16 TNA DEFE 11/202 British Embassy Tokyo to Ministry of Defence, London CAB 90, 27 October 1950. For Chiefs of Staff from Bouchier
17 TNA DEFE 11/202 Foreign Office to Peking Telegram No. 1698, 1 November 1950
18 TNA DEFE 11/202 Washington to Foreign Office Telegram No. 2950, 1 November 1950
19 TNA CAB 128/18 Cabinet Conclusions, 6 November 1950
20 TNA DEFE 11/203 COS (W) 894 for Lord Tedder from Chiefs of Staff, 6 November 1950
21 TNA DEFE 11/203 AWT 71 for Chiefs of Staff from Lord Tedder, 8 November 1950
22 TNA DEFE 11/203 TOK 38 Chiefs of Staff for Bouchier, 9 November 1950
23 TNA CAB 128/18 Cabinet Conclusions, 9 November 1950
24 TNA DEFE 11/203 Peking to Foreign Office Telegram No. 1761, 7 November 1950
25 TNA DEFE 11/203 New York to Foreign Office Telegram No. 1674, 8 November 1950
26 TNA CAB 128/18 Cabinet Conclusions, 13 November 1950
27 TNA DEFE 11/203 Foreign Office to Washington Telegram No. 5028, 13 November 1950
28 TNA DEFE 11/203 New York to Foreign Office Telegram No. 1720, 14 November 1950
29 TNA DEFE 11/203 Washington to Foreign Office Telegram No. 3079, 14 November 1950
30 TNA DEFE 11/203 Foreign Office to Washington Telegram No. 5066, 15 November 1950

31 TNA CAB 21/1985 Situation in Korea, 14 November 1950
32 TNA CAB 21/1985 Memorandum, 14 November 1950
33 TNA DEFE 11/203 Chiefs of Staff Committee Confidential Annex to 180th meeting, held on Wednesday, 15 November 1950
34 TNA DEFE 11/203 Chiefs of Staff Committee COS (50) 180th meeting held on Wednesday, 15 November 1950
35 TNA DEFE 11/203 Foreign Office to Washington Telegram No. 5099, 16 November 1950
36 TNA DEFE 11/203 Washington to Foreign Office Telegram No. 3089, 15 November 1950
37 TNA DEFE 11/203 Foreign Office to Washington Telegram No. 5123, 17 November 1950
38 TNA DEFE 11/203 Washington Telegram No. 5124, 17 November 1950
39 TNA DEFE 11/203 Washington to Foreign Office Telegram No. 3131, 18 November 1950
40 TNA DEFE 11/204 Chiefs of Staff Committee Confidential Annex to COS (50) 182nd meeting held on Monday, 20 November 1950
41 TNA DEFE 11/204 Chiefs of Staff Committee Confidential Annex to COS (50) 182nd meeting held on Monday, 20 November 1950
42 TNA CAB 21/1985 H Godfrey to Air Marshal Elliot, 22 November 1950
43 TNA DEFE 11/204 Telegram to Washington Repeated to UKDEL New York Telegram No. 3148 (of 21 November) Chinese intervention in Korea
44 TNA DEFE 11/204 Peking to Foreign Office Telegram No. 1882, 22 November 1950
45 TNA CAB 128/18 Cabinet Conclusions, 20 November 1950
46 TNA DEFE 11/204 Foreign Office to Washington Telegram No. 5194, 22 November 1950. Following personal for Ambassador from Secretary of State
47 TNA DEFE 11/204 Washington to Foreign Office Telegram No. 3159, 23 November 1950
48 TNA DEFE 11/204 Washington to Foreign Office Telegram No. 3165, 24 November 1950
49 TNA DEFE 11/204 COS (W) 907, 25 November 1950. For Tedder from Chiefs of Staff
50 TNA DEFE 11/204 CIGS to First Sea Lord and Chief of the Air Staff, 27 November 1950
51 TNA DEFE 11/204 Washington to Foreign Office Telegram No. 3195, 28 November 1950
52 TNA DEFE 11/204 Washington to Foreign Office Telegram No. 3209, 29 November 1950
53 TNA DEFE 11/204 AWT 76, 29 November 1950. For Chiefs of Staff from Lord Tedder
54 TNA CAB 128/18 Cabinet Conclusions, 29 November 1950

55 FRUS 1950, Volume VII (Korea). The Charge in the United Kingdom (Holmes) to the Secretary of State, 28 November 1950
56 TNA CAB 128/18 Cabinet Conclusions, 29 November 1950
57 FRUS 1950, Volume VII (Korea). Memorandum of a Conversation, by the Deputy Director of the Office of Northeastern Asian Affairs (Johnson), 29 November 1950
58 TNA CAB 128/18 Cabinet Conclusions, 29 November 1950
59 TNA DEFE 11/204 New York to Foreign Office Telegram No. 1895, 29 November 1950
60 FRUS 1950, Volume VII (Korea). The United States Representative to the United Nations (Austin) to the Secretary of State, 29 November 1950
61 TNA DEFE 11/204 Washington to Foreign Office Telegram No. 3208, 29 November 1950
62 TNA DEFE 11/204 New York to Foreign Office Telegram No. 1894, 29 November 1950
63 FRUS 1950, Volume VII (Korea) Editorial Note pp. 1261–1262

# 4

# Attlee in Washington

Although it was clarified, quite quickly, that the President had not been advocating the use of the Bomb in Korea (Attlee later told the Cabinet that 'Truman didn't realise he'd dropped such a brick'[1] during his Washington press conference) the ripples of consternation that flowed in public and diplomatic discourse enabled the Cabinet to decide, on 30 November, that it would be 'useful' if the Prime Minister could visit Washington for conversations with Truman. A message was sent accordingly to the President 'who at once replied that he would be very glad to see Mr Attlee'. On 2 December the French Prime Minister, Pleven and the French Foreign Minister, Schuman, came to London at their own request to inform Attlee and Bevin of the views of the French Government on matters which were likely to arise during Attlee's visit to Washington.

The Prime Minister left London by air at 9.30 pm on 3 December and arrived at Washington at 9.30 am (local time) on 4 December. He was accompanied by a high powered delegation including Field Marshal Sir William Slim, Sir Roger Makins and Robert Scott of the Foreign Office, Sir Edwin Plowden (Chief of the Economic Planning Staff), Robert Hall of the Economic Section of the Cabinet Office, DHF Rickett (Principal Private Secretary to the Prime Minister) and Philip Jordan (Adviser to the Prime Minister on Public Relations). Attlee was met at the airport by the President, Acheson, Sir Oliver Franks and a number of other high officials. The conversations between the President and the Prime Minister began on the afternoon of the day of the Prime Minister's arrival. In all, six formal meetings were held at which the President and the Prime Minister were attended by their principal advisers. There were also a number of personal talks between the Prime Minister and the President and a series of meetings between officials on both political and economic questions.²

Once the initial formalities were over, Attlee's party travelled to the British Embassy where Franks informed the Prime Minister that there had been a significant change of plan: whereas it had been intended that the talks should open on the following day at 4 pm, the US administration had now asked that in view of the latest developments in the Korean military situation they should begin that day. The meeting, explained Franks, was likely to open with a statement of the military position by General Marshall and General Bradley, and would then move on to an immediate decision on the following questions:

(a) what directives should be issued to General MacArthur;
(b) what action should be taken through the United Nations, e.g. to secure a ceasefire;
(c) these two questions would then be related in subsequent stages of the talks to the more general background. The position in the UK was that while the Chinese intervention in Korea had been placed on the agenda of the Assembly on United States initiative any discussion of it was to be held up until after the Prime Minister's talks with the President.

Franks outlined the latest appreciation of the military situation in Korea: there was now thought to be no possibility of holding a line across the Peninsula. Bridgeheads would be formed in the Seoul-Inchon and Hamhung areas. This was 'plainly an exceedingly unfavourable situation in which to open negotiations with the Chinese.' Franks explained that in talking of United States reactions he did not distinguish between the views of the administration and the broad bulk of public opinion: 'A great number of people in the United States did not realise their present military weakness and there was no national tendency to look to the Atomic Bomb to provide a solution.' The military problem of supply in any war against China, and the danger of intervention by the Soviet Air Force were not understood. The President would, therefore, have a domestic situation to deal with. Public opinion would be influenced by the heavy casualties suffered by US forces and the fact that the United States had never had to accept defeat. In this unprecedented situation, argued Franks, 'we could help the United States Administration with our advice if we could present it in a form which would carry conviction. It was important to avoid anything in the nature of a post-mortem on recent military developments, we should concentrate on the political side. This would lead us at some stage to discuss the conditions on which negotiations might be opened'. There would be little incentive to the Chinese to negotiate now that they held nearly half Korea, and they would tend to think of the United Nations as synonymous with the United States who had refused to recognise them. Therefore, said Franks, 'we must consider whether at the least [the] United States Government must not be prepared to withdraw recognition from Chiang Kai-Chek. Secondly, we must consider the position of Formosa. Whatever the strategic relations Formosa still had a strong emotional and psychological hold on the American mentality'. Attlee, in his comments, added that negotiations with the Communists could only be opened if:

(i) the United States were prepared to drop all talk of indicting the Chinese Government as an aggressor.
(ii) To withdraw recognition from [Nationalist] China.
(iii) To find a solution to the problem of Formosa.

Slim, meanwhile, felt that negotiations, difficult as they might be, were essential: 'It would be a serious matter to withdraw the United Nations forces from Korea. It could not be done unless we could hold bridgeheads at least for some weeks. But in order to induce the Chinese to negotiate the United States must be prepared to offer them something.' In further discussions there was a general recognition that any withdrawal from Korea could stir up public feeling that the South Koreans had been abandoned to their enemies and this would be a serious, but not necessarily fatal, blow to the prestige of the United Nations. There might also be a tendency on the American side to argue that such a successful example of 'war by proxy' might tempt the Russians to try the same methods in Germany. The view that Europe came first would also be under attack on the American side from General MacArthur and his adherents.[3]

Attlee next met with the President at the White House. In his opening remarks, Truman expressed his appreciation of the Prime Minister coming to the United States. The objectives of the United States and the United Kingdom were parallel, and he hoped they always would be. Accordingly, he believed these discussions would be very useful. The situation in Korea, was so serious that he felt it was necessary to begin the talks as soon as possible, although he had wanted to give the Prime Minister time to rest after his arrival; but after he had consulted with the Secretary of State and the Secretary of Defense, it had seemed that he ought to ask the Prime Minister to begin that afternoon since he did not want to come to any conclusions until after he had talked with him.[4] Truman felt that the meeting was 'badly needed'. The situation was such that it was important to reach a common understanding as soon as possible. He then asked General Bradley to give an outline of the military situation in Korea.[5] After this Slim enquired whether it was the intention to hold the beachheads or to evacuate them. Bradley said this made little difference at the time. Slim asked whether they could hold.[6] Bradley answered that no orders had yet been given to MacArthur whether to evacuate at once or to hold the bridgeheads for as long as possible. If he were so ordered, the Inchon-Seoul bridgehead might be held for some weeks with the troops which would be available. It was much more doubtful whether the Hamhung bridgehead could be held. There was no marked shortage of equipment. Pusan, where 145,000 Communist prisoners as well as three South Korean divisions were concentrated, had to be held as long as possible. Bradley warned that there could be 'no possibility' of holding a line across the peninsula at any point in view of the great numerical superiority of the enemy and the power of infiltration which this gave him.[7]

Slim remarked that it was very important to hold a beachhead in North Korea. This would constitute much more of a bargaining point. Bradley, though, thought it not much of a bargaining point considering the size of the beachhead and the size of the enemy force. Slim suggested that, nevertheless, while it was held, it might make 'the Chinese think we are building up'. Attlee inquired 'whether we could keep our air cover'; Bradley said there had been no trouble so far. The President interjected to say that the Prime Minister would see that 'we have very grave military decisions to make'. The United States had responsibilities in the East and the West: 'We naturally consider European defense primary, but we equally have responsibilities in Korea, Japan and the Philippines as the British do in Hong Kong and Singapore. It must be clear that we are not going to run out on our obligations even though these are hard to meet.' Accepting the President's invitation to respond, the Prime Minister agreed the British must take a 'broad view on a wide horizon'. A first point was the maintenance of the prestige and authority of the United Nations. The President expressed agreement with this. The United States, continued Attlee, was the principal instrument for supporting the United Nations, and the United Kingdom was giving what help it could.[8] Both the United Kingdom and the United States wished to limit the Korean affair to an assertion of the authority of the United Nations: 'We all realised the danger that the conflict might spread and lead to a world war. There was the very real risk too that if our forces became too deeply committed in China we should be left exposed in Europe where we had not yet succeeded in building up our strength. This would merely be playing into the hands of the Russians.' His Majesty's Government, explained the Prime Minister, hoped a line might be held so that an opportunity for discussion with the Chinese might be found. But as things were 'we were now on very weak ground for negotiation'. As to reinforcements these could only arrive from the United Kingdom after an interval of some months, and from what Bradley had said, it was apparent that that would be too late. Attlee urged the Americans to:

> take account of public opinion both in the United Nations and in America, Europe and Asian; and the United Kingdom, through its Commonwealth associations, was perhaps specially able to gauge opinion in Asia.
>
> If we became involved in war with China we should be playing the Russian game. His Majesty's Government had tried to look at the matter from the Chinese standpoint and see what they might ask for in any negotiation. They resented their exclusion from the United Nations and felt that, as a consequence, they had no obligations towards us. There was perhaps also a good deal of fear in their attitude – fear of the United States and of European nations generally. Above all they were a young nationalist movement, flushed with success, and it was almost inevitable that they should have imperialist ambitions. They felt strongly about Formosa and a little less strongly about Hong Kong. But for the same reasons they would not wish to throw themselves completely into the hands of Russia. The first aim of any negotiation must be to secure a cease-fire. We might then find that the Chinese would expect recognition as the Government of China and a settlement on Formosa. We must consider what was the farthest limit to which we were prepared to go and what chance there would be of it being accepted. Otherwise we might find ourselves on a slippery slope. Lastly, there was the question of the method of approach, whether through the United Nations Organisation or through India or in some other way. Whatever happened the United Nations would have lost much face and the position was serious and distasteful to all of us. But the overriding consideration was the security of Western Europe.[9]

One could not tell whether the Chinese wished all of Korea to be governed by the North Koreans or what solution they sought, argued the Prime Minister. Attlee hoped that these questions could be carefully considered. It was necessary to decide 'what kind of things we wanted to negotiate and how far we could go. We should consider the limits on negotiation and the method that should be used; for example, whether we should proceed in the United Nations through third parties.' The whole matter was serious and very distasteful. The United Nations might lose face 'as we all would, especially in the Far East, but we must weigh the advantages on one side and the other'. The British people had had to face some hard situations in their history. In Attlee's view 'we must not get so involved in the East as to lay ourselves open to attack in the West. The West is, after all, the vital part in our line against communism. We cannot take action that will weaken it. We must strengthen our hand in the West as much as possible'.

Acheson, at the request of the President[10] replied that, in his view, the central moving factor in this situation was not China but Russia:[11] 'we had to bear in mind that the central enemy is not the Chinese but the Soviet Union'. All the inspiration for the present action came from there. There had no doubt been some arrangement between the Chinese and the Russians to make the Chinese think they had strong Russian support. While their counterattack went well, there was little limit to what they would try to do; 'If they can drive us out, they will do so. No one knows how much further they might be inclined to go. The situation is already serious.'[12] There would not be many who would advise the President to embark upon an all-out war with China on land, sea and air, but on the possibility of negotiation they were far less optimistic said Acheson: 'Certainly we should try to get a cease-fire if we could but … the Chinese would almost certainly reject it and we should not be prepared to pay any high price for it. Even if we recognised the Chinese and gave them a seat in the United Nations Organisation and reached some settlement over Formosa was there any reason to think that their ambitions would stop there?' Their next demand, believed Acheson, would be participation in the Japanese Peace Treaty and further demands would follow. In all their actions the Chinese had showed themselves subservient to Moscow 'of whom they were apt pupils'. If Formosa were 'handed over' it would be exploited to the full in both a political and a military sense and the political repercussions in Japan and the Philippines would be very serious. So also would be the military consequences. This, concluded Acheson, 'was the very worst moment at which we could seek to negotiate with the Communist forces in the world. But if we did not negotiate would our position be very much worse? If we were pushed out of Korea we should refuse to recognise the territorial gains which resulted and do our best to make the government of China by the Communists as difficult as we could. We should certainly hold Formosa and reinforce our positions within the limits of what was possible in the Far East, though some of them, such as Indo-China, might have to be given up'.[13] If the Communists were successful in Korea, this might so weaken the French in Indo-China that they would pull out of there.[14]

When Attlee asked what public opinion would think of such a partial state of war – would there not inevitably be a demand for all-out fighting – Truman answered that such a demand existed now. Formosa and the immunity of the enemy airfields in Manchuria were a thorn in their side. He had little hope that anything could be achieved by negotiation. In reply to a further question on the attitude of the Japanese, Acheson remarked that 'if we threw in our hand they would make haste to change sides. If we stuck it out, even though we were losing, they might stay by us. He could not see that the Chinese actions would be altered by the concessions which it was proposed that we should make'. Attlee, though, suggested that the Chinese might prefer a middle position which would enable them to avoid becoming wholly dependent on Russia. Acheson and General Marshall, however, reiterated the view that China was little more than a Russian satellite.[15] The Prime Minister commented that opinions differed on the extent to which Chinese Communists were satellites. He inquired: 'when was it that you scratch a communist and find a nationalist', to which Truman responded that the Chinese were satellites of Russia and would be satellites so long as the present Peking regime was in power. He thought they were 'complete' satellites. The only way to meet Communism was to eliminate it. After Korea, it would be Indo-China, then Hong Kong, then Malaya. There was no chance to approach a solution without 'seeing clearly the course we should follow'.

Attlee seemed sceptical and remarked that this was the 'bandwagon psychology.' Acheson's answer was 'we would be better off if we took a strong attitude'. It was hard to tell whether the Chinese Communists would remain satellites in the long run, but he wondered whether they would not act in the same way now regardless of the answer to that question. It was a mistake to count on their goodwill. It was a saying in the State Department that with communistic regimes 'you can't bank goodwill; they balance their books every night'; Attlee expressed some agreement: if the Chinese Communists were satellites, they would play the Russian game. If they were Chinese nationalists, they might prefer to 'get into the club' so that if the Russians went too far in Manchuria or elsewhere they would not be already in Russian hands. General Marshall then referred to the several meetings he had with Mao Zedong and many more with Chou En-lai when he was in China. He recalled the latter saying to Mrs. Marshall, at the dinner table, with great emphasis, that there was no doubt they were Marxist Communists and resented people referring to them as merely agrarian reformists. Pictures of Stalin and Lenin were everywhere when Marshall visited their territory. They made not the slightest attempt to conceal their Moscow affiliations. They regarded the

Russians as coreligionists. This feeling was thoroughly indoctrinated in their troops. When Attlee remarked that Tito was also a full Communist, the President said he relied on the view of General Marshall who had dealt with these people for a year. They were fully tied to Moscow. The Chinese people did, of course, have national feelings. The Russians could not dominate them forever; but that was a long-range view 'and does not help us just now'. On Wake Island he recently told General MacArthur that he wanted to avoid giving any provocation to the Chinese in Manchuria and the Russians in Vladivostok. MacArthur had agreed and gave his opinion that the Chinese would not intervene: MacArthur had at that time arranged to shift two divisions to Europe because he was sure the Korean campaign would be cleared up, as it would have been were it not for the intervention of the Chinese Communists. However, they were now in. They intended to push the United Nations out of Korea if they could. Truman hoped 'we could find a way to prevent this. We had never taken a move or given General MacArthur an order unless it came from the United Nations'. Truman emphasized 'we do not want to act independently.' It was for this reason that he particularly welcomed these talks. Attlee added that the problem was to find out 'how best we could avoid playing the Russian game'. Truman said this was exactly right.

Marshall then commented on the Japanese reaction. He had in mind their great triumph for a time and then their collapse: 'We had been much worse off after Pearl Harbor and had then destroyed them. That memory would influence their reaction. They had a fearful lesson.' This led Attlee to add that it was also necessary to consider the effect of Western action on Asiatic opinion. The President agreed this was indeed vital. The trouble was that Asiatic governments seemed to condone Chinese action in Tibet and Korea and blame the United States for all that happened. Russian propaganda along this line had even gotten through to India. He had tried to make the US position perfectly plain, pointing out that 'we are not trying to take anything away from anybody but to restore things to those who ought to have them'. The Prime Minister noted that 'Asiatics think that this is their show'. He recalled the attitude which he had found in India almost twenty years ago in regard to the Japanese. Truman acknowledged that it was hard to offset this propaganda which had taken hold out there: 'We had to find a common policy for ourselves and … in order to get a common front and must then attempt to keep from all-out war.' The Russians only understood the mailed fist, 'and that is what we are preparing for them. The situation is very serious, and we must find a common course which we can all hold to'. He suggested that it might be desirable to continue the discussion the next day to 'see if we could reach a common conclusion which would avoid all-out war'. Attlee, though, wondered 'how we could avoid being bled in the East so that we could save the West. It would be wise today to consider the most immediate problems'. Truman accepted that if an approach was to be made on the question of a cease-fire, this could not be long delayed. Attlee agreed to this but warned 'if we delayed very long something would blow up'. Truman then announced he wished to read to the Prime Minister certain points:

1. It would be militarily advantageous in the immediate situation if a cease-fire order could be arranged provided that considerations offered were not so great as to be unacceptable. This might insure full support of the United Nations. Arrangements for a ceasefire must not impose conditions which would jeopardize the safety of United Nations forces nor be conditioned on agreement on other issues, such as Formosa and the Chinese seat in the United Nations.
2. If a ceasefire should be effected which permits a stabilisation of the situation, United Nations should proceed with the political, military and economic stabilisation of the Republic of Korea while continuing efforts to seek an independent and unified Korea by political means.
3. If the Chinese Communists reject a Cease-fire and move major forces south of the 38th parallel, the United Nations forces may face a forced evacuation of Korea. The consequences of a voluntary acceptance of a successful aggression and of a voluntary abandonment of our Korean allies would be such that any United Nations evacuation must be clearly the result of military necessity only.

The President here interposed that 'we cannot get out voluntarily': 'All the Koreans left behind would be murdered. The communists care nothing about human life.' The President then continued reading:

4. If the situation in the preceding paragraph develops, the United Nations must take immediate action to declare Communist China an aggressor and must mobilize such political and economic measures as are available to bring pressure upon Peiping and to affirm the determination of the United Nations not to accept an aggression. Also, there is the possibility of some military action which would harass the Chinese Communists and of efforts which could be made to stimulate anti-communist resistance within China itself, including the exploitation of Nationalist capabilities.
   In addition to the measures indicated above, the United States

and United Kingdom should consult immediately about other steps which might be taken to strengthen non-communist Asia. These steps might include:

(a) Restoration of considerable self-government to Japan, the acceleration of efforts to obtain a Japanese peace settlement, the strengthening of Japanese capacity for self-defense, the greater utilization of productive capacity to strengthen the capabilities of the free world, and the prompt admission of Japan into international organizations. United Kingdom reluctance to move on these points should be discarded in light of the new critical situation.

On this last point, Truman stated that he attached great importance to this and would like to discuss it at more length with the Prime Minister later. The President then continued:

(b) Appropriate military arrangements between nations in Southeast Asia capable of effective mutual support.

Truman wondered whether there was very much that could be done under this point before continuing:

(c) Special efforts to convince non-communist Asia of the nature of the threat which confronts it and to urge upon the governments concerned the need for concerted Asian action to resist communist aggression in that area.

The President thought a good deal could be done on this. He concluded with the following two points:

(d) Intensification of economic and military assistance to encourage the organization of resistance to Communist encroachment.
(e) Intensification of psychological and covert activity against communist regimes and activity in Asia.

Truman revealed he had been considering some kind of Marshall Plan for South-East Asia. A special plan was now underway for the Philippines and he hoped that it would be rapidly approved by Congress. All of these points were worth consideration and further discussion. When the President had concluded, Acheson commented that the Prime Minister knew the present position in the United Nations. Six powers had put the item on the agenda and had filed a memorandum without indicating any course of action: 'We might now put in the 6-power resolution which had been vetoed in the Security Council. It was important to take some action to avoid seeming not to know what to do.' Perhaps there should be a resolution just calling for a cease-fire now. It might be necessary to take the position very soon in the United Nations, and this should be done after complete agreement was reached between the Prime Minister and the President.[16] Sir Oliver Franks then intervened to add some perspective to the proceedings; he noted that there seemed to be a number of lines of thought in the discussion –

(a) The military situation was such that we ought not to assume that the bridgeheads could be held; and our position would be one not so much of diminishing strength as of definite weakness.
(b) The Prime Minister had tried to guess what would be in the mind of the Chinese if they came to negotiations. They would go beyond Korea and bring in the question of Formosa and that might well lead us on to a slippery slope.
(c) Mr Acheson had outlined another possibility under which we would hold on in Korea as long as we could and leave, not as a result of negotiations, but because we were forced out. We should then have to consider what to do to the Power that had forced us out.
(d) A proposal for a cease-fire, if possible at all, would have to be carried out very quickly. It to some extent cut across the two alternative courses already mentioned, but it seemed to be something which ought to be aimed at on its own merits.[17]

The President thought this was very clearly put. Acheson agreed it was very accurate. The only question which was posed by Sir Oliver was how a cease-fire fitted in. If the United Nations put forward such a suggestion, it would have said the Chinese Communists must cease and at the same time would say to the Chinese: 'We tell you that our forces will cease fire also.' At least that would result in 'stopping the killing of people while you talk. We would pay little for that. If they say we should be behind the 38th parallel, the answer is we soon will be anyway. Such a United Nations position which would be acceptable to us would mean that we are not the aggressors and that we are ready to stop if the Chinese will'. At this point the President suggested that, if it was generally agreed, the discussion could be adjourned until the following day.[18]

After the conclusion of the first meeting Franks, accompanied by Sir Roger Makins and Robert Scott came to Acheson's office for further conversation. Acheson recalled that there was some point in Sir Oliver's summary during the meeting which he wanted to touch on and to clear up any possible confusion. Franks had seemed to indicate an understanding that the US position was so weak that 'we had to proceed on the assumption that we were licked in Korea'. Acheson emphasised that he did not take this view 'and it should not be treated as a foregone conclusion that we are out of Korea'. He then went on to develop the United States' 'general thought'. Foreign policy in the East and in Western Europe could not be separated: 'We must have a single foreign policy for both sides of the world.' He touched on the problem of American opinion, pointing out that he was not referring to vociferous extremists but to the sound judgement of reasonable people: 'If we surrender in the Far East, especially if this results from the action of our Allies, American opinion will be against help in the West to those who had brought about the collapse. In order to avoid this kind of reaction we must take a steadfast position in the Far East.' Acheson pointed out that he was not falling back on the catchword 'my public opinion won't let me'. He was, however, appraising an important factor, namely, the trend of general American thinking. The Secretary pointed to the size of the US effort in terms of taxes, military service, etc. If as a result of the military defeat in a campaign in Korea 'we make a surrender which would lose to us all of the results of the Pacific war, American opinion would not accept such a situation'.

In his response, Franks emphasised that he did not dispute the fact that the United States had prime responsibility in the Pacific area and that the UK 'did not wish to make us weak on the western side of the Pacific'. In saying this he referred to the American position in the island chain. The Ambassador accepted the idea that the United States must take a two-ocean view and he did not wish to weaken that approach. Makins added that he believed that 'our two countries differ in our estimate of Chinese attitudes and intentions'. Acheson protested that a surrender to the Chinese would probably result in the loss of the island chain to which Franks had referred: 'If we surrendered Formosa, the Japanese would react to our surrender to the display of Chinese force. If we give up Korea by agreement the Filipinos and Japanese would run for cover.' Acheson believed the Russians had a general plan 'to oust us from our island defenses.' He then read a series of questions which had been prepared for the President but which Truman had not read calling attention to the appearance of indecision which would result from a delay by the Security Council and the General Assembly action in the United Nations. The following steps could be considered in the General Assembly: 'We might go ahead introducing the six-power resolution. We would then be taking the same position we took in the Security Council – no stronger; no weaker.' Someone might then introduce in the

Assembly a simple cease-fire resolution. 'We could press ahead with that resolution and get it passed in twenty-four hours, leaving the six-power resolution in abeyance.' It was probable the Chinese would not accept the cease-fire 'and that others would then urge us to pay a price. We should ignore such arguments'. If the Chinese did accept, 'we would reorganize our defenses as vigorously as possible.' If thereafter the Chinese attacked, we would be in a better world position and if we have to take a Dunkirk we will at least prove that we are not ready to surrender but are standing up to attack. After that we would have to go ahead and make trouble for the Chinese'. It would be much easier to hold opinion on that course than by desertion and surrender, stated Acheson: 'We must avoid rewarding the Chinese for their aggression and equally avoid putting an Army on the Chinese mainland and pulling in the Russian Airforce by all-out bombing of China.'

Scott then spoke about the importance of holding Asian opinion. While he agreed in the course of the discussion that concessions made to the Chinese now would probably not change their general policy, e.g. in regard to lndo-China, Malaya, the Huk troubles in the Philippines, etc., there was a chance to reduce the tempo of their activities and this was important. It was apparent, to the Americans, at this point, that in the minds of Scott and of the other UK representatives, 'Asian opinion' meant the views of India. The participants then dwelt at some length on the importance of Indian manpower to the UK in previous wars. Acheson though, indicated 'rather strongly' his view that the Indians could not be relied upon. Franks observed that it seemed to him that the United States was seeking a middle way between branding the Chinese as aggressors and negotiating with them. In this policy 'we end up merely by harassing them'. The Secretary of State pointed out that the American experience with the Russians, which should be applied here, showed that their basic theory of negotiating was to exchange something intangible for something tangible. In this case, 'we might be asked to give up Formosa, which is a tangible asset, in exchange for the hope that we might influence their future conduct'.[19]

Acheson suggested to Franks that he attempt to work out with Attlee a means of getting a more relaxed attitude at future meetings with the President and ask the Prime Minister to allow his subordinates at the meeting to initiate discussions on the subjects which came up. He felt the meeting with the President was 'rather rigid' and too many people were in attendance. The point he wanted to get over to the British was that the United States could not separate its foreign policy into two compartments – the far East and the European; Americans would not accept a surrender in the Far East in accord 'with the desire of some of our Allies and then cooperate in Europe with the same Allies who have urged us to be conciliatory in the Far East'. The American demand was that 'we must be vigorous everywhere'. The Secretary tried to point out to the British that the consequences of their proposal was greater than they thought: 'you can not, as the British seem to want to do, make a distinction between little aggressions and big aggressions. The British seem to be saying that we would take action to put down little aggressions but if a big aggression came along they would say that is a different matter and not act against it'. Franks felt that the Americans were basing their position on a 'moral position but since our power had collapsed they felt we would have to change our moral position'. Acheson replied by saying that he did not want to argue this but would rather examine the question to see whether this was a position which 'we could defend vigorously.' The British countered by claiming the US position was one of getting thrown out of Korea and maintaining a position to harass China which 'could get us nowhere even though we were to carry it on for years'. In addition, they pointed out that such action would make the British position in Hong Kong untenable. The British thought that this would weaken everyone and alienate the United States' friends. They said that the Asians now thought that Washington were wrong about Formosa and that this, of course, would further alienate them. They believed that if the Americans pursued this course, the Asians would probably not join the Soviet camp but would probably rather neutralise themselves into a third force. Acheson countered by saying that the Asians would probably do that anyway 'and he did not think we should pay a price for Asian opinion.'[20]

When the second Truman–Attlee meeting began the two sides were now in a position to agree, with regard to the UN, that if a cease-fire resolution were introduced in the General Assembly, the United States and the United Kingdom should, in principle, be prepared to support it.[21] The discussion then returned to the situation on the ground in Korea and Truman again reassured Attlee after the Prime Minister asked 'where we would go from there'? The President replied that 'we should hold the line in Korea if that can be done'. His military advisers told him that the line was too long to be held with the forces at their disposal. However, 'we cannot voluntarily back out of Korea. If that is to be the result we must be forced out'. He hoped that if there were a cease-fire 'we could hold the line'. For if 'we abandoned Korea the South Koreans would all be murdered and 'we could not face that in view of the fact that they have fought bravely on our side and we have put in so much to help them. We may be subjected to bombing from Manchuria by the Russians and Chinese Communists which might destroy everything we have'. Truman was worried about the situation. He did not like to go into a situation such as this 'and then to admit that we were licked'. He would rather fight it to a finish. That was the way he had felt from the beginning. He would like that to be on the record. Truman 'wanted to make it perfectly plain here that we do not desert our friends when the going is rough'. He thought that the Prime Minister felt the same way in his heart.[22] Moved by this, Attlee replied that the 'United Kingdom stood with the United States in the bridgehead and would maintain our present forces there'.[23] He declared 'We're in this with you and we stand together.' 'We had started by looking at the immediate position and have decided on the next steps in the UN. While we are partners in this matter and while our position is very important, we must remember that we are acting as members of the UN. What will the UN say next?' asked the Prime Minister. The UN took a firm line against aggression. It was vitally important to the whole future of the UN that it should not admit any condonation of aggression 'but we must all admit the limits on what we can do. We were all agreed yesterday on our major strategy in that we do not wish to be bogged down in an all out war with China'. The President agreed. The Prime Minister continued: 'We therefore do not want to bomb the industries in Manchuria and the various centers in China. As a matter of fact the Chinese get on without large industrial centers. In this respect they are like the Huns. They can also be supplied by the Russians.' Attlee wondered whether it was agreed that 'we had ruled out that kind of a war.' In regard to a blockade of China it should be noted that the Chinese were not greatly dependent upon the West 'and they could hurt us more on this than we could hurt them'. Furthermore, the Prime Minister warned it would be 'very hard to hold our own people' and UN opinion on such a policy directed more against the civilian population than against the armed forces of China: 'We would be led gradually into a shooting war against China or into negotiation. The suggestion which had been put forward seemed merely to hold the line without getting us anywhere.' Attlee thought 'we should talk very frankly about these matters in this meeting'. Here the President signalled that he entirely agreed.

The Prime Minister continued that the British appreciation of Chinese intentions differed from those of the Americans. The United States thought that the Chinese were completely subservient to the USSR and that they were not only Communists but Stalinists. There was a great difference here: 'They can be Marxists and yet not bow to Stalin.' He agreed that it was quite true that the Chinese were hard-shelled Marxists-Leninists but it was quite possible that they were not Soviet imperialists. There was a chance of Titoism. He had discussed this situation at length with Nehru – the President commented that he had also – and Attlee recalled that Nehru said that the Communists took advantage of economic and social conditions to appear as deliverers. They failed in Europe where the standard of living was high but in Asia they had allied themselves with nationalism. It was easy to say that China was entirely in the hands of the Russians. This was a 'fatalistic attitude' he declared. At 'least you can hope that if you back nationalism you can get Chinese imperialism opposed to Russian imperialism'. The Indian nationalists had waged a violent campaign against the British. The British gave them what they wanted and a very considerable change had occurred, and the Indians now recognised the values of Western civilisation. Attlee had seen a very great change in the orientation of leading Indians. It was not hopeless that the Chinese were not fully imbued with Soviet ideas. This, concluded Attlee, represented the general line of British thinking. After the Prime Minister concluded the President asked Secretary Acheson if he cared to comment.[24]

Acheson did not disagree with the Prime Minister's analysis 'as a statement of long-term tendencies. But could we act on it in the immediate future? The next three years was the critical period and we could not afford to make sacrifices of our vital military interests', for example by giving up Formosa in exchange for doubtful advantages in the distant future. If a cease-fire were accepted and negotiation proved possible 'we should restrict the negotiations to Korea itself. If, on the other hand, we were forced out of Korea our attitude must remain hostile and not friendly, whatever form our hostility might take. To alter our attitude because a small aggression had given place to a large aggression would fatally undermine the whole moral basis of American policy and public opinion would be confused'. The American people, believed Acheson, could not be encouraged at one and the same time to draw back in the Pacific and to adopt a vigorous forward policy in Europe. When Attlee pointed out that, at Cairo during the Second World War, Formosa had been promised to China, Acheson agreed but stressed that there was now a different Government in China and one, moreover, 'which had broken its side of the bargain'.[25] Attlee declared, frankly, that opinion in the UK had no sympathy with Chiang Kai-shek or on the question of Formosa. The United States must consider its opinion but both the United States and the UK must act as members of the UN.[26] With the discussion emphasising the gaps between the two delegations, at this point Sir Oliver Franks stepped in and, ignoring the obvious areas of disagreement, concluded that the discussion seemed to show considerable agreement; he pointed out:

> First, that we would not contemplate a voluntary withdrawal from Korea and would try to keep our forces up to strength. Secondly, that if a cease-fire could be brought about negotiations might be possible.

If, however, there was no chance of negotiation, we were far from convinced that the right course would be to try to maintain a state of war and to take such measures as economic sanctions and subversive activities against China. Lastly, if the chance of negotiations arose we were not convinced that their scope could be confined to Korea. The withdrawal at least of recognition from Chiang Kai-shek and perhaps also the seating of the Communist Government in the United Nations might have to be considered.

Attlee responded that it might be possible to distinguish between the question of recognition and the status for the time being of Formosa. He suggested that the United States might continue to protect the Island, but that they should cease to recognise the sovereignty of Chiang Kai-shek over it. A United Nations Commission might be set up to supervise its administration. Truman thought that this was a proposal worth considering 'and he would like to reflect upon it.'[27] The meeting effectively drew to a close at this point.

This was the background to the Truman-Attlee meeting that would decide the Anglo-American position on the use of the atomic bomb. By now the President was worried about the differences between the two sides and stressed his desire to show a solid front and to reach agreement before the conversations ended. Then Franks stepped forth once more and, ignoring the Anglo-American divisions – again – simply noted that the differences appeared to be greater than they really were. He listed the following points of agreement:

(a) We agreed on the strategic importance of the Pacific Island chain. The United Kingdom was influenced by the military arguments for the retention of Formosa and was not suggesting its immediate surrender.
(b) We had reached agreement on what we should try to do in Korea.
(c) We were agreed that we should negotiate with China if a favourable opportunity arose. The United Kingdom was perhaps more anxious to seek such an opportunity but had no special ideals on timing. We agreed that if negotiation was possible it should be used but we should not offer advance concessions nor start on a slippery slope of concession.
(d) The United Kingdom did not like the suggestion that if we were thrown out of Korea we might have to transfer hostility to China with many possible repercussions. We were therefore pleased to know that the policy of limited war was not yet firm.

Franks, continuing, said that there was one point on which 'we had not convinced the United States Government namely, Chinese membership of the United Nations'. The British, he explained, regarded it as only a recognition of a fact and did not think it should be a stumbling block in negotiations.[28]

The mood of the meeting had been transformed by Franks' summing up who declared that 'as time moved on our differences could be dissolved and that we would find a way'. He was optimistic 'we would be able to think up some idea for a solution, for example, in regard to Formosa'. As a result of the talks the British hoped that the United States would weigh the views which had been expressed on behalf of the United Kingdom 'with the problem of some decent negotiation'. A grateful President agreed that British views undoubtedly helped; the area of difference was not as great as had appeared. Attlee agreed that this was the case.[29]

Truman closed this part of the discussion by expressing the hope that it would be possible to disclose a large measure of agreement in the communiqué to be issued the following day.[30] He then revealed he had just talked with Attlee and that they had discussed the atomic bomb and its use.[31] A paper prepared for Truman laid out how (a) that by law only he could authorize its use, and (b) that he had not authorised its use. The British position was that the bomb should not be used without consultation – and probably without agreement – with them and perhaps others. Probably, also, they were strongly opposed to its use in China. The recommendations made to the President were:

(a) That no *commitment* be made restricting the action of the U.S.
(b) That our *desire* not to use the bomb be stressed.
(c) That our realization of the dire consequences for all of its use be stressed and our great sense of responsibility: We are, indeed, trustees for the future of the world in this respect.
(d) That our desire and expectation to move in step with the British be stressed. (Their role in this matter requires this.),
(e) That, if necessary after the preliminary discussions, further consideration of our position be undertaken.[32]

In their private talk together the President had reminded the Prime Minister that the Governments of the United Kingdom and the United States had always been partners in this matter and that he would not consider the use of the bomb without *consulting* with the United Kingdom. The Prime Minister had asked whether this agreement should be put in writing, and the President replied no that it would not be in writing, that if a man's word wasn't any good it wasn't made any better by writing it down. The Prime Minister expressed his thanks.[33] Equally, if not more important, was the agreement, at this meeting, on raw materials for the British economy creating US–UK machinery in the form of a small central body responsible for assuring action in this field.[34]

Despite the position agreed, opinion was divided as to how well the talks had gone. Twice, before the talk with the President and the Prime Minister, Tedder and Slim had said to Acheson that Attlee had 'muffed the ball on his kick-off on the defense business' in the meeting the previous afternoon. It had been hard for them to do anything 'since their chief did not lead off'. They asked Acheson if there was any way they could retrieve the situation. The Secretary replied it was up to them to handle it. Nevertheless, at a dinner in Sir Oliver Franks' residence, both the President and the Prime Minister said they were pleased with the conversations. The British brought up again the defence matters discussed in the meeting the day before and the Secretary used this opportunity as a cue to say he did not feel they had got very far. There were two points he felt which should be borne in mind. First, was that when the British left, unless the President and Marshall were convinced that the UK was doing everything possible in the direction of their own defence effort, the British had not accomplished much. Acheson was blunt and told them that there was a feeling in Washington that the British were not doing all they could do. He added that if the President and Marshall were convinced that the British were doing all they could, this would help a great deal in meeting the feeling in the United States to the contrary. The second point was that the only way 'we can do anything with NATO is for the United States and the United Kingdom to go ahead and act and force the others to follow'. Acheson thought much of the talk on these subjects had been off the point. He admitted that the British had problems but regardless of the difficulty, the question was whether what was being done was adequate. The British indicated they understood.

Attlee then said he wanted to raise a difficult and a delicate question. He raised the question of General MacArthur's direction of the effort in Korea: there was a feeling in Europe that MacArthur was running the show and also a feeling that the other participating countries had little say in what was done.[35] Attlee commented that this had aroused 'some anxiety' in Britain. He made it clear that he had no desire to conduct a post-mortem but the Americans showed a desire to discuss the position at length. In response, Truman admitted that some of MacArthur's statements had been 'very unfortunate'.[36] Bradley and Marshall then discussed the matter with Attlee arguing that MacArthur was doing what he was required to do by the United Nations which had given him the direction to hold Korea and conduct elections there. They emphasized that he was doing exactly what he had been told to do. Marshall discussed the joint control, by the Department of State and Defense, over MacArthur's activities. He said that the British could not say they were not consulted and mentioned the questions of 'hot pursuit' across the Chinese border, bombing of Manchuria, etc., on which consultation had taken place. The British then proposed some sort of committee to direct the war. Bradley objected that a war could not be run by a committee. The President commented that the United Nations had asked the United States to set up a Unified Command; he was in charge and would run it as long as the United Nations wanted him to and emphasised that he would have to continue running it unless the United Nations asked him not to. He added that the orders to MacArthur were only concerned with the safety of his command; if others came over to bomb the troops there, the President warned that every airfield in sight would be bombed 'in order to protect our troops'.[37] Attlee agreed the war could not be run by committee but raised the question of what consultation would take place in the event of the question of withdrawal from Korea arising. This seemed to him to be a matter which raised important political issues. Truman repeated his view that he would not talk about withdrawal and would not allow his troops to leave Korea unless they were forced out. They should hold on as long as possible. He and the Prime Minister had already agreed that 'we should hold on in Korea'. In these circumstances the conclusion was that the actual conditions in which a withdrawal might have to be ordered were military rather than political since the policy was now agreed.[38] The President was clear: 'we stay in Korea and fight'.[39]

The remaining issue to be decided was the content of the final communique – and the most controversial section was going to be that concerning the atomic bomb. Acheson called for R. Gordon Arneson, Special Assistant to the Secretary of State to join him at the White House and advise him as to what should be said in the Joint Communique concerning this matter. The President withdrew briefly from his final meeting with Attlee and went to his office to discuss with Acheson, Secretary Lovett, Secretary Snyder, Harriman and Arneson the language to be incorporated in the Joint Communique. During the discussion, Lovett recalled that the Quebec Agreement had provided that the United States had to obtain United Kingdom consent before using the atomic weapon. Members of the Joint Congressional Committee on Atomic Energy, particularly Senator Vandenberg and Senator Hickenlooper, had been very disturbed at this provision and had urged most strongly that steps be taken to abrogate it. Negotiations were undertaken at the end of 1947 (Lovett was then Under Secretary of State) to supplant the Quebec Agreement with other arrangements. A salient objective of these negotiations was to terminate the provision concerning United Kingdom consent. The resultant *Modus Vivendi* of January 7 1948, provided, among other things, that the commitment concerning the use of atomic weapons was to have no further force or effect. As the discussion proceeded, Arneson drafted the language which was subsequently incorporated in the final Joint Communique. The President approved the suggested language and asked Acheson to secure British acceptance thereof. Acheson discussed the matter with Sir Oliver Franks and, with British concurrence, these sentences were inserted as the penultimate paragraph of the Communique.[40] The key section did not include the term 'consult' as recorded in the British – and indeed the original American – minutes; instead it stated:

> The President stated that it was his hope that world conditions would never call for the use of the atomic bomb. The President told the Prime Minister that it was also his desire to keep the Prime Minister at all times informed of developments which might bring about a change in the situation.[41]

In his assessment of the talks, to Bevin, Attlee made it clear Acheson was 'obviously under heavy fire' and how, during the talks, twenty Republican Senators tabled a motion demanding that all agreements reached between the President and the Prime Minister should be laid before the Senate for its approval by virtue of its treaty making power:

> For these reasons you will appreciate that it was not possible to reach specific agreements in writing, to which it would be possible to refer later. For the same reasons the administration no doubt felt impelled to lay more emphasis than they might otherwise have done on the maintenance of their attitude towards China. Nor could they in the communiqué be as forthcoming as they were across the table in their assurances about the atomic bomb.
>
> We are agreed on the importance of avoiding a major war with China and I think that we have at least shaken the American Service Chiefs by impressing on them the dangers of limited war with China. Marshall said he had serious doubt about the concept. It remains to be seen how far the administration can hold the position against pressures which are likely to continue. During the meetings Acheson was clearly

contemplating a position where a resolution branding China as an aggressor could be introduced into the United Nations and he argued, though with more eloquence than conviction, in favour of the concept of a limited war. If a resolution were passed (which is not of course certain) we could not exclude the possibility that the United States administration would think it necessary to agree to some punitive measures against China.

We did not try to decide on action in a hypothetical situation and we clearly could not take decisions on the conduct of the operations in Korea and on the exact conditions on which a cease fire could be obtained. But I think that we have at any rate established a position in which the door is open for settlement by negotiation if a favourable opportunity occurs. I pressed home the point that if we manage to stand firm in Korea and if we are agreed not to be led into a major war in the Far East a settlement must inevitably follow at some time. Acheson obviously appreciated the logic of this argument since he was at pains to insist that our policy could only be judged by its likely results.

Attlee reflected that the Americans appeared reassured by his statement that the British did not necessarily contemplate the immediate cession of Formosa to Communist China and that they regarded the Cairo declaration on the future of Korea and Formosa as a single entity: 'It was not to be expected that we should persuade the Americans over recognition of China or Chinese representation in the United Nations' he concluded; it was the only point of difference recorded in the published US–UK communiqué: 'The most that we could achieve was recognition that the problem is one for solution by the United Nations. This was admitted at our final session but Acheson, no doubt for internal political reasons, objected to a statement to this effect in the communiqué.'

Attlee deemed it significant that the Americans 'implicitly and on occasion explicitly assumed that we are their principal ally and that we must be prepared in the last resort to continue the struggle together and alone'. How far this attitude could be interpreted in terms of strategic plans 'I do not know'; but 'we clearly must continue to support strongly the Atlantic concept of defending Europe as far to the east as possible'. The Prime Minister assumed 'we shall be successful in establishing still more firmly the informal contacts between our military staffs in Washington, which are already a great asset to us and in associating political representatives with these contacts as a regular thing'. These informal contacts would also provide a further channel through which 'we can try to influence the instructions issued to General MacArthur'. For Attlee the significance of the talks was that: 'the United Kingdom was lifted out of "the European queue" and we were treated as partners, unequal no doubt in power but still equal in counsel'. Finally, 'I believe the President's personal assurances about the use of the atomic bomb to be perfectly sincere. They meet one of the main points which was causing us concern before I left London.'[42]

But, in the course of subsequent comparison of minutes of the meetings, it was learned that the British minutes of the fifth meeting included a passage along the lines of the first statement which the President had made on the subject – promising to consult the UK on the use of the atomic bomb. The Americans argued that this statement should be deleted since the President had 'corrected' it and his correction constituted a change in the record of the conference itself and that the United States position on this matter was as reflected in the text of the Joint Communique. In subsequent conversations with F.W. Marten of the British Embassy, Arneson had occasion to make the same point, namely that the official United States position as agreed by the President, and as accepted by Attlee, was set forth in the penultimate paragraph of the Joint Communique 'no more and no less'.[43] The State Department, in the exchange of records, stated their opposition to accepting any passage referring to the undertaking to consult. The British, therefore, handed them a record from which this passage had been deleted but made clear to them orally that the United Kingdom record, held in London, contained the undertaking as given by the President. The State Department tried to maintain that the undertaking to consult Britain about the use of the atomic weapon was revoked and superseded by the undertaking to inform the UK contained in the communiqué: 'We have made quite clear to them that this was not our understanding' recorded Sir Roger Makin in a minute to Bevin. But, after consulting No. 10, the Foreign Office decided not tried to pin the Americans down in writing 'since to do so might defeat its own object by causing them to take steps to endeavour to have the undertaking modified. As things stand at the moment, therefore, the Prime Minister has received a personal undertaking from the President which we can feel sure will be honoured while President Truman remains in office. More than that we cannot hope to obtain at present' conceded Makins.[44]

This minute was counter-signed by Sir William Strang, the Permanent Under-Secretary at the Foreign Office, before submission to Bevin, who asked 'From [the] public point of view or from that of action in the future, does not this leave us just where we are now?' Makins explained, on 10 February 1951, that 'It is true that we are not in a position to quote publicly any new American assurances that the United States Government will consult us before using the atomic bomb. If we were to quote exactly what passed at Washington, we should embarrass the President and Mr. Acheson, who would almost certainly have to deny our version and maintain that they are only committed to inform us. This question is virtually forced upon them by the legislative history of the question in the United States.' At the same time the Prime Minister had made it clear in the House of Commons (first on the 12th and again on the 14th December) that he considered the assurances which he received to be perfectly satisfactory. It was also true that 'we have not committed the United States Government to any written undertaking to consult us, to which we could refer … if differences of opinion arose in the future.' The difficulty here was that, although the President's undertaking to consult and his announcement to consult were made during full meetings, the discussions leading up to his remarks were conducted between him and the Prime Minister alone. There was no record of what passed: 'We cannot therefore show conclusively to the Americans that the undertaking to consult is not superseded by the undertaking to inform, although we have already made it clear to them that this is our understanding.' Equally the assurance was only binding on Truman and was only valid so long as he was in office. Makin concluded that, 'while we cannot regard the problem as entirely satisfactory, it has been much improved through the Prime Minister's talks in Washington'. Bevin read this minute and commented that he still did not feel happy about the situation. He wondered whether there was any anger that anything that had been said by the Prime Minister or himself in the House would give rise to misunderstanding in the future.[45]

## Notes

1 TNA CAB 195/8 C.M. 85 (50), 12 December, 1950
2 TNA PREM 8/1200 The Prime Minister's Visit to Washington, New York and Ottawa, December 1950
3 TNA PREM 8/1200 Note of a Meeting held in the Ambassador's Study, 4 December 1950
4 FRUS 1950, Volume VII (Korea). United States Delegation Minutes of the First Meeting of President Truman and Prime Minister Attlee, 4 December 1950
5 TNA PREM 8/1200 Meetings of the President of the United States and the Prime Minister; United Kingdom Record of the First Meeting at the White House on Monday, 4 December 1950
6 FRUS 1950, Volume VII (Korea). United States Delegation Minutes of the First Meeting of President Truman and Prime Minister Attlee, 4 December 1950

7. TNA PREM 8/1200 Meetings of the President of the United States and the Prime Minister; United Kingdom Record of the First Meeting at the White House on Monday, 4 December 1950
8. FRUS 1950, Volume VII (Korea 1950). United States Delegation Minutes of the First Meeting of President Truman and Prime Minister Attlee, 4 December 1950
9. TNA PREM 8/1200 Meetings of the of the United States and the Prime Minister; United Kingdom Record of the First Meeting at the White House on Monday, 4 December 1950
10. FRUS 1950, Volume VII (Korea). United States Delegation Minutes of the First Meeting of President Truman and Prime Minister Attlee, 4 December 1950
11. TNA PREM 8/1200 Meetings of the President of the United States and the Prime Minister; United Kingdom Record of the First Meeting at the White House on Monday, 4 December 1950
12. FRUS 1950, Volume VII (Korea). United States Delegation Minutes of the First Meeting of President Truman and Prime Minister Attlee, 4 December 1950
13. TNA PREM 8/1200 Meetings of the President of the United States and the Prime Minister; United Kingdom Record of the First Meeting at the White House on Monday, 4 December 1950
14. FRUS 1950, Volume VII (Korea). United States Delegation Minutes of the First Meeting of President Truman and Prime Minister Attlee, 4 December 1950
15. TNA PREM 8/1200 Meetings of the President of the United States and the Prime Minister; United Kingdom Record of the First Meeting at the White House on Monday, 4 December 1950
16. FRUS 1950, Volume VII (Korea). United States Delegation Minutes of the First Meeting of President Truman and Prime Minister Attlee, 4 December 1950
17. TNA PREM 8/1200 Meetings of the President of the United States and the Prime Minister; United Kingdom Record of the First Meeting at the White House on Monday, 4 December 1950
18. FRUS 1950, Volume VII (Korea). United States Delegation Minutes of the First Meeting of President Truman and Prime Minister Attlee, 4 December 1950
19. FRUS 1950, Volume VII (Korea). Memorandum of Conversation, by the Ambassador at Large (Jessup), 4 December 1950
20. FRUS 1950, Volume VII (Korea). Memorandum of Conversation, by the Director of the Executive Secretariat (Williams), 5 December 1950. Subject: Meeting in the Secretary's Office
21. TNA PREM 8/1200 United Kingdom Record of the Second Meeting on Board the USS 'Williamsburg' on Tuesday, 5 December 1950

22 FRUS 1950, Volume VII (Korea). United States Delegation Minutes of the Second Meeting of President Truman and Prime Minister Attlee on the 'Williamsburg' Tuesday, 5 December 1950
23 TNA PREM 8/1200 United Kingdom Record of the Second Meeting on Board the USS 'Williamsburg' on Tuesday, 5 December 1950
24 FRUS 1950, Volume VII (Korea). United States Delegation Minutes of the Second Meeting of President Truman and Prime Minister Attlee on the 'Williamsburg' Tuesday, 5 December 1950
25 TNA PREM 8/1200 United Kingdom Record of the Second Meeting on Board the USS 'Williamsburg' on Tuesday, 5 December 1950
26 FRUS 1950, Volume VII (Korea). United States Delegation Minutes of the Second Meeting of President Truman and Prime Minister Attlee on the 'Williamsburg' Tuesday, 5 December 1950
27 TNA PREM 8/1200 United Kingdom Record of the Second Meeting on Board the USS 'Williamsburg' on Tuesday, 5 December 1950
28 TNA PREM 8/1200 Annex 5 Meetings of the President of the United States and the Prime Minister; United Kingdom Record of the Fifth Meeting at the White House on Thursday, 7 December 1950
29 FRUS 1950, Volume VII (Korea). United States Delegation Minutes of the Fifth Meeting of President Truman and Prime Minister Attlee
30 TNA PREM 8/1200 Annex 5 Meetings of the President of the United States and the Prime Minister; United Kingdom Record of the Fifth Meeting at the White House on Thursday, 7 December 1950
31 FRUS 1950, Volume VII (Korea) Memorandum for the Record by the Ambassador at Large (Jessup), 7 December 1950. Excerpt from Meeting between the President and Prime Minister in the Cabinet Room of the White House
32 FRUS 1950, Volume VII (Korea). Position Paper Prepared for the Truman–Attlee Talk. Use of the Atomic Bomb Present Position
33 FRUS 1950, Volume VII (Korea). Memorandum for the Record, by Mr R. Gordon Arneson, Special Assistant to the Secretary of State, 16 January 1953. Subject: Truman–Attlee Conversations of December 1950: Use of Atomic Weapons
34 TNA PREM 8/1200 Annex 12 Text of Report to the President and Prime Minister on Raw Materials circulated by the United States Delegation at a Meeting of Officials on 7 December and Agreed by the United Kingdom Delegation
35 FRUS 1950, Volume VII (Korea). Memorandum by Mr Lucius D. Battle, Special Assistant to the Secretary of State, of a Meeting Held on 6 December 1950
36 TNA PREM 8/1200 Annex 11 Record of Conversation held at the British Embassy on 7 December 1950
37 FRUS 1950, Volume VII (Korea). Memorandum by Mr Lucius D. Battle,

Special Assistant to the Secretary of State, of a Meeting Held on 6 December 1950
38 TNA PREM 8/1200 Annex 11 Record of Conversation held at the British Embassy on 7 December 1950
39 FRUS 1950, Volume VII (Korea). Memorandum by Mr Lucius D. Battle, Special Assistant to the Secretary of State, of a Meeting Held on 6 December 1950
40 FRUS 1950, Volume VII (Korea). Memorandum for the Record by Mr R. Gordon Arneson, Special Assistant to the Secretary of State, 16 January 1951
41 FRUS 1950, Volume VII (Korea). Communique Issued at the Conclusion of the Truman–Attlee Discussions
42 TNA PREM 8/1200 Prime Minister to Foreign Office Telegram No. 1287 (CRO), 10 December 1950
43 FRUS 1950, Volume VII (Korea). Memorandum for the Record by Mr R. Gordon Arneson, Special Assistant to the Secretary of State, 16 January 1951
44 DBPO: Korea No. 111 Minute from Sir R. Makins to Mr Bevin, 19 January Anglo-American Consultation on the Atomic Bomb
45 DBOP: Korea note 2 p. 311

# 5

## Divisions

### January 1951

In Korea the Chinese launched another offensive, this time on New Year's Eve. As UN forces fell back to the 38th parallel, Seoul was captured for the second time by the Communists. On 2 January 1951, Kenneth Younger fired off a minute, to Bevin, warning: 'It looks as if the Americans will try to force our hand by putting forward a condemnatory resolution in the General Assembly at a very early date. It is this move we must try to postpone for the time being'. Younger did not think – as Jebb had seemed to suggest – 'that if we subscribe to a resolution condemning the Chinese as aggressors, we could still resist subsequent suggestions for taking limited sanctions against China.' If this were a private arrangement with the Americans to this end, Younger did not believe for a moment that the Americans would hold to it; 'nor do I see how we could make it public, since to label someone as an aggressor and then refuse to do anything about it is clearly a betrayal of the United Nations Charter' he added. Younger, therefore, adhered to the opinion that 'we must resist a general charge of aggression against China unless we are prepared subsequently to engage in some form of sanctions against her.' In his view what HMG now had to do was:

(a) To make up our own minds whether we are in any event prepared to be dragged by the Americans into a limited war:
(b) If, as I would hope, we are not prepared for this, we should tell the Americans so firmly now:
(c) To tell them that they must hold their hand in the U.N. until we have consulted the Commonwealth:
(d) To suggest for their consideration a resolution (not to be introduced

until we have had a chance to sound the Commonwealth) which would condemn the Chinese action in Korea and would call upon member states not to aid the North Korean or Chinese forces and to give all assistance to the U.N. forces, but that we should avoid a general condemnation which would involve us all in measures against China which go beyond Korea itself.[1]

Younger was not alone in his concerns: the same day, John Strachey, the Secretary of State for War, wrote to Bevin articulating his fears relating to US policy. It was evident, to Strachey, that during the past three months Anglo-American relations, 'upon which so much depends', had been subjected to strain. It seemed only too possible that they would be subjected to further strain in the coming year. It was appropriate, therefore, to examine the causes of this strain, and the way in which the British Government should seek to deal with the matter, he argued.

The root cause of the difficulty lay in the fact that America had recently begun to pursue policies in both Asia and Europe 'which, we apprehend, threaten to involve us in early and general war. We have already had to authorise our Chiefs of Staff to work on the hypothesis that war is "possible in 1951 and probable in 1952"'. General war in 1951 or 1952 would, however, 'occur in a situation almost certainly fatal, in the literal sense of that term, to this country. Nor can any degree of rearmament which it is humanly possible to achieve in two years alter that situation fundamentally'. But would America be prepared to modify her present policies sufficiently to avoid widespread war in Asia or to avoid the outbreak of war with Russia in Europe before the possibility of a successful defence by the NATO states had been created, asked Strachey. On the one hand 'we can accept present American policies and join in a war with China which both we and America have already declared to be disastrous, while simultaneously risking a Russian challenge in the West which, our most expert advisers have appreciated, is not a bluff and which cannot be met'. Or, on the other hand, 'we can publicly refuse to follow America in her policies in both Asia and Europe and start to move independently in U.N.O. and elsewhere'.

The risks involved of the second of these courses were not underestimated: 'If we were in fact forced to make independent moves, which America will oppose, such as for example, voting against the imposition of sanctions on China or refusing to start the actual process of German rearmament until at least the nucleus of adequate land forces in Europe exist, a most serious situation would undoubtedly arise.' There was indeed a possibility, (perhaps a probability) that faced by inflexible British determination, 'backed as we can legitimately hope' by the Commonwealth and many other members of the United Nations, America would give way. 'But in a matter of this magnitude it is, of course, impossible to bluff. If we once say that in certain circumstances we shall take an independent course, we must, if the worst comes to the worst, be prepared to take it' warned Strachey.

What, then, were the risks involved in following America into general war with China and into a high degree of risk of war with Russia before any force capable of preventing the Russians reaching the Channel in a few weeks had been created? It was surely no overstatement to say that war with China and Russia during 1951 or 1952 would involve not the risk but the virtual certainty of national disaster for Great Britain? 'Let us face the simple, military fact that it is probable, almost to the point of certainty, that this country cannot physically survive a third world war which begins before land and air forces which can prevent Russia occupying the Channel coast have been created. Our responsible military advisers tell us that long range weapons of the V.I and V.II type, which are at Russia's disposal, would render the whole Southern and South-Western parts of Britain, including London, uninhabitable or at least "unworkable".' These, rather than atomic weapons, were surely the 'real and potentially fatal menace to the existence of this country if we fail to avoid the outbreak of war before we can prevent Russia occupying the Channel coast'. In the 'real circumstances' of 1951 the accusation that 'if we refuse to follow the American lead, we are proposing a policy of appeasement is irrelevant. It can never be right to take a fatal course however serious may be the disadvantages of the alternative' concluded Strachey. For America what was at stake was a feared loss of prestige weighed against the risk of an immediate war which she reasonably believed she could survive and would ultimately win. 'For us what is at stake is the same feared loss of prestige set against the risk of an immediate war which almost certainly involves our physical destruction. The question is, whose interests are to prevail? Our life and death interests or America's important but non-vital interests?' If these facts were faced, continued Strachey, 'who will deny that by far the wiser course in present circumstances is to accept whatever degree of dispute with America proves necessary' rather than to accept her present policies in Asia and Europe? Naturally 'we must cause the very minimum of public dispute between ourselves and America which we can; but if we always enter negotiations in the spirit that "we must not, at all costs, lose America", we are defeated before we begin. For our attitude of mind will at once become apparent to the Americans and they will know that they need not yield'.[2]

Strachey's covering letter to Bevin suggested: 'Put this memo into the waste paper basket if you feel you can't bear to read another thing! But one gets so anxious one can't help putting one's thoughts onto paper. I think I'm shoving at an open door in your case. Don't think of answering … John.'[3] But Bevin did take the memorandum seriously enough to circulate it to senior Foreign Office officials and ask for their comments. Sir Pierson Dixon's comment was: 'But at least there is an element of doubt whether the Russians would succumb to the temptation' to invade Western Europe. There were many restraining factors although there could be little doubt, on the other hand, that the danger of a Russian attack would be great if the United States, Britain and the Commonwealth were seriously divided: 'The worst condition of all would be an Anglo-American quarrel, followed by America pursuing a policy of war against China by herself, and leaving us and the Europeans without American help.' In such a contingency some might advocate a policy of neutrality, a compounding with the Soviet Union: 'That surely is unthinkable; and if so we have no choice in the long run but to retain the friendship and support of the U.S.A. It follows that we could not press our views about the Far East to a point where we might be abandoned by the U.S.A.' warned Dixon.[4] Sir William Strang, meanwhile, stressed: 'Our true objective should be to deter the Americans from dangerous courses without … a public row or a break in our relations of confidence. This is difficult to do, but that is what Foreign Ministers and Foreign Offices are for … With patience and firmness and skill we may even succeed over Korea. To face a Government and people with a public challenge is often the worst way to bring them to your way of thinking. But some of these "sorcerers' apprentices" think otherwise.'[5]

The confirmation of an American desire for the condemnation, in the UN, of China as an aggressor duly arrived from Washington. As Younger confided to his diary, on 7 January: 'The international situation is peculiarly worrying and depressing at the moment. As I write, we have reached the point where the UN "Cease-fire group" have reported failure & the Chinese have launched their expected second offensive below the 38th parallel. They are being pretty successful, so much so that we all doubt whether the U.S. military really intend to hold on in Korea at all.' He feared the measure would not get the support of Asian countries, notably India and would thus split both the UN and the Commonwealth. Younger was trying to persuade Bevin to speak 'very brutally' against the proposed US resolution, lobby against the Americans at Lake Success and also to try to get a combined front with the Commonwealth Prime Ministers who were at present in conference in London: 'It is on this that I am depressed about our own government' confided Younger. Although the whole Cabinet was 'solid on the merits of the policy, there is great reluctance to be tough with the Americans about it. So far we have done little more than express our view to the Americans. We have given them no cause to think that, if they disregard us, we will cause them any trouble. Nor have we made any public statement either officially, or by calculated press leakage, of our position.' Younger put this to Bevin who 'obviously disliked it but did not rule it out'. However, he took Younger along to see Attlee and he thus had the chance to say it all over again to him. Bevin made practically no comment, 'except that when Ernie wailed almost tearfully that this was the end of the US/UK alliance, the P.M. pulled him up rather sharply and said he did not think so at all'. Younger tried to get Attlee to say whether HMG were in any event prepared to vote for the limited sanctions that the United States were proposing or to tell the Americans privately now that London were not prepared to do so, 'but I could not get him to go so far.' In the end HMG did send a telegram to Washington telling Franks that UK support for a resolution condemning China as an aggressor, and calling for consequent measures, could not be assumed. Younger's 'impression of Ernie' was that he 'has been lamentable. Sometimes he seems very unwell, sometimes not so bad; but every time I have seen him so far he has seemed to me to be morally a broken man. I think the weakness is partly physical, & that he simply hasn't the stamina for taking difficult decisions. Just now the line of least resistance is to drift along behind the Americans, making ineffectual protests all the way. That is certainly what Ernie would do'.

Younger was influenced by fears that the US resolution might lead to the Communist states leaving the UN, which would then become in effect an anti-Communist alliance 'pure & simple'. That in turn would lead to the defection of a number of Asian states '& [the] UN would be at an end'. An 'equally big question' was whether action of this kind against China would be considered by Russia to make eventual world war so certain that she would decide to move in Europe soon. Everyone agreed that there would at present be no counter to a Soviet move in force in Europe. Presumably, Younger thought, the Americans would want to atom bomb Russia (no doubt from UK bases), but whatever that might do to Russia, it would not prevent the Red Army from reaching the Channel ports. Once that had happened, the Americans would have to consider whether to drop atom bombs on Western Europe too. 'I suspect they would bomb the Ruhr, but not France — anyway at first. How big is the risk of setting all this in motion through rash action in the east, is very hard to say. If [the] USA succeeded in leading the Western nations and the Commonwealth into war with China, I think a Russian might well take that as a certain pointer to world war within a few years. On that assumption, she [Russia] might prefer to deny W[estern] Europe to the Americans now, while it can be easily done, rather than wait until the Atlantic pact has begun to mean something in real military strength.' But Younger's worst anxiety was his 'lack of confidence in Ernie. I believe he would like simply to follow Acheson quietly, because he has as good as said so in an office meeting. He also said that if we didn't go with the Americans on this "we would be letting the Americans down" ... I was pretty rude to Ernie, & only restrained myself because there were half-a-dozen officials present.' So far, Younger observed, the Foreign Office had been 'pretty good on this, but I can see that the "don't be rude to the Americans" school is gaining. I don't think anyone, except perhaps Rob Scott, is likely to stick to his guns very firmly'.[6]

This was the domestic background, in Whitehall, as the Commonwealth Prime Ministers' Conference began in London. Across the Atlantic Sir Oliver Franks saw Acheson, on 7 January, and outlined the thinking Bevin had been doing on the situation in the Far East preparatory to the Commonwealth meeting. From this Acheson gained the impression, 'perhaps wrongly', that the Foreign Secretary was fearful that the naming of the Peking Government as aggressors would be followed by hostilities against China itself: 'I am not clear as to whether if you felt this it was because you concluded that that would be the attitude of the US or whether you concluded it was an inevitable sequence of events' he told Bevin. Acheson sought to assure Bevin 'first that we here intend to do everything we can to prevent hostilities spreading from Korea to wider areas in the Far East'. What Peking 'will do we, of course, do not know. But we do not believe for a moment' that Communists either in Peking or elsewhere would extend the theatre of war by reason of their being named as aggressors. Therefore, it seemed to Washington that whether or not hostilities could be prevented from spreading depended upon the deliberate choice of Peking or those who inspired that regime. Acheson continued: 'We are deeply concerned that failure of the UN to recognise the present Chinese Communist action in Korea as aggression and to name it as such will be the beginning of the end of the UN just as the end of the League of Nations stated with their failure to take any action against Japan and Italy in similar circumstances.' As Acheson read the barometer of US public opinion, he was deeply apprehensive that a failure of the UN to recognise this aggression would create a wave of isolationism in the United States which would 'jeopardise all that we are trying to do with and for the Atlantic Pact countries. I believe, therefore, that the UK and the countries of Western Europe have this additional and vital interest in supporting UN action of the *strength* I have indicated.'[7]

# Divisions: January 1951

The day of Acheson's message to Bevin also saw another message, this one from Attlee to Truman, cross the Atlantic. Although the UN Eighth Army, in Korea, was now under the morale boosting command of General Matthew Ridgeway, disconcerting rumours were reaching London of a military pull-out. The Prime Minister declared to Truman: 'I am greatly disturbed by present developments in the Far East, and feel that I should open my mind to you in order that there may be no possibility or misunderstanding between our two Governments. My colleagues and I have been basing their policy on the assumptions that we should fight it out in Korea and try to localise the conflict. This was my understanding of the common position which we reached together in Washington in December.' It was on these assumptions, and on the assumption that 'if we could hold a line' and build up a position of strength in Korea the Chinese might then be in a mood to respond to a suggestion for a negotiated settlement, that His Majesty's Government had been pressing that the possibility for a negotiation with China should be kept open. This accounted for the UK attitude on future action in the United Nations. But: 'It now appears from the information we are receiving that the intention of the United Nations command is to evacuate rather than fight it out. I feel compelled to ask you to give me an authoritative indication of the intentions of the United States Government in this respect.'

It might be, accepted Attlee, that it was militarily impossible to hold on in Korea. This possibility was 'recognised between us in Washington last month. Moreover, we are not blind to the possibility that China may intend to spread hostilities in the Far East'. But looking at the world situation as a whole, and bearing in mind that the Soviet Union was the principal enemy, 'we think it unwise to provoke China unnecessarily to further aggression. The wiser course, it seems to us, is to harbour our forces and build them up in order to meet Communist attacks wherever they may come'. It was true that Acheson, in his message of 8 January, to Bevin, stated that the United States intended to do everything they could to prevent hostilities spreading from Korea to wider areas in the Far East. But the kind of action against China for which the United States Government appeared to be pressing at the United Nations would, in Attlee's view, almost certainly provoke China to extend hostilities. There could be little doubt that, for example, a campaign of subversion or guerrilla warfare against China involving the use of Chiang Kai-shek's men would certainly have that effect: 'I do not know whether such a project is intended by the United States government, and I should like to know whether they would intend to recommend such action by the United Nations after China had been declared an aggressor.' It was for all these reasons, Attlee had felt 'bound to explain to you frankly, that we have been opposing the introduction at this stage of a resolution in the United Nations condemning China as an aggressor' and calling on the UN Collective Measures Committee (CMC) 'to consider what measures should be taken' as a result. In any case HMG considered it desirable, in order to consolidate opinion in the United Nations, which was at present disarrayed, and ensure the greatest measure of support on the part of the free world, that an immediate step should be taken at the United Nations which, while recognising the facts of the situation in Korea, would show that all concerned were prepared to go to the utmost limit in giving the Chinese a chance to reach a peaceful settlement. Such an immediate step might take the form of a resolution based perhaps on the latest set of Principles drawn up the by the UN Cease Fire Committee. This might include a clause condemning Chinese intervention in Korea. There was a good deal of support among 'our Commonwealth friends here for the notion that the Big Powers have a special responsibility in this crisis. It would be of the greatest assistance to me if you could possibly let me have a reply in time for tomorrow's meeting' with the Commonwealth Prime Ministers, asked Attlee in conclusion.[8]

In his reply, Truman reassured Attlee: 'First, there has not been any change in the position on which you and I agreed, that resistance to aggression in Korea should continue in Korea unless and until superior force requires the evacuation of our troops. Any other information you have received regarding the intentions and determination of the Government is wholly incorrect.' The present tactical situation did not reflect any change in this position, but, rather, the essential adjustments to cover the increased jeopardy to UN troops resulting from a recent marked decrease in the effectiveness of the sorely tried South Korean divisions. Secondly, the desire and intention of the US Government to confine hostilities to Korea was correctly and, Truman thought, plainly stated by Acheson in his message to Bevin. Should the Chinese Communists extend hostilities as, for example, by an attack on Hong Kong or Indo-China or Japan or by massive air attacks from Chinese territory on UN Forces, 'I should assume that you would agreed that our desire and intention might be impossible of fulfilment.' Thirdly, explained Truman, we do not intend to recommend to the UN a campaign of subversion or guerrilla warfare against the mainland of China by Chinese National Forces.' Fourthly, regarding action by the UN appropriate to the present situation in Korea, Truman's chief concern was that it should be honest and honourable and directed to preserve the very essence of the great principle for which the UN was created – the principle of collective security. In his message to the Congress the day before the President, as he pointed out to Attlee, had said: 'If the democracies had stood up against aggression in Manchuria in 1931, or the attack on Ethiopia in 1935, or the seizure of Austria in 1938, if they had stood together against aggression on those occasions as the UN has done, the whole history of our time would have been different.' By all means, continued Truman to Attlee, 'let us keep all doors open for peaceful settlement. That is our duty under the Charter of the UN. But, if the truth be that aggression has occurred, let us not shrink from stating that truth, because of the fact that the power which launches it is formidable. If we take that attitude the great common problems which you and we have are insoluble'.[9]

The President's message arrived in London as the Commonwealth Prime Ministers gathered; one of their chief concerns was, naturally, the Korean situation. Attlee had sent his message to the President in order to have an authoritative interpretation of the American view on Korea and regarded the exchange of messages with Truman as private and so copies were not circulated to the other premiers.[10] But the Prime Minister remained troubled. On 10 January, Attlee asked for Bevin to see him. The Prime Minister revealed that he too had been talking to a number of military and other personalities who were thoroughly alarmed about the present American attitude to world affairs which they were afraid 'would end by dragging us into war'. It had been represented to him that if the Americans turned over a great part of their industrial capacity to war production it would be very difficult for them to turn back to normal civilian production without causing economic chaos and there would be a strong temptation to resort to a preventive war. They had, of course, announced that they were going to spend enormous sums on tanks, aeroplanes, etc., and it was suggested that this would be interpreted as meaning that they intended to fight China or Russia or both. Attlee said that he would welcome Bevin's views on this problem. The Secretary of State replied that he must have time to think the matter over. His first reaction, however, was that it was to 'our advantage' that the United States should be strong and he did not think that their great productive effort need necessarily lead to war. He thought that the US Government could be prevented from taking any rash action if handled wisely. He undertook, however, to consider the matter further and let the Prime Minister have his views.[11]

After thinking this over, Bevin gave his answer to Attlee, on 12 January. The Foreign Secretary conclusion was: 'It is not, I think, in the character of the American people to provoke a war, or to commit an act of aggression, nor does their constitution lend itself to action of this nature.' He did not think 'we should accept the argument that the large war production programme which the United States are now embarked on will force the United States into aggressive action because they will not be able to reconvert to civilian production without economic chaos'. In spite of all predictions to the contrary, United States economic activity had been steadily maintained and expanded in the post-war years, and was much better controlled than often appeared. It had shown considerable flexibility. There was a risk that the United States Government, by some ill-considered or impulsive action, or series of actions, might find themselves in an exposed position from which they might drift into hostilities, especially in the Far East. But, argued Bevin, this risk could be mitigated by wise diplomacy, though it may continue to exist. Despite this optimistic note, the Foreign Secretary warned: 'We are, however, in a very dangerous situation in which some risks must be taken. There is no ground for changing the view which we formed after long deliberation that neither the Commonwealth alone, nor Western Europe alone, nor even the Commonwealth plus Western Europe (if such a coalition could even be held together) were strong enough, either economically or militarily, to hold out against the forces actively opposing them.' The full participation of the United States was essential to sustain the free world which Soviet Russia was trying to undermine: 'It must therefore be the least of all risks that America should be strong, resolute and actively co-operating with other free nations. This must offer the best chance of avoiding a war.'

There was a risk, which must not be underrated, conceded Bevin, that if the United States met with strong opposition from her associates, especially on a matter in which the majority of Americans felt that a moral issue was involved, e.g. condemning aggression, they would become disillusioned with collective security and the United Nations and would retire into a kind of armed isolation. The effects of this were unpredictable, 'but I would expect them to be disastrous, at all events for the United Kingdom. We have to imagine what it would be like to live in a world with a hostile Communist bloc, an unco-operative America, a Commonwealth pulled in two directions, and a disillusioned Europe, which would be deprived of support in the form of American troops and American involvement in active European defence'. To Bevin the situation was critical: 'We are in fact faced with a problem which tests our statesmanship and diplomacy to the fullest extent.' Now was the time to build up the strength of the free world, morally, economically and militarily with the United States, and at the same time to exert sufficient control over the policy of the 'well-intentioned but inexperienced colossus on whose co-operation our safety depends'. It was particularly difficult in the Far East where, at the outbreak of the Korean conflict, 'we had agreed to differ in our policies. These are harder to align in a period of emotional tension. It can only be done by influencing the United States Government and people, not by opposing or discouraging them'.[12]

And, at this point in time, the Commonwealth gathering, in London, was the mechanism to do this. The gathered Prime Ministers, set out their own proposals: they felt that formal condemnation by the United Nations of China as an aggressor would have 'serious and far reaching implications', and that further efforts must yet be made to find a peaceful solution on lines acceptable both to the Chinese and the Americans. After considerable discussion, the Prime Ministers agreed generally that the most promising line of approach would be for the General Assembly to endorse the need for an immediate cease-fire. After this, further steps for restoration of peace should be considered. The Prime Ministers called for all non-Korean forces to be progressively withdrawn and an opportunity given for Koreans to express their free will regarding their future Government.[13] Bevin emphasized to Washington that the Commonwealth Prime Ministers did *not* intend that a cease-fire should be made a pre-condition of negotiations. This, after all, was a proposal which, by implication, had already been made to, and rejected by, Peking. The proposed resolution might, however, be so worded as to suggest a cease-fire simultaneously with the beginning of the talk.[14] In informing the UK UN delegation, the Foreign Office suggested a possible compromise might be for a committee (on which the CPG as well as the United States would participate) to be set up and held in readiness for negotiations to immediately make the cease-fire effective.[15] Bevin, meanwhile, had been giving thought to the question of a possible further reply, by Attlee, to President Truman's last message. He was not in favour of trying to send a message on behalf of all the Prime Ministers for the following reasons:

(1) It would be difficult to do this without revealing to them your previous exchange of messages with the President, and to do this might, I think, be regarded by the President as a breach of confidence. It is most important that we should preserve this channel of communication for messages of this kind.
(2) I think it would be difficult to get agreement among the Prime Ministers on the terms of such a message, since Nehru would be pulling in one direction and Menzies and Holland in another.
(3) We have to be very careful not to give the Americans the impression that the Commonwealth are ganging up to put pressure on them.[16]

Attlee did decide on a reply and took Bevin's advice; in it he welcomed Truman's reassurance as to the intentions of his Government on Korea:

'This came in very opportunely during our meeting of Prime Ministers, though I did not reveal these exchanges to them.' All the Prime Ministers, he continued, felt the deepest anxiety about the intentions of the Chinese Government. There was unanimous agreement that in order to probe Chinese intentions it was wise to make an offer of a meeting to include the 'Big Powers' through the United Nations, at the same time fully recognising, of course, that talks could not take place whilst fighting was in progress. Attlee continued: 'I would like to say how deeply impressed I am by the careful attention you have given to the viewpoints of the other nations, and the great effort made to reconcile the views so as to get in the end a common agreement. We ought even now, perhaps, to be considering the situation that will arise in the near future. It may be that the Chinese will respond to this very fair offer.' If that happened no doubt their two Governments would maintain the closest possible touch as to the next steps. But Attlee had no illusions, and feared that 'we may be faced by a negative attitude on the part of the Chinese. I think that we shall have to consider very carefully what our aims should then be and what steps we should take to achieve them'. With Bevin, Attlee had given careful thought to the request, transmitted to them on the 4 January, to denounce China as an aggressor, but he felt that the issues and consequences affected 'not only our interests but the interests of so many countries so vitally that we should not embark precipitately on a policy which might not sway the Chinese Government, but which would certainly impose serious new strains on us'. The dominating factor was, of course, the military situation in Korea.[17]

As part of the American effort to reassure the British, there was increased activity between the US and UK Chiefs of Staff. In Washington, General Bradley saw Lord Tedder on 12 January in what was, essentially, a personal meeting with the Joint Chiefs and Bradley. The Joint Chiefs confirmed that the policy was still to fight but due to Chinese superiority in numbers coupled with large reserves available in North Korea and Manchuria, they planned on withdrawals southwards to a final beachhead position if necessary. But they doubted the feasibility of holding an adequate beach-head at all under Chinese pressure. Further they doubted the wisdom of attempting such a course. They actually disliked holding such a position because:

(a) However many enemy are destroyed in assaults upon it inevitably there will be heavy American casualties. In this they see no point particularly against the background of present public opinion in America as expressed in the press and in Congress and letters to

Congressmen. When I [Tedder] quoted the Anzio beach-head as an even more difficult proposition they remarked that Anzio had a future whereas a beach-head on Korea would have no military future.
(b) A small beach-head such as this would be a hostage to fortune in the event of a major war ensuing.
(c) They are anxious about the security of Japan ...
(d) Retention of U.S. troops in Korea will inevitably delay build-up in Europe. Two of their regular divisions in Korea are overdue in Europe.

In summary, Tedder concluded that the Joint Chiefs, while concerned at the 'very adverse' effect of leaving Korea, appeared 'really to be in favour of getting out of that country on military grounds'. Tedder found it a 'friendly and frank meeting.' It was clear that some of the implied criticisms from the Chiefs in London 'had touched them on the raw but I do not think left a sore though they felt some of them unjustified. They were I think sincerely surprised to find that the daily briefings Bouchier's reports and my talks with Bradley are not an adequate substitute for real joint thinking. The fact is that real exploratory discussion and joint examination of a problem is not in their make-up – I do not believe they do it amongst themselves'.[18]

As result of Tedder's meeting it was clear to the Americans and British that closer relations were necessary on the strategic front. In the British Chiefs' discussion of what to do next, Sir William Slim pointed out that the most surprising thing to him was that the Americans had not even thought out what they would do if they did evacuate. Slim was still sure that MacArthur intended to evacuate Korea in spite of the statements of the State Department and of the President to the contrary, and that MacArthur would obtain the support of the Joint Chiefs for this. What the British required from the United States was a full military appreciation of the extent to which it might be possible to hold on in Korea, but his personal sense was that, in view of the present attitude prevailing among the Americans, it was now unlikely to be possible to hold on. Slim's impression was that MacArthur still had at the back of his mind the ultimate idea of using Chiang Kai-shek's forces in Formosa against the Chinese mainland, once the United Nations' forces had left Korea.

Slim was sure that the retention of a footing in Korea would undoubtedly strengthen the United Nations' bargaining position on vis-a-vis Communist China, but if this was not possible the presence of considerable US forces in Japan and Chiang Kai-shek's 500,000 Chinese troops in Formosa would still be some kind of inducement to the Chinese to negotiate. They were bound to feel uncomfortable as long as these forces were so close and must necessarily regard them as a potential threat. The CIGS felt that 'our object in these circumstances must be to keep the potential threat in being and not dissipate … forces with possible adventures against the China coast, in order that we might take advantage of them as a bargaining counter to bring China to a reasonable frame of mind for negotiations'. Sir John Slessor, however, did not entirely agree with Slim's view about the 'threat in being' from Japan and Formosa and its effect on the Chinese; he thought it might not really prove such a valuable bargaining point particularly after the Chinese had seen the showing made by United States' troops in Korea. As to the troops of Chiang Kai-shek, Slessor had little confidence that if put into China they would fight – they would probably just go off home; the Chinese Communists no doubt also realised this.

For the Foreign Office, Robert Scott added his Department felt strongly that the retention of a footing in Korea was of the utmost importance in relation to inducing the Chinese to negotiate. 'We should therefore do everything possible to persuade the Americans to do this. The Foreign Office would like (subject to Sir Oliver Franks' agreement) Slessor to put across to the Americans the thought that the real way to uphold United Nations' prestige was by resisting in Korea and holding out, and not by putting forward yet another resolution in the United Nations condemning China as an aggressor – a course which was generally held to be not only valueless but positively dangerous.' If it was militarily impossible to hold out in Korea, 'we must at least ensure that the utmost care was given to the next moves'. The State Department were, so far as could be made out, against a 'limited war'; and the Foreign Office would like to know how much the Joint Chiefs agreed with this and the possible effect of MacArthur's views, 'whatever they might be'.

In accepting his mission, Slessor wanted the agreement of his fellow Chiefs (subject to Franks' approval) for an opening gambit with the Americans on the following general lines. He proposed to speak with complete frankness and to invite the Americans to do the same. The maintenance of Anglo/American solidarity was the first and essential concern; there were signs of potentially the greatest crisis arising in this vital matter. The whole country – Government, Services and public – was gravely concerned and puzzled about the conduct of the campaign in Korea and concerning United States' intentions. The Commonwealth Prime Ministers' conference had shown that there was equal concern and bewilderment among the Commonwealth countries. It was against this background and climate of opinion – of which the US Joint Chiefs should be made aware – that Slessor proposed to speak. There was an increasing unwillingness to 'tag along behind the United States': the feeling, he would explain, was that MacArthur had been given far too free a hand and that 'we had been kept in the dark'. In the light of the President's recent reply to the Prime Minister, re-affirming the United States' intention to resist in Korea, 'what were we to make of the contradictory indications which we were receiving not only from our own sources but also from highly placed United States Service sources (including General Bradley) of an intention to evacuate Korea?' And:

> We should like:-
> *Information* on:-
> (i) General MacArthur's orders.
> (ii) General MacArthur's reply to General Marshall's Signal asking both for clarification of the situation and for his intentions.
> (iii) An appreciation of our ability to hold on in Korea by Generals Marshall, MacArthur and Ridgeway.

On the question of consultation, Slessor would state: 'We do not propose to recriminate – we too have suffered reverses and been forced to carry out evacuations. We have never pressed General MacArthur directly for his intentions or views, but have stuck scrupulously to our correct channel through the United States Joint Chiefs of Staff. We have left the United States to act without interference as the agents of the United Nations. We have, however, been committed to various ways by their unilateral actions.' The first 'we heard of their original intentions in Korea was five hours before the broadcast on 25th July. We did not like crossing the 38th parallel, but did not argue about it'. Nor did the Chiefs expect their tactical suggestions to be given too much attention and appreciated that decisions in such matters must be taken on the spot, 'but we do expect to be consulted on matters of major policy'. Slessor also wanted to make the point that the British could not accept without protest recent United States advice to their nationals to leave Hong Kong 'where we had weakened the garrison in order to assist in Korea. We have a far greater stake in property and lives in the Far East than the United States. It cannot be pretended, for instance, that withdrawal from Formosa directly threatens the security of the United States. We speak not just as inhabitants of a small island but from the point of view of the vast interests not only of ourselves but also of the Dominions in this area. We must consider the threat to Hong Kong, the effect on Malaya – our greatest dollar earner – the appalling effect of loss of United Nations prestige on Burma and on the Asian Dominions. It must be remembered that the whole balance of power in the Far East has been upset by the emergence, for the first time, of China as a vast, fairly efficiently run, and reasonably united country'. Slessor's colleagues agreed although, it was suggested that something should be added to the effect that 'we have no doubt of General MacArthur's military ability but we have a less high opinion of his political insight and of his intelligence service'.[19]

Slessor flew to the States and, on 16 January, Franks, Tedder and the CAS had a two-hour meeting today with Bradley, Sherman and Rusk. Though there were no decisions or even implied commitments on either side, Slessor found it a 'most useful exchange of views which I hope will lead to further joint examination of the various problems confronting us.' Both Rusk and Bradley emphasised the temper of American public opinion with regard to China and the strong pressure which would be brought on the administration to ensure that some form of 'retaliation' were taken against the Chinese aggressors in the event of the UN being forced to withdraw from Korea. The Americans were obviously worried as to what action should be taken if it proved possible to stabilise a line in Korea and a stalemate resulted. In their view it would obviously be militarily unsound to tie up large UN forces for an indefinite period. In this connection Bradley pointed out that the Chinese might well equip and train up to 500,000 North Koreans using good Russian equipment and would then withdraw the majority of the Chinese forces. Although it might be equally possible to arm large numbers of South Koreans this would necessitate the diversion of American equipment from Europe. To Slessor it was clear that the Americans felt that China 'has already embarked on a phased programme of aggressive expansion with Indo-China, Formosa and possibly Hong Kong as the next steps and that U.N. action vis a vis China by political military or economic means should be designed to divert slow up or possibly stop this programme'.[20] Although Slessor was reassured that the American Government's position was still to hold in Korea, 'if this proved militarily possible', all of them agreed, including the CAS, that to continue to hold a bridgehead for an indefinite period gave the UN no military advantages. It would lock up Allied Forces who would in due course require relief by new formations. Nor did it appear that a bridgehead of this size had any political advantages since it would not provide an adequate platform for negotiations. The Joint Chiefs made it clear that whatever the outcome of military operations they did not intend to reinforce with any major formations though they would keep existing formations up to strength.

With regard to future action, Slessor found Tedder's opinion, that the Americans had not thought the problem through, was accurate. They were clear, however that no action against China, outside Korea, should be taken whilst UN forces were still operating in the country. The US Chiefs made it plain that, 'if we were driven out of Korea, in the U.S. there would be strong popular demand for action in the support of a resolution in the U.N. branding China as an aggressor'. As a result of the discussion Slessor thought 'they now accept the view that this might well take the form of economic sanctions backed up by naval blockade the sanctions to be on a selective basis applying only to certain semi-strategic materials such as rubber steel and oil thus avoiding the difficulties we stressed e.g. India's reliance on Chinese supplies of rice. It was agreed that a joint examination should be undertaken of the possibility and effects of applying sanctions based on this concept'.[21] Bradley accepted that the CAS should also receive a full briefing on the US strategic bombing plan including proposed targets. Bradley, though, made it clear that one of the vital bits of information which must by law be withheld was the size of the atomic stockpile a fact known only to some twenty people in the United States.[22]

On 17 January the Chinese appeared to reject the cease-fire proposals and Anglo-American tensions resurfaced once more. The Foreign Office, on 18 January, telegraphed instructions to the UK UN delegation stating that the UK found the terms of the Chinese reply unacceptable and authorising Jebb to have a 'good smack at it'. HMG hoped, though, that the United States would not insist on introducing a new resolution, denouncing the Chinese as aggressors, that day. If the United States did insist, and a resolution was introduced by the US UN delegation, the UK wished to have it amended. The British would prefer to have a condemnatory resolution handled separately from any resolution calling for further UN action and not combined in one document.[23] But Acheson informed Franks that he was afraid that 'they could not do what Mr. Bevin requested' and would suggest that Austin, at the UN – after saying that the Chinese people were aggressors – would call for 'future measures' to be considered. He could not promise to go further to meet Bevin's position for two reasons: the first was that 'we had talked with 45 Delegations along the general lines of the paper we had sent to Mr. Bevin about ten days ago. These Delegations understand that this is our general attitude, and if we don't go through with it, we will add to the general confusion'. The second reason was that in order to do 'everything possible to keep everyone together we brought ourselves to the verge of destruction domestically'. The Secretary pointed out that 'we could have all the preliminary talks with the British which were necessary'. But he 'did not think we could back off from the matter now'. Acheson thought someone 'must have gotten Mr. Bevin stirred up on this question, because he could not see that Mr Bevin's attitude was a sensible one'.

Franks revealed to Acheson he had told Rusk he would get off a telegram and do what he could to 'straighten Mr. Bevin out on this'. Franks 'did not see how any damage could come of it'. Acheson interjected that he did not see how anything but good could come from the proposed US action, and to this Sir Oliver replied that he was not certain about this, although he agreed that good would come from the public opinion point of view.[24] If the British felt uncomfortable with US actions so did the Americans; Austin outlined the dilemma, to Acheson, on 20 January: 'we were in a difficult situation at the present moment. We felt it was absolutely essential that a resolution be tabled today. Our greatest allies, the British and French, were not able to join with us … on the text … We were extremely anxious to do whatever we could to avoid giving appearance that [the] Russians had succeeded in splitting the US away from its major allies and from Europeans. We did not wish either to split the Commonwealth'.[25]

When the news from Franks was relayed to London it turned out that it was the Ambassador who had misread how concerned his Government was with events at the UN. On 22 January, Bevin reluctantly informed the Cabinet that it had not proved possible to 'restrain' the United States Government from putting forward in the Political Committee of the United Nations a resolution condemning Chinese aggression in Korea. This, after noting that the Chinese People's Government were continuing their large-scale attacks in Korea and had rejected all proposals for a peaceful settlement, called upon the United Nations:

(i) to conclude that the Peking Government were engaged in aggression, which should be ended by the withdrawal of Chinese Communist forces;
(ii) to affirm the determination of the United Nations to continue its action in Korea against aggression;
(iii) to invite all States to assist the United Nations in Korea and to refrain from assisting the aggressors;
(iv) to invite the Collective Measures Committee to consider and report to the General Assembly what additional action could be taken against this aggression; and
(v) to invite the President of the Assembly to designate two persons with whom he would cooperate at any suitable opportunity in using their good offices to enable the United Nations to achieve its objectives in Korea by peaceful means.

His Majesty's Government, Bevin told the Cabinet, had now to define their attitude towards this resolution and to decide whether their representative at the United Nations should be instructed to vote in favour of it. The Foreign Secretary invited the Cabinet, in considering this difficult situation, to keep three broad considerations in mind. First, what practical consequences would follow if China were formally branded as an aggressor by the United Nations? There was no doubt, he continued, that China had in fact committed aggression in Korea; and the United Kingdom Government were committed to support United Nations action in resisting aggression in Korea. But much more than this might flow from a formal condemnation of China as an aggressor. The United States Government might prefer to withdraw their troops from Korea, and direct their attack upon the mainland of China. They might even wish to use Chiang Kai-shek's forces in hostilities on the mainland, and to foment a new civil war in China in which they would be supporting Chiang Kai-shek against the Communist forces. Commonwealth Governments would not wish to be drawn into support of such policies as these.

Secondly, Nehru had taken the view that the latest reply from the Peking Government did not amount to a final rejection of the offer to seek a settlement through negotiation. There was in fact some ambiguity on at least one point in that reply. When the Peking Government said that they could not accept a cease-fire without preliminary negotiations, it was not clear whether they had in mind negotiations about the details of the cease-fire or negotiations about the wider issues of Formosa and their admission to the United Nations. If they referred to the latter questions there seemed to be no possibility of a compromise. But, if they meant only that there must be some preliminary negotiations about a cease-fire before it could be put into effect, this was a request which merited serious consideration. Bevin had therefore instructed His Majesty's representative in Peking to seek clarification of this point; and the Cabinet might think it wise to defer taking a final decision until this was available.

Thirdly, full account should be taken of the state of public opinion in the United States on this question. The fact was that Americans were exceedingly reluctant to admit the Chinese Communists on equal terms to a conference on the outstanding issues in the Far East. This was largely due to an emotional feeling that China was now showing nothing but ingratitude for all the generous help which the United States had extended to her over many years.[26] Bevin referred to a 'serious war psychosis' in the United States: 'They don't want a deal' with Communist China '– don't want to speak to them'. Having 'poured' money into China through missionaries and 'social work' they looked at the results and felt the 'Chinese nation has let them down'.[27] This made it difficult for the United States Government to take a realistic view of the current situation. But some means should, if possible, be found of handling that situation without any open rift between the Commonwealth and the United States. Against this general background the Foreign Secretary invited the Cabinet to consider the message from Franks regarding the proposals which the United States Government would put to the Collective Measures Committee if their resolution were passed. It was satisfactory that the Americans were not intending to ask that Committee to recommend military action against the mainland of China. On the other hand, the Committee would be asked to explore the feasibility of general economic sanctions, and the Americans evidently hoped that there would be some selective embargo on key exports to China. This Committee would be in a position of considerable influence, and it was unfortunate that it included a number of countries which would follow the United States lead. Although its findings would, in form, be only recommendations to Governments, it would in practice be difficult for member states to refrain from accepting recommendations carried by a two-thirds majority on that Committee. The Foreign Secretary, in conclusion, explained that his advice to the Cabinet was that they should defer a final decision until His Majesty's representative in Peking had reported the results of the enquiries which he had been instructed to make of the Chinese People's Government.

The Prime Minister, summing up the discussion, concluded that the Cabinet would not wish to take a final decision regarding their attitude towards the United States resolution until they knew the results of the enquiries which were now being made in Peking. The Cabinet must, however, decide what line should be taken at the United Nations, by Sir Gladwyn Jebb, in the debate on that resolution which was to be resumed later in the day. He read to the Cabinet a draft of the instructions which the Foreign Secretary was proposing to send to Jebb.[28] The problem, lamented Attlee, was the moral aspect that aggression had to be condemned especially aggression by 'one of the big 5' as he put it – whose aggression the UN Charter had never purported to deal with.[29] In discussion it was recognised that it would be difficult for Jebb to speak again on the resolution before he knew whether or not he would be instructed to vote in support of it. It would be preferable that, if this were at all possible, he should defer making his speech until the following day. If, however, he had to speak that day, he should avoid saying anything which might prejudge the Cabinet's final decision. From that point of view, it would be better that he should not express support for the paragraph of the United States resolution which condemned Chinese aggression in Korea. It was suggested that on this point he might confine himself to saying that the Chinese had committed aggression in Korea, but, notwithstanding that, the United Nations had offered to seek a settlement by negotiation and it was a matter for regret that the Peking Government had not yet accepted that offer. The Cabinet, finally, endorsed the decision that HMG should not join in sponsoring a resolution condemning Chinese aggression in Korea and agreed to defer a final decision regarding their attitude towards the United States resolution, pending the results of the enquiries which were now being made in Peking.[30]

The Cabinet were informed, the next day, 23 January, that the Chinese Peoples Government had answered the enquiries, made by the Indian Ambassador in Peking on behalf of the Governments of Canada and India, and by His Majesty's Chargé d'affaires, Sir John Hutchinson. The Chinese stated that, if the principle that all foreign troops should be withdrawn from Korea was accepted and was being put into practice, they would advise their 'volunteers' in Korea to return to China. Regarding the conclusion of the war in Korea and the peaceful settlement of the Korean problem, they thought it possible to proceed by two stages. First, there could be a cease-fire for a limited time, to be settled at the first meeting of a Seven-Power Conference and to be put into effect at once so that negotiations might proceed further. Secondly, in order that the war in Korea might be concluded and peace in East Asia ensured, agreement must be reached upon the following political problems: measures for the withdrawal of all foreign troops from Korea; measures enabling the internal affairs of Korea to be settled by the Korean people themselves; withdrawal of United States forces from Formosa and the Straits in accordance with the Cairo and Potsdam declarations, and other problems concerning the Far East. Finally, the Peking Government declared their right to represent China in the United Nations must be ensured.

In New York the Indian representative had read this reply to the First Committee of the United Nations Assembly and proposed that further discussion should be adjourned for 48 hours. Jebb supported this proposal; Austin spoke against it in 'intemperate' terms. After a debate, the proposal was carried by 27 votes to 23. Those voting against it had included the representatives of the United States, the Latin American countries, Greece, Turkey and the Philippines. Six representatives abstained from voting including the representatives of Australia and New Zealand. Jebb now asked for early instructions, from London, on the line which he should take when the debate was resumed the following day. In particular, he was anxious to know whether in the last resort he was to vote for the United States resolution, or to abstain. Other delegations were anxious to know what line he was proposing to take, and he would lose the opportunity of influencing them unless he could give an early reply to their enquiries.

In London, Kenneth Younger, in the absence of Bevin, informed the Cabinet that 'our first objective must presumably be to gain further time in which to explore to the full the possibilities opened by this further reply from the Peking Government'. It would, however, be helpful to Jebb if the Cabinet could also give him an early indication of the line which he would have to take if discussion were eventually resumed on the basis of the United States resolution. Attlee's summing up of the Cabinet's position was that in the discussions at the United Nations 'our policy must be to avoid precipitate action and to support any reasonable proposal designed to bring the Peking Government into conference'. The latest reply from the Peking Government suggested that the door to negotiations had not been finally closed; and 'we must do our utmost to keep it open'. Jebb was to be instructed to ascertain whether the Indian delegation were thinking of putting forward any positive proposal which would offer an alternative basis for discussion, so as to delay further debate on the United States resolution. As regarded that resolution 'we should continue to argue, as we had from the outset, that condemnation of China should be discussed separately from any proposals for the application of sanctions. We should wish to express our views separately upon different paragraphs of the resolution. We could not assent to the paragraph stating that the Peking Government had rejected the United Nations proposals. Nor could we support the proposal that the Collective Measures Committee should be invited to consider the application of sanctions against China'. On the other hand, HMG should be prepared to support some condemnation of Chinese action in Korea. For the moment Jebb should avoid committing himself to support any formula which formally branded China as an 'aggressor'; though Attlee recognised that in the last resort 'we might find ourselves unable to avoid the use of that phrase.' It followed that Jebb could not indicate at this stage how he would eventually vote on the United States resolution. The wording of the resolution was likely to be amended in various respects; and it would be impossible for him to say whether he would support it until it became clear in what form it emerged from the debate.[31]

Sir Pierson Dixon was deployed to see Gifford, the US Ambassador, to explain the Cabinet's decision, the substance of which was to be contained in Attlee's statement in the Commons that afternoon. Dixon emphasised two substantive reasons for the decisions: (1) a reluctance to drive a wedge between the West and the Asians, who opposed the US draft resolution and felt this was an Asian question in which they had strong legitimate interest; and (2) a feeling that there was still a slight chance of a negotiated settlement and consequent desire to keep the door open. Dixon said the fundamental reason, however, was that the Cabinet felt it could not carry the country with it in supporting the present US resolution. Jebb was being instructed to obtain postponement of the debate and Franks was being instructed again to review the position to Acheson and 'plead for no action until there is further chance to "test Peking sincerity"'. At same time Dixon said the Cabinet decision permitted the UK to vote for a resolution condemning the Chinese for 'intervening in support of aggression' but a delay was being sought in order avoid Jebb voting against objectionable parts of the US draft. Dixon did not deny the 'unrealism' of expecting any 'sincere' or constructive results from further approaches to Peking and indicated he would send further instructions to Franks authorising him to attempt to work out mutually acceptable amendments to the US draft resolution which might bring it within the limits of the Cabinet decision and thus save the UN from maintaining a completely pusillanimous posture vis-a-vis the Chinese.[32]

Acheson, in turn, urged Gifford to point out to the British the relative 'mildness' of the US proposals, in the face of the 'great provocation' by the Chinese: in spite of the heavy American losses in Korea, resulting in public pressure for quick and effective action, the United States had acquiesced in the desire of other powers to defer sterner measures during attempts to negotiate cease-fire arrangements. This 'forbearance has evidenced our desire [to] explore all reasonable possibilities for peaceful settlement'.[33] When he met Franks, Acheson urged the UK to support the resolution on the basis there would be 'ample opportunity' for bilateral consultation with a view reaching, 'if possible', a common position.[34]

On 25 January, Hubert Graves, from the British Embassy, informed the State Department that the Cabinet's conclusion was that Jebb should vote against the US resolution unless paragraph 2 was suitably amended and paragraph 8 deleted. Paragraph 2 of the US resolution stated, in effect, that the Chinese Peoples' Government had rejected *all* UN efforts to reach a peaceful settlement of the Korean problem. The Cabinet believed that amendments must be made based on the latest Chinese proposals which appeared in fact to accept *some* of the UN proposals. The Cabinet would accept an amendment along the lines that 'the CPG have not yet accepted *all* UN proposals' or 'noting the disappointing response of the CPG, etc.'. If such an amendment were made, Jebb could then vote for paragraph 2. The Cabinet, however, was most strongly opposed to paragraph 8, which called for the Collective Measures Committee to consider action against China. Jebb could not vote for the US resolution if this paragraph remained in it. Graves concluded that the latest instruction was, in his judgment, London's final word on the matter and represented the very great difficulty in which the United Kingdom found itself. He felt certain, and Franks wanted him to emphasise this, that the Cabinet had the full benefit of Acheson's views and that the present position was not based upon any difference in understanding between London and Washington. Rusk told Graves that 'we were greatly disappointed by this position, that we would consider what might be done with respect to some change in paragraph 2, but that there was no hope that we could agree to a deletion of paragraph 8'. Rusk added that Washington would very much hope that the United Kingdom would not find itself more or less alone with the Soviet bloc in opposition to the US resolution since that would create a 'most difficult situation indeed'.[35]

In London the Cabinet met, once more, to consider developments. Younger revealed that the Indian Ambassador in Peking had now obtained a further elucidation of the attitude of the Chinese Peoples' Government. From this it appeared that the Peking Government were now ready to give an assurance that Chinese volunteers would be withdrawn from Korea as soon as the principle of withdrawing all foreign troops had been accepted and was being put into practice. Secondly, they were agreeable that the terms and period of a cease-fire should be arranged as the first item of business of the proposed conference. Thirdly, they were ready to agree that a conference should determine the principles on which the internal administration of Korea should in future be based. Fourthly, as regarded Formosa, they now confined themselves to demanding the withdrawal of United States troops from the island and from the Straits. And, lastly, as regarded their recognition and admission to the United Nations, they asked merely that this should be affirmed in the course of the conference. The Indian representative at the United Nations would presumably disclose this further information when the debate in the First Committee was resumed later in the day. On the other hand, continued Younger, before this information was received, many of the Western powers had seemed to be coming round to the view that they would in the end be obliged to vote in favour of the United States resolution. All the other non-Asiatic members of the Commonwealth, and most of the European countries, now seemed to be willing to support that resolution. And there seemed to be some reason to fear that, if it were carried, the United States Government would not in fact be content, despite their protestations, with having China branded as an aggressor, but would go on to press for the application of political and economic sanctions against China. The mood of the Cabinet, at this stage, remained that this latest message from Peking was further evidence that the door to negotiations had not been finally closed, and that the possibilities of arranging for a conference should be fully explored before a vote was taken on the United States resolution.[36]

But, as Younger warned his colleagues, the moment for a decision was almost upon them: it now seemed likely that before the end of the week the First Committee of the General Assembly would have to vote on the United States resolution on Chinese intervention in Korea, substantially in the form in which it had been tabled on 20 January; and the United Kingdom representative should now be told how he should vote. It was almost certain that the resolution would be taken paragraph by paragraph before it was put to the vote as a whole. Three points arose on particular paragraphs of the resolution. The second paragraph recorded that the Peking Government had rejected 'all United Nations proposals' for a peaceful settlement. As a statement of fact this was no longer true, believed Younger, and efforts were being made to secure amendments designed to bring the paragraph into closer relation with the facts. If the paragraph was not amended in a satisfactory manner, Jebb should presumably vote against it. The third paragraph recorded that the Peking Government had itself engaged in aggression in Korea. This paragraph would have accorded more closely with the interpretation of events in Britain if it had followed the Prime Minister's statement in the House of Commons on 23 January and had condemned China for supporting an act of aggression; but the distinction did not seem sufficient to justify an adverse vote on the paragraph as it stood. The main difficulty arose in regard to the eighth paragraph, which requested the Collective Measures Committee to consider additional measures to meet the Chinese aggression. In the absence of any clear indication of United States intentions about the form of pressure they would wish to exert on China, there would be considerable risk in voting for that paragraph.

When it came to voting on the resolution as a whole, it seemed that Canada, Australia, New Zealand, South Africa and France – though disliking several of its paragraphs – would in the last resort vote in favour of it. The Cabinet might feel that, if the paragraph recording that China had rejected all proposals for a peaceful settlement had not been amended, then Jebb should not vote for the resolution. If acceptable amendments had been made in that paragraph, but not in the paragraph proposing the convening of a committee on collective measures, it might be possible for Jebb to vote for the resolution as a whole but to give a clear indication that this vote did not in any way alter HMG's belief that discussions should continue and that the imposition of sanctions was not likely to serve any useful purpose. It would also be important to take all practicable measures to ensure that, under the final paragraph of the resolution, machinery was created through which negotiations with China could be commenced. Younger also reminded the Cabinet that the Foreign Secretary had indicated at an earlier stage that in his opinion the United Kingdom Government ought in the last resort to vote for the United States resolution; but it had not been possible to take Bevin's view on the present situation given his health.

Hugh Dalton, asked: 'Are we to be led by stages to war' with China? This would be a grave error in strategy – as the Chiefs of Staff had pointed out; it was inconsistent with the position set out by the Prime Minister; it was unacceptable to public opinion; and played into the hands of Russia. When Herbert Morrison suggested Attlee approach Truman, the Prime Minister replied that the President could not go against the opinion prevailing in Congress: 'He has allowed them to go too far' complained Attlee. Aneurin Bevan warned that if Britain voted for the resolution but 'say we don't believe in it, we proclaim ourselves as satellites' of the United States. Younger pointed out the criticism that would ensue if a Great Power, like Britain, abstained on such a major issue: 'If we can't vote for, we ought to vote *against*' as a matter of 'self-respect'. He acknowledged that Bevin had favoured, in the last resort, standing with the United States; but if Britain voted with the Americans 'when everyone knows we oppose the policy' HMG's international standing and influence 'is destroyed for ever. If ever we stand' against the United States, he continued, 'this is the time, For all our friends agree with us on the merits'. Morrison then declared that, on balance, he agreed with Younger. While Attlee pushed for abstention, Younger argued that a vote for the resolution closed the door on further negotiations: 'How then can we justify not voting against' he asked.[37]

After debating this, the majority of the Cabinet came to the conclusion that Jebb should vote against the resolution. Abstention, for example, was a 'weak' course for a Great Power to take on a major issue. The Government believed that the resolution as a whole represented a 'mistaken approach' to the problem of Chinese intervention in Korea. HMG had already made it plain to the world that this was their view; and if, notwithstanding this, they now voted in favour of the United States resolution, it would be equally plain that they had voted against their convictions, for the sole purpose of supporting the United States Government. Thereby they would forfeit their independence and their self-respect; and they would deprive themselves of any power to influence the United States Government on any future occasion. If, however, an adverse vote had to be given, no opportunity should be lost of explaining the basis of the Government's policy. If this were done effectively, there was no reason to believe that, after the wave of annoyance in the United States had spent itself, the enduring common interests of the two countries would not reassert themselves. Thus Younger was tasked, by the Cabinet, with arranging for Jebb to be so instructed.[38] This decision did not go down well with senior Foreign Office officials: Sir William Strang informed Younger: 'I was brought up on the League of Nations and have very little direct knowledge of the United Nations and its ways; but I am told that an abstention has come to be regarded as a proper method of expressing disapproval when you do not wish to be unnecessarily offensive, whereas to give an adverse vote is a very strong step to take. We do not really yet know for certain which other Delegations, if any, other than the Soviet bloc, are certain to vote against. Do we really want to risk a position in which we might be almost the only Power other than the Soviet bloc giving an adverse vote? Would it not meet our position if we instructed Sir G. Jebb to abstain? Would not abstention also translate more accurately our attitude to a resolution parts of which we accept and parts of which we do not?'[39]

The Americans, meanwhile, attempted to overcome British objections suggesting, on 26 January, that paragraph 8 might be amended to read as follows: 'The General Assembly. Requests a committee composed of the members of the Collective Measures Committee as a matter of urgency to consider additional measures to be employed to meet this aggression and to report thereon to the General Assembly, taking into account in its report the results of the efforts of the good offices committee provided for in the following paragraph.'[40] Jebb turned this down and instead submitted the following 'counterlanguage' which Franks also gave to the Americans: 'Sets up a committee composed of members of the CMC to consider, whenever the GA should find that the efforts made by the good offices committee referred to in the aforesaid Para have failed, additional measures to be employed to meet the situation resulting from the armed intervention in Korea by the CPG of the PRC.'[41] The British also presented revised language with regard to paragraph 2 as well. Rusk informed Franks it would be possible to revise paragraph 2, and the US Mission in New York would be instructed to work this out in New York with Jebb.[42]

But, on paragraph 8, both Franks and Jebb were informed by the Americans that their suggested language was 'completely unacceptable' as Washington felt strongly it had to stand on the principle that the CMC must at least began a study of 'further steps'. The Americans, though, indicated to the British that they would be willing to put 'some brake' on the time of the CMC reporting to the GA.[43] Rusk suggested an addition to paragraph 8 as follows: 'it being understood that the Committee is authorized to defer its report if the Good Offices Committee, referred to in the following paragraph, reports satisfactory progress in its efforts'. Rusk explained that this was a draft which had no official status and had not been seen by Acheson. Another State Department official, Hickerson, indicated, however, that if it would resolve the difficulty of the UK on the US resolution, he would recommend to Acheson the acceptance of such language. Franks promised to communicate the language to London in an effort to obtain its acceptance 'but said he must tell us frankly that his instinct was that he would not be successful'. During the course of the conversation, Franks explained that he wanted to give the Americans his personal views as to the fundamental causes of the British hesitation on this matter; what he was going to say might be oversimplified and the Americans should realise it was his own opinion. He cited three main points:

1. Mistrust of the command in Korea and over U.S. intentions, and, above all, of U.S. impulsiveness.
2. The influence of Nehru at the recent Commonwealth Prime Minister's meeting. He said he knew that in London, and he thought in other parts of the Commonwealth, all aspects of this question were now viewed in the light of what Nehru had said at the Commonwealth Conference.
3. Although admitting that it was nothing very solid, there was a feeling in London that the latest message from Peiping contained more hope than we seemed willing to credit it with.

It was of interest, to the Americans how, during the meeting, Franks did not seem overly impressed by the argument that a failure in the UN to act promptly and firmly might have any adverse effect, in view of the sensitive state of US public opinion, on the efforts now being made to strengthen NATO.[44] Truman later approved the new language on the condition that, by so doing, the UK could vote favourably on paragraph 8 or if it would mean that the French and other Western Europeans would vote for it rather than abstaining.[45]

The major issue between the Americans and the British, as Washington saw it, was whether or not the CMC should begin to study the question of consequences. Acheson was certain that the 'US cannot yield on this point'. If the UK could not accept this language it was probably better to proceed even though the British were forced to vote against the US resolution. The US Embassy in London was instructed, by Acheson, to inform the British that the language handed Franks was 'our irreducible minimum beyond which we cannot make further concessions'. One problem with the British approach was that it was almost impossible to determine when a conciliation effort 'has failed': an argument could always be advanced by those who wished to do so that 'there is still hope. Our approach along the line of "satisfactory progress" is more practical' concluded Acheson. A further general argument Ambassador Gifford was authorised to use in his discretion was that the Unites States would greatly regret to see an open split in the UN on the US resolution as this was exactly what the Soviets wanted. Furthermore 'we believe it important to avoid such [a] split because of probable repercussions on US efforts to strengthen the NATO countries in view of current sensitive state of US public opinion.' Gifford could express the hope that the British had given adequate consideration to these factors and add that 'for our part, we have made one concession after another' on the resolution but the point 'has been reached where we can concede no more'.[46]

Attlee reported the developments to the Cabinet and how, on paragraph 2, for a peaceful settlement, the United States Government were now understood to be ready to accept an amended wording referring merely to the 'disappointing' response of the Peking Government to the proposals. If this paragraph could be amended accordingly, it would be 'sufficiently close to our own view to enable us to vote in favour of it' declared the Prime Minister. As regarded paragraph 8, Attlee reported that an amended version had now been suggested by the Israeli delegation which reversed the order of paragraphs 8 and 9 of the United States resolution and had the effect of proposing, first, that a Peace Observation Commission should consider ways and means of achieving a peaceful settlement and, secondly, that if those efforts failed the Collective Measures Committee should then consider additional measures. This amendment 'also would go far towards meeting our point of view'. Acceptance in the last resort of the principle of imposing sanctions upon an aggressor was 'inherent in our membership of the United Nations, and this proposal deferred the consideration of sanctions until after a further effort had been made to reach a peaceful settlement' explained the Prime Minister. Sir Gladwyn Jebb had added that, although the Israeli proposal contemplated that the Peace Observation Commission should make this further effort, the task might equally well be entrusted to a Committee of Three proposed in the final paragraph of the United States resolution.[47] When it was put to Attlee that a split between east and west in the Commonwealth was even more dangerous than a split between the UK and the United States, the Prime Minister's reply was: 'Be realistic ... We ... Can't throw over *all* our friends for fear of Asian attitude.' It was quite unrealistic to suppose that all references to sanctions would be deleted. He urged his colleagues: 'Don't risk losing all by pressing for too much.' When Dalton remained opposed to supporting the American resolution, Attlee emphasised that support did not commit HMG to sanctions: 'I've already told Truman I won't support mil[itary]. Measures' [sic] and that economic measures were 'futile'.[48]

Attlee carried the day and the Cabinet agreed that, if paragraph 2 of the resolution were amended in the sense proposed, 'our representative could be instructed to support it.' Discussion then turned on the significance of the Israeli suggestion for amending paragraph 8 and 'whether we should support this if it proved acceptable to the United States Government'. Younger pointed out that, if the Cabinet approved the acceptance of the amendment, 'our first task must be to urge the United States Government to accept it'. The Committee of Three was a much more suitable body than the Peace Observation Commission to make the final endeavour to reach a peaceful settlement, since the latter included China. However the question of Chinese representation on the Commission would become an immediate stumbling block, for the United States could not fail to demand that China should be represented by the National Government. Younger wished to make it clear that, while he personally did not feel that the difference between abstaining and voting against the resolution would be of any great importance in relation to United States public opinion, his advisers were of the opposite opinion.

Attlee, summing up the discussion, concluded that the balance of opinion in the Cabinet seemed to be in favour of supporting the proposed amendments to paragraphs 2 and 8 of the resolution if it proved possible to secure their acceptance by the United States. If the amendments were proposed 'we should vote for them; and, if they were carried, we should vote for the resolution as a whole'. His colleagues would realise, however, that the situation was fluid, and that he might find it necessary to decide at short notice how Jebb should be instructed to vote on the resolution as a whole if amendments had been made in rather different terms from those now under discussion. In those circumstances he must be guided by the views expressed in the Cabinet's discussions at the present meeting and on the previous day. The Cabinet's earlier decision to vote against the resolution in its original form need not, Attlee thought, preclude the possibility of abstaining from voting if the resolution eventually emerged in a form different both from the original version and from the amended version which the Cabinet were now prepared to support. Thus the Cabinet decision was to invite Younger to instruct Jebb that if paragraph 2 were amended as now proposed and if paragraph 8 were amended on the lines suggested by the Israeli delegation, he should vote in favour of both these paragraphs as so amended, and also in favour of the resolution as a whole.[49]

Acheson, meanwhile, called Franks, by telephone, on 27 January shortly before 11 a.m. After thanking Sir Oliver for his efforts to help clarify the rather confused situation at the UN, Acheson explained that he had been talking with Rusk and Hickerson and others, and also with the President. He said, with regard to paragraph 8 of the US resolution, he was authorising the adding of further language at the end of it to the effect that the Collective Measures Committee was authorised to withhold its report if the other Committee was getting along well with its work. Acheson felt Washington could go no further than that. He also mentioned that Jebb's proposals were not acceptable to the Americans. Franks asked if there was anything the Americans wanted him to say personally to Attlee. Acheson suggested that a lot of 'special messages' should not fly back and forth between the President and the Prime Minister. Franks agreed with this. Acheson added that he had raised this whole matter with the President and the full Cabinet and that both were unanimous in their agreement on the resolution. Acheson thought the 'whole thing' too serious for him to be taking positions without complete Cabinet backing, which he now had. He had reached the 'end of his elasticity' and said that 'our position was not one taken by just a few people in the State Department but represented an entire government position'. Acheson also mentioned his appearances before the House and Senate Foreign Affairs Committees the preceding day and observed that these committees were in support of the position he had taken adding that some of the Committee members wanted to be more 'rambunctious' than the United States was being. Franks replied that he would do the best he could 'on this problem'.[50]

In London, Attlee realised the crunch point had now been reached and the US Embassy was informed that, although the Prime Minister had not cleared it with the Cabinet, he, personally, was in favour of accepting the revised paragraph 8 with the additional language on the understanding that the United States would not put obstacles in the way of those nations which felt that negotiations were still possible or useful.[51] At Cabinet, Younger told his colleagues of the further developments in Washington and New York: while the position on paragraph 2 was not yet entirely clear, it seemed likely that the United States Government would be willing to accept an amendment satisfactory to HMG. There had been further discussions about paragraph 8 and, while the idea of amending it on the lines proposed by the Israeli Delegation had been abandoned, the United States amendments represented 'a substantial concession to our point of view and that we should accept it if we could be assured that there was a genuine disposition on the part of the United States to allow an attempt to be made to bring negotiations about'. Instructions had therefore been sent to Jebb, with the Prime Minister's concurrence, authorising him to agree to this compromise, provided that the United States would give an assurance that they would not oppose proposals, on the lines of those put forward by the Canadian representative, for the consideration of a specific programme to achieve a negotiated settlement. The United States had subsequently expressed to Franks their general agreement with the principles of the Canadian proposals. They had also indicated that they were willing to discuss them with the Canadians and the British in order to put these forward in a mutually agreeable form, but they could not pledge their support in advance to any resolution which might be brought forward on the basis of the Canadian suggestions.

Attlee added that, if a compromise on these lines was agreed with the United States, 'we should have substantially achieved our two principal objectives', to keep the door open for negotiations with the Peking Government and to ensure that any decision on the imposition of sanctions was reached only after further negotiations had taken place. The Indian Government remained opposed to any mention of sanctions in the resolution, and had reiterated their view that such a mention would bar the way to any further negotiations with the Chinese; but the acceptance of the compromise would re-establish a common policy between the United States and the older members of the Commonwealth, and would also emphasise 'our acceptance of our obligations' as a member of the United Nations. The United States had, moreover, agreed to HMG making public reference to the American desire to reach a peaceful settlement of the Korean conflict, and he felt that a statement to that effect would do 'much to reassure public opinion in this country about American intentions'.[52] On 1 February the United States resolution on Korea was submitted to the First Committee of the United Nations Assembly in the form agreed and Jebb was able to vote in favour of it; the resolution was carried by 44 votes to 7. Eight States abstained from voting for it.[53]

## Notes

1 DBOP: Korea Younger to Bevin, 2 January 1951
2 TNA FO 800/517 Anglo-American Relations memorandum
3 TNA FO 800/517 Strachey to Bevin, 2 January 1951
4 TNA FO 800/517 Dixon minute, 6 January 1951
5 TNA FO 800/517 Strang minute, 8 January 1951
6 Geoffrey Warner, *In the Midst of Events: The Foreign Office Diaries and Papers of Kenneth Younger February 1950–October 1951* (London: Routledge, 2005), pp. 53–55
7 TNA PREM 8/1438 Acheson to Bevin, 8 January 1951
8 TNA PREM 8/1438 Prime Minister's Personal Telegram Serial No. T.9/51, 8 January 1951
9 TNA PREM 8/1438 Prime Minister's Personal Telegram Serial No. T10/51, 9 January 1951
10 FRUS 1951, Volume VII (Korea and China Part I). The British Embassy to the Department of State. Substance of a Telegram Now on the Way from

Mr Bevin to Sir Oliver Franks (Parts thereof telephoned by Mr Parrott at 11: 30 a.m., 10 January 1951)
11 TNA FO 800/517 Minute to Strang, 10 January 1951
12 TNA FO 800/517 Bevin to Attlee, 12 January 1951
13 DBOP No. 108 Mr Bevin to Sir … N Charles (Ankara), 12 January 1951
14 FRUS 1951, Volume VII (Korea and China Part I). The British Embassy to the Department of State Substance of a Telegram Now on the Way from Mr Bevin to Sir Oliver Franks (Parts thereof telephoned by Mr Parrott at 11: 30 a.m., 10 January 1951)
15 FRUS 1951, Volume VII (Korea and China Part I). The Ambassador in the United Kingdom (Gifford) to the Secretary of State, 11 January 1951
16 TNA PREM 8/1438 Bevin to Attlee, 12 January 1951
17 TNA PREM 8/1438 Prime Minister's Personal Telegram Serial No. T11/51, 13 January 1951
18 TNA DEFE 11/207 Chiefs of Staff from Lord Tedder, 12 January 1951
19 TNA DEFE 11/207 Chiefs of Staff Committee Confidential Annex to COS (51) 10th Meeting
20 TNA DEFE 11/207 JSM 782 Personal for Chiefs of Staff from Slessor, 16 January 1951
21 TNA DEFE 11/207 JSM 780 Personal for Chiefs of Staff from Slessor, 16 January 1951
22 TNA DEFE 11/207 JSM 780 Personal for Chiefs of Staff from Slessor, 16 January 1951
23 FRUS 1951, Volume VII (Korea and China Part I). The Ambassador in the United Kingdom (Gifford) to the Secretary of State, 18 January 1951
24 FRUS 1951, Volume VII (Korea and China Part I). Memorandum of Telephone Conversation, by Lucius D. Battle, Special Assistant to the Secretary of State, 18 January 1951
25 FRUS 1951, Volume VII (Korea and China Part I). The United States Representative at the United Nations (Austin) to the Secretary of State, 20 January 1951
26 TNA CAB 128/19 Cabinet Conclusions, 22 January 1951
27 TNA CAB 195/8 C.M. 5(51), 22 January 1951 C.M. 5(51), 22 January 1951
28 TNA CAB 128/19 Cabinet Conclusions, 22 January 1951
29 TNA CAB 195/8 C.M. 5(51), 22 January 1951 C.M. 5(51), 22 January 1951
30 TNA CAB 128/19 Cabinet Conclusions, 22 January 1951
31 TNA CAB 128/19 Cabinet Conclusions, 23 January 1951
32 FRUS 1951, Volume VII (Korea and China Part I). The Ambassador in the United Kingdom (Gifford) to the Secretary of State, 23 January 1951
33 FRUS 1951, Volume VII (Korea and China Part I). The Secretary of State to the Embassy in the United Kingdom, 24 January 1951
34 FRUS 1951, Volume VII (Korea and China Part I). The Secretary of State to the Embassy in the United Kingdom, 24 January 1951 (second telegram)

35 FRUS 1951, Volume VII (Korea and China Part I). Memorandum of Conversation, by the Assistant Secretary of State for Far Eastern Affairs (Rusk), 25 January 1951
36 TNA CAB 128/19, 25 January 1951, at 10 a.m.
37 TNA CAB 195/8 C.M. 8(51). 25 January 1951 [5 p.m.]
38 TNA CAB 128/19 Cabinet Conclusions, 25 January 1951, at 5 p.m.
39 DBOP: Korea No. 117 Minute from Strang to Younger, 25 January 1951
40 FRUS 1951, Volume VII (Korea and China Part I). Memorandum by the Director of the Office of British Commonwealth and Northern European Affairs (Raynor) to the Assistant Secretary of State for European Affairs (Perkins), 26 January 1951. Subject: Possible Modification of US Resolution in UN on Chinese Communist Aggression
41 FRUS 1951, Volume VII (Korea and China Part I). The Secretary of State to the Embassy in the United Kingdom, 27 January 1951
42 FRUS 1951, Volume VII (Korea and China Part I) Memorandum of Conversation, by the Director of the Office of British Commonwealth and Northern European Affairs (Raynor), 26 January 1951. Subject: Korean–U.N. Problem
43 FRUS 1951, Volume VII (Korea and China Part I). The Secretary of State to the Embassy in the United Kingdom, 27 January 1951
44 FRUS 1951, Volume VII (Korea and China Part I). Memorandum of Conversation, by the Director of the Office of British Commonwealth and Northern European Affairs (Raynor), 26 January 1951. Subject: Korean–U.N. Problem
45 FRUS 1951, Volume VII (Korea and China Part I). The Secretary of State to the Embassy in the United Kingdom, 27 January 1951
46 FRUS 1951, Volume VII (Korea and China Part I). The Secretary of State to the Embassy in the United Kingdom, 27 January 1951
47 TNA CAB 128/19 Cabinet Conclusions, 26 January 1951
48 TNA CAB 195/8 C.M. 9(51), 26 January 1951
49 TNA CAB 128/19 Cabinet Conclusions, 26 January 1951
50 FRUS 1951, Volume VII (Korea and China Part I). Memorandum of Telephone Conversation, by Lucius D. Battle, Special Assistant to the Secretary of State, 29 January 1951
51 FRUS 1951, Volume VII (Korea and China Part I). The Ambassador in the United Kingdom (Gifford) to the Secretary of State, 28 January 1951
52 TNA CAB 128/19 Cabinet Conclusions, 29 January 1951
53 TNA CAB 128/19 Cabinet Conclusions, 1 February 1951

# 6

# MacArthur goes

On 28 January, MacArthur was reported to have stated: 'This is exactly where I came in two months ago to start this crusade. The stake we fight for now, however, is more than Korea – it is a free Asia.'[1] The implication was that his 'crusade' extended beyond Korea. The Cabinet discussed the statement, the 'latest of a series of unauthorised statements by the United Nations Commander-in-Chief, which gravely embarrassed the Governments which had contributed to the United Nations forces in Korea.' Moreover, a statement of this kind was 'bound to exert a most unfavourable influence on the public reception of the Government's policy toward the United States resolution. Could we not publicly dissociate ourselves from this view and take steps both to repudiate it and to prevent further statements of this kind?' was a question being asked in Cabinet. After discussion the Cabinet agreed that, if the report of MacArthur's statement was confirmed, Jebb should be instructed, at his discretion and subject to his appreciation of the state of American public opinion, to refer publicly to it in the United Nations, making it clear that it had been made without the knowledge or approval of the United Kingdom Government.[2]

It was a few days later when Sir Oliver Franks was, personally, able to draw the State Department's attention to MacArthur's alleged statement – and found the Americans had received an almost identical version. Franks reported to London how: 'They agreed that this particular statement was ill-judged and that it would have been far better if the General had confined himself to purely military matters. Unfortunately he is a man who frequently allows himself an adornment of language which leads him outside the bounds of his subject. They added that whilst his remarks were to be regretted it was unfortunately the fact that words cannot be recalled.'

In fact the State Department was keen to assure London that MacArthur's 'careless expression does not represent in the slightest degree any shift or change in the policy of the United States Government'.[3]

British unease over McArthur's statement was not helped when press reports claimed that some South Korean forces had already proceeded beyond the 38th parallel. Younger, in the absence of Bevin, 'strongly recommended' to the Cabinet that United Nations forces should not seek to advance beyond the 38th parallel. This view had already been expressed informally to the political and military authorities in Washington, and reassuring replies had been received. Younger now recommended, however, that the United States Government should be asked formally to confirm that the United Nations forces would not advance beyond the 38th parallel without a fresh political decision, and that this would be a matter, not for the United States Government alone, but for the United Nations and, in particular, those member States who had contributed to the United Nations forces in Korea. Finally, he recommended that, if the United Nations Forces established a line south of the 38th parallel, even minor penetrations and assaults beyond it should, if possible, be avoided. The First Sea Lord, attending the Cabinet on behalf of the Chiefs of Staff, reported that he had no official information about these reported movements by South Korean forces. He pointed out that any restriction against proceeding north of the 38th parallel could not, however, be absolute. If the United Nations forces established a line on the basis of the 38th parallel, there would probably be some points at which the line must go slightly beyond it by reason of the nature of the terrain. Equally, the United Nations Commander must have some discretion to press tactical counterattacks beyond the 38th parallel. And he must be free to launch air attacks on enemy troop concentrations and lines of communication to the north of the parallel. Nevertheless, the Cabinet agreed that the United States should be asked formally to confirm that United Nations Forces in Korea would not advance beyond the 38th parallel without a fresh political decision taken, not by the United States Government alone, but by the United Nations.[4]

Washington was, though, anxious to reassure London and Acheson, in particular, cabled Bevin that he 'agreed wholeheartedly that there should be full consultation amongst the powers principally concerned on this 38th parallel question and endorsed your suggestion that United Nations forces should again only cross that line after careful consideration and full consultation.'[5] This news, though good, only made the question of what to do next more urgent. The Joint Planning Committee of the Chiefs of Staff Committee was tasked by the Foreign Office to answer certain questions regarding British policy in Korea. The questions could be summarised as follows:

(a) Is it desirable from the military point of view to hold some position in Korea?
(b) Is it militarily possible to do so?
(c) What is militarily the best line to hold?
(d) Is it militarily advisable for United Nations forces to recross the 38th parallel?
(e) What arrangements should be made for a cease fire in the event of China agreeing to accept one?

In order to examine these questions the Planning Committee felt it was necessary, firstly, to define the British – and, therefore, the UN – object in Korea:

1. The overall object with which United Nations forces went into Korea was to demonstrate that the United Nations cannot be flouted with impunity and that aggression does not pay.
   Within this overall object our immediate object in Korea now is to achieve such a position of military strength as to allow political negotiations for a free and unified Korea to proceed.
2. It is against this background that we examine the question put by the Foreign Office.

In deciding future action the Planning Committee took due note of a Chinese policy statement to the effect that they would not negotiate if branded as aggressors. They had now been so branded and the Planning Committee therefore felt that, more than ever, they would only negotiate if faced with a 'really unfavourable' military position. It was clear that neither 'our immediate nor our overall object in Korea can be achieved unless we can hold some position in Korea'. However, the Committee concluded that the final view on this question could only be given by the operational commander on the spot – which meant MacArthur; nevertheless, it was also true that the Chiefs of Staff had always stated that they saw no military reason why a position covering a substantial area of Korea should not be held and recent events had merely reinforced this view since:

(a) The morale of the American forces has now improved.
(b) The Chinese are showing signs that the weight of the Allied air attack against their extended lines of communication is beginning

to make itself felt. Their supply difficulties may be aggravated as the rivers unfreeze.

(c) The Chinese are reported to be suffering a high rate of wastage from sickness and frostbite.

The Best Line to Hold

Militarily the choice resolves itself into one between :-

(a) Holding a bridgehead in Southern Korea.
(b) Advancing to and holding the northern frontier along the Yalu river.
(c) A position on the northern "waist" of Korea, north of Pyongyang.
(d) A position on the southern "waist" of Korea covering Seoul and Inchon.

If the whole of Korea were occupied the Planning Committee concluded that the United Nations resources would be stretched on internal security and rehabilitation tasks and it was inconceivable that the Northern frontier could be manned in sufficient numbers to halt a surprise Chinese attack. The UN should, moreover, be at a great disadvantage in being unable to attack the enemy airfields and lines of communications: 'There is no doubt in our minds, in view of the above, that the southern "waist" is the sounder military position. Indeed the dividing line between where we can hold a solid line and where our ability to do so would be in doubt may well lie between these two positions.' Since the Southern waist covered a sufficient area 'to enable us to achieve our object we would therefore be opposed to any advance north of this position.'[6]

This was what the Foreign Office wanted to hear for, as Sir William Slim explained to Robert Scott, he feared that the crossing of the 38th parallel would mean that 'our chances of negotiation with the Chinese would be seriously prejudiced, and it might also result in disasters similar to those which followed the first crossing of the Parallel'. The most suitable place for the cease-fire line, he thought, might well be the 38th parallel itself. Scott agreed wholeheartedly when told this, although Slessor thought it unrealistic to use the 38th parallel as the actual cease-fire line since it was, in fact, no more than a line on the map and bore no relation to the military situation on the ground. He suggested – and the Chiefs of Staff ultimately agreed – that the cease-fire line should be based on the Southern 'Waist' as suggested by the Planning Committee. A major crossing of the 38th parallel would be unnecessary in order to hold this line, although there might be some penetration north of the parallel for a short distance when the exact tactical trace of the line had been decided. For the same reasons some enemy forces might, in places, remain a short distance south of the line.⁷ The end result was that the Foreign Office and the Chiefs were agreed: no advance deep into North Korean territory.

As this was discussed in London there was a changing of the guard in Tokyo as Joe Gascoigne departed for diplomatic pastures anew. It was customary for a diplomat to meet with MacArthur before departure for a final chat. On 4th February, Gascoigne called on MacArthur to bid him farewell after an 'association with him of four and a half years'. He was accompanied by his Diplomatic Counsellor, George Clutton, whom Gascoigne wished to present to the Supreme Commander 'before he assumed charge of this mission on my departure on 7th February'. On this occasion the General repeated once again that the campaign in Korea was a mission in a vacuum.

Following their audience with MacArthur, Gascogine asked Clutton for his impressions of the man, 'who, for so long, has been the outstanding figure in Japan and the Western Pacific'. Although Clutton had followed the Supreme Commander's activities closely since his arrival in Japan, the previous May, and although he had frequently seen him from distance, this was the first time that he had met him face-to-face. In the first place, the 'tremendous force' of the General's personality struck Clutton in the same way as it had done so many others. He felt that here, beyond question, was a great man who still had greatness in him. The General's charm, 'though patently turned off and on like a tap and, in some respects (for instance, the hand-clasp) grating, was difficult to resist, and his plausibility and persuasiveness in stating his case was so great as, at times, to make his argument well-nigh convincing'. Physically, the General appeared a much slighter and frailer figure than he seemed in his photographs, on the parade-ground or driving through the streets of Tokyo. But Clutton was also struck by the General's physical vigour, his youthful appearance, and the clearness and brightness of the eyes in a face, comparatively, little lined. At the same time, Clutton told Gascogine that he had a feeling of meeting someone slightly unreal and that, within the surprisingly youthful body, 'there was a mind no longer as young as the body and which was beginning to indulge in those searchings of conscience and the memory that occupy the old during the wakeful periods of the night'. While the General's argument was lucid enough, his refusal to allow Gascogine 'to get a word in edgeways, his insistence on remaining in his chair and continuing to talk despite the fact that I had four times risen to my feet to take my leave and his use in argument of facts and figures which he must have realised we knew to be untruthful or exaggerated, all seemed to Mr. Clutton essentially the habits of an old man'. Again, throughout the interview, the General was on the defensive, explaining his actions and rebutting his critics; but here Clutton felt that he was not defending his actions in the context of the political and military situation of the day so much as defending his place in history, which was the only thing that now mattered to him. In his final despatch to the Foreign Office, Gascoigne reflected:

> As I am leaving Japan tomorrow on transfer to another post, I feel that it is appropriate for me to add an expression of my own feelings towards this remarkable American General – despite the numerous occasions upon which I have had cause to report to you about him.
>
> During the period of my mission in this country, my personal relations with MacArthur have been, overtly, of the best, even if at times our official views were diametrically opposed. I have, all along, had to work with a dictator whose every word was law, even in Washington. The possibility therefore of our carrying out any useful work at all in connection with the occupation of Japan depended upon the maintenance of good relations with MacArthur himself, for his numerous satellite generals and officers most completely reflected his likes and dislikes upon all with whom they had to work. Since the beginning of the Korean war, and more emphatically of course since the disasters which befell us in Korea in late November and December 1950, the General has, indirectly, shown bitter resentment towards our China policy; furthermore, the attacks which have been made against him in certain organs of the United Kingdom press have wounded him deeply, for, after the manner of all dictators, he is supersensitive to public criticism. At the present time it would seem, as seen from here, that MacArthur may be losing some of his influence in Washington, although, as a 'political' General, he will always, presumably, be in a position to make mischief through his Republican friends.
>
> Despite the fact that MacArthur, in his personal and official relations, has of late treated me in a fashion which is not becoming to the attitude which should be adopted by him towards the representative of a great power (during my last interview he was careful not to make any reference at all, although I gave him an opening to do so, to the sustained co-operation and endless patience which H.M.G. have shown, through me, with his work in Japan), I cannot but feel deep respect for this man who has, it must be remembered, performed valuable work for the Allies both in war and, generally, in his administration of Japan during the period of occupation. That he has made serious mistakes both in Japan itself, in his recent conduct of the Korean war, and in his attitude towards Chiang Kai-shek, there can be no doubt; and this is due in great measure, I believe, to his jealous nature and his over-weening

conceit and confidence in his own judgment. Nevertheless, when the dust settles upon this Far Eastern scene, it will, I believe, become clear that, in the main, his successes outweigh his failures, and one thing is, I am sure, completely clear, namely that he recognizes the overriding necessity for Anglo-United States co-operation despite the fact that by many of his actions he has tended to bring about the uneasiness in our relations in this part of Asia.[8]

The last word, however, would be, as one would expect, MacArthur's. A few days later, from Hong Kong, Gascoigne wrote to Sir William Strang, in the Foreign Office, to tell him: 'I think that you ought to know that your criticism of MacArthur has been taken to heart.' About a fortnight previously Strang had cabled Washington, instructing Franks to approach the State Department officially, to complain about the 'd— silly statement which the Supremo had made to the effect that the United Nations troops in Korea were fighting for the "freedom of Asia".' During Gascoigne's final meeting to bid MacArthur his final farewell the General had discussed the situation with the Ambassador as usual, 'but froze up completely when I had made my last little friendly utterances. I naturally wished to part with him on amicable terms, but he refused to reciprocate in any way!' Gascoigne remarked:

> That was the first gun. He fired his second gun by, undoubtedly, letting it be known that no Americans were to see me off at the airport – a custom which is rigorously followed in Tokyo even if one is only going away on leave.
>
> The latter incident, which will have been noted by all my foreign colleagues who were at Haneda to see me off, was a serious one – it was a direct hit at H.M.G. & it goes far to show the *small mindedness* of this, admittedly, great man.
>
> It is immensely disappointing to me to think that, after all that you, in London, have done since 1946 to meet MacArthur half way, & to make my job easier by not thwarting this man, he should now repay us in this fashion. Of course, he is governed by his vanity, & your rebuke through the State Dept must have wounded him very deeply.[9]

The Foreign Office was 'somewhat disturbed by the reports appearing in the press of President Truman's statements at his press conference on 15th February about crossing the 38th parallel and the powers of the United Nations Commander in this connexion.' The President did not rule out an advance beyond the parallel. As reported in the *The Times* it appeared to

Bevin that 'President Truman's statements seem to be at variance with the earlier indications given by Dean Rusk that there should be full consultation amongst the powers principally concerned on the 38th parallel question'.[10] In Washington, Franks set about trying to find out if there had been a change in American policy. He found that there was a rigid rule that there should be no verbatim record of Presidents' remarks at press conferences. But he had been allowed a copy of Rusk's account of what was said. Truman had been advised to refrain from commenting on the 38th parallel question but after trying to remain silent he was 'tempted to enter the contest.' The offending comments concerned the limiting of MacArthur's freedom of action. Rusk reassured Franks that this remained the chief consideration in the administration's mind at present. But, at the press conference, the President had added that, with the military position being what it was, it would be impossible for United States authorities to say anything which would effect the creation of a safe haven for the enemy north of the parallel. This could be interpreted as leaving open the possibility of a US advance beyond it once more. Following this clarification, Rusk hoped that Bevin would not 'freeze your view on this question publicly' as this would tend to give the Chinese an assurance of a sanctuary. Furthermore it would cause critics of the administration to challenge the position, with the result that some 'thawing statement' would have to be made in order to keep the Chinese guessing.[11]

Shortly afterwards Herbert Morrison succeeded Ernest Bevin, as Foreign Secretary, following the latter's resignation on 9 March, due to illness; Bevin finally succumbed and died on 14 April. His successor had to deal with the continuing fall-out of MacArthur's mischief making. On 15 March, the General made a public statement on the 38th parallel issue in a telegraphic interview with Hugh Baillie, President of the United Press. In response to a question on how many troops would be needed to hold the 38th parallel inviolate, the General responded that 'the conditions under which we are conducting military operations in Korea do not favour engaging in positional warfare on any line across the peninsula'. The terrain was such that to establish a conventional defence system in reasonable depth would require such a sizeable force that 'if we had it, and could logistically maintain it, we would be able to drive the Chinese Communists back across the Yalu, hold that river as our future main line of defense, and proceed to the accomplishment of our mission in the unification of Korea'. The problem involved required 'much more fundamental decisions than are within my authority or responsibility to make as the military commander-decisions which must not ignore the heavy cost in Allied blood which a protracted and decisive campaign would entail.'[12]

In London, Morrison informed the Cabinet, on 22 March, that he had been reviewing the current situation in Korea. Unless some fresh political initiative were taken, there seemed to be some risk that McArthur might again advance north of the 38th parallel and seek to justify that course on military grounds. The Cabinet invited Morrison to 'take whatever steps were necessary' to ensure that the United States was 'not left in any doubt' about the strength of the views held by British Government against allowing United Nations forces in Korea to advance north of the 38th parallel.[13] As if on cue, on the morning of 24 March, McArthur left Tokyo for one his fleeting visits to the Korean battle front – but before his departure he issued a statement on the military situation in Korea, once again unauthorised by his superiors. In the statement, MacArthur declared that he was impressed by the 'clear revelation that this new enemy, Red China, of such exaggerated and vaunted military power, lacks the industrial capacity to provide adequately many critical items essential to the conduct of modern war'. MacArthur then announced he stood ready, at any time, to confer in the field with the Commander-in-Chief of the enemy forces.[14]

To many, MacArthur's emphasis on Chinese weakness suggested he was attempting to create a momentum for an extension of the war into China. In New York, Sir Gladwin Jebb was aghast at the General's latest proclamation, cabling London: 'I am not quite sure what has been happening in Washington, but I take it that MacArthur's latest pronouncement was not in fact an agreed statement and does not therefore reflect the collective view of the nations with troops in Korea? In the absence of any statement to the contrary we must however assume (with the Chinese) that it reflects the views of the United States administration, or at any rate of the President under whom MacArthur operates.' On this assumption Jebb's comments were as follows:-

(a) The thesis that, although the Peking Government lacks manufacturing bases for successful ground operations, the only way to produce their military collapse is to attack such bases seems to be a contradiction in terms.
(b) If MacArthur thinks that in spite of his optimistic estimate of the result of so doing, the General Assembly is going to authorise him to extend the war beyond the confines of Korea, he must be only conscious of public opinion in the Philippines, some of the banana states, and the lunatic fringe of the Republican Party.
(c) The suggestion, if such it be, that he should now conclude, not apparently an armistice but a sort of military treaty with the 'enemy Commander-in Chief' in order to 'realise the United Nations

objectives in Korea', whatever he may deem them to be, is hardly likely in itself to appeal to a majority of members of the United Nations, nor is it evident what authority the General has for doing anything of the kind.

(d) Apparent suggestion that some agreement on Korea could be negotiated with the Government of Peking without any consideration being given to the problems of Formosa or Chinese representation in the United Nations is directly contrary to the 'principles' of the United Nations for which the United States voted.

Generally speaking, unless the evidence was that the Chinese were 'folding up' and engaged in evacuating Korea, Jebb concluded that the only effect of the declaration would probably be to reduce the possibility of an agreed solution to a vanishing point and increase the dangers of all-out war with China along with the risk of Soviet participation. Unless repudiated, Jebb concluded the declaration also effectively precluded any agreed statement of objectives such as that recently proposed by Rusk. As against this, Jebb admitted that there was no evidence whatever that Peking was prepared to arrive at any solution of the Korean question acceptable to the United Nations.[15]

In Korea itself, Adams, the British Representative, therefore had, on 26 March, a conversation with Ambassador Gieben, the Netherlands delegate on the United Nations Commission based in the country, during the course of which the Dutchman described an interview he recently had with MacArthur in Tokyo. Gieben said that at a previous meeting he was treated by the General to a 45-minute monologue, but that on this occasion he was given opportunity to express his own views which were received with interest even when quite out of line with MacArthur's opinions. Gieben gained the impression that the General 'anticipates little likelihood of being able to bring the campaign to a satisfactory conclusion unless enemy bases in China are bombed, and that he is critical of British attitude to the Chinese in their relations to the Korean war'.[16]

This, it seemed to the Foreign Secretary, made a new approach to the Korean issue all the more pressing. Morrison, in a message to Franks, asked the Ambassador to approach the State Department with the possibility of a fresh initiative on a negotiated settlement in Korea. A separate approach might be made to the Soviet Government and would be on somewhat different lines from an approach to Peking. MacArthur's latest statement was an additional reason for considering some entirely new procedure as it was now unlikely that any further statement by the Unified Command alone would be taken seriously by the Chinese.[17] Morrison, at this stage, was still inclined to give MacArthur the benefit of the doubt and considered 'in fairness' to the General and to the United Nations 'something more specific (not for publication) is called for in order to allay uncertainty and to stop his periodical and dangerous incursions into the political field. If we can take his public statements at face value, MacArthur himself would welcome a clear directive from the President, and it may be that some of his public utterances have been prompted by a desire to draw precisely this'. The inference from some of his statements, Morrison thought, was that 'the United States Administration are to blame for not giving him clear guidance on military objectives in the light of Chinese intervention'. The need for clarity was reinforced by a report which reached Morrison that the US 7th Fleet was going to cruise off the Chinese coast near Formosa for about a fortnight from 7 April. 'This coat trailing' was in his view not militarily necessary to the prosecution of the Korean campaign, 'but may have a most harmful effect on the possibility of a negotiated settlement with China.'

Though Morrison understood that the object of the cruise was not to land forces on the coast of China, 'it is a clear hint that the conflict may be extended beyond Korea' which was emphatically against the policy of His Majesty's Government. Moreover, it might result in incidents, with unforeseen consequences for which the United States Government would have to shoulder the responsibility. Morrison instructed Franks to suggest to Acheson that the President, as Chief Executive of the Unified Command, should give an explicit directive to MacArthur. As one of the member states of the United Nations supporting action in Korea, 'His Majesty's Government consider themselves entitled to make proposals regarding the political directives issued to the Commander of the Forces on the spot.' Morrison left the manner of the approach to Frank's discretion. As regarded the reported naval operations off the China coast, 'you should ask State Department whether they can confirm the report and, if confirmed, leave them in no doubt whatsoever of the serious view taken of the project by His Majesty's Government and the grave responsibility that will fall on the United States Government for the consequences'.[18] On 5 April, Franks went to Rusk's office and showed the Assistant Secretary of State Morrison's telegram from London which he said reflected the 'MacArthuritis' in London.[19]

While Franks approached the State Department, Lord Tedder, also on 5 April, raised with Bradley the question of the need for a clear directive to MacArthur as to what action he was authorised to take if attacked by Chinese air forces. The Americans were concerned at the build-up of Chinese air forces, maintenance and preparation of airfields coupled with the vulnerability to air attack of all U.N.O. forces in Korea. Tedder reported to the British Chiefs that Marshall felt strongly that 'we ought now (repeat) now to have ready clear instructions to MacArthur as to what he may or may not do in such circumstances'. Tedder reassured the Chiefs that press reports in Washington claiming that MacArthur already had authority from the Joint Chiefs to attack Chinese air bases were 'quite unfounded'. Bradley wanted the British and Americans to agree together as to what action was to be permitted. Bradley's own feeling, supported by Admiral Sherman and, Tedder believed agreed by Marshall, was that in the event of Chinese air attack MacArthur should be authorised to attack Chinese air bases in Manchuria. Such action would be confined strictly to air bases.[20]

But, to the Chiefs of Staff, in London, all this appeared part of a carefully constructed attempt, by the Supreme Commander to extend the conflict beyond Korea. Slim felt that MacArthur was attempting to involve the United Nations in a 'real war' against China. MacArthur was 'exaggerating' the admittedly large Chinese build-up which might or might not be intended for an offensive. Slim just did not believe there was much likelihood of a 'massive' air attack, although the Chinese would probably make some attempt in the air if they staged an offensive, 'as they certainly would if we were to go up into North Korea'. What worried Slim was that such an air attack by a small number of bombers 'might have a startling effect on the completely unprepared Allied army'; but it ought to be promptly, effectively, and finally dealt with by the large American air forces. If 'we were to keep on or about the 38th parallel', that would be near the useful limit of M.I.G.s from Manchuria, and Chinese bombers would have 'no hope' without heavy escort. Slim believed that, with his bomber force, MacArthur should be able to deny all airfields in North Korea to the enemy 'if he started to do so now'. The Chief of the General Staff considered that 'we should be very careful not to give General MacArthur a "blank cheque" which enabled him to carry out unrestricted retaliation in China or Manchuria without specific authority from Washington'.[21]

In a message to Franks, the British Chiefs noted that while the Americans were talking in terms of 'massive' air attacks by the enemy: 'We have no evidence that the enemy is capable of anything like "massive" air action, though no doubt it is possible that some Russians might participate under Chinese markings.' The Chiefs' estimated total of operational aircraft in the general area and in adjoining North Korea, including Russian, Chinese and North Korean was about 300 fighters and ground attack aircraft. This was less than the American estimate 'but ours have been consistently more accurate in the event'. The Americans estimated about 150 TU–2 bombers in the same area. 'We put it at about 50 probably on training.'

In the Chiefs' view 'massive' enemy air action was only possible if the Russian Air Force intervened openly, 'which we think it would do only if MacArthur is allowed to take the sort of action against objectives in Manchuria and China proper which it is obvious he is still itching to do but to which we remain resolutely opposed'. In this connection 'we fear history is repeating itself and that MacArthur and [his intelligence chief] Willoughby are hard at work doing what they did in November and December, namely, building up a legend of vast but entirely mythical hordes of Chinese to justify extending operations in China or to explain away any reverses that U.N. forces may suffer in a future enemy offensive'. But the main consideration in 'our minds has always been that militarily the U.N. forces in Korea have far more to gain than they can possibly lose by avoiding any action which would bring upon them the air onslaught' which Rusk had also suggested to Franks. 'We have had a straight tip that to extend bombing to Manchuria would mean the intervention of the Russian air force. The result would be not only that Ridgway would lose the complete air superiority he now enjoys in the battle area, but also his communications – which with their ports and shipping are more vulnerable than those of the Chinese in Manchuria – would also be liable to attack.' However, if the Chinese, with or without Russian assistance, became a menace by bombing from bases across the frontier, 'we do not consider that we could sit back and allow them to do so with impunity. We consider that a few light raids from across the frontier should not immediately be followed by counter-attacks on their airfields of departure, because we think it more than likely that the enemy bombers would suffer so severely at the hands of American fighters as to discourage further attempts without running the risks involved in spreading the war to Manchuria'. But if enemy air intervention became 'really serious' on the lines that Rusk envisaged 'we think we should have no reasonable alternative to counter-attack, though we think it should be confined to the enemy air-bases. We doubt whether that in itself would mean open intervention by Russia ... we agree that it would be a good thing to have ready a carefully prepared announcement to be issued in the appropriate manner if and when the necessity arose, to the effect that, while most anxious to localize hostilities, we can not accept without appropriate action the extension of the area of conflict that would be represented by strong enemy air attacks from bases outside Korea. We agree that such a warning must come from Washington and not be left to MacArthur.' In general, the Chiefs thought that in any politico-military discussion on Korea, Franks and Tedder should take a strong line in the following sense:

> We are increasingly disturbed at the apparent inability of Washington to exercise any control over MacArthur. No one suggests that the detailed conduct of a campaign can be exercised from 7000 miles away. But that is quite different from continuing to allow a local commander freedom to intervene politically and publicly in matters of major strategic policy, in a sense contrary to the declared policy not only of the U.S. Government but also of other Governments intimately concerned, to avoid the extension of hostilities beyond Korea. We strongly suspect that MacArthur is doing his utmost to force us into war with China … We think it of great importance that MacArthur should at once be given … orders that he is not (R[repeat]) not to undertake any operations outside Korea, including counter-attacks on enemy airfields, without specific authority from Washington. We should expect to be consulted and our agreement obtained before that authority is granted.

Such was the concern that the Chiefs now regarded the MacArthur issue that while they had consulted Foreign Office at the official level there had not been time to refer the message to Ministers – quite an extraordinary step.[22]

But unknown to the British the curtain was about to come down on MacArthur's military career. The final straw, for President Truman, came on 5 April, when Congressman Joseph W. Martin, Jr., of Massachusetts, the Republican minority leader in the House of Representatives, read the contents of a letter, dated 20 March, which he had received from MacArthur. MacArthur claimed that his views and recommendations, with respect to the situation, created by 'Red China's entry into war against us in Korea have been submitted to Washington in most complete detail'. Generally, these views were well known and clearly understood, as they followed the conventional pattern of meeting force with maximum counterforce, 'as we have never failed to do in the past'. He commended Martin's view that the utilisation of the Chinese forces on Formosa against the Communists was 'in conflict with neither logic nor this tradition'. MacArthur found it 'strangely difficult for some to realize that here in Asia is where the Communist conspirators have elected to make their play for global conquest and that we have joined the issue thus raised on the battlefield; that here we fight Europe's war with arms' while the diplomats there 'still fight it with words; that if we lose the war to communism in Asia the fall of Europe is inevitable, win it and Europe most probably would avoid war and yet preserve freedom. As you pointed out, we must win. There is no substitute for victory'.²³

The day after McArthur's letter was revealed, Franks and Tedder met with Bradley, Admiral Sherman and Paul Nitze (Director of Policy Planning at the State Department), to discuss the retaliatory action to be taken against a Chinese air attack on UN forces in Korea. Bradley then read the directive which he proposed to clear with the Secretary of Defense, the Secretary of State and the President, with the view to obtaining their authorisation to issue, upon a determination by the JCS, that the situation contemplated by the directive had in fact arisen.²⁴ In it the Joint Chiefs recommended to General Marshall that he obtain Presidential approval for them to send the following message to MacArthur if and when the enemy launched, from outside Korea, a major air attack against UN forces in the Korean area: 'You are authorized with the U.S. forces assigned to the Far East Command to attack enemy air bases and aircraft in Manchuria and the Shantung peninsula ...'²⁵ Franks had 'certain preliminary' comments. He felt there were far-reaching political implications to the decision involved, and that his government would feel that this was a decision which would have to be taken by the responsible Ministers. His Majesty's Government felt that if the 'state of facts' occurred it would be desirable to give a preliminary warning, the warning to be endorsed by as many of the U.N. governments as possible.²⁶

Naturally, the JCS proposals rang alarm bells among their British counterparts, for this appeared to give MacArthur even greater latitude, even encouragement, to attack Chinese territory, with the consequent implications for world peace. For Slim this was the final proof that MacArthur, personally, wanted war with China; his own statements amply bore this out. Furthermore, as had been 'proved' in November and December 1950, he had few scruples about colouring both intelligence and operational reports to suit his own ends. It was, therefore, highly dangerous to base any decision solely on information derived from this source. On the other hand, at least so far as operational reports, were concerned, Slim was concerned the British had no other proper source on which to rely. The inference, to Slim, from this was that Korea should be removed from MacArthur's sphere of command, 'and that quickly.' In the present circumstances Slim thought it would be 'most inadvisable' to delegate to the Joint Chiefs of Staff responsibility for deciding what constituted a 'massive air attack': 'They were scared of General MacArthur: his definition of the scope of air attack would be what they would work on, and this definition might well be coloured to suit his own wishes.'²⁷

Franks was despatched to the State Department, on 6 April, to see

Dean Rusk who made a number of comments on MacArthur. The first was that whatever statements from different sources might appear in the press MacArthur had in fact got directives and that these directives were very much on the general lines of Morrison's own suggestions. Rusk said, informally, that he understood how the impression formed in London by the report of the projected cruise of the United States 7th Fleet off the China coast, might easily arise. Nevertheless, it was a mistaken impression. So long as the 7th Fleet had the duties entrusted to it in relation to Formosa by the President, it was necessary that they should engage in reconnaissance from time to time in order to carry out these duties properly. The purpose of the projected cruise was reconnaissance. Despite this reassurance Franks left Rusk in no doubt about the nature of the impression in British minds 'and I used the words "coat trailing"'.[28] Morrison discussed Franks' report with the Defence Committee; while HMG sympathised with the American position 'we do not rate the likelihood of such attacks as seriously as they do … Our principal difficulty, however, is General MacArthur. His policy is different from the policy of the United Nations. He seems to want a war with China. We do not' the Foreign Secretary declared to Franks. London's general comment on the proposal was that this was a decision which must be taken by Governments and could not be left to military authorities.[29]

Within the Foreign Office sympathy for MacArthur was articulated by Sir Pierson Dixon who pointed out that: 'Much as we may criticise General MacArthur, it must be admitted that there is an underlying ambiguity as to the political objectives governing the military conduct of the campaign in Korea and this ambiguity, I think, partly justifies the Supreme Commander's attitude though not his indiscretions.' The truth was 'we are in a jam' in Korea and perhaps inevitably, covered this up by not openly facing the ambiguity: 'The fact is that we can neither get out nor get on. We can only get out, that is liquidate the Korean affair honourably and without further fighting, if China negotiates. We can only get on, that is conquer and hold the whole of Korea up to the Yalu, if we attack Chinese bases, supply centres and communications in China.' That at any rate seemed to be MacArthur's thesis based no doubt on the experience of his last disastrous general offensive. 'We do not want to do this because war with China might bring in the Russians and develop into a general war' summarised Dixon. 'We are thus on the horns of a dilemma, which H.M.G. try to solve by harping on the possibility of negotiations (as a means of getting out), and MacArthur, with some support now from the administration, by harping on the need to attack China proper (as a means of getting on).' While insisting that the war must not be extended to China, 'we continue to insist that our objective is a free and independent Korea.

If the Chinese would negotiate with the same objective in view, well and good'. But it seemed highly unlikely to Dixon that the Chinese would agree to negotiate 'so long as we maintain that objective, because they know that we are stuck and on the horns of a dilemma'. If then the Chinese continued to refuse to negotiate, 'and we maintain our objective of a free and independent Korea, are we to go on and try to conquer and hold all Korea by force as the sole means of attaining our political objective? If it is decided to do so, General MacArthur will have some justification in saying that in order to attain the political objective he must attack China'. The real solution of the dilemma, it seemed to Dixon, was to 'modify our political objective. This would mean abandoning the concept of a free and independent Korea and accepting the concept of a divided Korea'.[30] Dixon had called it just right.

Then suddenly, on 10 April, Acheson asked Franks to send Attlee and Morrison an urgent personal message. 'He said that he fully realised that in doing so he risked overdrawing on any fund of goodwill he might have with you' Franks informed Morrison. 'He begs you so far as is possible to arrange that members of His Majesty's Government do not make comments or criticisms on General MacArthur during tomorrow, Wednesday'. Acheson referred particularly to three sentences in a draft statement the Foreign Secretary was about to make in the House of Commons – shown to the Americans in advance – and expressed 'his earnest hope that you would be willing to omit this critical reference to General MacArthur'. He went on to say that events would occur and become known on the following day (Thursday British time) and possibly late on Wednesday Washington time which Acheson believed would give full justification to his present request. He felt it of the greatest importance that during the next day, Wednesday, 'in view of this coming event', criticism of MacArthur should not emanate from Britain. Franks assured Acheson that he would find a way of sending this message which would ensure that it gave rise to no speculation in London. Franks told Morrison he had 'no doubt that some major announcement about the position of General MacArthur will be made known at the times suggested above and that in this very difficult situation Acheson is thinking of Anglo-American relationships in urging the importance of not allowing words said in London in any way to connect with or seem to influence the event he foresees'.[31] At 1 am, the following morning, Acheson rung Franks up at the request of the President to say 'that at 1 a.m. this morning (Wednesday Washington time) General MacArthur is relieved of all his commands'. The action had been moved forward because of a threatened leakage. Acheson remarked to Franks, on a purely personal basis, 'that the less said by all of us the better. Inevitably he had Britain especially in mind because of what has been written here [in the US press] recently and because the sensation in Washington will be considerable'. Within three minutes of the call Franks despatched the dramatic news to London.[32]

The news was, of course, political dynamite in the United States. Jebb happened to be dining in Los Angeles with Mr. and Mrs. Douglas Fairbanks, Jr., when Truman's announcement that he had dismissed General MacArthur came through on the radio: 'There was quite a distinguished company, including the American equivalent of the Astronomer Royal and the "Queen" of the American stage, Miss Ethel Barrymore. The general effect on them all was as if a bomb had exploded' reported Jebb to London; but after a few minutes the Americans dining with the Briton became 'very markedly divided on whether Truman was right or wrong. I had the general impression that the initial reaction was unfavourable to the President but that, after a pause for reflection, reason tended to prevail'.[33]

Franks was the main source for assessing American opinion in the immediate aftermath of MacArthur's decision. The Ambassador discovered that the President's decision had provoked a wave of emotional feeling which, 'although characteristic of this country, is evidently on a larger scale and of greater intensity than anything experienced in recent years' – the first dropping of the atomic bomb and the announcement of Russia's possession of it included. MacArthur 'occupies such a unique position in the American mind that his sudden supercession has affected everyone personally, and has aroused feelings of violent partisanship and idolatry'. Should the General decide to return immediately to Washington 'there is every possibility that this head of steam will explode into unbridled manifestations of mawkish public feeling, which will cause intense embarrassment to the administration and alarm amongst many of America's allies'. If, however, MacArthur's reported intention of travelling by sea and arriving in about three weeks time 'is fulfilled there is reason to believe, on the basis of past experience, that the storm will blow itself out sufficiently before he appears without doing any serious damage'.

There were, however, indications to Franks that the reported jubilation in France to the news had struck rather a sour note in the light of her contribution in Korea, and the restraint of the British press had by contrast been favourably noted by normally friendly commentators. 'We have not, on the other hand, come off scot-free. "Good old Harry", the alleged comment of a high Foreign Office official has been widely and unfavourably quoted.' In certain quarters well-disposed to the General his dismissal was being ascribed primarily to British pressure. So strong was this feeling in a state college in East Texas that its President cancelled the visit of a member of Frank's staff who was to address the students. The impression that 'we are the real niggers in the wood-pile' had also been fostered by the current reports in the press regarding British insistence on the inclusion of the Peking regime in the Japanese Treaty negotiations and that the Treaty should provide for the return of Formosa to China. Franks was confident, though, that the basic issue, namely the maintenance of the superiority of the civil over the military authority, put the President in a strong position, and was one which must appeal strongly to the American imagination.[34] Franks was absolutely right for, although the returning hero received adulation throughout America, MacArthur was holed below the waterline during the subsequent Washington hearings into the background of his dismissal. The Joint Chiefs testified that they supported the President in removing MacArthur and highlighted the latter's insubordination to his Commander-in-Chief. MacArthur was indeed, as he once said himself, about to become one of those old soldiers who faded away.

Lord Tedder and Sir Oliver Franks, meanwhile, met with Omar Bradley and Dean Rusk to try and reach US–UK agreement on the thorny issue of UN retaliatory bombing strikes. Tedder noted that even though there was close collaboration on intelligence matters between the British and Americans in Washington, he found that there was more difference between London's views and Washington's than he had previously thought existed. London doubted whether the Chinese had the capability of a new offensive in the near future.[35] Bradley, though, was concerned about the relatively small number of anti-aircraft units available to UN forces. In the whole of Korea, there were only two batteries of 90 mm guns though there were considerably more batteries of light AA including one British and one Turkish battery. With regard to the Communist air build-up, Bradley warned that in the last few days some 40 or 50 additional jet fighters had arrived in Antung bringing up the total of these aircraft on this field to between 80 and 100. He then gave the British the news that took them by surprise: the directive to retaliate with US forces in the event of a major attack had been approved by the Secretary of Defence, the Secretary of State and the President. This approved Directive was now locked in his safe. It must be realised, the General explained, that if the final decision to retaliate had to await an enemy attack, such a decision might be long delayed. General Marshall might be in Southern Pines and the President 'down the river' in the Presidential yacht, the *Williamsburg*. Bradley pointed out that as far as the United States were concerned it was accepted that the policy decision was a Governmental one and that decision had been approved by the US Government. It remained for the Joint

Chiefs of Staff to decide what was a 'major' attack. They would of course refer to the US Government if time permitted but had authority to act in an emergency. He then again stressed the importance of the time factor. To get 14 UN Governments – with forces in Korea – to agree to retaliatory action after an attack would impose an impossible delay. Furthermore, the Russians would know that such consultations were taking place. The United States would be quite prepared to seek political reaffirmation of the policy before retaliation if time were available and would doubtless consult the U.K. if the necessary authorities were immediately available. But Bradley asked that serious consideration should be given to the number of American planes which would be lost if a second attack were carried out before any retaliation took place: 'Our planes in Korea were wing tip to wing tip and immensely vulnerable as indeed were the Allied carriers.'

Bradley acknowledged that more airfields could be built in Korea or Japan but only at the expense of airfields being built in Europe and North Africa. The morale of UN forces in Korea could not but suffer if a week went by before any retaliation took place whilst consultations with all the nations concerned and possibly in the UN were taking place. He agreed that the decision to initiate retaliatory action was a political one. And on the American side, this political decision had already been taken. Indeed, the President, in discussing the matter, had said that he felt it was a decision that should have been taken some time ago. The Joint Chiefs were prepared to seek political reaffirmation of the decision if time permitted, and indeed, in consultation with the British if this did not cause undue delay, but the Joint Chiefs now had authority to act without any further consultation.

Rusk then added he fully recognised the gravity of this decision but what, he asked, would happen if action was delayed whilst Washington and London considered the matter, Washington saying 'yes' and London saying 'no'. In reply, Tedder explained that, on the UK side, there was undoubtedly concern that the initial reports of air action from bases outside Korea might prove to be exaggerated. It was his experience that the initial impression of a first air attack was often far more alarming than later proved to be the case. To this Rusk asked whether the decision to retaliate was to be based, in the British view, on the scale of the enemy attack or on its effect. Tedder pointed out that Admiral Sherman, in a previous discussion, had referred to a 'damaging attack'. Rusk, however, was inclined to feel that it was the decision to attack the U.N. forces from outside Korea 'rather than the effects of the attacks which should govern our reaction.' Bradley added that if the enemy were to break the present 'ground rules' it would be essential 'either for us to change our "ground rules" or to get out of Korea'. The United States recognised the political nature of the decision to retaliate. As he had said before, if time permitted the Joint Chiefs would wish to reaffirm this political decision perhaps in consultation with the UK and indeed the French. Was it the British view that all the fourteen nations with forces involved should also be consulted? Bradley pointed out that the Russians might realise that if the Communists broke the local 'ground rules' 'we would be forced to do the same. The Russians would then be faced with the choice of accepting our retaliatory action or starting a third World War in which latter event there was nothing we could do but accept the fact.' If the Russians participated in the air attack, 'World War III would have started'. UN troops would have to 'get out' but, to do this without heavy loss, 'it was essential to use our air at once and to the maximum extent'. Bradley wondered whether such a Russian air attack, for example on Japan, would still be regarded by the UK as resulting in a conflict which could be localised as far as HMG was concerned. In this connection, a Russian attack on Japan would certainly result in a full-scale war between Russia and the United States. Rusk added that the United States had been taking for granted the fact that the UK would also be involved in this eventuality in a full-scale war with Russia in view of the Allied nature of the occupation of Japan.

All Franks could do when faced with this argument was to say he was sure he would not be expected to give an immediate answer. Previous conversations had revealed a 'community of view' on 'some cases' in which certain action would precipitate general war.[36] Franks repeated that his government was interested in the application of the policy; but this carried real risks of an enlargement of the war, starting in the Far East. His government must look at it from the point of view of a country which would suffer most of the casualties in a full-scale war. They felt that they ought to be in on the decision. Speaking personally, Franks felt that if one looked at it from the British viewpoint, this looked right. He agreed that if one looked at it from the point of view of its effects in Korea it might be hard to say that it was right. If the UK had to go along with everything that followed from the decision, then HMG must be in on the decision. When Bradley commented that 'when we know that they have changed the ground rules we know they are prepared for general war', Franks answered that if such were to be their decision, it was vital that the 50 million people in the UK 'go in in good heart'[37] into World War III.

As Franks later communicated to London, the most disturbing part of the meeting was Bradley's statement that Truman's approval had already been obtained to the draft directive for retaliation. He therefore made further enquiries the following morning, 13 April, and found that the statements were correct: 'Actually General Marshall took the decision with the President while our first meeting was in progress. The reason given me for the hurry which I am sure is genuine is that it was necessary to put a stop to uncertainty about where responsibility lay as between Washington and Tokyo. It was felt that not taking a decision at that time was also a decision and too dangerous at that. The position now therefore is that Presidential approval has been obtained but the whole matter is not finalised pending the outcome of our discussions.'[38]

Morrison now pushed, once more, the opportunity for a political initiative at the UN. The Foreign Secretary believed that, in order to rally world opinion following MacArthur's removal, 'the present is the psychological moment for making a broad declaration re-affirming our objectives in Korea coupled with specific proposals for a settlement. There is the feeling everywhere that the political issues are being allowed to drift'. What was needed was a broad declaration of policy by all the governments contributing forces in Korea. Less than this, believed Morrison, 'will not satisfy the needs of this country and others'. The Foreign Secretary remained under strong pressure to make such a statement, in Parliament, but had refrained from doing so 'in the hope that agreement would be reached to a declaration in the names of all countries who are bearing the burden of the Korean conflict'.[39] Rusk, however, confirmed to Oliver Franks that the present State Department view was that no further immediate steps were necessary or desirable. In reply to a question as to whether this view had been reached on domestic or international grounds, Rusk said 'both'. Franks then asked Rusk whether the international considerations related to the repercussions of MacArthur's dismissal. Rusk acknowledged that this was in part the case. The Americans did not wish, by a new appeal at this stage, to give the impression that United States policy had changed. There were also the hard facts of the present military position in Korea. The one inference Franks drew from the foregoing was that whereas the dismissal of MacArthur might appear to the British as providing a good opportunity for a further attempt to reach a negotiated settlement the 'reaction here is very different'. Reflecting on this, to Morrison, the Ambassador thought that the United States administration, 'whose enemies will try to make the maximum political capital out of the MacArthur affair' would find it difficult to participate in anything that looked like an international appeal to Peking until the excitement had died down. Franks supposed that it might help if the representatives in Washington of the countries who supported Morrison's proposals would press the State Department 'but I do not think it would help much'.[40] There was, at least, some good news from the point of view of British influence, when reports filtered through from Tokyo concerning the manoeuvres of the 7th Fleet off the China Coast: Washington had issued instructions that greatly curtailed operations and removed all semblance of its being a demonstration of force.[41]

Franks had a short conversation with Rusk on 15 April regarding retaliatory air attacks. Rusk's remarks were made on a purely personal basis though after consultation with others on the American side. Rusk explained that he was, for the moment, unable to see means of reconciling two entirely valid and serious points of view. They were all taking this problem most earnestly. To his mind the problem stripped of all forms and superficiality appeared like this. If the Americans, because they waited to obtain full agreement with London, 'whether the wait was due to the natural delay of consultation or disagreement between us', permitted repeated heavy air attacks to develop on their troops in Korea without retaliation, this circumstance, because of the reason for it, 'was enough to break the alliance of our two countries'. On the other hand he saw, well enough, given the possible consequences of the Korean War ceasing to be localised and the impossibility of seeing in advance how wide the war might become, 'that our demand that the British Government should share in the actual decision about what to do flowed from the proper responsibilities of the British Government to the British people. Here too things would go very wrong between our countries'.

Rusk gave Franks the impression that he was 'searching about for ways by which to ensure great rapidity of consultation and agreement or alternatively some method of … defining the field of the actual decision to retaliate in such a way that practically all the political responsibility was carried in the hypothetical previous general agreement reached in advance of the particular occasion'. He speculated, for instance, on the possibility of limiting the operational decision to a UN attack on Antang airfield, if it were true that it was only from that airfield that serious damage could be done, with the other Manchurian airfields being used for staging purposes only. This illustration, cautioned Franks, should, however, be taken only as an indication of the way his mind was searching about for a solution:

> I add one comment on my own. Apart from the military reasons which are the basis of American preoccupation with the possibilities of major heavy air attacks in Korea, there is one domestic political point that might become relevant. The chief political risk the President runs in having removed MacArthur does not rise from anything that may

happen in the United States. It arises from the possibility of a successful enemy attack in Korea in the near future which might seem to vindicate MacArthur. This will tend to make the Americans very sensitive in the next few weeks to what the enemy in Korea does by land or air.[42]

The nearest a US–UK agreement on retaliatory bombing came to was with Tedder's suggestion for 'suitable machinery for immediate consultation'. For Morrison this would 'be better in every way than the alternative of agreement in advance to restrict attacks to specified air fields as suggested by Rusk'. Morrison's interpretation of Tedder's suggestion was that when the Joint Chiefs considered the risk of massive air attack was imminent, necessary arrangements were to be made to bring into force previously agreed machinery to facilitate an immediate political decision from the US and UK Governments once the first attack had taken place. As to consultations with the other Governments providing forces in Korea, the Foreign Secretary attached importance to as many being consulted as considerations of time and security permitted. In particular the Old Commonwealth Governments and France should certainly be brought in: 'I fully realise the difficulties which this may involve but in view of the crucial implications of any decision this point needs to be faced.'[43] The Americans were equally keen to find some mechanism to circumvent Anglo-American differences. At a meeting between State Department officials and the Joint Chiefs, on 18 April, General Vandenberg insisted: 'The British are the main obstacle.'[44]

Sir William Elliot (in Washington to become the head of the BJSM) and Tedder discussed the possibilites with Bradley, on 18 April, who explained that the US view was that if circumstances permitted political confirmation of the Joint Chiefs decision to act would be secured – in which case there would equally be time for the UK to be consulted or at least informed. If, on the other hand, circumstances demanded immediate action, he, Bradley, would ensure immediate contact between himself and Elliot. The meeting was a brief one, sandwiched between other important engagements of Bradley's and there was no opportunity of discussing the wider issue of consultation with France and the Dominions.[45]

On 30 April, Acheson sent a personal message to Morrison 'about some of our common problems, especially those relating to the Far East. We each ought to understand the other's position – what we think; why we think it.' There were now 'many indications' that a major air attack might be launched at any time against the United Nations forces from bases on Chinese territory wrote Acheson. He reassured Morrison: 'We realize fully that the Governments which have forces in Korea are deeply concerned in this decision, and for this reason we have been holding consultations to reach the widest possible agreement on the procedure to be followed.' The particular circumstances of an attack could not be anticipated, 'but I think we can anticipate that the decision of how to meet the attack, if there is a major one, would have to be made at once'. As a practical matter, consultation after the event between Washington and London – to say nothing of additional consultations with the other Governments – would require the passage of hours, even days, during a time of grave peril to UN forces.[46]

On 2 May, Morrison told the American Ambassador he appreciated the personal message from Acheson 'very much and that he thought it [an] excellent statement of our position and quite convincing'. However he wanted to study it carefully.[47] In fact Morrison had, effectively, made up his mind. He wrote to Attlee about the 'most far-reaching' implications involved in the possible bombing of Chinese territory: 'We have – quite rightly – been insisting on close consultation, and this information was provided in the process of consultation, with the request that we should associate ourselves with the political decision now.' That was the position until the receipt of Acheson's message. In view of this latest development in American thinking Morrison told Attlee: 'I do not think that we can let this matter drift.' Already HMG had taken a number of decisions. With the approval of the Defence Committee, the United States authorities were informed that 'we doubted the reliability of their intelligence reports as our advisers did not credit the Chinese with the necessary air forces; that the decision was of great importance and must be taken by governments at the time and not in advance; that it might mean an extension of the war perhaps into global war; and that other governments (at the very least, the old Commonwealth Governments and France) should be consulted. One of the reasons for our reluctance to give a definite answer – our distrust of General MacArthur – is now no longer valid'. Franks had warned Morrison, on 25 April, that the Americans would not delay striking back, and that the probability was that if an emergency arose there would be no time for effective consultation. This forecast was borne out by Acheson's message, in Morrison's view. As he put it to the Prime Minister: 'I earnestly trust that the occasion will not arise. If however it does, the onus and responsibility will be on China and on Russia, without whose assistance large scale Chinese air attacks would be impossible.' On the merits of the case, Morrison saw no alternative but to meet this new threat by the most effective military means at the UN's disposal, i.e. by bombing the bases from which the attacks had been launched. If China took the grave decision to extend the war she must accept the consequences, and the Foreign Secretary believed that it would be 'a profound mistake for us to flinch from taking the decision, unpalatable as it is'. This general conclusion, which Morrison reached with reluctance, was in his view inescapable:

> if we are not to surrender all along the line, is strengthened by my anxiety about the results if we take a contrary decision or even if we delay taking this decision. If we hesitated for even a few days, after the Americans had unilaterally authorised retaliation, the domestic and international consequences for us might be very serious. Our best prospect of controlling the situation would be to announce at once where we stood and seek to influence others in the same direction.
>
> I do not doubt that in the long run we would find ourselves participating in action against China if she were to provoke this by heavy air attacks on United Nations forces in Korea; and I believe that the people of this country would understand and endorse that course. It would in fact be a choice of evils, in which the alternative (neutrality) would be against our own long-term and world-wide interests and against the interests of the United Nations. If this is the decision to which we would come in the long run, there are great advantages in coming to it at once.
>
> If you agree in general, I would suggest that you consider putting proposals on these lines to the Cabinet:-
> 
>     (a) that we should now take a decision in principle that, in the event of heavy air attacks from bases in China on United Nations forces in Korea, His Majesty's Government will associate themselves with the decision to authorise retaliatory action against these bases;
>
>     (b) that we should now so inform the United States Government, stressing that this is a decision in principle only, and that it requires your confirmation at the time in the light of the information supplied to us regarding the nature and weight of the attacks on United Nations forces. We might also inform the United States Government that in our opinion the Governments of Canada, Australia, New Zealand, South Africa, and France, should be consulted by them at this stage. Finally, we might inform the United States Government that in view of the gravity of the decision, and as on our side it will be taken by you at very short notice if necessary, we consider that on their side it should be confirmed by the President in spite of his previous authorisation of the action;
>
>     (c) that in order to enable you to take this decision at (if necessary) very short notice the Cabinet should delegate authority

to you to take it, perhaps in consultation with the Minister of Defence and me. You would no doubt wish to seek the advice of the Chiefs of Staff, who in turn would require the fullest factual information immediately from the United States Chiefs of Staff before advising you.

In certain circumstances (such as breakdown in telecommunications or pursuit of enemy bombers to their bases by UN fighters) this system of consultation might prove inadequate. This to Morrison's mind made it all the more important that the decision in principle should be taken now 'so that we shall not be caught unprepared'. This proposal differed from the arrangements outlined in Acheson's message. Though the Foreign Secretary was sure that the decision would (in Acheson's words) be 'soberly and wisely made', the issue might be no less than that of extending the Korean campaign into a world war, 'and I do not see how (so far as we are concerned) we can delegate authority to another government. Believing, as I do, that we could not and should not dissociate ourselves from the action should it be forced upon us by Chinese initiative I see only one course open to us: to take a decision in principle now, and to set up machinery for confirmation at extremely short notice'.[48] With Attlee's support, on 3 May, Morrison put the case to the Cabinet and asked it to delegate, to the Ministers concerned, the authority to agree to any United States proposal for retaliatory action. The Cabinet endorsed his request.[49]

When Gifford came to see Morrison, on 4 May, Morrison confirmed that the replacement of General MacArthur had allayed an element of apprehension on the British side for 'we were confident that the United States Government shared our anxiety to avoid being involved in a major war in the Far East'. He was able to tell the Ambassador now that if there were heavy air raids (he stressed that they should be 'material') on United Nations forces from bases in China, then His Majesty's Government accepted in principle that it would be militarily necessary and reasonable for the United Nations forces to bomb the bases in China from which these raids came, 'though none of us should under-estimate the possible consequences'. The only point of difference between Acheson's proposals and HMG's own policy concerned the mechanism for consultation: 'We were a little nervous lest this action might be taken precipitately.' Moreover, it was an extremely grave decision, the responsibility for which must be borne by Governments. It was not a question of lack of confidence in the President and in the United States administration, but of the proper placing of responsibility for this serious decision. 'We could not say: we leave it to the President to take this decision automatically on our behalf without consultation with us. We were with the United States in Korea and if it were necessary to bomb bases in China we would share the consequences with the United States, but we must take the decision for ourselves.' The mechanics of consultation must therefore be worked out in such a way as to give HMG an opportunity to confirm their decision without holding up action which might be militarily urgent: 'We had on our side made arrangements for a very quick decision and could give this decision if necessary in, say, two days.'[50] On 10 May, Morrison formally replied to Acheson and confirmed British agreement. Air attacks from bases in Soviet territory, however, would raise separate and even graver problems, 'and our present decision does not cover this contingency'.[51]

The situation in Korea was soon transformed by the announcement of a truce leading to talks on an armistice – although this did not halt further periodic offensives by the Chinese or a continuous low-level war of attrition between the UN–Communist lines. Unfortunately the talks, conducted by the Americans on behalf of the UN, proved torturously slow and complicated. So when Morrison and Acheson met in Washington, in September, the latter read from a position paper setting forth a proposed US course of action in case there was no armistice. In addition the Americans believed 'we must accelerate the military preparations. The free nations must get themselves in a state of readiness for general war'. Acheson did not wish to alarm anyone, but he believed there was a clearly increased likelihood of general hostilities: the United States had evidence of a considerable build-up in the Chinese air force, and at least two armoured divisions had appeared in North Korea. The Americans wanted the removal of restrictions against attacks in North Korea, especially against the Yalu River dams and the power installations on the North Korean bank of the Chinese frontier. Here Morrison asked 'why we had originally embargoed action against these objectives'. Acheson explained that 'we thought such action might be provocative to the USSR'. However, the Communists had now removed most of the equipment which generated power for North Korea so that the entire output was going into Manchuria. In addition, one of the dams served as a main highway into North Korea. With regard to air attacks, such as on Rashin, a North Korean ice-free port in the Sea of Japan, these would be approved on an individual case basis, and the emphasis in this connection was to keep UN aircraft clear of the Soviet border. Morrison was unfamiliar with Rashin so Acheson explained its location and proximity to Manchuria and Soviet territory. The UN had bombed it approximately three weeks before, destroying the rail road marshalling yards and large quantities of war material. Morrison asked if there had been any Soviet reaction, and Acheson replied that there had not been any evidence of it but that there might well have been concern on the part of the Russians. Alarmingly, Morrison was also 'not clear on whether the JCS was an entirely American military group'; this point was made clear to him. The Foreign Secretary agreed that if UN forces were heavily bombed, 'we would have to strike back, but the UK didn't want to do things needlessly. As diplomats, it was our business to avoid World War III'. As for the situation on the ground in Korea, Morrison explained that the British were satisfied to depend on Ridgway's discretion regarding tactical moves. He felt that it was necessary for a field commander to have such discretion; he well understood the point regarding troop morale because London had experienced a similar problem when undergoing the terrific German bombings and 'a job to do' was vital in maintaining morale.[52]

In London, Manny Shinwell, the Minister of Defence, was concerned that to carry out attacks right on the Chinese border was greatly increasing the danger of spreading the war. Since the targets concerned, though militarily important, did not seem vital to a battle on or below the waist of Korea, he thought it would be better only to authorise such discretion in the event of renewed heavy-scale fighting by the enemy supported by heavy air attack. He also felt that once this discretion was given to Ridgway he would sooner or later be certain to exercise it; hence Shinwell wanted additional safeguards.[53] But as Morrison explained, in a telegram to Attlee, the American proposal was not connected with the possible bombing of United Nations forces, but was intended to destroy dams which were important communication routes for the Chinese and power plants on the Korean side of the frontier which served the Chinese military effort in the Manchurian base areas, in the event of renewal of heavy fighting in Korea. If the renewal of fighting was accompanied by heavy air attacks – which must be from bases outside Korea: 'we are (as you know) already committed to support policy of retaliation subject to consultation' stated Morrison. Discretion given to Ridgway would not be used by him unless there was heavy new fighting and he would still be subject to present standing instructions to respect the frontier. Morrison acknowledged the Minister of Defence's concerns but, on thinking it over, could not see how 'we could justify maintenance of the restrictions against bombing dams and power plants as targets of military importance, if heavy ground fighting is resumed, and if in Ridgway's opinion operations would have military value. It is a difficult problem, and there may be accidents, though I would continue to impress on the Americans the need for strict instructions and great care. But on balance I think that the risks of approving these operations are less than the risks involved in laying ourselves open to the charge that (despite break-down in the armistice talks) we are content to let our troops operate at a disadvantage, rather than risk a frontier incident'.[54]

Upon his return to London, Morrison asked the Foreign Office and the Chiefs of Staff to consider the following question: *'Whether discretion should be given to General Ridgway to take the initiative in a series of battles of manoeuvre and be given latitude to penetrate as far as the "waist" in North Korea.'* The Chiefs' reply was to consider that this proposal went beyond the 'Military Action in Korea in the event of a breakdown in the Armistice Talks' (D.O. (51) 102) document, which was approved by the Defence Committee on 10 September. The relevant conclusion of that paper read as follows:

> Should a Chinese offensive collapse and the Chinese are thrown into disorder, General Ridgway should have discretion to undertake tactical advances as is thought militarily desirable to follow up the retreating Chinese. Should he wish to make a major advance, such as to advance as far as the 'northern waist' this will require the approval of Governments.[55]

The Chiefs of Staff took the view that while the American proposal was bound to increase the risk of the frontier being violated, from the military standpoint it was reasonable that Ridgway should receive the authority proposed, in the event of a resumption of large-scale fighting in Korea.[56] While the Chiefs adhered to the views expressed in the D.O. (51) 102 document, they were still not in favour of a major advance to the 'waist' and did not feel that this should be undertaken without specific Governmental approval, they were, however, of the opinion that in 'certain special circumstances' an advance by manoeuvre as far as the 'waist' might be undertaken. Morrison informed Acheson that subject to further consideration he agreed that Ridgway should have such discretion to manoeuvre. In the Foreign Office, Sir Roger Makins recommended to Attlee that 'we should agree with the views of the Chiefs of Staff; but your specific approval is required to this since the limited discretion which we propose should be given to General Ridgway goes slightly beyond the provisions of D.O. (51) 102'.[57]

On the other issue, of bombing the Yalu, Morrison had signalled approval while in Washington, without referring back to the Chiefs in London. British Military Intelligence, in contrast to the Americans, had just completed study of recent aerial photographs of Yalu River Dam and drew the conclusion that the dam was not being utilised as a communications line between China and Korea; that the construction of the dam itself was such as to preclude the passage of vehicular traffic; that there were no railways or serviceable roads on the Manchurian approach to dam; and that the precipitate nature of the terrain was such that road construction would be impractical. The railway bridge was shown to be some six miles downstream from the dam. The British study drew the inference that 'no useful military purpose' would be served in destroying the dam by bombing. Gifford reported from the US Embassy in London that the British Chiefs of Staff were understood to be 'indignant' over the fact that Morrison on his own initiative agreed that Ridgeway, in the event resumption of a full-scale Communist offensive, should bomb the Yalu Dam without further reference to the British Government.[58]

The British had, by now, now put in place the arrangements for the consultation process to take place in the event of the feared Chinese air attack. Sir Norman Brook, the Cabinet Secretary, issued instructions concerning the action to be taken by the Cabinet Office Duty Officer if he received, outside normal office hours, a message from the United States Government asking for agreement to the retaliatory bombing of Chinese air bases. Ultimately, the Cabinet authorised the Prime Minister, after consultation with the Foreign Secretary and the Minister of Defence, to take a decision on this point on their behalf if there was not time to summon a meeting of the Cabinet.[59]

It was presumed that a request would come through the diplomatic channel to the Foreign Office. The Ministry of Defence might receive a parallel message through the British Joint Services Mission in Washington preceded by the code word 'HURDLE'. HURDLE stood for:- 'American request for our agreement to carry out retaliatory bombing against Chinese bases is about to be passed to us by telegram.' On receipt of such a message the Foreign Office or the Ministry of Defence were at once to inform the Secretary of the Cabinet. He would take instructions from the Prime Minister as to whether to summon a meeting of the Cabinet or to arrange for a meeting between the Prime Minister, the Foreign Secretary and the Minister of Defence. He would also seek instructions about the attendance of the Chiefs of Staff. If the request for retaliatory bombing was received during the week-end, in a holiday period, or after normal office hours, the Foreign Office or the Ministry of Defence had to at once communicate with the Cabinet Office Duty Officer through the Cabinet Office switchboard. The Duty Officer would, again, immediately inform the Secretary of the Cabinet and would obtain through the Prime Minister's Private Secretary instructions whether to arrange a meeting of the Cabinet or a meeting between the Prime Minister, the Foreign Secretary and the Minister of Defence. The Resident Clerk, Ministry of Defence, would be informed of the arrangements by the Cabinet Office Duty Officer. The Resident Clerk would then be responsible for arranging for the Chiefs of Staff to hold a preliminary meeting of their own, if required, and for informing them of the Prime Minister's instructions about their attendance at the Ministerial meeting.[60] This, then, was the procedure – the British feared – might herald the beginning of World War III.

## Notes

1. TNA DEFE 11/207 Outward Saving Telegram from Commonwealth Relations Office, 1 February 1951
2. TNA CAB 128/19 Cabinet Conclusions, 29 January 1951
3. TNA DEFE 11/207 Washington to Foreign Office Telegram No. 301, 30 January 1951
4. TNA CAB 128/19 Cabinet Conclusions, 1 February 1951
5. TNA DEFE 11/207 Washington to Foreign Office Telegram No. 331, 1 February 1951
6. TNA DEFE 11/207 Chiefs of Staff Committee Joint Planning Staff Policy in Korea. Report by the Joint Planning Staff
7. TNA DEFE 11/207 Chiefs of Staff Committee Extract from C.O.S. (51) 24th Meeting held on 5 February 1951
8. TNA FO 371/92061 United Kingdom Liaison Mission in Japan, British Embassy, Tokyo, 6 February 1951
9. TNA FO 371/92061 Gascoigne to Strang, 11 February 1951
10. TNA DEFE 11/208 Foreign Office to Washington Telegram No. 648, 17 February 1951
11. TNA DEFE 11/208 Washington to Foreign Office Telegram No. 523, 19 February 1951
12. FRUS 1951, Volume VII (Korea and China Part I). Editorial Note pp. 234–235
13. TNA CAB 128/19 Cabinet Conclusions, 22 March 1951 at 10 a.m.
14. TNA DEFE 11/209 Korea to Foreign Office Telegram No. 59, 27 March 1951
15. TNA DEFE 11/209 Jebb to Foreign Office Telegram No. 365, 24 March 1951
16. TNA DEFE 11/209 Adams to Foreign Office Telegram No. 59, 27 March 1951
17. FRUS 1951, Volume VII (Korea and China Part I). Telegram by the British Secretary of State for Foreign Affairs (Morrison), to the British Ambassador in Washington (Franks)
18. TNA DEFE 11/209 Foreign Office to Washington nd
19. FRUS 1951, Volume VII (Korea and China Part I). Memorandum of

Conversation by the Assistant Secretary of State for Far Eastern Affair (Rusk), 5 April 1951. Subject: Korea
20. TNA DEFE 11/210 Chiefs of Staff from Lord Tedder. AWT 130, 5 April 1951
21. TNA DEFE 11/210 Chiefs of Staff Meeting nd
22. TNA DEFE 11/210 Chiefs of Staff Meeting nd
23. FRUS 1951, Volume VII (Korea and China Part I). Editorial Note pp. 298–299
24. FRUS 1951, Volume VII (Korea and China Part I). Memorandum of Conversation, by the Director of the Policy Planning Staff (Nitze), 6 April 1951. Subject: Korea
25. FRUS 1951, Volume VII (Korea and China Part I). Memorandum by the Joint Chiefs of Staff to the Secretary of Defense (Marshall), 6 April 1951
26. FRUS 1951, Volume VII (Korea and China Part I). Memorandum of Conversation, by the Director of the Policy Planning Staff (Nitze), 6 April 1951. Subject: Korea
27. TNA DEFE 11/210 Washington to Foreign Office Telegram No. 1023, 6 April 1951
28. TNA DEFE 11/210 Addressed to Foreign Office Telegram No. 1023 of 6 April
29. DBPO Korea No. 141 Morrison to Franks, 9 April 1951
30. DBPO Korea No. 142 Minutes by Sir P. Dixon, 9 April 1951
31. TNA FO 371/9007 Washington to Foreign Office Telegram No. 1074, 10 April 1951
32. TNA FO 371/9007 Washington to Foreign Office Telegram No. 1082, 11 April 1951
33. DBOP: Korea No. 145 Letter from Sir G. Jebb (New York) to Mr Morrison, 14 April 1951
34. TNA FO 371/9007 Washington to Foreign Office Telegram No. 1105, 12 April 1951
35. FRUS 1951, Volume VII (Korea and China Part I). Memorandum of Conversation, by the Director of the Policy Planning Staff (Nitze), 12 April 1951. Subject: Korea
36. TNA DEFE 11/210 U.K. Record of Meeting Held in General Bradley's Room, The Pentagon, on Thursday, 12 April 1951 at 1630 Hours
37. FRUS 1951, Volume VII (Korea and China Part I). Memorandum of Conversation, by the Director of the Policy Planning Staff (Nitze), 12 April 1951. Subject: Korea
38. TNA DEFE 11/210 Washington to Foreign Office Telegram No. 1122, 13 April 1951
39. TNA DEFE 11/210 Foreign Office to Washington Telegram No. 1437, 11 April 1951

40 TNA DEFE 11/210 Washington to Foreign Office Telegram No. 1109, 12 April 1951
41 TNA DEFE 11/210 Bouchier to Chiefs of Staff TRAIN 19, 12 April 1951
42 TNA DEFE 11/210 Washington to Foreign Office Telegram No. 1150, 15 April 1951
43 TNA DEFE 11/210 Foreign Office to Washington Telegram No. 1548, 17 April 1951
44 FRUS 1951, Volume VII (Korea and China Part I). A Memorandum … at a Department of State-Joint Chiefs of Staff Meeting, 18 April 1951
45 TNA DEFE 11/210 AWT 141 Chiefs of Staff from Lord Tedder, 18 April 1951
46 FRUS 1951, Volume VII (Korea and China Part I). The Secretary of State to the Embassy in the United Kingdom, 30 April 1951
47 FRUS 1951, Volume VII (Korea and China Part I). The Ambassador in the United Kingdom (Gifford) to the Secretary of State, 3 May 1951
48 TNA FO 800/639 Morrison to Bevin, 3 May 1951
49 TNA CAB 129/19 Conclusions of a Meeting of the Cabinet held in the Prime Ministers Room, House of Commons, SW1, on Thursday, 3 May 1951 at 4.30 p.m.
50 TNA FO 800/639 Conversation between the Secretary of State and the United States Ambassador Morrison to Sir O. Franks (Washington), 4 May 1951
51 FRUS 1951, Volume VII (Korea and China Part I). The British Embassy to the Department of State Text of a Message from Mr Morrison to Mr Acheson, 10 May 1951
52 FRUS 1951, Volume VII (Korea and China Part I). United States Delegation Minutes of the Second Meeting of United States-United Kingdom Foreign Ministers, 11 September 1951
53 TNA FO 800/639 Foreign Office to Washington Telegram No. 4261, 13 September 1951. Following for Secretary of State from Strang
54 TNA FO 800/639 Washington to Foreign Office Telegram No. 2930, 13 September 1951. Following personal for Prime Minister from Secretary of State
55 TNA FO 800/639 Roger Makins to Prime Minister 'United States proposals for action in the event of failure of the cease-fire talks and the resumption of heavy fighting in Korea', 25 September 1951
56 TNA FO 800/639 Following for Secretary of State from Strang
57 TNA FO 800/639 Roger Makins to Prime Minister 'United States proposals for action in the event of failure of the cease-fire talks and the resumption of heavy fighting in Korea', 25 September 1951
58 FRUS 1951, Volume VII (Korea and China Part I). The Ambassador in the United Kingdom (Gifford) to the Secretary of State, 31 October 1951
59 TNA CAB 21/3321 Retaliatory Bombing on Chinese Bases, 16 May 1952

60 TNA CAB 21/3321 Instructions for the Cabinet Office Duty Officer, 21 May 1952

# 7

## The long war

In October 1951 the Conservatives returned to power: Winston Churchill was, once more Prime Minister and Anthony Eden his Foreign Secretary. One of the many issues – and potential divisions with the Americans – remained Korea. In mid-November, Churchill's concern was expressed to Eden: 'No one here knows what is going on in Korea or which side is benefiting in strength from the bombing and grimaces at Panmunjom. We must try to penetrate the American mind and purpose. We may find this out when we are at Washington. Nobody knows it now. The other side clearly do not want an agreement. It is important to think out how prolonging the deadlock can benefit them. Obviously it diverts United Nations resources. But what else do they hope for' wondered Churchill. Meanwhile 'a war is being carried on, and British troops are engaged, with sharp losses' complained the Prime Minister.[1]

This set the scene for talks between London and Washington, on 28 November, when British and American delegations met in Rome, led by Eden and Acheson, and where General Bradley argued that, after an armistice was agreed, 'we had to face the problem that the enemy could build up its forces materially once freed from UN air interdiction and thereby create a very serious threat to the UN forces'. The real question was 'whether we could not assure General Ridgway of some other form of security, such as perhaps a blockade or other measures which might be taken against the communists'. Eden reflected that was a 'very big' question and one he could hardly answer on the spot. Acheson reassured the Foreign Secretary 'we did not expect him to answer it then but that we thought he would want to discuss it in full with our people before making his decision'. When Eden asked if the Americans had in mind a public statement, to warn the Communists of the consequences of breaking an armistice, he was told it 'would have to be'. As to the nature of the statement, Acheson explained that 'what we had in mind was a US–UK statement, or possibly a US declaration supported by the UK. We did not contemplate making this statement through the UN'. Eden, though, wanted the United States to work out just what it was it wanted to say. Acheson replied he did not have any language 'but that what we had in mind was a public statement outlining the serious nature of an attack'. It would be made without time limit, but it would be understood that it was not an unlimited future commitment regardless of other circumstances. Eden asked whether the Americans would want to do more than bomb the Communist airfields; he was told that some form of naval blockade would be necessary. Eden suggested, that from a purely personal standpoint, he felt that bombing beyond the Yalu would be 'less difficult' for his government than the blockade.[2] This last point was accepted by the Prime Minister who told the Chiefs of Staff that the Soviets would 'start World War III when they wanted to: she certainly would not do so merely to honour her pledge to China'. Consequently, Churchill was not concerned about the bombing of targets in Manchuria; as for the possibility of war with China, he considered it not a country 'against which one declared war; rather a country against which war was waged'. In practical terms the meeting agreed that any warning statement should be phrased in general terms as was the case with Berlin – precision would be imprudent.[3]

After reflecting, back in London, on the American position Eden considered that any warnings should not be made only by the United States and the United Kingdom. It seemed to the Foreign Secretary that the statements should be made by the United States, United Kingdom and as many as possible of the countries contributing forces in Korea. These warning statements should be in very general terms and, in the British view, should if possible be identical. It would be 'unwise' to be precise about the nature of the 'counter action which we should feel obliged to take, but we might, for example say that in the event of such a major breach, it might prove impossible to localise hostilities as hitherto. We should of course like to discuss the draft'. Eden's preliminary views on the other two measures mentioned by the Americans were as follows: on the question of a naval blockade he noted that China was not dependent to any real extent upon seaborne imports for the maintenance of her present war effort in Korea, and in the short term this war effort could be maintained in the face of a sea blockade by a combination of the overland supplies from the USSR and the production of China's own war industry. The Admiralty did not feel that a sea blockade would produce effective results except over years rather than months. They also felt that unless the Soviet ports were included, it would be futile. This last point had, to Eden's mind, raised the gravest issue, as it would be a direct hostile act against the Soviet Union 'which is exactly what we are both so anxious to avoid. Therefore we are not at all convinced that a sea blockade would be a useful measure'. On the question of bombing north of the Yalu, Eden noted that neither the JSC nor the British Chiefs were sure that decisive results would follow from the bombing of the Chinese airfields, bases and junctions: 'However', stated Eden, 'we would much rather proceed in this way than by the sea blockade. It is here to be noted that munitions sent through Soviet ports might be intercepted in this way.'[4] These conversations confirmed to Churchill that the Communists were stringing out the armistice negotiations with the United States in order to gain time: 'The question is for what? The six months parlaying have enabled the Chinese Communists to add sixty thousand to their strength to build up their artillery and above all to let the Russians teach them how to fly the Russian planes' he noted. The United Nations' position was actively and relatively far worse than it was six months ago. The Prime Minister commented to Eden: 'We may be grateful that we have only a small say in these matters. I am glad we do not have the responsibility of having to guess the Communist motives. There can however be no doubt that so far time has been almost entirely on their side.'[5]

On 16 December, the United States Ambassador talked to Eden about Korea. Gifford's first point was that the State Department thought they could now find a formula, within the framework of the revised draft which HMG had proposed, for the terms of a warning statement to the Chinese and North Koreans in the event of a breach of any armistice concluded in Korea. They still thought HMG's draft rather weak and preferred to say that it 'would not', rather than 'might not', be possible to confine hostilities within the frontiers of Korea. But Gifford, in Eden's opinion, was 'obviously pleased' that the State Department had moved away from their original 'menacing form of words'. The Ambassador explained that the United States realised that it was not possible for HMG to agree in advance on the minimum steps which might be taken in the event of a major breach of an armistice. This matter would have to be 'hammered out' if such an event occurred. Meanwhile it was understood, commented Eden to Oliver Franks, that 'we were not committed to the steps which they had proposed, while they themselves still held to their proposals. This need not prevent us from issuing the warning'.[6] The final statement was agreed between Eden and Acheson. [7]

As Churchill and Eden prepared for their first joint journey to the White House, in January 1952, the Foreign Secretary informed his Prime Minister of the limited expectations they could expect in terms of assistance, from the Americans, with regard to British concerns particularly with Egypt and Persia: 'I do not think that there is a real bargain to be struck between American policies in the Far East and ours in the Middle East. In the Far East we have met the United States on the major present problem, which was the warning in respect of Korea. About that they are fully satisfied.'[8] During the Churchill–Truman talks, in Washington, there was broad agreement on Korea although the British rejected, once more, the desirability and effectiveness of a naval blockade, the Foreign Secretary describing it as 'futile'.[9] The British, however, did signal a clear shift from the previous Labour Government, with Churchill describing British diplomatic relations with Communist China as a 'fiction'. He added that had he been in power he would have broken relations with China when the Chinese attacked the UN forces in Korea. However, when he was returned to power the phase of armistice talks had been initiated and he did not think that such a British action would be desirable now because of its possible effect on the negotiations. Referring to Formosa, Churchill said that it would be 'shameful' for the UN to leave the 3–400,000 anti-Communist Chinese to the tender mercy of the Communists. These Nationalist forces on Formosa had been on 'our side in the Second World War and had fought on our side afterwards'. However, he personally did not want to see Chiang Kai-shek's Government recognized as the legitimate government of mainland China. Eden then added that he did not agree with the late British Government's position concerning China and, in particular, with its belief that a Chinese brand of Titoism could be fostered. He thought it unwise to base a national policy on such a tenuous possibility.[10]

While the political talks had not reignited the wartime-type relationship which Churchill had sought[11] the British Chiefs were taken aback when Slim attended high-level military talks, in Washington, on 11–12 January, with the Americans and French, where there was a suggestion that a warning that should be issued, cautioning the Chinese that 'further active aggression' in Indo-China would result in retaliation not necessarily limited to the area of aggression. The Americans pushed for the bombing of targets in China and a blockade of the Chinese coast. Sir William Elliot informed Churchill that the British military chiefs were opposed to these proposals for fear they could, almost involuntarily, involve the Soviet Union and lead to global war.[12] Sir William Strang's assessment of the Washington talks was that the objective seemed to be entice the British into a war with China.[13]

In the meantime the armistice talks dragged on. By March 1952, Eden felt it looked less and less as if the Communists wanted a settlement but he wondered: 'maybe they don't want a renewal of the war either'.[14] He informed Churchill that the Foreign Office was fully supporting the Americans in their efforts to find a way to avoid having to hand back any prisoners of war to the Communists against their will; although: 'We do not know whether any Chinese or North Korean prisoners are being allowed to slip away and disappear.' And, 'mercifully', they were not at the point where an armistice in Korea could be obtained only at the price of agreeing to force some prisoners to return to Communist territory. The humanitarian argument, Eden believed, 'does not work only one way because we must not forget the fate of our own men whose release can be brought about only by an armistice'. Having said that Eden reassured the Prime Minister: 'I naturally agree that it revolts the conscience to contemplate the forced return of prisoners who would go, not to freedom, but to slavery or death.'[15]

The Foreign Secretary was conscious, though, of how the Foreign Office, upon examining the legal basis of voluntary repatriation concluded that it could not be argued on the basis of the Geneva Convention. Eden was shocked: 'I did not know that our legal grounds were so poor but this doesn't make me like the idea of sending these poor devils back to death or worse.'[16] This was of no consequence to the Prime Minister who informed his Foreign Secretary: 'It is, as I have written before, a matter of honour to us not to force a non-Communist prisoner of war to go back to be murdered in Communist China. This is not a matter of argument, but one of the fundamental principles for which we fight and, if necessary, die.' The Prime Minister complained of a telegram received from Bouchier as showing 'a taint of pro-Communism. Indeed it is so redolent that I wonder whether he is not playing irony. Why, for instance, had he "hoped" that they [POWs] would all wish to go back to the Communists? ... Why is he "disappointed" that a great many of them think this would be odious? Why should he be worried lest the numbers who do not wish to go back to the Communists are "too large a total for the Communist authorities to stomach?" Of course, he may only be talking the conventional jargon into which they have got, but if these are his sincere opinions, he is an insult to the British employment or uniform' declared Churchill.[17]

Eden reassured Churchill that Her Majesty's Embassy in Washington had impressed on the State Department 'that before any irrevocable decision was taken on the prisoner-of-war issue we should expect to be consulted'. Since Eden had last written to Churchill on the subject, on 31 March, the United Nations Command had taken a census of prisoners in its hands, and this census showed that only 70,000 Communist prisoners out of 132,000 wished to be repatriated. This information had been passed on to the Communists. First reactions by the Communists were, as was to be expected, unfavourable, 'but we have not yet reached deadlock, nor have we exhausted the possibilities of compromise'. If the Communists really wanted an armistice, continued Eden, the outcome of the present exchanges 'may be a compromise acceptable to us without offence to our conscience. If, however, deadlock is reached, we shall have to take a definite stand and make our views known to the Americans. Meanwhile, the Americans know that we expect to be consulted before they take a final decision, and I think we can leave it at that for the moment'.[18] Churchill had felt, for some time, that the POW question 'raised the largest issues. The Americans have now definitely pronounced, as I hoped and thought they would, against handing over prisoners of war to the Communists against their will. I do hope there will be no question of our differing from the Americans on this point of moral principle as I think the consequences might be very far reaching' he told Eden.[19]

So, despite the dubious legal position HMG's stance was set out by Selwyn Lloyd, the Minister of State at the Foreign Office, at the UN in October. Following the contention of the Soviet delegate – Vyshinsky – that the attitude of the United Nations Command to forcible repatriation of prisoners was in violation of the Geneva Convention, Lloyd focused on the article – 118 – to which Vyshinsky referred; the relevant sentence of read as follows: 'Prisoners of war shall be released and repatriated without delay after the cessation of active hostilities.' Lloyd focused on the actual words. The Convention did not speak merely of repatriation. The phrase used was *'released* and repatriated'. It would be necessary to continue to detain the prisoners and to hand them over under armed guard: 'Can it possibly be said that a prisoner has been released if he has in effect to be conveyed in chains to the authorities of his own country?' asked Lloyd. Vyshinsky also referred to the wording of article 7 of the Convention. No reference was made to forcible repatriation. This article was to the effect that prisoners could not renounce the rights secured to them by the Convention. This provision was, of course, inserted to protect the prisoners themselves against attempts by the detaining Government to procure such a renunciation under pressure. It was certainly not the intention, continued Lloyd, in any phrase in the 1949 Geneva Convention to impose on States an obligation to hand over individuals to political persecution or to limit in any way the long-established right of States to grant asylum on political grounds. The notion of forcible repatriation introduced an element quite foreign to the normal conception of repatriation and not in any way implied by it. But apart from the argument on phrases and words, surely it was the *spirit* of the Convention which was of more importance than its wording, argued Lloyd. 'If one studies its detailed provisions article by article and paragraph by paragraph one is forced irresistibly to the conclusion that the Convention was drawn up in the interests of the prisoners of war themselves and in protection of the individual rights of individual prisoners. It was not drawn up to define the rights of States' he claimed. The idea that individual prisoners should be 'forced by bayonets stuck against their backs to go back to a country in which they fear for their lives, is completely out of keeping with the tenor and spirit of the document. I cannot believe that any unbiased, thinking, reasonable person can dispute the proposition which I have just sought to put'. The Geneva Convention, therefore, did not impose an obligation on anyone to repatriate prisoners by force.

Vyshinsky had also referred in particular to a treaty between the USSR and Great Britain. He said that in that treaty of 1920 the Russians agreed that if any Britons did not wish to be repatriated they should remain in Russia: 'I think his words were "it would be nice to have them in Russia"' recalled Lloyd. He thought that they might make good citizens in the Soviet Union, and therefore the Soviet Union were willing to have them stay: 'In other words M Vyshinsky does admit the principle that in certain circumstances a prisoner can make a choice, and that portion of his argument which maintained that no prisoner could be expected to make a choice, that no one in captivity could exercise a free choice seemed to me to founder completely upon that example of which he seemed to approve, which he drew from the past of the Soviet Union' argued Lloyd.[20]

In August 1952, at an informal discussion with Sir William Elliot, General Bradley said that it had been brought to his notice that an impression was gaining weight in certain journalistic circles in Washington and New York that the British were becoming very critical of the use of the napalm bomb by the United Nations' Air Forces in Korea. This was causing some concern to himself and his colleagues. Bradley fully realised that hostile Parliamentary Questions on this subject did not necessarily reflect the general British view, but the impression was gaining ground that this feeling of uneasiness was also held in official circles in Whitehall. In order to forestall newspaper articles expressing these views, which were now being prepared and which would 'harm' Anglo-American relations, Bradley wished to be able to make an 'off the record' statement that there was no foundation for the belief that the British Government were critical of the way the napalm bomb was being used in Korea. He would like to be able to say that the British Government were in agreement with and supported the use of this weapon as at present employed. Upon learning of this the Chiefs of Staff were 'extremely anxious' to meet Bradley's wishes and prepared a draft statement, which met Bradley's point. Churchill's Minister of Defence, Alexander, passed on the Chiefs' views to the Prime Minister,[21] along with the draft 'off the record' statement, which would say: 'The British Government has given us no grounds for believing that they are critical of the use of NAPALM in Korea. The British Service authorities regard it as a legitimate and useful weapon for use against military targets, particularly tanks and strong points.'[22] Churchill's response was dismissive and angry:

> I do not like this Napalm bombing at all. A fearful lot of people must be burned, not by ordinary fire, but by the contents of the bomb. We should make a great mistake to commit ourselves to approval of a very cruel form of warfare affecting the civilian population. Napalm in the war was devised by us and used by fighting men in battle action against tanks and against heavily defended structures. No one ever thought of splashing it about all over the civilian population. I will take no share in the responsibility for it. It is one thing to use Napalm in close battle ground troops, or from the air in immediate aid of ground troops. It is quite another thing to torture great masses of unarmed people by it.
>
> The statement about giving 'due warning to civilians to evacuate', etc., is not worth much. If people have to go to their work every day and live in their homes, they have not much choice. My own feeling is that Napalm ought not to be used in the way it is being done by the American Forces. This is I am sure the overwhelming feeling of the House of Commons, but I do not take my opinion from them. I certainly could not agree to our taking any responsibility for it, otherwise than in the general duty of serving with and under the United Nations Command.[23]

Alexander responded by emphasising how the American press were 'trying to work up a case to prove that there is disagreement between the British and American Governments on the use of napalm, which may culminate in an article which would be most damaging to Anglo-American relations'. Unless something was done to dispel the impression that there was 'a serious disagreement between us everyone will assume that the Press criticism is justified'. Alexander pointed that not only did the Americans think that napalm was a legitimate and effective weapon of war, but that the Chiefs of Staff agreed with them: 'We have no reason to believe that the Americans have used napalm against anything other than legitimate military objectives. The spate of Communist propaganda about the bomb suggests that it has been a very effective weapon.' Alexander felt it was 'desirable' to allow Bradley to say 'something which will be sufficiently definite to dispose of the idea that there is a serious difference of opinion between ourselves and the Americans on this subject.'²⁴ In reply, Churchill told Alexander:

> I do not see how Press articles and jabber of that kind compares with splashing about this burning fluid on the necks of humble people living where they have to. We are a subordinate factor in the U.N. operations in China. I do not suggest a protest at the present time but I am not going to take any direct avowed responsibility – nor will the House of Commons – for the [un]discriminating use of napalm not in warfare between fighting men but to torture civilian populations. There is nothing doing in all this I can assure you. I do not mind at all if the American Press complain that I am not loyal to the napalm stunt. The most we can do is to let them go on and say anything. Even this will cause serious trouble. I am quite willing to telegraph to General Bradley myself and show him where we stand if you think that this would be worth while. Anyhow there must be no approval by any British Government of which I am the head.²⁵

The Foreign Secretary then intervened and pointed out to Churchill that, in a message which he sent to Bradley, on 3 July, 'you expressed confidence that every effort would be made to avoid needless loss of life and suffering by the use of napalm bombs in crowded areas.' Eden entirely agreed with the Prime Minister on this point, adding 'we should take no share in the responsibility for any use of napalm bombs in crowded areas'. The Foreign Secretary, therefore, suggested that, in reply to Bradley's approach:

> we should remind him of the passage referred to above in your message of the 3rd July and continue as follows: that we regard napalm as a legitimate weapon for use against military targets, that we should deplore giving Communist propaganda any opportunity to speculate about differences in the policy of our two Governments on this subject; but that, as there is some impression among the public here that napalm is in fact being used against crowded areas in Korea where these contain military targets, we should be grateful for an authoritative account of the precise manner in which napalm is being used by the United Nations Command before committing ourselves to any form of words about our attitude which General Bradley could use as suggested.

On 29 August, Eden was able to communicate to Alexander – 'Prime Minister agrees with this minute. So proceed. AE';²⁶ but, just in case

Alexander thought there might be room for manoeuvre with the Prime Minister's position, Churchill sent him one more message on the subject: 'My opinion is unchanged.'[27]

Churchill was also concerned by Communist claims that the Americans had employed bacteriological warfare (it first appeared in Communist propaganda at the Warsaw Peace Congress in November 1950) in Korea.[28] In Britain, the Dean of Canterbury became the leading attacker of US policy in Korea accepting the claims of biological warfare completely; the main instrument for spreading tales supporting the allegations was the Communist *Daily Worker*. The allegations had such force that Churchill, who did not believe them, wanted to be certain there was no truth in them before he condemned them as propaganda: he demanded a report from the Ministry of Defence and from Lord Cherwell, his scientific adviser, about them. After studying the *Daily Worker* and the 'Dirty Dean', the Prime Minister wrote: 'I think this is a good example of how the Communists use lies and make them truths or facts by repetition. I am rather thinking of taking this up myself in a world broadcast but I must be on very firm ground beforehand. I cannot see that the United States attempted to destroy the population of China by spreading plague bacilli. People think they can deal with this by pooh-poohing it, but the lie goes on. I thought it might be good perhaps for me to deal with it on behalf of the free world.'[29]

In his report on the germ warfare claims, Cherwell's general view was the Communists in the Far East had been suffering from serious epidemics resulting from lack of hygienic precautions and medical care. 'No doubt it occurred to them that they could escape responsibility and at the same time make useful anti-American propaganda by attributing these epidemics to American germ warfare.' It would be extremely easy for them to fake evidence going to show this had occurred. Anybody could photograph containers which could have carried insects or the like, and groups of insects, and say the two were causally connected with some aircraft that might have been heard passing in the night. 'No normal mind would consider such suspect pieces of evidence as valid proofs' concluded Cherwell. He pointed out how the Communists had paraded insects reputedly infected with cholera and plague which they asserted rapidly produced outbreaks of disease: 'As has been pointed out, these things are nonsense from a scientific point of view.' Cholera was a waterborne disease and was not carried by insects, and plague was only spread to humans when the rats which carried the plague fleas had died in such numbers that the fleas were reduced to adopting human hosts. Other similar examples of 'equal absurdity' had been mentioned in the press: 'It is strange that the Communist propagandists should be so stupid as to allow allegations of this sort to be put forward when any competent biologist must know they are rubbish. It shows either that they are extremely ignorant or extremely careless in faking their evidence.' Curiously, in opposing this propaganda Cherwell doubted whether it was wise to say, as *The Times* had done, 'No one in the West believes for a moment that the Americans, or any other people of the United Nations, have ever considered using so vile a method of warfare'; he warned 'No one knows what the future may bring.'[30]

It was the task of the Foreign Office's Information Research Department (IRD) to counter the Communist propaganda. The IRD considered the evidence adduced in support of the charges as of two kinds – 'that which might be expected to impress anyone of average intelligence, and that which would scarcely deceive a child'. In between those two categories there had been a mass of material which was from the scientific viewpoint not conclusive, 'but cannot be said to disprove the charges, and this is dressed up in scientific guise to impress the layman'. In the first category came the so-called confessions of two American airmen, Enoch and Quinn, and certain 'evidence' brought back and quite plausibly presented by a Mission from the International Association of Democratic Lawyers in April; into the 'ludicrous' category fell the Dean of Canterbury's stories of children collecting infected insects with chopsticks; and into the third came a collection of so-called scientific micro-photographs, many of harmless insects and others meaningless without their context, but designed to give superficial scientific support to the charges. The basic factors facing the IRD in considering counter-measures were '(i) that it is virtually impossible to prove a negative; (ii) that it is the Americans alone who are being accused. The tactics should accordingly be, on (i) to show that the Communists are not seriously trying to prove anything; (ii) to maintain the fullest possible unity with the Americans and support them to the full in countering the charges against them.'

As a matter of tactics, the IRD considered that it was important for governments 'not to appear to be in the least alarmed or moved by the campaign'. Ministerial statements and speeches should accordingly expose the bases of Communist policy as a whole, and treat the bacterial campaign as a 'normal Communist phenomenon'. Parliamentary Questions could be arranged to deal with specific developments such as the discovery of new 'evidence'. But for the rest, it was important that counter-publicity on the particular issue of germ warfare 'should originate in non-governmental circles, and especially among scientists. The official machinery can then be discreetly used to publicize their comments'.[31] The scale of the problem facing the IRD, and the West generally, was illustrated when even Churchill wanted to know if a new story being disseminated by the

Communists, led him to ask: 'I want to know however, whether there is any truth in the story or whether it is one of those Soviet lies which become truths after continuous repetition.'[32]

Churchill also became irate at the prospect of appointing a British Officer as a Deputy Chief of Staff to General Clark: the Prime Minister complained the appointment would be responsible to the United Nations Supreme Commander and should not impart any secret information to Her Majesty's Government except with Clark's approval. The Deputy would, however, receive guidance from HMG about their views and would seek opportunities of acquainting the Supreme Commander with them as the occasion served.[33] Churchill was disturbed by 'the dangers of the step we have taken in accepting the invitation to appoint an officer who will be on General Mark Clark's staff and not free to report to us and yet whose presence will give the General a right to say that we have been "consulted". Thus we have a more direct responsibility without real power'.[34] On 9 July, Selwyn Lloyd warned Eden that the 'Prime Minister has more than once expressed doubts about the appointment of a British Deputy Chief of Staff to General Mark Clark's Headquarters. He said again this morning that he had not yet made up his mind to agree to it'. The Minister of State thought this 'most unfortunate. The matter having been raised and publicised, I am sure we have got to go through with it. I think the danger in the appointment is over-emphasised, provided it is clearly understood that this officer's first loyalty is to General Clark.' He would have no authority to consult Her Majesty's Government at all. The link between him and HMG would be a Liaison Section in Tokyo, and he would not inform the Liaison Section of General Clark's intentions without the General's permission:

> The advantages we should get from this appointment would be:-
> (1) A different point of view would be available to General Clark in taking decisions.
> (2) It would enormously help the work of the Liaison Section and, incidentally, that of Dening [British Ambassador in Japan].[35]

On 22 July, Churchill accepted that the matter should finally be decided by the Cabinet the next day: 'I still think that it is liable to criticism as being "much ado about nothing". Moreover I feel that we shall be held to be sharing responsibility more directly than we do now or need to do' complained the Prime Minister. He took a swipe at the Foreign Office support for the appointment having only just found out the Chiefs of Staff were opposed to it: 'In all the circumstances I should prefer to say we do not propose to take advantage of General Mark Clark's friendly offer upon full consideration of all the circumstances. Or; in view of the new hope of a favourable outcome of the Truce negotiations it would be premature to make the appointment at the present time.'[36] Eden objected that: 'I do not see how we can now change our plans. I do not think that we shall in practice be any more committed by this appointment than we are at present, provided that the statement is made in succinct terms, indicating plainly that the Deputy Chief of Staff will be responsible solely to General Mark Clark.' The Foreign Secretary warned: 'If we were to change our minds now it would be very confusing for the House of Commons and for public opinion in this country and the Commonwealth.' Apart from the change of order, counter-order, disorder, it might be suggested that there was some new discord in Anglo-American relations insisted Eden.[37] Although, in Cabinet, Churchill referred to the appointment of a 'Ridiculous mouse, but A.E. still wants it' and the fact that Parliament 'will scoff at this',[38] the Foreign Secretary got his way. Air Marshall Barnett was the man ultimately chosen for the job and, in the end, would prove his usefulness as a discreet provider of information about US intentions.

But these were side issues to the main one of prisoners of war that continued to stall the armistice talks. The issue of the non-forcible repatriation of POWs dominated debate at the UN. On 29 October, Selwyn Lloyd called on Acheson, at the latter's request, for a general talk at the UN. Lloyd mentioned that Menon, the Indian UN delegate, was working on a proposal to support the principle of no forcible return and increase the possibilities of an armistice. Lloyd believed that Menon was doing this in good faith in a real effort to be helpful. Menon's thoughts were as follows: that the armistice agreement on prisoners should be somewhat vague, such as an undertaking. Prisoners should be returned and repatriated in accordance with the Geneva Convention. This should be carried out and interpreted by a 'protecting' Power which might in fact be a group of powers, say the final armistice inspecting Powers, with a neutral chairman. These Powers, having the constructive possession of prisoners, would then administer their disposition. Menon thought that this would produce an armistice and that if there were any disagreements about its administration they would be with the protecting Powers and not with the UN Command.

Acheson, however, told Lloyd that he strongly opposed an approach of this sort and said that an attempt to have a vague principle, which meant different things to the two sides, would not succeed and would be very dangerous. It would not succeed because the Unified Command would have to make it absolutely clear that the principle of no forcible POW return was in effect. This would, of course, defeat the purpose which

Menon had in mind and from which, in Acheson's judgement, there was no escape. Lloyd agreed with this. Acheson then said that to have a provision in the armistice which was so certain to present controversy would cause grave hazards for the Unified Command and the troops in Korea: 'Our defensive position would be weakened after the armistice and if a breach of the armistice occurred as a result of a dispute in so confused a manner as Mr. Menon's proposal, it would gravely undermine the idea of the greater sanction' declared Acheson, who thought that it was clear that 'we could not accept any such proposal and earnestly hoped that Mr. Menon could be dissuaded from making it'.[39]

The British, however, did not play ball and, instead, formulated a text of a resolution based on discussions with the Indians. This resolution 'goes so far to meet the Communist point of view as to in fact contemplate the ultimate abandonment of the principle of no forced repatriation' complained Acheson to Truman. The prisoner of war commission contemplated under the resolution would have to hold indefinitely prisoners resisting repatriation and 'subject them to Communist haranguing until they give up and decide to go home'. That was, the resolution provided for no disposition of the prisoners other than being held indefinitely under the control of the commission or returning to Communist control.[40] On 16 November, Acheson, Lovett and Bradley met with, among others, Lloyd and Mike Pearson (from Canada) to outline their objections to the Indian proposals. Lovett and Bradley spoke on three principal points which the JCS, who had looked over the proposals, indicated were essential. These were: (1) there should be no forcible repatriation and this should be clearly stated in the body of the resolution; (2) the suggested umpire should be a member of the POW Commission and the draft should be cleaned up to indicate a definite time limit for the retention of prisoners and an alternative choice ie., a second door for them to leave detention; and (3) it should be understood that the resolution, if and when passed, would constitute a recommendation to General Clark and that it would be up to him to implement the details involved.

This led Lloyd to ask what agreements were pending in addition to the non-forcible repatriation item. Acheson replied that the matter of the prohibition of building airfields was not mentioned in the present armistice agreement and that the question of a Soviet member of the Commission had been set aside on the understanding that it would not be made an issue if the Communists agreed on non-forcible repatriation. This was the 'package deal'. Bradley then referred to the three objectives in the minds of the military. As drafted, the Menon proposal did not present a clear picture and that if it was not clear there was not a clear armistice to be had. A second point was the security of United Nations forces. If the Communists continued a major build-up, this would be dangerous and they would also have unlimited access for propaganda and infiltration. Conversely, 'we would have no pressure against them because a major factor in our favor would be eliminated when our air pressure came off'. He was setting forth this position not because he did not want an armistice but rather because he wanted a definite one. Once the fight had stopped, 'it would be hard to get our people to go back into action'. With respect to the Menon proposal, if the prisoners were kept incarcerated, this amounted to forcible repatriation because after several years the probability was that they would break down and indicate a desire to return to the homeland. This was 'clearly not in accordance with our principle'. The third military point was that the resolution should be passed in the General Assembly and then passed to Panmunjom, and would be implemented by the Unified Command as to detail. With respect to prisoners who would not accept repatriation, he thought that there should be no future General Assembly responsibility for the prisoners, that they should be disposed of, i.e., released, and that the provision in this regard was much 'too fuzzy'.

Lloyd countered that the British point of view was different in that, like it or not, they felt it highly desirable to get the Indian resolution passed if possible. He had spent many hours with Menon and the 'two large points' mentioned had, he thought, been agreed. The first of these was reference to the fact that force should not be used was now contained in the body of the resolution. This point the Chinese would not like and they would turn it down. The second point as set forth (in Menon's paragraph 12 of the resolution) indicated that disagreements should go to negotiation in the GA or in the POW Commission as an instrument of the GA. Lloyd was not satisfied that the resolution showed another way (i.e., a second door) out of the repatriation camp. He thought that, therefore, it was essential to get a change here.[41]

On 18 November, Eden spoke on the telephone to General Eisenhower, the victorious Presidential candidate for the Republican Party. Eisenhower understood that the Indian resolution was unsatisfactory; Eden asked if the General had seen the text to which Eisenhower replied he had not. Eden then explained that, in his view the terms on non-forcible repatriation were satisfactory although some amendments might be necessary as to the procedure for the final release of POWs. The Foreign Secretary had the impression the General was not against the resolution but against what he had been told was in it. Eden offered to send Eisenhower a copy of the resolution, which the President accepted.[42] Two days later, when Eden met with the General, the Foreign Secretary formed the impression that Eisenhower 'seemed definitely more favourable in his approach' to the Indian initiative than Acheson had been: he said that the essential point was that the POWs should not be forced 'to go back' nor kept in prison indefinitely. If both these points were met he would be satisfied. Eisenhower stated 'we could not maintain our position in Asia without the help of the Asians'. That was why he considered the Indian initiative so important. Eisenhower asked Eden to send a message to Nehru thanking him for the initiative he had taken without committing himself to the details of the text.[43]

By 20 November, Acheson realised that the momentum in the UN was moving away from the US position to Menon's. He told Truman: 'We have now reached a point at which the only question is whether we can lead the … powers to amend Menon resolution along the lines worked out with the Joint Chiefs of Staff … As I mentioned to you, our basic problem has not been with Menon, but with the British, Canadians and French, who feel strongly we should accept Menon's resolution even though it waters down considerably the principles on which we have taken our stand at Panmunjom.' The British, Canadians and French had grave apprehensions about what the new Eisenhower administration might do regarding Korea, and therefore showed a 'desperate anxiety' to exhaust all possibilities for an armistice now, however remote. They argued that even if an armistice were not to result, Menon's resolution would still attract solid Asiatic support. They were 'very soft on our principles, particularly on our insistence that all POWs who do not wish to return home be freed within a short period of time.'

Following Truman's instructions, Acheson 'laid it on the line' when he saw Eden – who had arrived in New York – earlier in the day. Acheson asked the Foreign Secretary 'whether he was with us or against us'. Eden assured Acheson that he 'wanted to be with the Americans. Acheson told Eden that Washington could not accept an arrangement for the prisoners which left them with no alternative except repatriation or continuing to rot in a POW camp, 'as is now provided in Menon's resolution'. Eden agreed that the British could not either, but he stressed the importance of not changing Menon's resolution so much that Menon might be unable to vote for it himself. When Acheson warned Eden that he might have to choose between 'our vote or the Indian vote', the Foreign Secretary replied 'that in that case he wanted ours'. This led Acheson to speculate to Truman: 'I think we may be able to work this out.' It was clear that a General Assembly resolution would have to be based on the Menon draft, 'but I believe we shall be able to get many or most of our amendments accepted'. The crucial amendment, on which Acheson told Eden there must be movement, was that there must be an absolutely flat time limit after which POWs who resisted repatriation would be released. The British seemed to be 'moving in our direction, but have not yet come far enough. I believe that with patience and continued pressure we can bring them along, and this will help to assure acceptance of our amendments by the Assembly' Acheson wrote to the President.⁴⁴

The following day Acheson was able to report to Truman 'some brightening of the prospects here in the UN debate on Korea as a result of developments during the past twenty-four hours. For one thing, the British have prepared the way for agreement with us on modifications that must be made in the Menon resolution'. The Americans were pleased to note that Eden, in his speech before the UN Political Committee that day, indicated a considerable measure of agreement with the considerations 'we had been urging upon him with some force'. While endorsing the Menon resolution, Eden indicated support for major modification to make the POW Commission effective by strengthening the position of the umpire, and for the release of prisoners not repatriated to a UN agency to care for and resettle them. The other hopeful development was that Sir Percy Spender, of Australia, was taking a strong initiative behind the scenes to solidify support among other Powers for a series of modifications of the Menon resolution.⁴⁵

Austin, Eden and Lloyd, met on 22 November, where 'the three of us had a frank and friendly discussion for more than an hour' recalled the American. Eden still believed that the Indian resolution in the form tabled by Menon was 'not too bad'. He felt it was a 'large accomplishment' that the Indians had recorded their support for the principle of non-forcible repatriation. Although Eden was not able to appreciate the full force of US objections he, as well as the vast majority of the British public, felt that the Indian initiative was of 'tremendous importance'. Eden shared US doubts that the Communists would accept an armistice but he attached importance to the fact that the Communists would have to accept or reject the proposals. Eden requested Austin to keep in confidence that he had been seeing Menon during the past two days and had been attempting to persuade Menon to accept the substance of the US proposals. Eden was frank in saying that in so doing he felt that he was representing the US points of view rather than his own, since he himself was prepared to accept the present Menon draft rather than to risk loss of Indian support. But it was clear to Austin, from his remarks, that the Foreign Secretary had not been endeavouring to persuade Menon to accept US amendments in the form in which they had given them to Eden.⁴⁶

On 25 November, Eden made it clear to Acheson that the UK saw the present posture of the Korean problem as a major tactical and political problem in the Cold War transcending the POW issue. Lloyd also expressed the feeling 'we have been losing ground in [the] cold war in past 6–8 months'.[47] This was what motivating their championing of Menon's resolution. By the following day, Eden, although reluctant to support any amendments to Menon's draft, was able to work out, with Acheson, a wording for paragraph 17 which provided that responsibility for the 'care and disposition' of any prisoners not repatriated, or not provided for by the proposed post-armistice political conference, should be transferred to a United Nations agency at the end of 120 days; that was 30 days after the conference began. Acheson told Eden that 'we did not like this, but that we could live with it and would accept it if it meant that both he and Menon would support the resolution. Otherwise, we would prefer our own draft of paragraph 17' which did not mention a political conference. Eden avoided firm commitment, but said he would work on Menon along these lines and advise Acheson later of both Menon's and his own reactions. In a later telephone call, however, the British said they had not meant to leave the impression they were going to get in touch with Menon, and urged that Menon not be 'crowded' at this time.

As a result of a talk between Gross, Lloyd (Eden being absent) and Menon, all three agreed to consider an amendment which Menon would either propose or accept, and which would provide that 120 days after the armistice was signed – that was, 30 days after the 90 days – the disposition of the prisoners, as well as their care and maintenance, should be transferred to the UN. This was the 'heart of the matter from our point of view', noted Acheson, since it terminated the jurisdiction of the political conference and terminated it one month short of the period which some had advocated. Acheson authorised Gross to confirm US adherence to this settlement of the matter, provided Menon agreed. Acheson, on 26 November, told the President: 'Events in the past twenty-four hours have moved swiftly here and with all the elements of an old-fashioned melodrama.' Vyshinski's speech in the Political Committee, 'set everyone in the Committee on their ears'. He not only rejected Menon's resolution, but all other resolutions except his own.[48]

In the evening of 26 November, Gross talked at some length with Menon, who was discouraged because the Americans were insisting on changes in paragraph 17, in the face of Soviet attacks on his resolution. Menon had also received word from the Chinese Communists that his resolution was not acceptable. Menon was, therefore, seriously thinking of withdrawing it. Later, Gross spoke to Selwyn Lloyd and pressed him very hard to talk with Menon, as soon as possible, to urge him to accept the essential US changes. It had been Gross' understanding, at a morning meeting with Eden, that either the Foreign Secretary or Lloyd would talk with Menon during day. Lloyd replied he did not think it was 'wise' for him to talk with Menon for another day or so, but if Gross insisted, he would do so. Gross said he thought it was important and Lloyd then agreed to talk with Menon. Shortly after midnight Lloyd called Gross at home to report on his conversation with Menon. Lloyd read Gross the following text which he said he 'thought' Menon agreed to:

> If at the end of a further 30 days there are any prisoners of war whose return to their homelands has not been effected under the above procedures or whose future has not been provided for by the political conference, the responsibility for their care and maintenance until the end of their detention and for their subsequent disposition shall be transferred to the UN, which in all matters relating to them shall act in accordance with international law.

Lloyd also read to Gross a suggested alternative text:

> If at the end of a further 30 days there are any prisoners of war whose return to their homelands has not been effected under the above procedures, or whose future has not been provided for by the political conference, responsibility for them shall be transferred to the UN, which in all matters relating to them shall act in accordance with international law.

Gross told Lloyd he did not think this second text would be acceptable. Firstly, it would be necessary under this form of words to have it clearly understood that the General Assembly would adopt a subsequent resolution, designating the UN agency which would have authority to care for and dispose of non-repatriated prisoners of war. Lloyd expressed agreement with this and said he was sure Menon would understand, but commented that they should not move ahead at once with a follow-up resolution. Gross commented this would have to be done by the Assembly in time to take on the responsibility. Secondly, Gross felt the phrase 'until the end of their detention' must come out of the text. Lloyd thought he could persuade Menon to delete these words. Thirdly, Gross inquired as to the significance of the last clause 'which in all matter relating to them shall act in accordance with international law'. These words seemed to Gross to be undesirable, since, if they meant anything they implied that when and if this question came back to UN, the whole subject of non-forcible repatriation could be re-opened on the basis of arguments thrashed over during the past few weeks. Lloyd explained that Menon attached great importance to these words, 'which for some reason', that he conceded was obscure, the language gave Menon 'an excuse' to accept modifications in paragraph 17. Gross stated to Lloyd he could not make any commitment whatever on the drafts but would talk to Acheson in the morning and would call Lloyd before 10 a.m.

The following morning Gross reported all the foregoing to Acheson who authorised him to tell Lloyd that the United States would, if necessary to maintain Menon's support for his own resolution, accept the first alternative formulation, subject, however, to the deletion of phrase 'until the end of their detention' and of the last clause reading 'which in all matters relating to them shall act in accordance with international law'. However, Acheson also authorised Gross to accept the text as it stood, if he considered it essential in order to avoid breaking with Menon. Gross spoke with Lloyd, who agreed to see Menon as soon as possible and urge him to delete the phrase relating to detention. As for the deletion of the last clause, Lloyd thought Menon would find this impossible because of the importance he attached to having 'an umbrella' under which he could justify his acceptance of the changes. Gross then suggested to Lloyd that he urge Menon to agree to the insertion, following the words 'in accordance with', the clause 'the principles of this resolution and'. Lloyd accepted this suggestion and said he would do his best with Menon. Gross pressed Lloyd to persuade Menon to circulate his revised paragraph 17 as soon as possible. Lloyd replied he would try to do so but that Menon had told him he felt he had to cable to New Delhi, although Lloyd personally doubted that Menon in fact had to do so. Nevertheless, Lloyd would commend Menon to accept these changes.[49]

Later, that morning, Acheson, Gross, Lloyd, and Mike Pearson met to discuss progress. Pearson counselled consideration of the shorter alternative formulation, which Acheson had already rejected. Lloyd and Pearson thereupon agreed to press upon Menon acceptance of the longer version but with the omission of the words Acheson objected to.[50] Menon could not persuade his delegation to accept a change in the period to 30 days; instead the Americans asked the Danes to put in an amendment to Menon's new revision, changing 60 days to 30 and Menon agreed that he would support the resolution even if this amendment was adopted.[51] On 1 December the First Committee voted on the Indian draft resolution approving each paragraph by considerable margins. Then, a Danish amendment proposing a 30-day instead of a 60-day time limit for the political conference to dispose of the remainder of the prisoners, was adopted by a large majority.

The Committee overwhelmingly rejected the amendments of the Soviet Union to the Indian resolution; and then passed the Indian resolution as a whole and as amended by a vote of 53 to 5, with 1 abstention.[52]

## Notes

1. TNA FO 800/780 Prime Minister Personal Minute Serial No. M.53e/51, 16 November 1951
2. FRUS 1951, Volume VII (Korea and China Part I). Memorandum of Conversation. by the Deputy Director of the Executive Secretariat of the Department of State (Barnes), 28 November 1951
3. Peter Lowe, *Containing the Cold War in East Asia. British Policies Towards Japan, China and Korea 1948–53* (Manchester: Manchester University Press 1997), p. 240
4. FRUS 1951, Volume VII (Korea and China Part I). The British Embassy to the Department of State, 3 December 1951. Telegram from the British Secretary of State for Foreign Affairs to the British Embassy in Rome
5. TNA FO 800/780 Prime Minister's Personal Minute Serial No. M.154e/51, 13 December 1951
6. TNA FO 800/780 Conversation between the Secretary of State and the United States Ambassador. Eden to Sir O. Franks (Washington) Telegram No. 1451, 16 December 1951
7. TNA FO 800/780 no title to memo
8. TNA FO 800/780 Eden to Churchill, 4 January 1952
9. FRUS 1952–1954, Volume VI (Western Europe and Canada Part I). Memorandum by the Secretary of State of a Dinner Meeting at the British Embassy, 6 January 1952
10. FRUS 1952–1954, Volume VI (Western Europe and Canada Part I). United States Delegation Minutes of the Third Formal Meeting of President Truman and Prime Minister Churchill, The White House, 8 January 1952
11. John Young, *Winston Churchill's Last Campaign. Britain and the Cold War 1951–1955* (Oxford: Clarendon Press, 1996), p. 86
12. Kevin Ruane, 'Containing America: Aspects of British Foreign Policy and the Cold War in South-East Asia 1951–54', *Diplomacy & Statecraft*, 7:1, pp. 141–174 (1996), p. 147
13. Ibid., p.149
14. TNA FO 800/780 Secretary of State's reply to the Prime Minister's Personal Minute, 3 March 1952
15. TNA FO 800/780 31 Eden to Churchill, 31 March 1952
16. Lowe, *Containing the Cold War*, p. 250
17. TNA FO 800/780 Churchill to Eden, 15 April 1952
18. TNA FO 800/780 Eden to Churchill, 22 April 1952
19. TNA FO 800/780 Churchill to Eden, 28 April 1952

20 Korea No. 1 (1953) *A Summary of Further Developments in the Military Situation, Armistice Negotiations and Prisoner of War Camps up to January 1953* Cmd 8793 Extract from a Speech by the Right Hon Selwyn Lloyd, CBE, TD, QC, MP, Minister of State, in the First Committee of the United Nations General Assembly, on Thursday, 30 October 1952
21 TNA PREM 11/115 Napalm Bombing In Korea, 20 August 1952
22 TNA PREM 11/115 Draft 'Off The Record' Statement for General Bradley on the British Attitude to the use of Napalm Bombs in Korea, 20 August 1952
23 TNA PREM 11/115 Prime Minister to Minister of Defence, 21 August 1952
24 TNA PREM 11/115 Alexander to Prime Minister, 28 August 1952
25 TNA FD 1/4908 Prime Minister to Minister of Defence, August 1952
26 TNA PREM 11/115 Eden to Prime Minister, 29 August 1952
27 TNA FD 1/4908 Prime Minister to Minister of Defence, 30 August 1952
28 TNA PREM 11/250 The Communist Germ Warfare Campaign
29 TNA PREM 11/250 Prime Minister's Note, 21 September 1952
30 TNA PREM 11/250 Cherwell to Prime Minister, 25 September 1952
31 TNA PREM 11/250 The Germ Warfare Campaign. Memorandum by Information Research Department
32 TNA PREM 11/250 Prime Minister's Personal Minute Serial No. M.498/52, 5 October 1952
33 TNA FO 800/782 Prime Minister's Personal Message Serial No. M.360/52 to Minister of Defence Proposed appointment of a British Deputy Chief of Staff to General Mark Clark's Headquarters, 3 July 1952
34 TNA FO 800/782 Prime Minister's Personal Message Serial No. M.355/52 to Strang, 3 July 1952
35 TNA FO 800/782 Lloyd to Eden, 9 July 1952
36 TNA FO 800/782 Prime Minister's Personal Message Serial No. M.398/52 to Foreign Secretary, 21 July 1952
37 TNA FO 800/782 Foreign Secretary to Prime Minister, 21 July 1952
38 TNA CAB 195/10 C.C. 71 (52), 22 July 1952
39 FRUS 1952–1954, Volume XV (Korea Part I). Memorandum of Conversation by the Secretary of State, 29 October 1952. Subject: Korean Question
40 FRUS 1952–1954, Volume XV (Korea Part I). Memorandum by the Under Secretary of State (Bruce) to the President, 13 November 1952. Subject: Korean Resolution in the United Nations General Assembly
41 FRUS 1952–1954, Volume XV (Korea Part I). Draft Memorandum of Conversation of a Meeting Held in New York, 16 November 1952
42 TNA FO 800/781 Record of a Telephone Conversation between the Secretary of State and General Eisenhower, 18 November 1952
43 TNA FO 800/781 Conversation between the Secretary of State and General Eisenhower, 20 November 1952

44  FRUS 1952–1954, Volume XV (Korea Part I). The Secretary of State to the President, 20 November 1952
45  FRUS 1952–1954, Volume XV (Korea Part I). The Secretary of State to the President, 21 November 1952
46  FRUS 1952–1954, Volume XV (Korea Part I). The United States Representative at the United Nations (Austin) to the Department of State, 22 November 1952
47  FRUS 1952–1954, Volume XV (Korea Part I). The Secretary of State to the Department of State, 25 November 1952
48  FRUS 1952–1954, Volume XV (Korea Part I). The Secretary of State to the President, 26 November 1952
49  FRUS 1952–1954, Volume XV (Korea Part I). The Secretary of State to the Department of State from Gross, 26 November 1952. Re: Korea
50  FRUS 1952–1954, Volume XV (Korea Part I). The Secretary of State to the Department of State, 26 November 1952
51  FRUS 1952–1954, Volume XV (Korea Part I). The Secretary of State to the President, 26 November 1952
52  FRUS 1952–1954, Volume XV (Korea Part I). Editorial Note pp. 700–701

# 8

# Breakthrough

In the aftermath of Stalin's death, and the emergence of a collective leadership in the Kremlin, Churchill, who had taken over the Foreign Office in the wake of Eden's illness, was apt to think, as he informed Eisenhower: 'I believe myself that at this moment time is on our side.' An apparent change of Soviet mood was 'so new' and 'so indefinite' and the causes for it so obscure that there could not be much risk in letting things develop. 'We do not know what these men mean.' Hitherto they had been the aggressors and had 'done us wrong at a hundred points'. Nevertheless great hope had arisen in the world that there was a change of heart in the vast, mighty mass of Russia and this might carry them far and fast and perhaps into revolution: 'It has been well said that the most dangerous moment for evil Governments is when they begin to reform.' All this came to a particular point upon Korea, wrote Churchill, who was worried that the President's speech, to be delivered to the American Society of Newspaper Editors and listing five principles defining the US position in the Cold War, would have a negative impact on the new Soviet leadership: 'I was hoping that at least we should secure at this juncture a *bona fide*, lasting and effective truce in Korea which might mean the end of that show as a world problem. It seems to me very unlikely that the terms you require for the later political settlement of Korea as set out in your statement would be accepted as they stand by the other side. I fear the formal promulgation of your five points at this moment might quench the hope of an armistice.' Churchill urged – but failed – to persuade the President to wait until the full character and purpose of the Soviet change was more clearly defined and also was apparent to the whole free world, adding: 'I always like the story of

Napoleon going to sleep in his chair as the battle began saying "Wake me when their infantry column gets beyond the wood".[1]

Despite Churchill's concerns, there was a thaw in the armistice talks. Negotiations as a whole resumed on April 26. At the outset, the Communists submitted a proposal for sending all prisoners not directly repatriated to an agreed neutral State where for six months after their arrival representatives of the States to which they belonged would 'explain' to them matters related to their return; if after this period any non-repatriates remained, their disposition would be referred to the proposed political conference. Discussion subsequently centred upon the questions of what neutral State should be nominated, of whether non-repatriates should be removed from Korea, and how long the non-repatriates would remain in neutral custody. On 7 May, the Communists put forward a new proposal providing for establishment of a Neutral Nations Repatriation Commission to be composed of the four States already nominated for membership on the Neutral Nations Supervisory Commission, namely, Czechoslovakia, Poland, Sweden and Switzerland, as well as India as agreed by both sides. This Commission was to take custody of the prisoners in Korea.[2]

Although these proposals were rejected by the Americans, a cautious optimism emerged in London. But, on 8 May, Churchill informed Sir Roger Makins, who had succeeded Franks as ambassador in Washington, that he had learnt that the United Nations Command planned a major bombing attack on one or possibly two targets near the Yalu River almost immediately. He feared that these operations at this moment 'will be thought to be an attempt to spoil agreement at Panmunjom. Are they really necessary whilst things hang in the balance in the negotiations? If there is no overriding military necessity I can see only harm resulting from this plan'. The Prime Minister urged Makins to see Beddell Smith urgently 'and tell him my views. You could ask whether these operations could not be deferred'. The problem, though, was that this report had come from Air Vice Marshal Barnett, the British deputy to General Clark, in Tokyo. 'We have not heard of the plan directly from Washington' explained Churchill and 'We do not want to compromise Barnett's relations with General Mark Clark but as the same time I have strong views on the unwisdom of this operation, of which we might well have been informed from Washington. I leave it to you how best to convey these views to General Bedell-Smith.'[3]

Makins, however, replied that it was not possible to make representations to Bedell Smith 'about a top secret operational matter of which we have no knowledge except through Air Marshal Barnett, without divulging the source. There is no other source from which we could have got this information, and if we use it General Mark Clark is certain to be informed from Washington'. Makins, therefore, wanted to be sure that the importance of the representations outweighed any prejudice that might result to Barnett's position in Tokyo. The only alternative way of handling the matter that Makin could suggest was for Churchill to send a message in general terms to the President saying that in view of the progress made in the armistice negotiations, 'you hope that nothing will be done in the military sphere which could prejudice them'.[4] From Toyko, Sir Esler Dening, the British Ambassador, confirmed that there could be no doubt that if representations were made on specific information obtained from Barnett 'his usefulness will be gravely impaired, since [the] Americans will undoubtedly refrain in future from disclosing information which is likely to result in their getting a rap over the knuckles from Washington'.[5] Makins was duly informed by the Foreign Office: 'You need take no action.'[6] A few days later Makins was instructed to approach the Americans on more general lines and ask them, when deciding upon military action, to bear wider considerations in mind. 'You should make this point forcibly to the United States Government', he was instructed.[7]

A further crisis was averted when the British wobbled over issuing the agreed warning statement should an armistice emerge. Makins had recently been instructed to inform the State Department that the conditions under which the armistice might be signed could be different from the expectations when the warning statement was originally prepared. The right time, the British suggested, to decide whether a warning should be issued and on what terms, would, it was argued, be after an armistice was signed.[8] Makins had barely finished drafting telegrams and the passage in his weekly summary dealing with trade with China, when Bedell Smith rang him up, on 9 May. He had just come from a meeting with Congressional and administration leaders on the Far Eastern situation and had been astonished by the bitterness which had been displayed by some of the Congressional representatives, much of which had been directed against the United Kingdom. He said that the administration were going to do their best but that they would have the greatest possible difficulty in following through their chosen policy which, Makins inferred, was to secure an armistice in Korea involving some compromise on outstanding issues. At the best there were bound to be some violent expressions of opinion from the 'articulate minority on the hill'. Against this background, Smith reverted to the question of the warning statement and said that in the prevailing climate of opinion, 'if we were to change our attitude on this question, it would, in his view, certainly precipitate critical trouble in our relations. He wished me to be quite clear about his opinion on this point'. This conversation served to confirm Makins' impression that 'we are once more threatened with an emotional crisis in this country over the Far East. I do not suggest that we should be deflected by this from our policy, but I am sure that we should not change it, and that we should explain our attitude as clearly and as dispassionately as possible'.[9] In these circumstances the Foreign Office recommended that 'we should not press our suggestion further but confirm our acceptance of the issue of the warning statement in the form originally agreed upon'.[10]

Meanwhile the United Nations Command presented its POW counter-proposal on 13 May shortening the period of time in which the non-repatriates would remain in neutral custody, providing for the release of Korean non-repatriates immediately after the armistice, and proposing that only Indian forces take actual custody of the non-repatriates.[11] The counter-proposals also included a proposal that, on the day the Armistice became effective, all Korean prisoners of war who did not want to go back should be released to civilian status, although, if they changed their minds again at any time in the future, they would be allowed to return to their original side under article 59 of the Draft Armistice Agreement.[12] Jebb had already complained, from New York, that the Americans were 'singularly ill-advised' not to accept the original suggestion by the Chinese to transport all recalcitrant prisoners (at Communist expense) to a neutral state such as Pakistan. Not having accepted this they were now hoist with their own petard since the Communists had proposed what was to a large extent the plan supported by the United Nations in December.[13] In a note for Churchill, the Foreign Office pointed out that Jebb was correct. The Communists' 8-Point Plan of 7 May 'made an important step forward'. In fact the Foreign Office considered 'there were only two points which we thought it important to improve – the introduction of Czech and Polish troops, and the failure to mark out a clear future for prisoners refusing repatriation'. The United Nations Command's counter-proposals of 13 May did not bridge the remaining area of difference, but instead introduced new issues, such as the proposal to release all Korean prisoners of war immediately after an armistice, which the Communists could not be expected to accept easily.[14]

Churchill ordered the Washington Embassy to take these points up with the State Department immediately. Bedell Smith studied the Prime Minister's concerns and fully agreed that the two points in the Foreign Office note, to Churchill, were the crux of the present problem and, he reassured the British, the State Department were bending all their efforts to bridge this gap between themselves and the Communists which he described as deep but narrow. As regarded the introduction of Czech and Polish troops, Smith feared that this was something which it would be practically impossible to concede. The chief obstacle was Syngman Rhee. Rhee was now the master of 20 Korean divisions and, moreover, had the ear of very influential quarters in the United States. He was absolutely determined not to permit Koreans to be guarded by Communist troops or, indeed, to have any Communist troops in South Korea. Smith added that the Americans also had pretty strong security objections but Rhee was the principal stumbling block and was being extremely difficult.[15] Upon receipt of this news Churchill commented to the Minister of State and Sir William Strang: 'This is a very helpful and encouraging telegram. Evidently the obstacle is Syngman Rhee. Let me have in outline what you think I might send to encourage Bedell and back him up.'[16]

The following day, in Washington, Smith telephoned to the Minister of State, at the British Embassy, to say he wanted to consult the major allies in Korea in regard to the next move at Panmunjom. The meeting was arranged at the State Department which turned out to be exclusively Commonwealth representatives of the Australian, Canadian, New Zealand and the South African Embassies. With the Minister's consent Smith then read out the Foreign Office note, originally written for Churchill, agreeing the two points mentioned therein were the crux of the problem. But another important point was the US provision that the POW repatriation commission should take decisions on the basis of unanimity. He admitted that this was 'a straight – out matter of internal politics in the United States', but he was at pains to emphasize that this did not detract from its great importance. The feeling in Congress on this was extremely strong. Congressional leaders held very firmly to the view that if decisions were taken by a straight majority the inclusion of India would mean a 3 to 2 vote in favour of the Communist position. Smith mentioned in this context that there had been open threats by Congressional leaders to sabotage the aid programme to Korea if the administration took what they thought to be an objectionable line in Korea. He went on to emphasise the necessity for the Allies to stand together at this point, either to achieve an armistice (which he hoped would be the case) or to fail honourably with an agreed and unanimous point of view. The United States had tried to arrive at a final position representing the limits to which they could possibly go. There was, however, no intention to present this position to the Communists in the form of an ultimatum.[17] To Makins, Bedell Smith stressed that the State Department were most anxious to have Churchill's reactions to their proposals by 21 May. If there were strong objections from any of the Commonwealth Governments consulted these would be taken into account but otherwise the position described would be embodied in proposals to be submitted at Panmunjom.[18]

Before Churchill had replied, on 20 May, Smith asked Makins to see him that evening. Smith explained that, as the 'strongest reactions' to the United States proposals had been received from the United Kingdom and Canada, he wished to speak both to Makins and the Canadian Ambassador. Since the latter was in Canada he was, however, saying nothing to the Canadian Embassy. The President was sending Churchill a personal message but there were some points on which he wished to elaborate. The President had agreed with the Prime Minister that 'we should not let Syngman Rhee's attitude be decisive'. Nevertheless the Koreans were making the greatest single military contribution and to flout Rhee's views could involve serious risks. At a long and difficult meeting that morning Smith had found that Congressional leaders had spoken with great strength of conviction, but soberly and earnestly and with an awareness of the gravity of the issues involved. Agreement had finally been reached on the following set of proposals:-

(a) Decisions by the Neutral Commission to be taken by simple majority vote.
(b) The Koreans to be handed over to the Neutral Commission in the same way as the Chinese.
(c) After prisoners have spent 90 days in the custody of the Neutral Commission and the problem has been considered for 30 days by the Political Conference, all prisoners to be released: or at the option of the Communists the problem can be remitted to the General Assembly.
(d) The troops for the Neutral Commission to be provided by India alone.
(e) The terms of reference for the Neutral Commission as proposed by the United Nations Command to remain substantially unchanged.

It was to this last point about the terms of reference of the Commission that Bedell Smith particularly addressed himself. This was not an issue which lent itself to discussion among a large number of countries but it was one on which it was vital that HMG and the Americans should stand together. Although in one sense procedural, 'it was really much more than that. If we allowed coercion and force to be used against prisoners we should be jeopardising the essential principle of no forcible repatriation.' Clark would have some latitude in regard to the presentation of the proposals but not on the substance. If the Communists rejected the proposals or made no counter-proposals within the principles laid down, and showed no evidence of willingness to reach an agreement, Clark was to report to Washington. In this event the United States was resolved to instruct Clark to break off negotiations; to cease to recognize the demilitarized zone; to bomb Kaesong; to step up military and air operations; and to release the Chinese and Korean prisoners who did not wish to be repatriated. This plan of action had been approved in advance by the National Security Council. In reply to a question, by Makin, Smith said that it was not proposed to make any approach in Moscow at the moment. At the end of these explanations Smith emphasised that, after great travail with the Congressional representatives, the President had been able to concede all the points of principle to which Churchill attached importance. The administration had gone to their limit and he and the President felt deeply that a demonstration of unity between the principal Allies was wanted if an armistice was now to be obtained. Personally, Makin was convinced that the President and Smith had made a sincere and a sustained effort to meet the Prime Minister's views in the face of determined objections both from some Congressional leaders and some of their advisers: 'Though I recognize that it would have made things much easier if they had known their present flexibility some days ago, I hope you may now be able to give them some support and encouragement' concluded Makin.[19]

In his personal message to Churchill, Eisenhower explained that he had carefully considered the Prime Minster's message. The President felt that the position Bedell Smith had set forth was 'eminently reasonable' especially in view of the fact that 'we are the parties who are resisting an unprovoked aggression'. Eisenhower hoped his proposals provided the basis upon which 'we all could have taken a final stand. It is essential that a firm unified stand be taken if the Communists are to be convinced that the United Nations will never forsake the principle of non-forcible repatriation, either in statement or in fact. Upon this there can be no possibility of misunderstanding'. Although the United States had grave doubts, concerning the conviction of some of the Allies that it could depend upon a simple majority vote, 'we are prepared also to agree' to such a voting formula for the POW Commission provided that the terms of reference for the Commission were such as to ensure, beyond any reasonable doubt, that coercion and force would not be used against the prisoners. If an armistice was to be obtained upon any acceptable basis it would be essential, argued the President, that the Communists clearly understood that there could be no deviation from the essential elements of the position to be taken by the United Nations Command. Any sign of weakening in Allied unity or resolve would again be exploited by them to the disadvantage of 'all of us. I am sure that you will appreciate that any failure on the part of our principal Allies fully to support the position so clearly reasonable and fair and going so far to meet the views of those Allies would have most adverse effects upon American public and Congressional opinion at this critical time'. With respect to Rhee's attitude Eisenhower quite agreed that 'we cannot allow him to dictate policy to our two countries. Yet I beg of you not to forget that Korea is the one place where we have an inspired resistance by the peoples themselves to the Communist enemy. The Koreans are valiantly resisting in numbers that far exceed the combined contributions from all of us. The inspiration for that struggle largely comes from President Rhee'. Finally, the President wrote that he believed that a prompt public and unequivocal statement that the United Kingdom was fully consulted and fully supported the position which the United Nations Command was taking in the forthcoming Executive Sessions would assure an armistice promptly, if in fact the Communists wanted one on the basis acceptable to the Allies.[20]

In his reply, Churchill declared he was 'very glad' that the United States had gone so far to meet British view over the points of substance. The Prime Minister thought there was now a real chance of reaching agreement at Panmunjom. This remained the paramount consideration: 'We must persevere in the course of negotiation' he declared. There should be no resolve of ultimatum and no hasty decision to break off negotiations: 'We cannot decide more than one step at once.' But clearly the Prime Minister was unsettled by Bedell Smith's meeting with Makins and the suggestion that the war would be intensified if the Communists refused an armistice: while Churchill approved the proposals to be put forward at Panmunjom and was willing to declare publicly that HMG were consulted about this and supported American proposals, the Prime Minister warned that the grave decision to support a 'rupture of negotiations' and stepping up of operations if there had been no progress at the end of the week could 'only be taken when the break is inevitable'.[21] The following day, 25 May, the United Nations Command submitted the new proposals.[22]

Adding to Churchill's worry was another despatch, from Makins, this time relating to the opposite of an American intensification of the war – the prospect of a return to isolationism. This despatch concerned a speech by Senator Robert Taft that, warned Makins, was 'symptomatic of a feeling of exasperation which, as I have recently reported, is growing in public opinion here over developments in the Far East. I have not until quite recently given serious heed to suggestions that the United States might in certain circumstances decide to "go it alone"'. But Makins was now beginning to take the possibility more seriously. The achievement or otherwise of an armistice in Korea would be a crucial factor in checking or encouraging the trend.²³ But confirmation the British ought to be concerned with the more immediate problem of the American threat to intensify the war soon came. The United States Minister in New Dehli showed the UK High Commissioner, privately, a short note left behind by the US Secretary of State, John Foster Dulles, of his conversations with Nehru who had been assured that every endeavour would be made in the new proposals, to be put to the Chinese to bridge the main points of difference. If, however, in spite of these endeavours the new proposals were rejected by the Chinese, then negotiations would have to be broken off. The result would be that the American people would feel called upon to make 'not a lesser but a greater' military effort and this would almost certainly mean an *extension* of the war. There followed a note by Dulles that he hoped this would be relayed to the Chinese. The High Commissioner regarded it as noteworthy that Dulles deliberately referred to 'extension' and not 'intensification' of the war.²⁴

After reading this message from India, Churchill despatched a message to Eisenhower pointing out that, in the talk between Smith and Makins on May 23, the idea was mentioned that perhaps the United States might make some approach to Moscow to help agreement at Panmunjom: 'I think it would be a pity for the United States to make an approach to Moscow at this juncture and that it would only be taken by them as a sign of weakness. You are the overwhelmingly powerful figure in the ring and we are supporting you in your effort to make the Communists accept' declared Churchill. However, the Prime Minister thought it would be quite a different thing for himself to send a personal and private message to Soviet Foreign Minister Molotov 'and indeed I had thought of doing this anyhow'. The position would then be the United States maintaining a 'formidable front' and Britain, 'bound to them by unbreakable ties, giving a friendly hint. Let me know how you feel about this' the Prime Minister asked. Churchill ended his message welcoming Eisenhower's rejection of Taft's isolationist remarks: 'I look back with dark memories to all that followed inch by inch upon the United States' withdrawal from the League of Nations over 30 years ago. Thank God you are at the helm.'²⁵

As it turned out, Makins was told that the State Department had just informed a member of his staff the administration had decided in favour of an approach in Moscow and that the United States Ambassador was instructed to see Molotov that day. The Americans had no particular reason for believing that action in Moscow would be effective, but apparently decided that this particular stone should not be left unturned, and that if any action was to be taken in Moscow it must be before the Communists had reached a firm position and, therefore, during the course of that week.²⁶ From Moscow the British Ambassador, Sir Alvary Gascoigne reported that his American counterpart, Charles Bohlen, had 'merely' left with Molotov a paper defining the key points; but Bohlen orally impressed on Molotov that these constituted the furthest limit to which United Nations Command were prepared to go, and that they should therefore be looked upon with the utmost seriousness and studied with the greatest possible care. He was careful to avoid giving any suggestion of a threat. Molotov, although he was completely non-committal, did not challenge any of the conditions laid down in the six points, nor did he try in any way to disclaim responsibility in the matter of the negotiations. He merely promised Bohlen that he would refer the question to his government. While Bohlen had no inkling at all as regarded Molotov's real attitude towards this matter, he was impressed by his apparent interest in it, and particularly by the fact that he did not challenge any of the points made. As Bohlen said to Gascoigne, Molotov 'may have been "putting on an act"; if so he played the part well'. Bohlen revealed he was not informing any of his other foreign colleagues in Moscow about the approach.²⁷

Churchill went on and contacted Moscow anyhow, informing Molotov that, as acting-Foreign Secretary, he was 'very glad to re-open my former contacts with you … It would I am sure be a help if this Panmunjom prisoners-of-war business were got out of the way. Please do not hesitate to telegraph direct and personally to me whenever you feel inclined'.²⁸ But once again Churchill's efforts to play a role were superseded by events: on this occasion Gascoigne was informed, by the Americans, that the Soviet Government had taken note of Bohlen's statement of 28 May and that while the decision did not rest with the Soviet Government the latter were gratified to learn that a path was being laid which might lead towards successful negotiations. Gascoigne considered this important, showing that the prospects of a settlement seemed to be brighter. It was also interesting that the Soviet Government had been willing to show their hand in this way. There was no need for Molotov to have said anything further to Bohlen noted Gascoigne, who did not call for a reply. Bohlen, once again, declined to inform any of his foreign colleagues, apart from the British, of this news.²⁹

On 4 June the Washington Embassy learnt of a breakthrough in the armistice talks: that very day General Nam II, for the Communists, had read out an entirely new draft which proved to embody most of the language of the United Nations Command's proposals of 25 May, amounting, in effect, to an almost complete acceptance of these proposals. The terms of reference for the Neutral Commission were accepted with a few minor changes.

But Makins reported the Americans were warning that the attitude of Rhee and his Government were still unsolved 'and premature rejoicing would be unwise'. Clark would be seeing Rhee that night 'and much would hinge on the outcome of this meeting'.[30] That Clark was worried was confirmed from a report from Dening who, the day before, had been told by General Shoosmith (Clark's new British Deputy Chief of Staff and the only non-American on that staff) that he had had a 'bad hour' with Clark who was 'in very low spirits (partly due to fact that his wife, to whom he is very devoted, had a heart attack and is in hospital here) and very bitter about attitude of United Nations Governments and his own'. The point which Clark apparently stressed was that 'there is nothing he can really do about it if Syngman Rhee takes the bit between his teeth, now that he has 16 divisions'. Clark was also concerned about the fact that 35,000 North Koreans who did not want to go back were being guarded by South Koreans who had their orders, 'but may not in the last resort obey them'. Dening believed Clark's difficulties 'to be very real and rightly or wrongly he apparently thinks that they are not being taken into sufficient account by United States and other governments'.[31]

Nevertheless, on 8 June, an armistice was signed by the UN Command and the Communist representatives at Panmunjom. A Military Demarcation Line was to be established at the battle-line on the day that the armistice was signed. Each side would withdraw two kilometres from this line, leaving a Demilitarised Zone four kilometres wide. No reinforcements of men or equipment would be allowed, but each side might rotate its troops up to a limit of 35,000 a month. The building and repair of airfields was not forbidden. A Military Armistice Commission would be established, composed of senior officers of the two sides and assisted by joint teams of observers. This Commission would supervise the implementation of the Armistice Agreement inside the Demilitarised Zone, and would settle, through negotiation, any violation of it. A Neutral Nations Supervisory Commission was also set up, composed of senior officers from Poland, Czechoslovakia, Switzerland and Sweden and assisted by Neutral Nations Inspection Teams stationed at five ports of entry on each side. The task of the Neutral Commission was to supervise the implementation of the Armistice Agreement *outside* the Demilitarised Zone. Both sides also agreed to recommend that, within three months after the Armistice Agreement became effective, a political conference should be summoned to settle the question of the withdrawal of all foreign forces from Korea and the peaceful settlement of the Korean question, 'etc'. The United Nations Command stated at the time when this article was agreed: 'We wish it clearly understood that we do not construe the words 'et cetera' to relate to matters outside of Korea.'³² As part of the attempt to reassure Rhee, the UK Government also put its name to the Warning Statement that cautioned the Communist powers and sought to reassure the South Koreans that, that if there was a renewal of the armed attack, 'we should again be united and prompt to resist. The consequences of such a breach of the armistice would be so grave that, in all probability, it would not be possible to confine hostilities within the frontiers of Korea'.³³

Anti-truce demonstrations, organised by Rhee, took place on an unprecedented scale in Pusan on 11 June. For the first time, attention was paid to the British Legation when schoolchildren stopped at the gate and chanted slogans in English and Korean. One slogan was 'out with Churchill and sympathisers and traders with the Communists'. The demonstration, though, was orderly and good humoured.³⁴ More serious was the incident, on 18 June, when South Korean government officials engineered a breakout of some 27,000 Korean prisoners of war who had previously indicated they would resist repatriation to North Korea.³⁵ When Makins saw Dulles later in the evening, the Secretary of State read a 'refreshingly stern' message which Eisenhower had sent to Rhee.³⁶ On 19 June, Dulles asked the Ambassadors of all countries with forces in Korea to attend a meeting at the State Department. He began by giving a 'somewhat bowdlerised' account of the President's letter to Rhee. Makins was told that there was considerable evidence that the release of the prisoners 'was not an end in itself but a deliberate attempt to make it impossible to proceed with an armistice'.³⁷

On 20 June, Churchill despatched a personal message to Eisenhower: 'The following is only a thought of my own. Syngman Rhee arrested or dismissed from office. British send an extra brigade from Egypt to Korea. Winston.'³⁸ A parallel message was despatched, by Field Marshal Alexander, instructing Dening to personally ask Clark, if the United States decided to get rid of Rhee, would the South Korean Army remain loyal to the United Nations Command. Alexander emphasised that the British were 'considering how best we can help'.³⁹ When asked, Clark told Dening that, in his opinion, if there were a conflict of loyalties between Rhee and the United Nations Command, practically all the South Korean Commanders and their troops would side with their President. To force him to relinquish office would involve his replacement by a new President with insufficient prestige and authority to carry the nation with him. There simply was no one of this calibre known to Clark and to depose Rhee might well precipitate the very situation the UN wished to avoid, i.e. civil war in South Korea and the prospect of armed conflict between UN and South Korean forces.⁴⁰

Makins, meanwhile, saw the President on the morning of 21 June and passed on the Prime Minister's message. He found the President was in excellent form and very friendly. On Rhee, Eisenhower sympathised with Churchill's desire but said emphatically that any change must come or appear to come from within South Korea. The President felt strongly that the Western powers who had intervened in Korea to uphold freedom and democracy must not be seen to be setting up a puppet government. He had given much thought to this and had some hope that there were elements in South Korea who understood that the country was wholly dependent on the United States for its reconstruction and future support and that they would exert influence. Makin asked whether something would now be done through the South Korean Army. Eisenhower seemed to think the Army might in fact make a move. As to Churchill's offer of an additional British Brigade the President 'observed that this would have a gainsaying effect in the United States.' Finally Eisenhower said he would reflect further upon Churchill's offer. He entirely agreed that the matter should be kept in closest secrecy. Any hint that such a thing was under discussion could have a 'most serious effect'. Makins ended his despatch to Downing Street with the news that he understood 'very confidentially that the President and some of his advisors have in fact already discussed at length ways and means of dealing with Rhee and that there are also unconfirmed indications that a military coup in Korea is being prepared'.[41] Churchill, meanwhile moved to reassure the Russians, personally contacting Molotov to reassure the Russians that he was sure the United States Government were deeply angered by Rhee's outrage 'and so are we. We must not let our thoughts on larger issues be unduly disturbed by this sinister event. I mean to persevere in my policy of "bridges not barriers". We must all do the best we can'.[42]

## Notes

1 TNA FO 800/784 Foreign Office to Washington Telegram No. 1596; 10 April 1953. Personal and Secret message from the Prime Minister to President Eisenhower
2 Korea No. 2 (1953) *Special Report of the Unified Command on the Korean Armistice Agreement Signed at Panmunjom on July 27, 1953*, Cmd 8938
3 TNA PREM 11/460 Foreign Office to Washington No. 2040, 8 May 1953
4 TNA PREM 11/460 Washington to Foreign Office Sir R. Makins No. 991, 8 May 1953
5 TNA PREM 11/460 Tokyo to Foreign Office Sir E. Dening No. 509, 9 May 1953
6 TNA FO 800/783 Foreign Office to Washington Telegram No. 2061, 9 May 1953

7 TNA PREM 11/460 Foreign Office to Washington No. 2071, 11 May 1953. Following from Minister of State
8 TNA PREM 11/460 Warning Statement by Sixteen Nations after an Armistice in Korea (J.S.H. Shattock), 12 May 1953
9 TNA PREM 11/460 Washington to Foreign Office Sir R. Makins No. 1001, 9 May 1953
10 TNA PREM 11/460 Warning Statement by Sixteen Nations after an Armistice in Korea (J.S.H. Shattock), 12 May 1953
11 Cmd 8938
12 TNA PREM 11/460 Tokyo to Foreign Office Sir E. Dening No. 529, 14 May 1953
13 TNA PREM 11/460 New York to Foreign Office Sir G. Jebb No. 370, 9 May 1953
14 TNA PREM 11/460 Foreign Office to Washington No. 2138, 16 May 1953. Note for the Prime Minister by the Foreign Office
15 TNA PREM 11/460 Washington to Foreign Office Sir R. Makins No. 1052, 18 May 1953. Prime Minister's Personal Telegram Serial No. T153/53
16 TNA PREM 11/460 Prime Minister's Personal Minute Serial No. M.148/53, 18 May 1953
17 TNA PREM 11/460 Washington to Foreign Office Sir R. Makins No. 1060, 19 May 1953
18 TNA PREM 11/460 Washington to Foreign Office Sir R. Makins No. 1061, 19 May 1953
19 TNA PREM 11/460 Washington to Foreign Office Sir R. Makins No. 1097, 23 May 1953
20 TNA PREM 11/460 Eisenhower to Churchill, 23 May 1953
21 TNA PREM 11/460 Churchill to Eisenhower, 24 May 1953
22 Cmd 8938
23 TNA PREM 11/460 Washington to Foreign Office Sir R. Makins No. 1129, 27 May 1953
24 TNA PREM 11 From UK High Commissioner in India, 27 May 1953
25 TNA FO 800/783 Foreign Office to Washington No. 2247, 28 May 1953. From Prime Minister to President Eisenhower
26 TNA PREM 11/460 Washington to Foreign Office Sir R. Makins No. 1142, 28 May 1953
27 TNA PREM 11/460 Moscow to Foreign Office Sir A. Gascoigne No. 395, 29 May 1953
28 TNA PREM 11/460 Prime Minister's Personal Telegram Serial No. T183/53 Foreign Office to Moscow No. 322, 2 June 1953
29 TNA PREM 11/460 Moscow to Foreign Office Sir A. Gascoigne No. 406, 3 June 1953
30 TNA PREM 11/460 Washington to Foreign Office Sir R. Makins No. 1189, 4 June 1953

31  TNA PREM 11/460 Tokyo to Foreign Office Sir E. Dening No. 590, 4 June 1953
32  TNA PREM 11/460 Note for Prime Minister Korea: Armistice Agreement. Military Demarcation Line and Demilitarised Zone
33  TNA PREM 11/460 Korean Warning Statement
34  TNA PREM 11/460 Korea to Foreign Office Mr Graham, 11 June 1953
35  Cmd 8938
36  TNA PREM 11/460 Washington to Foreign Office Sir R. Makins No. 1282, 18 June 1953
37  TNA PREM 11/460 Washington to Foreign Office Sir R. Makins No. 1294, 19 June 1953
38  TNA PREM 11/460 Foreign Office to Washington Prime Minister's Personal Telegram Serial No. T 204A/53 No. 2481, 20 June 1953
39  TNA PREM 11/460 Foreign Office to Tokyo No. 785, 20 June 1953. Personal message to Ambassador Dening from Alexander
40  TNA PREM 11/460 Sir E. Dening. Tokyo. Telegram 637, 21 June 1953
41  TNA PREM 11/460 Washington to Foreign Office Prime Minister's Personal Telegram Serial No. T 210/5 No. 1304, 21 June 1953
42  TNA PREM 11/460 Prime Minister to Molotov, 26 June 1953

# 9

# Manchurian candidates

With the ending of hostilities British POWs began to return home. As they did so it became necessary to assess whether any of the returnees posed a threat to the State because of Communist attempts at indoctrination. The Prisoners-of-War Geneva Convention of 1949, drawn up by an international conference which included delegates from the Soviet Union and most of its satellite countries, did not apply *de jure* to the combatants in the Korean War, but the British Government considered 'it was reasonable to regard it as having set civilised standards which should be recognised by both sides'. Both the United Nations Command and the North Koreans declared that they intended to apply the convention *de facto* in their treatment of war prisoners. On the other hand the Chinese, British prisoners were told, did not hold under Communist leadership 'with any oppression of common peoples.' What was curious was that officers and senior non-commissioned officers (NCOs: who made up about 12 per cent of the total of British soldiers captured by the Chinese) remained almost completely unaffected by Communist propaganda and were segregated from the remainder, while among the junior NCOs and Other Ranks some two-thirds remained virtually unaffected. Of the remainder, most absorbed sufficient indoctrination to be classed as Communist sympathisers, but had most likely responded to the influence of normal home life upon their return. A small minority – about 40 altogether – returned home convinced Communists. But some had Communist leanings or affiliations before they went to Korea.[1]

Most British personnel had resisted Communist attempts to make them cooperate with them. But there were many soldiers who did cooperate and, even worse from the authorities' point of view, collaborated with the enemy. On 7 August 1951 the Chiefs of Staff had decided that all British POWs repatriated from the Korean theatre of operations should be interrogated in order to obtain important intelligence information. The responsibility for this interrogation was delegated to A.I.9., Air Ministry. The establishment of the unit to carry out these interrogation duties was approved by the Establishment Sub-Committee on 3 September 1951 and was called the British Repatriated Prisoner of War Interrogation Unit (BRPWIU). A number of factors that came to light led to a broadening of the charter of the interrogation unit. Briefly, these factors were the revelation that attempts were made by the Chinese and North Koreans to indoctrinate POWs with 'communist ideals' and the necessity to assess the results of the indoctrination programme on British POWs. The interrogation unit stationed in Japan assisted in the latter task and reports were duly made to the Joint Intelligence Committee. Preliminary and, of necessity, broad assessments showed that a considerable number of British POWs had been 'affected' to varying degrees by Communist indoctrination. At this stage it was considered desirable and necessary to exchange information with the US authorities on the indoctrination techniques used by the Communists in order that British and UN combat troops could be adequately briefed to resist this 'insidious' form of interrogation and propaganda in future.

The interrogation of repatriated British POWs revealed that while the number of British POWs seriously affected by Communist propaganda was not so high as was considered possible at the time that the preliminary assessment was made, the degree to which certain POWs had been affected was 'more serious than was considered likely at that time'.[2] The first 40 British POWs were released in April 1953, as sick and wounded, during an operation known as 'Little Switch'. In August and September 1953 a little over 1,000 were released during operation 'Big Switch'.[3] Major A.N. West-Watson, the Commander of BRPWIU, was certain that the Communist authorities had planned the release of United Nation POWs to suit their own purposes by releasing those from Camp 5 first. By this action the first POWs were in the main 'progressives' although there were a few 'reactionaries' and 'middle of the road' POWs among the later releases from the camp. West-Watson believed that the Communist plan was that these POWs would receive the best reception as they were the first out and, secondly, they would be the first to return to their homes and leave the Korean theatre before the remainder of the POWs were released. But this did not take place as expected and a large number of the POWs from another camp were released and arrived in time to catch the first troopship returning to the UK. It became evident at this time that the progressives 'no longer had the protection of the Chinese nor their majority in the party' and therefore the reactionaries and others immediately began to threaten some of the POWs they considered had been responsible for their ill treatment, while others were considered to have been too active as progressives. Although there was no serious outbreak of beatings, the feeling was there all the time and is probably still there on their return to the United Kingdom. The majority of the reactionaries are at a loss to understand why those whom they consider have misbehaved in the camps are being given the same treatment as themselves once they have been released. Although it has been explained to them that they must not take the law into their own hands they still feel a certain amount of resentment as nothing has so far happened' to those POWs who collaborated.[4] The problem for the Government was how to conduct disciplinary action against offending POWs. From information available it seemed likely that the following categories of offences had probably been committed:-

(a) Pre-capture
   (i) Cowardice
   (ii) Desertion or Absence.
(b) During captivity
   (i) Aiding the enemy by such method as informing against fellow PW.
   (ii) Endeavouring to seduce members of H.M. Forces fighting against the Communists from their allegiance.
   (iii) Aiding the enemy by spreading propaganda liable to damage the U.N. cause, either by means of pamphlets or by broadcasting.

The problem, however, was that it was 'not considered that the mere fact of becoming a good Communist constitutes an offence, provided such a man has not taken active steps to assist the enemy'. This was in accordance with Churchill's personal directions given when sick and wounded POWs were first repatriated. As for offences committed in captivity there were 'certain difficulties in bringing home this sort of charge':

(a) The offence under the Army Act is *Voluntarily* aiding the enemy. In a number of these cases it may be difficult to show that the action was voluntary, and the offender may well plead that he acted under fear or duress.
(b) The case of seducing men from their allegiance of which we already know rests on a document purporting to be signed by a number of PW. The proof of these signatures will not be easy.

Other factors that the Government had to take into consideration included the fact that public opinion seemed likely to be strongly in favour of bringing to justice any men who could be shown to have let down their fellow POWs, but in respect of the other offences it could easily be swayed in the reverse direction by:

(a) Trials of what seemed to be trivial offences and which savour of persecution on purely political grounds.
(b) Failure to obtain convictions.

It, therefore, seemed to be wise only to bring to trial men who had committed really serious offences and against whom there were cases with a good chance of conviction because: 'Left wing elements in this country have good legal resources at their disposal and we must expect men charged with this type of offence to have available exceptionally able defence. This further strengthens the grounds for only bringing strong cases.'[5] Only one soldier was prosecuted, for cowardice, as a result.

It became evident during the interrogation of POWs by BRPWIU that the Communists had started and maintained dossiers of the activities, writing, etc. of all POWs in their hands. These dossiers contained copies or the originals of propaganda documents, petitions, private letters, confessions, criticisms etc., made by the prisoner concerned. Many of these had never been used for the purpose they were originally designed. West-Watson considered it sufficient to say that in a great number of cases the prisoner was forced in one way or another to acquiesce to Chinese demands for an initial statement during the interrogation or indoctrination and from then they continued to build up their demands in spite of opposition. Some of course continued without further pressure being put on them. Although the exact reason for these dossiers was not evident, West-Watson believed that the Communists intended to use them to solicit the assistance of the ex-POWs on their return to Britain either to provide additional information by using this as blackmail or using it as a lever to force the person concerned to continue his activities on behalf of the Communists. In addition there was always the possibility that some selected students of Communism among the POWs 'may have already been detailed to act for the Communist movement in this country when they continue their service life or after they return to their civilian occupation'. West-Watson thought that it was 'probable that all the "Progressives" have been and still are loyal to their own country particularly now they have returned home. Their loyalty may be put to the test however, if they are confronted with evidence of their cooperation and collaboration with the Communists by the production or with the fear of production of documents from the Communist held dossiers. Others on the other hand may consider their sympathy with the World Communist Movement sufficient to warrant their assisting the Communist party when asked to do so'. It was evident, therefore, that unless any ex-POWs reported that they had been contacted by a member of the Communist Party 'to do something for them, however small, they will be a danger to security if they are employed where they could do so. Once they have started giving assistance it will be difficult for them to stop and easy for the Communists to increase their demands'.

So, it was apparent to West-Watson that the return to the United Kingdom of the ex-POWs presented many problems 'which might solve themselves while others would have to be solved by some more direct means'. The initial problem was whether any action could be taken against those whom it could be proved had collaborated with the enemy to the detriment of their fellow POWs. Secondly, it was evident that adequate safeguards must be taken by the Security Service, MI5, to ensure that none of the POWs, 'who had become adherents to the Communist faith', were put in a position where they could become a danger to national security at the same time as placing themselves in a compromising position. The third major problem was what action, if any, could be taken to recognise those POWs who had done more than was demanded of them as POWs and to have suffered in some cases considerable ill treatment from their captors. West-Watson deemed it probable that a considerable number of the more 'lightly indoctrinated' POWs would forget the Communist teaching on their return to their families and normality in England, 'but others may continue to further their knowledge and activities'.[6]

The repatriated POWs were graded either 'Black' or 'Grey', depending on the amount of Communist penetration which appeared to have taken place, and had 'affected the thoughts, sayings and actions of these people'. It had not been possible to lay down a rule of thumb method to decide into which grade these persons should be put, but broad definitions were used as a guide for the grading, and West-Watson was responsible for the final decisions. The grading was:

> *'White'* Any person who has not been a subject of special indoctrination and who appears to be completely unaffected by any Communist propaganda which has been directed at him.
> *'Grey'* All persons who cannot initially be graded as 'White' or 'Black'.
> *'Black'* Any person who has become a convert to Communism and who became a leader or propagandist of Communism within the Camp.

A final classification was included; that of 'Broadcaster'. This was included as, in many cases, the first reference that had been received of a POW turning towards Communism had been the mention of his name in a broadcast from Peking Radio or an actual broadcast by the man either sending Christmas greetings or taking part in some propaganda effort. The grading was decided upon purely as a result of the evidence available initially with changes and additions where necessary once the prisoners had been released and interrogated when direct evidence was available and personal assessments could be made.[7] The interrogation reports of the initial 40 Army officers and 915 other ranks, together with information already obtained, resulted in 90 other ranks being placed in the category of 'Black'. Specifically, to be graded 'Black', a POW had to fulfil all of the following conditions:

(a) To have made one or more broadcasts on radio PEKING expressing pro-Communist sentiments
(b) To have signed one or more peace petitions containing anti-UK or pro-Communist propaganda
(c) To have expressed persistent pro-Communist sympathies in his letters to relatives in the UK
(d) To have originated or signed chain letters to relatives in the UK asking them to sign peace petitions.

Interrogation reports on all returned POW were distributed to interested Service Departments and MI5. In the case of those thought to be of continuing security interest forms were made out giving:

(a) Personal details
(b) Provisional political grading i.e. Black, Grey, White
(c) Security Assessment i.e. High, Medium, Low Risk

These details were forwarded to MI5 and the Directorate of Military Intelligence at the War Office (MI 11) including those reports in their individual filing system which ensured that the security risk came to notice when applications were made for individuals to be granted access to classified material, i.e. through vetting. MI 11 also notified Records Offices of those soldiers to be placed on 'restricted postings' i.e. no posting without reference to MI 11, for all those who continued serving in the Service or who were on the reserve list.[8]

An example of the interrogations carried out by BRPWIU was that on Rifleman Spencer. He was one of two British members of the Central

Committee of the US–British War Prisoners Peace Organisation. His name appeared upon a number of statements issued by that Committee and a quotation was made in a statement alleged to have been made by Spencer. Just before leaving North Korea, he seemed to have made a farewell broadcast which, from its text, was considered fairly innocuous. In his favour it was considered important to note that:-

(a) No 'contaminated' letters have ever been received from Spencer;
(b) Spencer is NOT one of those who have made application for membership of the British Communist Party.

During his interview, in Tidworth Military Hospital, Spencer voluntarily and readily divulged a large quantity of extremely important information upon the subject of the Communist indoctrination methods. He also supplied, without pressure, some important information of value to AI9, concerning the defences of Camp 5 and barge and river traffic on the Yalu River. His interviewer gained the impression that Spencer was something of a 'creature of circumstances' in that his election to membership of the Central Committee was perhaps organised, 'Communist fashion'. It was very probable that he volunteered for some administrative post in order to better his lot with the Chinese and instead of being elected to the Sanitary, Food or other committees (which seemed to have been running elections at the same time as political elections) found himself on a political committee and in a job which he felt himself incapable of holding: 'He may, perhaps, have been running with the hares and is now hunting with the hounds. Whatever his motive for his past misdeeds, he was *very anxious* to help his interviewer and volunteered his services for the future.' It was felt that, considering Spencer's position in the political hierarchy of the prison camps, he was 'singularly unaffected by communism. He strikes one as being perhaps, somewhat spineless. He does not appear to be a dominating individual by nature; indeed, quite the opposite. If he undertook his political task for selfish motives, the streak of egocentricity is not apparent in his superficial personality'. Spencer's attitude during his interview could not be compared, for example, with other POWs: 'Surridge and Co; he is not in the same "class" as these swaggering doctrinaires and his interviewer concluded with the impression that Spencer did not warrant a rating of "Black".'[9] Unlike Spencer, Private R.W. Fish was deemed a security risk. He was considered to have embraced Communism for the following reasons:

1. He was a member of Camp No. 1 Study group;
2. From his conversations upon the subject of 'Self criticism' it was

obvious that he approved of this method of punishment and deplored those whose 'self criticisms' were 'insincere' (his wording);
3. He claims to have signed practically all the 'peace' and other petitions. (This is a peculiar claim, because no record is available in A.I.9 of Fish's signature on petitions held in the department. However, most petitions contain or refer to a number of signatures corrupted during transmission. Nevertheless it is strange that Fish's signature should not have appeared upon one of the many petitions, if his claim is correct.)
4. On his own admission he claims to have acquired considerable interest in politics, and he claims to have read a large amount of communist literature;
5. When pressed to disclose the names of the leaders of his study groups, his response was 'Don't you know them already'? When directly asked to provide names he very reluctantly disclosed two;
6. He claims to have been interrogated 15 times by the Chinese – 6 of these in Camp 1. It is significant to note that this claim is far above those of other repatriated PW, even allowing for gross exaggeration the claim is still outstanding. Allowing for exaggeration it is felt that the Chinese would not have imposed so many interrogations without reason.
7. In a letter received in A.I.9 on Friday 24th April, Fish was making contact with a woman unknown to him. The contact was made through the 'Daily Worker' in which a report appeared stating that the woman, who lived alone, was being troubled by Americans. Fish wrote a letter of sympathy to her and enclosed a chain letter for circulation.

As for Fish's general demeanour during the interview, although he was 26 years of age, 'he is immature and looks about 22 years of age. He is young and arrogant and seemed quite proud to announce that he had signed practically every petition, indeed, in making this announcement his attitude was almost one of defiance'. Although not uncooperative in supplying matters of general intelligence, he fidgeted uneasily when the subject of politics was discussed and was extremely reluctant to provide any information upon the subject of political indoctrination. 'He made no bones about his own part in this matter.'[10]

The authorities, usually Special Branch working with MI5, kept a close eye on any activities by 'indoctrinated' former soldiers; for example, on Thursday 1 October 1953 at 8.00 pm, a meeting to 'Welcome back our lads from Korea' was held, organised by the Ex-Service Movement for Peace. It was hoped by the organisers that a large audience would be attracted, but at 7.30 pm only William Henry Lovelock, Secretary of the Movement, and two other members were present. Eventually when the meeting commenced there were barely 50 persons present. All these appeared to be members or supporters of the Movement. The *Ex-Service News* was on sale, and a collection taken realised £8. 14. 8. The Chairman was Ted Hawkes, and with him on the platform were Edgar Young, Ernie Rowan and Vic Pegram. Hawkes made an apology for the small numbers present by saying that the high cost of travel made attendance for members, who lived all over London, very difficult, and that was the reason why so few indoor meetings of the Movement were held. Rowan was then introduced as a veteran of the Korea War, and he said that he wished to welcome back all those who had fought and suffered in Korea, but apart from that, and the account he gave of his experiences in Korea, it was noted that 'nothing was said by any speaker concerning the subject for which the meeting had been ostensibly held: "Welcome back our lads from Korea"'.

Rowan said that on his way home from Korea he had visited Hiroshima, but the damage there did not compare with the devastation caused in Korea. He gave an account of his life after demobilisation from the Army in 1945 – saying that all he wanted was to live in peace with his wife and two children and to look after his invalid mother. When he was recalled to the Army to go to Korea, he had no political opinions at all – and he affirmed that he still had no desire to meddle in politics. Out in Korea, however, it became evident to him that it was a political war, and the troops there used to call themselves the 'United Nations of America'. He gave an account of the suffering of women and children in Korea and condemned the war as having achieved nothing but misery, 'and to-day the opposing forces are back where they started from'. Rowan praised the objects of the Ex-Service Movement, arguing that the only way to preserve peace was for all ex-Servicemen to unite, irrespective of political opinions to ban wars for ever. If this was done by the four million ex-Servicemen in Britain, war would be impossible. Hawkes then invited questions, and the first person to speak from the body of the hall was a man who said he wished to protest against the undemocratic way in which the speakers had monopolised the proceedings and allowed so little time for discussion by the audience. He then proceeded to call for revolutionary action by the Movement on the lines of 'original Socialism'. It was noted, by the security services, that he 'appeared as though he was settled to speak indefinitely, and the Chairman had to silence him'.[11]

Despite this harmless episode, fears of the possible effects of indoctrination on POWs ran deep in the British security apparatus. An alarming prospect was thrown up, in December 1953, when Major H.S. Cousens, Deputy Director of Intelligence (Security), at MI11, reported a recent visit of members of his Branch to Washington; it was learned during unofficial talks with Lieutenant Colonel Whitehorne, Chief of Returnee Section, G–2 HQ US Army, that one American POW, while in North Korea, had undergone a course of instruction in espionage and had received orders that, on his return to the States, he was to 'lie low' for two years before commencing activities. This information came to light by chance followed by a prolonged period of intense interrogation 'and would not have been discovered in the normal course of interrogation of returnees'. Cousens felt this would be of interest to MI5 as it was considered that the interrogations carried out by BRPWIU 'would not have brought any information of this type to light'.[12]

As a result the psychological indoctrination techniques employed on certain POWs, by the Communists, now became the object of intense study by the Services. Mr Cunningham, the Senior Psychologist at A.19, investigated these cases. He noted that the 'critical issue is the use of sleep-deprivation and suggestibility as a means of precipitating the breakdown of the personality of a prisoner under interrogation'. The use of sleep deprivation in Communist interrogations had been 'satisfactorily proved' for some considerable time but the circumstances in which the Communists employed this conditioning technique were not so well known. Cunningham noted that there were two distinct methods by which a source was denied sleep: one was a complete deprivation over a short period of usually not more than 72 hours (and often less) and the other application was the deprivation of adequate sleep over a very long period as a means of debilitation. The effects of sleep deprivation upon the individual had been investigated by various scientists for some considerable time, the most significant experiments being conducted in America as long ago as 1936; as a result of POW experiences in Korea the results of these experiments had been obtained by A.I.9 from the Royal Aircraft Establishment, Farnborough. Cunningham, in his assessment of the Korean experience, observed how the use of suggestion as a technique of interrogation by the Communists had been the source of a great deal of rumour and speculation, especially by newspapers. An extension of this speculation was the use of hypnosis as a means of achieving confessions in an open court in the more sensational of the Communist trials. However, in two years of searching, concluded Cunningham, 'I have never before come across a shred of evidence to suggest, yet alone prove the deliberate use, by the Communists, of suggestibility in their interrogation techniques.'

But then the case of former POW Lieutenant D.A. Lankford RNVR, seemed, as far as Cunningham was concerned, to prove, 'beyond all doubt', the deliberate attempted use of direct suggestion. Lankford was asked by Cunningham to recall this particular aspect of his experiences carefully and in detail, and no indication was given to him of specific issues of interest. On his own initiative he mimicked the words, intonations and inflections of his former captors. Briefly, Lankford was captured North of the 38th parallel in 'compromising circumstances', and was subsequently evaluated by the Chinese as an espionage agent. His interrogation was very prolonged and intensive at Pyoktong. Lankford who had surrendered himself after an abortive escape, had been bound hand and foot for two weeks, and then, after a brief medical inspection was confined to a hut with his interrogators, Commander Lee and Interpreter Ying. Lee, through Ying, told Lankford that they would discuss only unimportant issues, beginning with a brief history of the Royal Navy and its customs. The list of unimportant things which would be discussed was 'innocuous' material such as the organisation of the Admiralty, British Fleets and their bases, especially Singapore, Fleet tactics off the West Coast of Korea, Flotilla organisation and communications, battle strategy of Carrier forces etc. Lankford pleaded ignorance, but the plea was not accepted. A day or two later, Lee extended the list of requirements to Naval operational planning, inter-service operational planning and the appointments of the various staff planning officers. Lankford would, said Lee, also discuss information on Naval Intelligence – its sources, collation and collection, as well as information on MI5. The answers that Lankford would give were verbal, in discussion, and subsequently committed to paper. This outline of the requirement occupied several days before Lankford was asked if he had anything to say. He pleaded ignorance and was promptly accused of lying.

The interrogation commenced in the forenoon and continued for 72 hours non-stop. The method of interrogation was direct-verbal questioning by relays of Chinese interrogators – the 'Conveyer' system working in pairs. During this period Lankford was sitting on a chair. After 72 hours of sleep deprivation he was left for a period to reflect and managed to obtain some sleep, after which the sleep deprivation was repeated. This second 'outburst' began in a leisurely fashion at first, questions being flung nonchalantly at the prisoner. As time progressed so also did the hostility. Lankford was subjected to a hostile bombardment of questions at great speed for an unknown number of days without respite. The interrogators worked on the Conveyor system, relieving each other at approximately 4-hourly intervals. Lankford was seated on a chair, was provided with meals twice daily, hot drinks and cigarettes.

On about the third or fourth day (Lankford was quite unable to recollect precisely the time factors involved) he could no longer keep awake and his head fell forward on to his chest. When this occurred, the interrogator would knock his head backwards to awaken him. Finally, he fell off the chair and fell asleep immediately. Lankford was certain in his own mind that he was asleep only for a few minutes before he was awakened and told that he had had 12 hours of sleep and must continue with the interrogation. From this point onwards, he was permitted to sleep and sometimes told to sleep at 20-minute intervals. On each occasion he was awakened immediately and told that he had been sleeping for 12 hours. After the continuous repetition of this technique, for an unknown period, each time Lankford was awakened and told that he had been sleeping for 12 hours he would repeat the words '12 hours' in singular reiteration. At this stage the interrogators told Lankford, 'You are going mad' in singular reiteration for a lengthy period. Eventually Lankford became amnesic for an unknown period. He was convinced that he remained thus for several days – but he had no means of accounting for the time.

On his return to consciousness – he was not at all certain if this was a gradual process or an abrupt awakening – Lankford was told by his interrogators that he had been very ill. A good meal of meat and eggs, chicken and boiled sweets was brought to him and he was told to eat it to help his recovery. Two days later, considerably shaken by his experience and particularly perturbed about the amnesia, Lankford decided to display a cooperative attitude to his captors and produced for them a large chart of an imaginary organisation of the Admiralty. This product was promptly destroyed in his presence by the interrogators who ordered Lankford to produce another with fewer inaccuracies. Lankford produced a replica of his former product and this was accepted.

Cunningham concluded that the proof that Chinese interrogators recognised the opportunity for the use of suggestion upon him was revealed in the reaction of Lankford to his repeated awakening to the suggestion that he had slept for 12 hours – to which Lankford repeated '12 hours'. Only an interrogator who had had some sort of training in psychology would recognise this symptom of a potentially suggestible state. The method of the Chinese reiteration of the suggestion 'You are going mad' (which was mimicked by Lankford) 'was a properly spoken patter for the establishment of rapport with a person to be influenced by suggestion'. Once again this indicated, to Cunningham, the deliberate use of a technique by a person familiar with some aspects of psychology. The use of complete sleep deprivation as a means of conditioning a prisoner for suggestion 'indicates an advanced psychological insight on the part of the Chinese interrogators.

No interrogator untrained in psychology would see the implications of this technique. It is possible that the technique has been developed as the result of deliberate research'.

Cunningham had not been able to discover any experiments which had been conducted either in the UK or America on sleep deprivation that directly demonstrated the increase of susceptibility to suggestion in persons deprived of sleep: 'A.S. Edwards, an American specialising in sleep-deprivation studies stated in results published in 1941, that gross deprivation produced large and definite increases in the static ataxia of his subjects. This result tends to support the hypothesis that deprivation enhances susceptibility to suggestion.' The US Navy office of Naval Research experiments on sleep deprivation showed results of increased body-sway of subjects deprived of sleep. 'This is a more direct indication of the connection between deprivation and suggestibility. I suspect that the mechanisms involved in heightening suggestibility by sleep deprivation in interrogation are not as simple as they would at first appear. The context of the situation must not be ignored.' Those who had suffered a prolonged period of savage interrogation at the hands of Communists 'are undoubtedly subject to psychological disturbances without sleep deprivation. Interrogation of this sort can cause a neurotic condition' and according to some of the research that Cunningham was aware of, 'neurotics are more susceptible to suggestion'. Furthermore:

> Sleep deprivation after the prisoner had already been subjected to interrogation for a prolonged period would, in all probability, enhance the neurotic symptoms and would thus heighten suggestibility.
>
> One further form of conditioning is said to heighten suggestibility ... suggestibility is commonest in persons living secluded lives. An extension of this hypothesis is therefore, that solitary confinement will play some part in increasing the suggestibility of the prisoner.

Cunningham believed the apparent purpose of the Chinese interrogators, in 'forwarding suggestions of madness' to Lankford was to influence him directly (consciously) or indirectly (sub-consciously) of his loss of reason. The actual way in which the suggestion was advanced, and the purpose, if it was indeed as it appeared, were 'incompatible. In other words, although there is ample evidence of the sinister attempt to employ suggestion, the attempt was apparently clumsy and psychologically, inadequate and misapplied'. It seemed as though the Chinese interrogators had a technique that, because of inadequate training, they misapplied and actually brought it to bear upon the off chance that it would work; but:

'It was quite ineffective in this instance.' Since the Chinese had available a doctor who examined Lankford prior to his interrogation they had the opportunity to determine, in advance of the interrogation, his suitability for suggestibility:

> It must therefore be concluded that although the Chinese are aware that the sleep-deprivation suggestibility technique is possible, and can apply it with deliberation, they are not able to pre-select prisoners upon whom it will work successfully. The selection test is a very simple one, so simple that it can be applied under almost any conditions. The effects of suggestion upon suggestible individuals often appear to laymen as sensational. Without embarking upon a complex description of suggestion, it may be briefly indicated that ... there are two kinds of suggestibility, primary and secondary. Primary suggestibility produces an involuntary motor reaction; that is to say it is possible to affect some bodily movement such as an increased body-sway, involuntary pressure of the hands and the involuntary activation of certain muscle groups.
>
> Secondary suggestibility can produce perceptual illusions and sensory illusions by indirect suggestion. This would seem to be the potentially dangerous kind of suggestion so far as interrogation is concerned since it is possible to suggest pain, obnoxious smells and malfunction of the sense organs.

Primary suggestibility was much more akin to hypnosis. In the actual hypnotic state it was possible to reinforce the personalities of the mentally ill. The converse was also probably true, that was to say, to precipitate the disintegration of the personality by post-hypnotic suggestion. 'One need hardly emphasise the dangers inherent in such a practice' observed Cunningham. There was as yet, no evidence of the use by the Communists of hypnosis. But indirect stimulation of secondary suggestibility, 'would, I think, over a period of time, produce a drastic and deleterious effect upon persons of weak attitudes to suggestion generally. That is to say those persons who are, in common parlance, weak characters, weak-willed, with constitutional defects of "will power", could be broken down by pernicious indirect suggestions of insanity, physical illness or drug psychosis'. It was possible, for example, to suggest to a 'weak' patient, the physical and mental symptoms of violent digestive disorders, visual and mental disorientation and even pregnancy; but the stimulation of such things was alleged to be more effective if it was indirect, so that the subject or prisoner was not aware of the influence being exerted upon him by others. Reverting to the Lankford case, Cunningham concluded that, had the Chinese interrogators been more knowledgeable, they could probably have produced a much more effective result by indirect suggestion. The technique that they actually adopted was apparently aimed at primary suggestibility or hypnosis. If this was the intention, then the personality of the interrogators and its effects upon the prisoner was a most important factor. In this instance it was apparently insufficient to affect Lankford. The danger from Communist attempts at suggestibility necessitated the use of counter measures to primary suggestibility and hypnosis that were relatively simple: 'So far as is known at present, suggestion has only been employed by the Communists upon prisoners from whom they require highly classified information, or whom they suspect of being clandestine agents or operators.' Cunningham recommended that special service operatives be subjected to psychiatric selection.[13]

The case of Lieutenant Colonel Carne, winner of the Victoria Cross during the Battle of Imjin, and CO of the Glosters, raised the possibility that the Chinese might have employed drugs on him; it was also a case in which it was possible to assess the impact of severe isolation on an individual as Carne was punished by his captors in this way. Unsurprisingly, AI9 invited Cunningham to make a study of Carne's case: had, for example, drugs been used on the British officer? In making an investigation into the alleged use of drugs, Cunningham searched for the symptomology of drug psychosis: 'But this in itself is not enough; one has to decide whether or not the symptoms described could have been caused by something other than drugs.' He concluded that, in this specific case, the symptoms described by Carne, 'can reasonably be attributed to the mental, physical and environmental stresses under which he lived for a protracted period.' Cunningham found it was impossible to state emphatically that drugs were not used, 'but there is much more evidence to indicate that they were not used than there is to support an allegation of their use'. Firstly, there was no motive for their use. The period during which Carne suspected their use was the period *after* his detailed military interrogation. Neither did there seem to be much evidence to support the hypothesis that they might have been used to force Carne to commit himself to political issues because there was no evidence to show that the Chinese made any real effort to make political capital out of their prisoner. Also, there was little doubt that drugs would not be needed to bring about a breakdown in the personality of Carne.

In his diagnosis, Cunningham concluded that the violent physical symptoms, which Carne reported having occurred during the period in which he suspected the use of drugs, seemed to be the symptoms of a common group of psycho-somatic disorders aggravated, probably, by the effects of diarrhoea and indigestible foods. Hysterical vomiting, nausea over food, excruciating pains in various parts of the body, disorientation (dizziness), all of which were transient, were symptoms common to those suffering under stress. They lacked the cohesion and permanence of a disease and were indicative of a neurotic condition, and seemed to be hysterical conversion symptoms. From the evidence which Carne had given concerning his partial blindness it was probable that this too was a hysterical conversion. According to his evidence, Carne's night vision (which was largely peripheral vision) was unimpaired at night but impaired by day. Cunningham pointed out that dietetic deficiencies effected night vision to a greater degree and more rapidly than day vision, 'and one would therefore expect that if his disability was due to dietetic deficiencies his night vision could be somewhat worse than his day vision'.

Cunningham concluded that the mental symptoms which again were transient experiences also lacked cohesion and persistence. Allegations of poisoning and persecution were common among prisoners of war. Carne's memory of events 'occurred during the period during which he alleges the use of drugs remains unimpaired; if drugs had been used it is extremely doubtful if he could have remembered these events or that he would have been conscious of any change in his personality'. The fact that, during the critical period, he was not suffering from violently disturbing dreams at night 'would seem to indicate that his anxieties had not reached the stage of a disease'. The compulsions concerning his wife ceased when he resorted to action expressing his aggression by attacking his guards. Cunningham noted that the common method used by Communists to motivate recalcitrant high-grade sources and the method used by the Chinese in this instance was to collect and fabricate sufficient evidence to implicate the source as a 'War Criminal'. This action gave the interrogators the preliminary and necessary 'hold' over the source and provided a means of intimidation since it put the source outside the protection of the Geneva Convention and permitted the detaining power to punish the source according to its own criminal law.

In the specific case of Colonel Carne, 'who is essentially a man of high moral values and is easily recognised as such', everything was done to humiliate him, to undermine those standards of conduct 'which are sacred to him and to *force him to act contrary to and in sharp conflict with his normal code of conduct.*' In a man of Carne's type of personality, concluded Cunningham, 'actions contrary to normal codes of conduct, even though effected under duress, are often seen by them as self-betrayal and weakness, giving rise to strong feelings of guilt. It often gives rise to a great deal of self recrimination, self-torture, which facilitates and precipitates the breakdown of their own personality'. The amount of physical duress applied to Carne to force him to act contrary to his normal standards of conduct was slight in comparison with that suffered by other British personnel in Chinese custody. But the various acts – the cold water thrown into his face, the removal of his trousers – 'would be extremely degrading and humiliating to him and probably just as effective upon him as the more degrading acts would be upon officers of lower rank and with less esteem to maintain'. Continuous mental stress and especially bitter self-recrimination produced a 'peculiar frame of mind at the height of which the source accepts the guilt and responsibility for the situation in which he finds himself. It is in moments such as these that the source is predisposed to actions and suggestions which are foreign to his normal conduct. Deeds performed while in this state are afterwards regarded with horror and disgust; so foreign do these things seem that the source refuses to accept the responsibility for them and rationalises the cause as the responsibility of others'. So, construed Cunningham, in the case of Carne the rationalisation he used to explain his behaviour centred upon the use of drugs, 'which not only provides a reason for his foreign conduct, but would also provide a reason for his physical experiences'. The greatest amount of physical duress which was inflicted upon Colonel Carne was punishment for breaches of discipline i.e. assaulting camp guards and personnel and in one instance provoking the guards knowing what the consequences of the act would be. In these circumstances, concluded Cunningham, the Chinese behaviour was 'not unreasonable'.

The method by which information was elicited from Carne was apparently identical to that used by the Russians upon high-grade German sources incarcerated in camp 7027 at Krasnorgorsk. In this specific instance, the interrogation was entirely written and there were no periods of verbal questioning. The technique took the form of a series of written compositions, beginning with a nebulous and fairly innocuous subject and continuing with more and more poignant and sensitive issues. The most important point that Cunningham noted, was that, in using this technique, 'the Communists have found a means of making the source actively participate in the interrogation of himself!' This technique was tentatively called the 'projection' technique. This was well known in psychological medicine and was a means by which the source supplemented a nebulous or ambiguous stimulus with data drawn from his own experience or imagination: 'For example, if I, as an interrogator, ask my source to tell me what HE thinks are my interrogation targets, (and presuming that the source is suitably motivated) the source will, unless he is especially cautious, furnish me with information drawn from his own experience and *orientate my interrogation of him for me.*' Thus, for instance, during an Evasion and Escape exercise interrogation, the interrogator asked his prisoner to state what he (the prisoner) thought the interrogator was looking for. The source stated that he thought the interrogator was after the location of his 'dropping zone', 'cut-out' and 'pick-up point'. In so saying the prisoner orientated the questioning of himself. As applied to Colonel Carne, the technique began with a demand that he should write a history of the British Army. The form which this composition should take was left entirely to the initiative of Carne. In leaving Carne the initiative the Chinese could reasonably hope that in drafting the composition he would reveal to them something of his knowledge of the British Army. This approach would also serve as a 'lead-in' question. Next, a more pertinent question was set, possibly framed on the basis of knowledge imparted in the first composition. The second question was that the Colonel should list the names of all the regiments in the British Army, and from this the third question was set, i.e. to group these regiments in their respective brigades and divisions and to number them appropriately. There followed questions on organisation, leading as it were, to the War Office organisation. All this led to the sensitive question of the syllabus of the Staff College. Cunningham considered that the use of this as a deliberate technique seemed to be confirmed by the fact that at the end of the year the Chinese demanded that the Colonel should list the subjects upon which he had been interrogated over the period of that year; the Chinese 'must have been perfectly aware of the answer to this problem. The chances are that the Chinese expected him to list a subject about which he had not in fact been interrogated thus furnishing them with another subject of interrogation'. The fact that some of the questions were reiterated after the lapse of a considerable period of time was 'another indication of the deliberate use of the technique. Not only does this trick provide a reliability check but it again affords the opportunity for the source to "project" his knowledge and indicate fresh intelligence targets'.

Cunningham thought the projection technique was especially apt for use upon sources concerning the 'knowledgeability' of whom the enemy was either in doubt or ignorance. Carne was to be the first senior British officer ever to fall into the hands of the Communists: 'The Communists would probably not know for certain what sort of knowledge they could reasonably expect to gain from a source of this calibre. It is perhaps impossible to frame searching questions without first having some idea of the scope and depth of the source's knowledge. The enemy would, of course, be aware that they had in their custody an important prisoner (this would be judged by his rank) but the areas of knowledgeability would be uncertain.'

It was fairly common for the Communists to treat the potentially valuable prisoner with restraint noted Cunningham; 'they would not kill the goose that shows promise of laying the golden egg, so to speak. Thus they make the prisoner orientate his own interrogation by the projection technique, motivating him indirectly'. In the end, Cunningham thought that the most significant feature of the Chinese interrogation of Colonel Carne was that 'they do not seem to have been capable of assessing the veracity of his answers. Had they been able to do this, there is every evidence from the reports of other repatriated prisoners, to indicate that there would have been some very unpleasant repercussions'.[14]

While Cunningham's conclusions appeared reassuring, the concept of a British 'Manchurian Candidate'-type figure, indoctrinated or 'brainwashed' by the Chinese in Korea, was revived by the George Blake spy scandal in the 1960s – Blake an MI6 officer captured in Seoul during the war, emerged as one of the Soviets' greatest agents. Further alarms were rung after another Communist agent – Vassal – was uncovered in Naval Intelligence. An immediate review of all ex-Korean POWs who had been cleared previously by Positive Vetting was ordered.[15] There were still, in 1963, a significant number of military men serving who had been POWs in Korea. In the Army the number of senior posts which did *not* entail regular and constant access to Top Secret information was considered 'negligible'. There were a few in the administrative services, but all the posts for Brigadier and above in the combatant services would require Positive Vetting. The position was broadly the same in the Royal Air Force and the Royal Navy. It was very difficult to find a suitable post for a senior officer 'who was not fully cleared'. The problem was that a committee set up to assess the threat, which included Sir Roger Hollis the Director General of MI5 and someone who would became the target of a witch-hunt himself, recognised that even a careful Positive Vetting could not ascertain whether the subject who had once been a captive 'had been brainwashed'.[16]

## Notes

1 TNA CAB 21/4020
2 TNA WO 32/20495 British P.W. Repatriated from North Korea – Interrogation Reports
3 TNA WO 208/4004 Report on the success of Communist indoctrination among British PW in North Korea, with particular reference to after effects on their return to the United Kingdom
4 TNA WO 208/4004 Major A.N. West-Watson Report on the success of Communist indoctrination among British PW in North Korea, with

particular reference to after effects on their return to the United Kingdom, 22 October 1953
5 TNA WO 32/20495 Disciplinary Action – PW Korea
6 TNA WO 208/4004 Major A.N. West-Watson Report on the success of Communist indoctrination among British PW in North Korea, with particular reference to after effects on their return to the United Kingdom, 22 October 1953
7 TNA WO 208/4004 List of British Commonwealth PW who appear to have absorbed Communism, 30 April 1952
8 TNA WO 32/20495 Army Personnel who have been in Communist Hands 1951–61
9 TNA WO 208/4004 Major CJ Young; Subject:- 3654392 Rfn EF Spencer, 14 May 1953
10 TNA WO 208/4004 Major CJ Young; Subject:- 22530141 Pte RW Fish, 14 May 1953
11 TNA WO 32/20495 The Ex-Service Movement for Peace. Korea "Welcome Home"
12 TNA WO 32/20495 Repatriated Allied P.W., 4 December 1953
13 TNA WO 208 4021 Supplementary Interrogation Report on Lieutenant D.A. Lankford RNVR by Mr Cunningham, BA (Hons) Senior Psychologist, Air Ministry, A.1.9, 15 January 1954
14 TNA WO 208 4021 Preliminary Appreciation of the Chinese Interrogation of Lieutenant Colonel J.P. Carne, VC, DSO by Mr C. Cunningham, BA (Hons) Senior Psychologist, Air Ministry, A.I.9
15 TNA WO 32/20495 Review Procedure: Ex-Korean PW
16 TNA WO 32/20495 Note of a Meeting held in Room 77, Treasury, SW1, on Thursday, 25 April 1963, at 3.15 p.m.

# Epilogue

## Bermuda

In the wake of the Armistice attention turned to an anticipated political conference on the future of Korea. As the British POWs returned home an odd distraction from the norm occurred with the release of Lieutenant Colonel Carne: as far as the British authorities he was released to were concerned, at this stage, it was assumed that he had been: 'subjected to treatment by the Communists including drugs, which made his brain as he put it, like a sponge capable of absorbing anything.' After this process and after the Armistice had been signed, he was brought before a Chinese General who formally told him about the Armistice. He asked the General whether he was meant to pass on what he had been told, to which the General said he knew nothing about that, but if Colonel Carne had anything to tell he should tell his own people when he got back. Just before the Armistice, his Adjutant, Captain Farrar-Hockley, was arrested on a trumped-up charge that he had plotted the assassination of the Camp Commandant (who was actually fired at several times by a Korean) and sentenced to 7 years' imprisonment. He was told of the sentence just after the Armistice, and was then told that the sentence would be remitted if he consented to become a Chinese agent and to provide information about US military forces. Carne was also informed:

(a) The Chinese would like the early unification of Korea but if this is not possible, they want a buffer zone larger than the present one which should be policed by Chinese and British forces. They would accept a British Command and, at a pinch, only British forces.
(b) They would like the United Kingdom to undertake the reconstruction of both North and South Korea.

Epilogue: Bermuda 263

    (c) The price the Chinese would be prepared to pay for the good offices of the United Kingdom would be :-
        (i) Cessation of the war in Malaya;
        (ii) the renewal of the lease of the New Territories at Hong Kong when it expires in (?) 1985;
        (iii) the possible grant of the mandate of Formosa to the United Kingdom provided the U.K. would maintain a sizeable Pacific Fleet;
        (iv) settlement of the Indo-China question.

Carne's account of this was 'rather confused' but, from what he said to officials at the British Embassy in Tokyo, it was deduced that the Chinese would use their good offices, together with the United Kingdom and perhaps some other countries, for a negotiated settlement between the French Associated States and the Viet Minn. Carne went on to say that 'if we did all these things the Chinese were prepared to put a lot of trade in our way', reported the Embassy, and he mentioned Centurion tanks, jet aircraft, naval craft and the equipment of six armoured divisions to the tune of some £300 million. When asked whether any mention was made of Russia, Carne was unable to say that it was, nor was he able to explain why, 'since Russia is hand-in-glove with the Chinese in Korea', the Chinese Communists should wish such a considerable role to be played by the United Kingdom. He was asked how, assuming that the Chinese really wanted him to communicate all this to HMG, they expected to get a reaction from it. Carne said that the Chinese had urged the early appointment of a fully-accredited Ambassador to China with whom they could discuss matters. ('This does not make sense' noted the Embassy.) Questions elicited the fact that while the Communists were, as Carne put it, making a sponge of his mind over many months, it was not until March 1953 (i.e. at about the time when they showed signs of seriously wanting an Armistice) that they put the above thoughts into his mind. He then recalled that they had given their reasons for not wanting an Armistice before. These were that they wanted to show the world that America could not fight, could not look after prisoners and was not fit for world leadership.[1]

Sir Eslner Dening's comment was that the 'whole thing might be pure fantasy except for the fact that Colonel Carne could hardly have invented it and does not strike one as that sort of person'. He appeared to Dening to be physically fit but to be suffering from intense mental fatigue, and he obviously had difficulty in marshalling his thoughts. It might be that the Communists 'overdid the job' so that it became impossible for him to register all that he was meant to record, reflected Dening; nevertheless, there did seem to be some political significance in his story, and the Communists presumably had some purpose in singling out the senior British officer in captivity with a record which must have been known to them, for the kind of treatment Carne said he received: 'I did not like to cross-examine Carne too closely in view of his mental fatigue, but I understand military authorities contemplate flying him home. I think this is a good idea, and you may wish to question him further when he arrives. For your confidential information I think it would be advisable to separate him from his former adjutant, Capt. Farrar-Hockley, also a released prisoner, who is so full of bright ideas that he may put them into the Colonel's tired brain, and thus further confuse his picture of what the Communists told him' telegraphed Dening to London.[2]

The view in London was rather different where: 'We are not disposed to take seriously the alleged Chinese offer reported by Colonel Carne, which appears to be no more than a crude propaganda effort to divide us from the Americans' wrote an official. The alleged offer might also represent the line adopted by the Chinese as most likely to disturb Carne's loyalty and patriotism. Moreover, the possibility could not be overlooked that Carne, after 19 months of solitary confinement and being subjected to drugs, was in no condition to judge the nature and importance of all that was said to him: 'If the Chinese had really wished to make such an offer they would surely have chosen a more direct and reliable channel. In any case, the substance of the alleged offer is so nonsensical as not to merit serious consideration. Even if the offer were a genuine feeler from the Peking Government it would, in our view, not be right to pay any attention to it coming to us in this way.'[3]

Attention in London was soon more focused on the upcoming Bermuda conference, in December 1953, postponed after Churchill's stroke earlier in the year, but where a well again Eden would be joining his Prime Minister together with Eisenhower, Dulles and the French Foreign Minister, Bidault. In the run-up to Bermuda a memorandum of 30 November, by the Chiefs of Staff – Sir John Harding (CIGS), Sir Rhoderick McGrigor (First Sea Lord) and Sir William Dickson (CAS) – recommended, that in the event of renewed Communist attack in Korea, the best military course of action would be to stand on the offensive there, using conventional bombing attacks against airfields and military targets in Manchuria to assist in preventing a breakthrough. In view of the great danger that the use of atomic weapons outside Korea might lead to general war, they recommended that only if military defeat appeared imminent should the use of tactical atomic weapons against the enemy within Korea be considered.[4] The Foreign Office was consulted during its drafting and was represented at the meetings at which the Chiefs of Staff discussed it. Before it was drafted the Chiefs of Staff asked the Foreign Office for a statement of the political objectives to which Her Majesty's Government would probably subscribe in the event of a renewed Communist attack. This was provided in a paper which was approved by Eden on 3 November. The key passage in the Chiefs paper stated: 'it will not be possible to obtain a clear cut victory in Korea without the unrestricted use of unconventional weapons against China. Such a course of action would not, however, be consistent with what are understood to be probable political objectives of Her Majesty's Government', and they concluded 'that the best military course of action, consistent with the probable political objectives of Her Majesty's Government, is to stand on the defensive within Korea, maintaining the present position and using conventional bombing attacks against military targets in Manchuria to assist in preventing a break through. Should a military defeat appear imminent it might be necessary to use atomic weapons tactically against the enemy *within* Korea'.

This conclusion produced consternation in the Foreign Office after the Chiefs, 'in spite of representations' from the former, agreed the paper despite the fact it 'seemed politically unrealistic and unhelpful to Ministers since it simply posed two extreme alternatives, neither of which it seemed stood any chance of being acceptable both to Her Majesty's Government and the United States Government'. The Chiefs had reached their decision on the basis that, in the event of a renewed Communist attack in Korea, the overriding necessity would in fact be to find a common US/UK policy which would ensure that 'we were both fighting the same war together by the same means for the same objectives'. From this point of view the Foreign Office had greatly preferred the original conclusion in the draft paper first submitted by the Joint Planning Staff. This had pointed the way to a possible compromise which might be militarily acceptable and might enable the British and American Governments to reconcile their policies, since it had suggested that 'provided we could authorise strategic bombing in Manchuria we might be able to dissuade the Americans from carrying the war further into China and thus increasing the risk of a general conflagration'. What worried the Foreign Office was that, in submitting the paper, the Chiefs had not made it clear that it was aimed at a situation when the Communists did '*not* intend a general war but are simply out to drive United Nations forces from Korea. If the Communists intend general war, then we too would set no limit to our operations. But if they intend another local war we also should try to keep it local, although recognising that some action outside Korea would be necessary to repel the Communist aggression'. In these circumstances the Foreign Office suggested that the overriding necessity would be to find some common ground politically acceptable both to HMG and to the Americans, in spite of the military imperfections of such a compromise: 'We should therefore prefer a conclusion more on the lines of that originally suggested by the Joint Planning Staff', which was as follows:

> We think that the most effective military course of action to repel Chinese aggression, consistent with an acceptable degree of risk of war with Russia, lies in employing the maximum land effort, supported by conventional weapons, within Korea, combined with conventional bombing attacks on airfields and communications in Manchuria, and possibly with localised blockade of the Chinese coast between the Kwantung peninsula and the Yalu. We do not believe, however, that this action is likely to achieve the 'clear cut' victory which is likely to be the American political objective.[5]

This was the Whitehall background to the Bermuda Conference, in December, where the American, British and French Heads of Government gathered to assess the post-Armistice situation, among many other issues, affecting the Western powers. Eisenhower remarked at the opening of the 'Big Three' meeting, in the afternoon of 4 December, that the United States Government had made it plain that they would 'hit back with full power' in the event of a Communist breach of the Korean truce and appeared to imply that they would use atomic weapons.[6] The President also remarked that the world was in a 'rather hysterical condition about the atomic bomb'.[7] That there was more than rhetoric to these comments became apparent at a private lunch on 4 December, where the President informed Churchill that if there was a deliberate breach of the Armistice by the Communists 'we would expect to strike back with atomic weapons at military targets. We would not expect to bomb cities but would attack areas that were directly supporting the aggression'. The Prime Minister, according to the American record, replied that he 'quite accepted' this and that the President's statement put him in a position to say to Parliament that he had been consulted in advance and had agreed.[8] Eden, perhaps not privy to his Prime Minister's apparent endorsement of the US stance, was not as sanguine when told of the conversation. The Foreign Secretary told Churchill of his alarm at this: 'This goes far beyond anything we have hitherto agreed. As you will remember we have agreed that if there were a breach of the armistice by China our reaction would be prompt, resolute and effective, and we have said that in all probability the conflict could not be confined to Korea. We have always recognized that it would probably be impossible to avoid bombing Chinese aerodromes beyond the Yalu. But we have never given, or been asked to give, approval to widespread bombing of China proper nor, of course, to the use of atom bombs, or to a blockade.' Eden wanted to raise this again with the Americans: 'We should ask them how they appraise the likelihood of a Chinese attack and what steps they propose to take in the event of such an attack, and whether they would consult us.' This was of vital interest to the UK, particularly having regard to the East Anglian US bases: 'First because the Chinese will not, I am convinced, attack in Korea except with Soviet approval. Secondly because once atomic bombs are used retaliation with the same weapons becomes an immediate danger.'[9] As Sir Pierson Dixon set out, in a minute, for the Foreign Secretary: 'We totally disagree with such action and would have to say so publicly and say that we had so informed the Americans if, in the event, we were asked whether we had been consulted in advance. The present notification does not constitute consultation.' British reasons for disagreement were:

a) An American–Chinese war could not be confined to China. Even a war with conventional weapons would be bound to hit the British Empire somewhere. The Chinese would no doubt immediately react on Hong Kong. But a much more serious aspect is that an American–Chinese war would be bound to develop into a general war. Russia is bound to go to China's assistance under the Sino-Soviet Treaty.

   It is, of course, the whole object of our world policy to prevent the outbreak of a general war. On this ground alone we are bound to disagree fundamentally with the American attitude.

b) We are equally opposed to *starting* atomic warfare. In any case we are bound to consider the vulnerability of our Islands to this form of attack. Owing to the US bases in the Islands, the British Isles are a first target for Soviet retaliation.

   In short, an American all out attack on China, including the use of the atomic weapon, would start a chain reaction which might lead to a Soviet attack on the British Isles as the opening phase of the extension of the war to the West.

It follows from this that the decision to go to war in *any* part of the world and the decision to use the atomic weapon *anywhere* must be a matter for joint consultation between the US Government and HM Government.

Unless we can persuade the Americans to agree to this we must seriously consider protecting ourselves by asking them to remove their bases from the United Kingdom.

We are in any case not prepared to accede to the recent American request that the two Governments should decide *now* to use the US bases in Britain against three different types of target in a certain order of priority. There can be no question of modifying our joint decision requirement on the use of the bases.

Conclusion

(1) We should in effect ask the Americans to renounce their plans for all out war against China, whether with conventional weapons or with atomic weapons; and should press them to work for a policy of accepting that the Western Powers must live with a Communist China. This admittedly means that we cannot 'win the Korean war': we must be content with attaining the UN objective, ie repelling the aggression over the 39th [sic] parallel.

(2) A joint Anglo-American review is urgently required of the whole world situation in its strategic and political aspects, striking the balance between the Far East (China) and Europe and the Middle East (Russia).[10]

W.D. Allen, in a second Foreign Office minute for Eden, highlighted three general points which should be borne in mind in connection with Dixon's minute. The first was that the action which the United States Government contemplated would, of course, be taken only in the event of renewed Chinese and North Korean aggression. In discussion of this matter with the Americans it might, therefore, be prudent not to make too much of HMG's desire for a more forthcoming American policy towards Communist China, particularly on the question of recognition: 'Our hope for some advance in the American attitude in this respect must, I think, be based on the assumption that China remains peaceable and gives some evidence of good behaviour.' Renewed Chinese aggression would at once destroy this assumption. In such circumstances 'we might find that, far from being able to persuade the Americans to move towards our point of view, we should be subject to strong American pressure to stiffen our own attitude'. Secondly, both Her Majesty's present Government and Her Majesty's late Government had gone some way towards committing themselves to act with the Americans in the event of renewed Chinese aggression. These commitments were referred to in the public statement issued from Downing Street on August 15. This statement included *inter alia* the following passage:

It was revealed to the House on February 26, 1952 that the late

Government had gone so far as to agree that if heavy air attacks from bases in China were made upon the United Nations force in Korea they would associate themselves with action not confined to Korea. There is therefore no change whatever in principle in the policies followed by the late Socialist Government or by HM present Government.

But these past undertakings did not of course commit HMG to endorse any particular course of action in hypothetical circumstances, least of all the use of the atomic bomb against China proper. Finally, Allen pointed out that action, such as that indicated by President Eisenhower, if carried out under the orders of the United Nations Command in Korea, would constitute action by the United Nations and not only by the United States against China: 'This fact strengthens our right to demand full and proper consultation.'[11]

So, at dinner, attended by Eisenhower and Dulles, on the one hand, and Churchill and Eden, on the other, the primary subject of discussion was the use of the atomic bomb and missiles. In the main, Churchill and Eden expressed the view that US thinking on the subject was 'several years ahead of theirs' and of the rest of the world. They warned of the danger of the United States taking action which would be morally repellent to most of the world. It would be much better, if there were an attack in any area which permitted of delay and possible localisation, if the Americans did not instantly react with atomic weapons but waited for public opinion to develop, which it probably would do very quickly.[12]

A few days later, Eden was still complaining to Churchill about American intentions: 'So far I am in the dark as to what they are, though I fear what they may be.' The Warning Statement of the 16 nations against a Communist breach of the armistice made it plain that it might not then be possible to confine the fighting to Korea: 'Specifically we had in mind that we might have to bomb Communist installations beyond the Yalu.' Now it seemed that the Americans 'have much more far-ranging plans. They are ready to use atomic weapons in Korea. Are they also ready to drop atomic bombs on a fairly wide range of targets in China and Manchuria avoiding only big cities? Do they also propose to blockade China and land Chiang Kai-shek on the mainland? And do they propose to do all or any of these things without consultation with the United Nations in whose name they are acting?' asked the Foreign Secretary. He was partly reassured that a private chat the Prime Minister had had with the President 'have borne fruit and it may be that the fears outlined' were not justified. But it seemed 'essential that we should know, for the reasons set out in my earlier minute and in Sir P Dixon's. The minimum requirement is that the United Nations should be consulted before steps are taken which could result in retaliation on East Anglia or unleash a third world war'.[13]

The clarification the British received, in the next plenary session, was not reassuring. Dulles observed that if the Armistice had not been obtained, the United States would have wished to increase the scale and intensity of its military operations: 'for that purpose they had 'already sent out to this theatre the means of conducting atomic warfare. They had reason to believe that the Communists were aware of this, and that it had influenced their attitude towards the armistice. Thus, the armistice had been secured by strength not weakness'. Dulles reassured the British that the Americans would certainly do their utmost to carry out the terms of the Armistice and to prevent the resumption of hostilities. But if this should happen, the Americans did not intend to allow the war to follow the same pattern as before the Armistice, viz., a pattern of entrenched lines and prolonged attrition. It was their intention to prosecute the war with greater intensity and vigour. While they would be careful to avoid any action which might lead to an outbreak of general war, or might involve the Soviet Union in the Far Eastern struggle, they intended to attack with the most effective weapons at their disposal the bases from which air attacks were made on United Nations troops, to apply the doctrine of 'hot pursuit' without regard to the Manchurian frontier, and in general to take whatever action was best designed to achieve rapid and conclusive results. In this connection the United States were influenced by the consideration that there were strong defensive positions which could be more cheaply held on a line further to the north than those which had been held hitherto. They believed that their previous intention to intensify the offensive had induced the Communists to accept an armistice. Similarly, they believed that their determination to apply this policy if hostilities were resumed would afford the best guarantee that the Communists would not renew the struggle. It might well pay them to resume the war on the old basis: it would not pay them to court an intensified American offensive. Dulles hoped that Washington might count on the British Commonwealth 'to give moral and military support for this policy'. They did not ask for military help from France, who were fully occupied with the war in Indo-China. The surest method of deterring an aggressor was to make it perfectly plain in advance that any aggression would be firmly resisted. Churchill had himself said on more than one occasion that the Second World War might have been averted if the democracies had made plain their intention to resist Hitler's aggression.

Instead of endorsing this position, as Dulles hoped, Eden replied that 'he was somewhat disturbed' by the indication which the former had given of the military policy which the United States were disposed to follow if hostilities should be resumed in Korea. He was glad to know that it would be their aim to avoid any action which might lead to a general war. But 'he feared that it might be difficult in practice to apply the vigorous policy which Mr Dulles had outlined without running the risk of extending the conflict.' So long as the United States were conducting these operations on behalf of the United Nations, pointed out Eden, was it not desirable that their military policy in conducting them should carry the approval of the United Nations? The idea of pursuing hostile aircraft to their bases beyond the Manchurian frontier was not new: it had been discussed on previous occasions and was generally accepted. But there were other aspects of Dulles' proposals which involved new departures in policy. Thus:

> the use of atomic weapons, even if their use were restricted to military targets, would be regarded in many quarters as a new departure of considerable importance. Although the Americans now seemed to be disposed to draw no distinction between atomic and conventional weapons, he was by no means sure that public opinion in other countries would not continue to draw a sharp distinction between them. Again, how far would attacks be pressed beyond the Yalu River and against what targets? What was intended as regards the blockade of Chinese ports – which had previously been regarded as dangerous because, to be effective, it would need to be extended to neighbouring Russian ports and as ineffective because supplies could equally well be brought to the Communist armies by rail?

This and similar questions ought, Eden suggested, to be jointly discussed before all could agree to support a new military policy. If hostilities broke out again in Korea, Britain would certainly wish to play a part, as before, in support of the United Nations, 'but she would wish to be fully consulted on the military policy which was to be applied and the means by which it was to be carried out'. She would also wish to have an opportunity of consulting the other Commonwealth Governments contributing forces to the Commonwealth Division in Korea. Speaking for the Prime Minister and himself, Eden felt that they must reserve their position until they had had an opportunity to consult with their Cabinet colleagues and with the other Commonwealth Governments concerned. Until then they could not commit themselves to support the new military policy which Dulles had outlined in his statement.

Eisenhower tried to reassure Eden that the United States were certainly not intending to take any precipitate action without due consultation with their Allies. Eden had suggested that there might be need for prior discussion of military policy by the United Nations. The President confessed that he was not clear precisely how much discretion was left to the United Nations Commander to modify the military policy underlying the operations under his command. He wished, however, to make clear the attitude of the United States Government towards the use of atomic weapons:

> The United States were spending $50 billions a year on defence – representing an annual contribution of $300 per head of population. They were maintaining eight divisions, and a total of 275,000 men, in Korea. As there were limits to the total amount which the American people were prepared to spend on defence, heavy demands in Korea must have the effect of reducing the defence resources which the United States could deploy elsewhere in the world. Thus, their problem was to find means of reducing the cost of the Korean operations so that they might be able to maintain the contribution which they were making elsewhere towards the preservation of world peace. They had spent many millions of dollars in developing the atomic weapon. Certainly they would never use it for an aggressive purpose. But it was natural that the American public should ask why it should not be used to repel a deliberate aggression against American troops. Any decision of principle which excluded the use of that weapon, within the limits of local military circumstances, would have the effect of impairing America's ability to help in defending the cause of peace throughout the world. Certainly there should be consultation on the circumstances in which it might be used and the targets against which it should be employed. But it would be a very serious matter if its use were to be excluded as a matter of principle in all circumstances.

At this point, Churchill asked what prospect there was that the Korean Armistice would be broken? Eisenhower imagined that the risk was not at present regarded as especially great – though the Communists were continuing to build up their forces in Korea. Churchill then asked whether he could assume that the proposals outlined by Dulles had been put forward not because it was thought likely that the Armistice would be broken. Eisenhower confirmed that this was not the main reason for these proposals. They were put forward mainly because the United States were anxious to reduce the strength of their ground forces in Korea and, in order to do this without risk, they thought it necessary to make it clear in advance that they would be prepared to use other methods of conducting the offensive if hostilities should be resumed. The President thought it right, however, to make it plain that the United States had no intention of authorising atomic attacks on Chinese cities. The atomic weapon would be used only against military installations, mainly airfields, supporting a renewed Communist offensive against United Nations troops in Korea. To this Churchill argued:

> what was now under discussion was a hypothetical situation. The United States Government were proposing to declare in advance that they would feel free in certain circumstances to use atomic weapons against military targets. It thus became important to consider what attitude the Russians would adopt towards such a declaration. Might they not make a counter-declaration, if the Americans did as they proposed, that they would also hold themselves free to use their atomic resources? Would not a Soviet declaration on those lines be likely to cause widespread alarm?

The President admitted that, in the United States, it was already taken for granted, not only in official circles but also by public opinion, that the Russians would use any weapon at their disposal at any time when it suited them to do so. If this belief had not been so widely held in the United States, public support would not have been forthcoming for the substantial programme of defence expenditure on which the United States Government had embarked.

Churchill answered that he accepted that, while he did not doubt that Eisenhower had rightly interpreted the Russian intentions, the fact remained that the Russians had never yet made any public declaration that they would engage in atomic warfare: 'If we now said publicly that we would use this weapon in certain circumstances, this might well provoke them to say that they would at once retaliate.' This would give them an obvious opportunity to imply that their atomic resources were even greater than they were: they would be able to bluff to the limit. It would surely be a very serious step to invite such a declaration – 'and all because of a hypothetical situation which we had no reason to expect to arise in the immediate future'. These considerations should be very carefully weighed. He would like to be sure, before such a declaration was made, that the Russians would not be able to turn it to their advantage. Churchill feared that they might gain the moral advantage of being able to say that they would not be the first to use these weapons and would do so only if compelled by an American initiative. 'It would be a different matter if our intentions could be made plain to the Chinese and the Russians without a public declaration.' Churchill was by no means sure that there would be a favourable public reaction to a public declaration if it were related to a hypothetical situation which had not yet arisen. If the Armistice were treacherously broken, the public mood might well be different and there might be such a surge of public feeling as would justify and support the kind of action which Dulles had outlined. 'What should we lose by postponing a final decision until the actual situation had arisen? We might then be able to count on the united support of all our friends throughout the world. But, if we made some premature announcement, which provided a counter-declaration by the Russians, we might well find that hostile and middle opinion throughout the world would unite in attributing to the Americans and their Allies the responsibility for exposing mankind to all the horrors of full-scale atomic warfare' argued Churchill. He suggested that, as the issues involved were so grave, they called for further thought and discussion.[14]

In the course of conversation, after dinner, Eisenhower spoke of the growing power of the atomic weapon: nobody could say that even the hydrogen bomb, terrible as its explosive power was, would be the end. Meanwhile, he continued, all the three Service in the United States were being equipped with atomic weapons. If war came or if there were be a serious breach of the Armistice in Korea, the people of the United States would never understand it if the weapon was not used. Churchill repeated that it was unnecessary to face this issue now and if the armistice were in fact broken, on a major scale, a new situation would arise and the mood of the world might be 'very different from what it is today'.

The discussion then turned to the text of the President's impending speech to the UN. Churchill and Eden urged the modification or elimination of the passage which made it clear that the US would use atomic weapons to repel aggression, developing the arguments used previously by the Prime Minister. The President promised to give attention to these arguments; he thought the divergence of outlook between the European nations and the US, on the use of atomic weapons, was in part due to the fact that the Americans had become temperamentally more accustomed to the idea of atomic weapons and more familiar with the prospect. To them atomic weapons were coming to be regarded as just another form of weapon, whereas to the European peoples they were still a terrible new departure.[15]

This sufficed for now. At a National Security Council meeting, back in Washington, Dulles noted that 'to our suggestions with regard to normalizing the use of atomic weapons' both the British and the French 'exhibited very stubborn resistance to any idea of the automatic use of atomic weapons, even in the case of a Communist renewal of hostilities in Korea'.[16] Duly noted, by the Americans, this concern may have been but from the British perspective this merely postponed the issue. But Churchill and Eden had to face the fact that their own Chiefs of Staff paper presented a 'dilemma' for: 'either we go for all-out war against China, including atomic weapons, which would be unacceptable to us and to world opinion generally; or we stand fast on a defensive line, which would be unacceptable to American opinion'. One option floated was propose to the 'Old Commonwealth' a reply to the United States on the following lines:

(b) the Communists must now know that a second deliberate act of aggression in Korea would very probably bring on a general war. They would not therefore launch an aggression in Korea unless they were prepared for the consequences of a general war. On the other hand, if they wanted to bring on a general war, they would surely start it by attacking us at points more vulnerable for us and less for themselves. The contingency for which Americans ask us to plan is therefore very unlikely to arise. It is almost impossible to see the circumstances in which it might arise. Detailed planning and advance commitments are not therefore feasible. The two extreme cases are at least clear: if the Communists unmistakably provoke general war, we resist with all the means in our power; and if there is any chance of confining renewed fighting within Korea and preventing a general conflagration, we should do everything possible to take that chance.

(c) we stand by the Hurdle and the Joint Policy Declaration commitments. The latter, with the explanatory statements issued since, is a sufficient deterrent. The position must now be clear to the Communists without further warning.

(d) If nevertheless the Americans insist on pursuing the subject further, we should ask them first: what is the result they hope to achieve by their resistance to a renewed act of Communist aggression in Korea. Once the objective has been defined and agreed, we should ask two further questions:
  (i) what measures are best calculated to bring about the desired result? And
  (ii) what risk is there of any such measures bringing in their train other results which we wish to avoid (e.g. threat to Hong Kong, general war)? It should be on these grounds that our plans of action should be decided.[17]

Churchill and Eden stated their 'strong dislike for further commitments in hypothetical circumstances', and reserved their position until they had

had an opportunity to consult with their colleagues and with the other Commonwealth Governments concerned. Eden recommended to Churchill that 'we should consult with the old Commonwealth Governments and tell them that, subject to their views, we propose to inform the Americans that we stand by the undertakings previously given to associate ourselves with the policy of retaliation against bases in China, in the event of heavy air attack on United Nations forces; but that to reaffirm the reservations made when those undertakings were given and would therefore expect to be consulted in advance before a decision to authorise retaliatory action was taken. This would apply in particular to the use of atomic weapons'.[18]

At one level British fears were unfounded: there was no renewal of hostilities in Korea. But fears of global war were still very real as far as Eden was concerned. The events at Bermuda demonstrated the length to which the Americans might be prepared to go – and the US threat to use nuclear weapons was a spur for Eden's celebrated performance in ending the Indo-China war at Geneva in 1954: by May of that year Eden regarded the Americans as the main threat to world peace. He refused to go along with Dulles' public call for 'united action' to prevent French defeat at Dien Bien Phu fearing American intervention would provoke Chinese intervention as had happened in Korea. The Eisenhower administration, therefore, had no option but to await the outcome of the Geneva Conference.[19] An American nuclear response in Korea had, by now, evolved into a potential nuclear response in Indo-China: as early as 24 January 1954, Robert Scott was concerned that the Eisenhower administration would 'not necessarily refrain from action if they cannot get our consent' and maintaining a 'united front' would be problematic.[20]

The fear, in London, was of American intervention in Indo-China and the consequences that would entail for Britain. A suspicion that the Americans were not thinking rationally about what was at stake was not allayed when, on 9 February 1954, Eisenhower, in a letter to Churchill, wrote of the 'stupid and savage individuals in the Kremlin', the 'Russian menace' and the requirement to 'throw back the Russian threat and allow civilization, as we have known it, to continue its progress'. The President concluded with his nightmare description of what faced the West: 'an atheistic materialism in complete domination of all human life' which he led him to appreciate how necessary 'it is to seek renewed faith and strength from his God, and sharpen up his sword for the struggle that cannot be escaped'. Eden was alarmed that Eisenhower's private remarks seemed to echo the public rhetoric of Dulles that could be, up to this point, interpreted as warning shots, only, to the Communists. Eisenhower's private comments opened up the possibility that there was more substance to the public rhetoric, perhaps even a desire for confrontation with the Communist bloc. Eden demanded the Prime Minister confront the President and inquire of him: 'I take it that you are referring ... to the spiritual struggle. Otherwise your words suggest that you believe war to be inevitable. I certainly do not think so and I am sure you do not either.' Churchill acquiesced but before he could react events were overtaken when it was announced that the Americans were in possession of a viable thermo-nuclear weapon.[21] How far the Soviets were from developing a comparable device was hardly the point: the fact was the nature of a future global war had been transformed by thermo-nuclear weapons and the possibility for the United Kingdom to survive in such a conflict were diminished considerably compared to the aftermath of an atomic attack on it. And for Eden it was the Americans, not the Communists, who appeared to be the greatest danger to world peace.

## Notes

1 TNA DO 35/5822 British Embassy Tokyo 7 September 1953 Statement made by Lieut. Colonel J.P. Carne, DSO. The Gloucestershire Regiment
2 TNA DO 35/5822 Dening Telegram No. 816, 8 September 1953
3 TNA DO 35/5822 G.D. Anderson minute, 24 November 1953
4 TNA CAB 21/3319 Memo to Prime Minister. Korea – Action in Event of Renewed Communist Aggression
5 TNA FO 371/105540 Action in the Event of a Renewed Communist Attack in Korea (CT Crowe), 4 December 1953
6 TNA FO 371/105540 PM/53/337, 4 December 1953
7 FRUS 1952–1954, Volume V (Western European Security Part II). First Restricted Tripartite Meeting of the Heads of Government, Mid Ocean Club, Bermuda, 4 December 1953
8 FRUS 1952–1954, Volume V (Western European Security Part II). Eisenhower-Churchill Meeting, Mid Ocean Club, Bermuda, December 4, 1953 Memorandum of Conversation, by the Secretary of State, 4 December 1953
9 TNA FO 371/105540 PM/53/337 Eden to Churchill, 4 December 1953
10 TNA FO 371/105540 US Policy in the Far East: US Bases in the UK Notes for discussion with the Americans at Bermuda, 5 December 1953
11 TNA FO 371/105540 Action in the Even of renewed Communist Aggression in Korea (WD Allen), 5 December 1953 to Sir P. Dixon
12 FRUS 1952–1954, Volume V (Western European Security Part II) Eisenhower-Churchill Meeting, Mid Ocean Club, Bermuda, 4 December 1953 Memorandum of Conversation, by the Secretary of State, 4 December 1953

13 TNA FO 371/105540 PM/53/339 Eden to Prime Minister, 7 December 1953
14 TNA FO 371/105540 Confidential Annex 4th Meeting, 7 December 1953, 10.30 am
15 TNA FO 371/105574 Informal Meeting held after dinner at the Mid-Ocean Club, 5 December 1953
16 FRUS 1952–1954, Volume V (Western European Security Part II). Memorandum of Discussion at the 174th Meeting of the National Security Council, 10 December 1953
17 TNA FO 371/105540 Minute, c. December 1953
18 TNA CAB 21/3319 Memo to Prime Minister. Korea – Action in Event of Renewed Communist Aggression
19 Ruane, 'Containing America', pp. 141–42
20 *Ibid.*, p. 155
21 *Ibid.*, p. 161

# Conclusion

Britain's Korean War demonstrated both the limits and opportunities for influencing the United States' policy during the early Cold War. The disagreements, during the conflict, between the United Kingdom and the United States, were merely one aspect of a series of difficulties between the two Powers: Persia, Germany, and Egypt remain the glaring examples. But disagreement did not equate with powerlessness to influence the Americans. And this – influence – was what the British, conscious of their real decline in power since the Second World War, required. On Korea this was essential as, unlike other issues, here was a real war with the potential to evolve from a limited military engagement, in a far away place, to Armageddon for the compact British Isles. The intensity of the US–UK 'special relationship' ebbed and flowed but remained a constant because of the common interest of both Powers to resist the threat of Soviet expansionism. The key aim of British strategy towards to the United States was the desire to be 'consulted' on matters of major policy: this might take various forms but the necessity for it was so the British would have the ability to influence American policy.

The dominant fear in the minds of the Chiefs of Staff and the Foreign Office, in the first, intense, ten months of the conflict, was that of an American expansion of the war that would bring in the Soviet Union. This focused, increasingly, on MacArthur's intentions. The British Government, through its Ambassador and its military representatives in Washington, consistently raised their concerns. These appeared, at certain times, to act as a check on MacArthur's ambitions to expand the war but his dismissal was not due to British or Allied representations but his constitutional challenge to his Commander-in-Chief. In the aftermath of the General's departure it became apparent that a desire to expand the war was not limited, in American circles, to the former Supreme Commander alone. But the war remained a limited one: when the British were asked, by the Truman administration, to agree to 'hot pursuit' across the Chinese border and to extend UN bombing into Chinese territory, HMG politely declined to agree; in London they were the thin end of the wedge: it should not be forgotten that the military balance of power in Europe, with an American political and military commitment to its defence was still a delicate flower that needed to be nourished, was firmly to the Soviet advantage. US miscalculation in Asia could ignite the gunpowder trail that would lead to a detonation Germany. The British did not have a veto over American strategy in Korea – but under the Truman administration they came pretty close to one with respect to the widening of the war into China. But once key military points were conceded, by the UK to the Americans, British leverage was eroded.

The British had some right to be consulted over events in Korea because they had troops there (despite the dwarfing of the UK-Commonwealth contingent by the US contribution, and American carping over this, it remained the case that the British had the second biggest allocation of forces in both military and naval terms). There is an intellectually coherent argument that military intervention should be driven by selfish strategic national interests only: clearly, with regard to Korea, it was not in Britain's selfish strategic national interest to intervene there; but it was in Britain's political interests to send ground troops. Attlee made this decision in terms of how much influence Britain could have with the United States – or, perhaps, more accurately, how much influence HMG might lose by not committing its forces. And the role of the 'man on the spot' – in this case Sir Oliver Franks – illustrates the importance of individuals in this decision. The greatest asset the Americans had, in terms of leverage with the British, was the spectre of isolationism; British policy towards the United States was conducted with an awareness of American domestic politics.

In the attempt to influence Washington, personalities mattered. Bevin was cautious, anxious not to risk a possible breakdown in the Anglo-American relationship. But the impact of Bevin's personality on policy, within the Cabinet, can be seen when he was absent and Younger took his place: Younger took a harder line towards certain American policies and, in the Foreign Secretary's confinement to a hospital bed, it is noticeable that the Cabinet came closest to a break with Washington over the naming of China as an aggressor in the UN. American concessions prevented this but there was, for a brief moment, a real possibility of a break between the two Powers. This was driven by the worry that the consequences would lead to general war with China and, consequently, increase the chances of global war involving the USSR. This remained the overriding concern of British policy towards the United States in regard to Korea. Morrison, as Foreign Secretary, was more amenable to American siren calls to show greater flexibility with regard to bombing policy. His lack of knowledge, historically, in foreign affairs, before his appointment – coupled with his extracurricular interests (some considered his concern in his pet project of the Festival of Britain as his main interest in 1951) – may account for his instinct to forge an understanding with Acheson, on retaliatory bombing, rather than sounding out the Chiefs of Staff as his predecessor would have done. In doing so Morrison gave up much of what the Foreign Office and Chiefs had achieved in their efforts to have an input into US military strategy since the beginning of the war: once this was conceded it could not be retrieved.

The Attlee–Truman talks, in December 1950, secured for the British the watershed agreement of the right to be consulted on the use of the atomic bomb: whatever the vagueness of the offer by the President it did represent a significant diplomatic achievement – even though it was based upon the *personal* guarantee of Truman to Attlee. The Prime Minister took the President – at the latter's insistence – as a man of his word. Despite some historians downplaying the significance of this agreement, herein lay the uniqueness and weakness of the 'special relationship' for such a personal assurance was not offered to any other Great Power; but it was an agreement with a limited lifespan – that of the Truman administration. A new president might have a different perspective as, indeed, was the case with Eisenhower. And, with the Republican administration, came a qualitatively different perspective. The Truman administration had judged that support from its key allies, in the Korean conflict, meant a certain restriction in the US room for manoeuvre; but while the Eisenhower administration also sought support from its allies, it judged that Allied, including British opinion, should not act as a block on US policy in Korea to the extent that had occurred under the previous Democratic administration. Nowhere was this more obvious, to the British, as in the matter of the possible use of atomic weapons in Korea – or elsewhere. Anglo-American interdependence had its limitations: ultimately it depended on American sufferance of British views. The British, in turn, had leverage by calling an American bluff over the latter's commitment to the defence of Europe – central to the US conception of its vital interests; but, as Churchill and Eden's concerns with regard to the European Defence Community would later illustrate, it was never a bluff the British would ever want to call.

Could Churchill and Eden have acted as a check on the American designs to use atomic weapons in a renewed Korean conflict? Certainly, the Eisenhower administration was, in internal discussions, confident it could force Western allies to acquiesce in such an outcome. That there was no renewal of Korean hostilities should not blind one to the fact that unilateral US atomic action was a real threat: the Suez crisis would demonstrate just how far Eisenhower would go to damage the position of his key European allies if he deemed it in the strategic national interest of the United States. The discussions at Bermuda convinced Eden, at least, that the greatest danger in the ignition of World War III lay with the American intention to use atomic munitions in Korea. This was the catalyst for Eden's subsequent determination to drive home a settlement in Geneva ending, for now, the conflict in Indo-China: the same dread of what the United States was capable of doing during renewed hostilities in Korea. In this sense Eden's spectacular success at Geneva was the result of his Korean concerns. This was based upon the simple, and shocking, deduction of Eisenhower and Dulles that nuclear weapons were merely a more powerful form of explosive. The advent of thermo-nuclear bombs made this assumption absurd particularly in view of the quantum leap in destruction that promised the extinction of the United Kingdom in a global conflict that might emerge from a regional conflict of, in relative terms, strategic unimportance. The preservation of world peace could not be left to the Americans for their plans entered an element into the Cold War that was unpredictable. Eisenhower did not even realise that, as head of the Unified Command, he was not acting for the United States alone. The British position of insisting on being 'consulted' by Washington was, initially, a holding position; it would, also, provide an opportunity to reiterate the strong moral and political objections Her Majesty's Government had to the use of atomic weapons. Whether this would have held back the Americans, in such circumstances, no one can say beyond speculating what effect the objections of Washington's two principal allies (Britain and France) in the fight against Communist expansion may have had.

The danger of the Korean War was that it was a theatre of real conflict between the West and Communism in which the United States seriously considered the use of nuclear weapons. It should not be forgotten that the United States remains the only country to have actually used nuclear weapons in war and against an Asiatic people. The legacy of Bermuda was witnessed in Eden's success at Geneva, spurred on by fear of the consequences of American impetuousness in their policy towards China. But only by having access to American thinking on future military strategy was it possible for Eden to comprehend the consequences of failure at

Geneva: it was not, of course, inevitable that the United States would intervene militarily in Indo-China, or that Korean hostilities would erupt once more; but the risks involved were frightening if either of these possibilities occurred. The Eisenhower administration appears to have been quite serious in their determination to expand the war in Korea and use atomic weapons if necessary. The President convinced himself that a quick, sharp use of overwhelming force in Korea, against China, would have overcome British – and other Allied – misgivings; but the risk the British could not afford to take was that the outcome might also have been a quick, sharp use of overwhelming force against Western Europe – and the United Kingdom's position as a base for a strategic nuclear strike against the Soviet Union in particular – that would decimate Britain. Any US atomic attack on China would make the activation of the Soviet-Sino Treaty a real possibility. It is here that one can see the benefits of the 'special relationship' for the British: however tilted absolute power was, in favour of the Americans, had HMG been excluded from the inner thoughts of US policy, the UK would never have been in a position, as Eden did, to negotiate a settlement that he considered essential for global stability and the most important issue of all for a statesman – the very survival of his country itself. This could not have been achieved but for the endless days, months and years of attempting to work with, and influence, the Americans. It bore fruit by delivering to the British Government, from its perspective, the opportunity to set an agenda that it believed would reduce the likelihood of the destruction of Western Europe and the UK. And diplomatic success does not come much bigger than that.

# Bibliography

## Primary sources

CAB   Cabinet Office
DEFE  Ministry of Defence
DO    Dominions Office
FO    Foreign Office
PREM  Prime Minister's Office
TNA   The National Archives
WO    War Office

Command Paper 8078 *Summary of Events Relating to Korea* 1950
Korea No. 2 (1953) *Special Report of the Unified Command on the Korean Armistice Agreement Signed at Panmunjom on July 27, 1953,*
*Documents on British Overseas Policy* (DBOP): Korea, June 1950–April 1951 Series 2
*Foreign Relations of the United States* (FRUS) Volume VII (Korea)
*Foreign Relations of the United States, 1951. Korea and China* Volume VII, Part 1
*Foreign Relations of the United States, 1952–1954. Korea* Volume XV, Part 1
*Foreign Relations of the United States, 1952–1954. Western European Security* Volume V, Part 2
FRUS 1952–1954 Volume VI (Western Europe and Canada Part I)

## Books and articles

Acheson, Dean, *Present at the Creation: My Years in the State Department* (London: Hamish Hamilton, 1969)

Aldrich, Richard J. (ed.), *British Intelligence, Strategy and the Cold War, 1945–51* (London: Routledge, 1992)

Ambrose, Stephen E., *Eisenhower the President* (London: Allen & Unwin, 1984)

Attlee, Clement, *As It Happened* (London: Odhams Press Ltd, 1st edn, 1954)

Ball, S., *The Cold War: An International History, 1947–1991* (London: Arnold, 1998)

Barclay, Roderick, *Ernest Bevin and the Foreign Office, 1932–69* (author published, 1975)

Bark, Dennis L. and David R. Gress, *A History of West Germany: Volume I, From Shadow to Substance, 1945–1963* (Oxford: Blackwell, 1989)

Bartlett, C.J., *British Foreign Policy in the Twentieth Century* (London: Macmillan, 1989)

Bartlett, C.J., *The Special Relationship: A Political History of Anglo-American Relations since 1945* (London: Longman, 1992)

Baylis, John, *Anglo-American Defence Relations, 1939–1984: The Special Relationship* (London: Macmillan, 1984)

Belmonte, Laura, 'Anglo-American Relations and the Dismissal of MacArthur', *Diplomatic History*, 19:4 (1995), pp. 641–667

Blake, Robert and William Roger Louis (eds), *Churchill: A Major New Assessment of His Life in Peace and War* (Oxford: Oxford University Press, 1993)

Boyle, Peter G. (ed.), *The Churchill–Eisenhower Correspondence, 1953–1955* (Chapel Hill: University of North Carolina Press, 1990)

Bullock, Alan, *Ernest Bevin: Foreign Secretary 1945–51* (London: William Heinemann 1983)

Carlton, David, *Anthony Eden* (London: Allen & Unwin, 1986 edn)

Charmley, John, *Churchill's Grand Alliance: The Anglo-American Special Relationship, 1940–1957* (London: Hodder & Stoughton, 1995)

Cummings, Bruce, *Origins of the Korean War, Volume 2: The Roaring of the Cataract, 1947–1950* (Ithaca: Cornell University Press, 2004)

Danchev, Alex, 'The Cold War "Special Relationship" Revisited', *Diplomacy & Statecraft*, 17 (2006), p. 579

Dimbleby, David and David Reynolds, *An Ocean Apart: The Relationship between Britain and America in the Twentieth Century* (London: Guild Publishing, 1988)

Dingman, Roger, 'Truman, Attlee and the Korean War Crisis', in Ian Nish (ed.), *The East Asian Crisis: the Problem of China, Korea and Japan*

(London: London School of Economics and Political Science, 1982), pp. 1–42

Dobson, Alan P., *Anglo-American Relations in the Twentieth Century* (London: Routledge, 1995)

Dockrill, Michael, 'The Foreign Office, Anglo-American Relations and the Korean War, June 1950–June 1951', *International Affairs*, 62:3 (1986), pp. 459–476

Dockrill, Michael and John W. Young, *British Foreign Policy, 1945–1956* (London: Macmillan, 1989)

Dockrill, Saki, 'Britain and the Settlement of the West German Rearmament Question in 1954', in Dockrill and Young (eds), *British Foreign Policy, 1945–56*

Donoughue, Bernard and G.W. Jones, *Herbert Morrison: Portrait of a Politician* (London: Weidenfeld & Nicolson, 1973)

Dutton, David, *Anthony Eden: A Life and Reputation* (London: Arnold, 1997)

Ellison, James, *Threatening Europe: Britain and the Creation of the European Community, 1955–58* (London: Macmillan, 2000)

Farrar, Peter N., 'A Pause for Peace Negotiations: The British Buffer Zone Plan of November 1950', in James Cotton and Ian Neary (eds), *The Korean War in History* (Manchester: Manchester University Press, 1989), pp. 66–79

Foot, R.J., *The Wrong War: American Policy and the Dimensions of the Korean Conflict 1950–1953* (Ithaca: Cornell University Press 1985)

Foot, R.J., 'Anglo-American Relations in the Korean Crisis: The British Efforts to Avert an Expanded War, December 1950–January 1951', *Diplomatic History*, 10:1 (1986), pp. 43–57

Gaddis, John Lewis, *Strategies of Containment: A Critical Appraisal of Postwar American National Security Policy* (Oxford: Oxford University Press, 1982)

Gilbert, Martin, *Never Despair: Winston S. Churchill, 1945–1965* (London: Heinemann, 1988)

Gladwyn, Lord, *The Memoirs of Lord Gladwyn* (London: Weidenfeld & Nicolson, 1972)

Goncharov, Sergei, John W. Lewis and Xue Litai, *Uncertain Partners: Stalin, Mao and the Korean War* (Stanford: Stanford University Press 1994)

Greenwood, Sean, *Britain and European Cooperation since 1945* (Oxford: Blackwell, 1992)

Greenwood, Sean, *Britain and European Integration since the Second World War* (Manchester: Manchester University Press, 1996)

Greenwood, Sean, *Britain and the Cold War 1945–91* (London: Palgrave Macmillan, 2000)

Greenwood, Sean, '"A War We Don't Want": Another Look at the British Labour Government's Commitment in Korea, 1950–51', *Contemporary British History*, 17:4 (2003), pp. 1–24

Greenwood, Sean, *Titan at the Foreign Office: Gladwyn Jebb and the Shaping of the Modern World* (Leiden: Brill, 2008)

Harris, Kenneth, *Attlee* (London: Weidenfeld & Nicolson, 1982)

Hastings, Max, *The Korean War* (London: Simon & Schuster, 1987)

Hennessy, Peter, *Never Again: Britain 1945–1951* (London: Jonathan Cape 1992)

Hennessy, Peter, *Having It So Good: Britain in the Fifties* (London: Penguin 2007)

Hennessy, Peter and Anthony Seldon (eds), *Ruling Performance: British Governments from Attlee to Thatcher* (Oxford: Blackwell, 1987)

Horne, Alistair, *Macmillan: Volume I, 1894–1956* (London: Macmillan, 1988)

James, Robert Rhodes, *Anthony Eden* (London: Weidenfeld & Nicolson, 1986)

Jian, Chen, 'The Sino-Soviet Alliance and China's entry into the Korean War', *Cold War International History Project Working Paper*, No. 1, June 1992

Jian, Chen, *China's Road to the Korean War: The Making of the Sino-American Confrontation* (New York: Columbia University Press, 1996)

Jong-yil, Ra, 'Political Settlement in Korea: British Views and Policies, Autumn 1950', in James Cotton and Ian Neary (eds), *The Korean War in History* (Manchester: Manchester University Press, 1989)

Kim, Youngho, 'The Origins of the Korean War: Civil War of Stalin's Rollback', *Diplomacy & Statecraft*, 10:1 (1999), pp. 187–189

Lafeber, Walter, *America, Russia and the Cold War, 1945–1992* (New York: McGraw-Hill, 1993)

Lamb, Richard, *The Failure of the Eden Government* (London: Sidgwick & Jackson, 1987)

Lowe, Peter 'The Frustrations of Alliance: Britain, the United States and the Korean War 1950–51', in James Cotton and Ian Neary (eds), *The Korean War in History* (Manchester: Manchester University Press, 1989), pp. 80–99

Lowe, Peter, 'An Ally and a Reluctant General: Great Britain, Douglas MacArthur and the Korean War 1950–51', *English Historical Review*, 105:416 (1990), pp. 624–653

Lowe, Peter, 'The Significance of the Korean War in Anglo-American Relations 1950–53', in Anne Deighton (ed.), *Britain and the First Cold War* (Basingstoke: Macmillan, 1990), pp. 126–148

Lowe, Peter, *Containing the Cold War in East Asia. British Policies towards Japan, China and Korea 1948–53* (Manchester: Manchester University Press, 1997)

MacDonald, Callum, *Britain and the Korean War* (Oxford: Blackwell, 1990)

Macmillan, Harold, *Tides of Fortune, 1945–1955* (London: Macmillan, 1969)

Marsh, Steve and John Baylis, 'The Anglo-American "Special Relationship": The Lazarus of International Relations', *Diplomacy & Statecraft*, 17 (2006), pp. 173–211

Moran, Lord, *Churchill: The Struggle for Survival, 1940–65* (London: Constable, 1966)

Morgan, Kenneth O., *Labour in Power 1954–1951* (Oxford: Oxford University Press 1984)

Northedge, F.S., *Descent from Power: British Foreign Policy, 1945–1973* (London: Allen & Unwin, 1974)

Parker, R.A.C. (ed.), *Winston Churchill: Studies in Statesmanship* (London: Brassey's, 1995)

Pelling, Henry, *Churchill's Peacetime Ministry, 1951–55* (London: Macmillan, 1997)

Pimlott, Ben, *Hugh Dalton. A Life* (London: Jonathan Cape, 1985)

Pimlott, Ben, *The Political Diary of Hugh Dalton 1918–40, 1945–60* (London: Jonathan Cape, 1986)

Ra, J.Y., 'Special Relationship at War: The Anglo-American Relationship during the Korean War', *Journal of Strategic Studies*, 7:3 (1984), pp. 310–317

Ramsden, John, *The Age of Churchill and Eden, 1940–1957* (London: Longman, 1995)

Reynolds, David, *Britannia Overruled: British Policy and World Power in the Twentieth Century* (London: Longman, 1991)

Reynolds, David (ed.), *The Origins of the Cold War in Europe: International Perspectives* (Yale: Yale University Press, 1994)

Roberts, Frank, *Dealing with Dictators: The Destruction and Revival of Europe, 1930- 1970* (London: Weidenfeld & Nicolson, 1991)

Ruane, Kevin, 'Anthony Eden, British Diplomacy and the Origins of the Geneva Conference of 1954', *Historical Journal*, 37:1 (1994), pp. 153–172

Ruane, Kevin, 'Refusing to Pay the Price: British Foreign Policy and the Pursuit of Victory in Vietnam, 1952–4', *English Historical Review*, 110:435 (1995), pp. 70–92

Ruane, Kevin, 'Containing America: Aspects of British Foreign Policy and the Cold War in South-East Asia, 1951–54', *Diplomacy & Statecraft*, 7:1 (1996), pp. 141–174

Ruane, Kevin and James Ellison, 'Managing the Americans: Anthony Eden, Harold Macmillan and the Pursuit of "Power-Proxy" in the 1950s', *Contemporary British History*, 18:3 (2004), pp. 147–167

Salmon, Andrew, *To the Last Round: The Epic British on the Imjin River, Korea 1951* (London: Aurum Press Ltd, 1st edn, 2009)

Salmon, Andrew, *Scorched Earth, Black Snow: The First Year of the Korean War* (London: Aurum Press Ltd, 2011)

Seldon, Anthony, *Churchill's Indian Summer: The Conservative Government 1951–55* (London: Hodder & Stoughton, 1981)

Shlaim, A., P. Jones and K. Sainsbury, *British Foreign Secretaries since 1945* (Newton Abbott: David & Charles, 1977)

Shuckburgh, Evelyn, *Descent to Suez: Diaries 1951–1956* (London: Weidenfeld & Nicolson, 1986)

Smith, Joseph (ed.), *The Origins of NATO* (Exeter: University of Exeter Press, 1990)

Stephens, Mark, *Ernest Bevin: Unskilled Labourer and World Statesman* (Stevenage: SPA Books, 1985)

Stueck, William, 'The Limits of Influence: British Policy and American Expansion of the War in Korea', *Pacific Historical Review*, 55 (1986), pp. 65–95

Stueck, William, *Rethinking the Korean War: A New Diplomatic and Strategic History* (Princeton: Princeton University Press, 2002)

Stueck, William (ed.), *The Korean War in World History* (Lexington: University Press of Kentucky, 2004)

Thomas-Symonds, Nicklaus, *Attlee: A Life in Politics* (London: I.B. Tauris & Co Ltd, 2010)

Thornton, Richard C., *Odd Man Out: Truman, Stalin, Mao and the Origin of the Korean War* (London: Brassey's, 2000)

Warner, Geoffrey, 'Anglo-American Relations and the Cold War in 1950', *Diplomacy & Statecraft*, 22:1 (2011), pp. 44–60

Warner, Geoffrey (ed.), *In the Midst of Events: The Foreign Office Diaries and Papers of Kenneth Younger. February 1950–October 1951* (London: Routledge, 2005)

Weathersby, Kathryn, 'Soviet Aims in Korea and the Origins of the Korean War', Working Paper No. 8, *Cold War International History Project*, November 1993

Whiting, Charles, *Battleground Korea: The British in the Korean War, 1950–51* (Stroud: Sutton Publishing Ltd, 1999)

Williams, Francis, *Twilight of Empire: Memoirs of Prime Minister Clement Attlee* (Westport: Greenwood Press, 1978)

Yasamee Heather, 'Britain, Korea and the politics of power by proxy' Foreign and Commonwealth Office Occasional Paper, No. 5, *Korea*, April 1992

Young, John (ed.), *The Foreign Policy of Churchill's Peacetime Administration, 1951–1955* (Leicester: Leicester University Press, 1988)
Young, John, *Britain and European Unity, 1945–1992* (London: Macmillan, 1993)
Young, John, *Winston Churchill's Last Campaign: Britain and the Cold War, 1951–1955* (Oxford: Clarendon Press, 1996)

# Index

38th parallel
  clashes on 2, 11
  crossing of 26, 37, 56–8, 61–4, 66, 68–71, 75–7, 79, 98, 102, 116, 118, 149, 170–1, 172, 175–7, 252
  division of Korea 10, 21, 49, 64, 69
  withdrawal to 12, 26, 28, 34, 39, 41, 48, 60, 135, 180

abstention 13, 160–1
air attacks 15, 83, 100–1, 142, 170, 171, 180–1, 183, 188, 189, 191–4, 196, 197, 199, 269, 270, 276
Anglo/American solidarity 1–3, 12, 19, 33, 37, 148, 279, 283
  weakness of 281
armistice 177, 196–8, 204–9, 216–21, 227–31, 233–4, 236–8, 262–3, 266, 269–70, 272, 274
Attlee, Clement (U.K. Prime Minister 1945–51)
  Acheson, Dean and 50, 120, 128
  China and 156, 163, 193
  escalation of war 101
  Formosa and 123–4
  India and 25, 36–8, 41, 43, 122–3
  influence on the U.S. 1951 4, 108, 110–14, 116, 125, 129–30, 141–3, 145–6, 195, 280–1
  justification for war 21
  provision of forces 50, 52–3
  UN resolution and 160–66
  USSR and 23–4, 39, 115
atomic weapons 4, 8, 20, 104, 109, 124–5, 127–8, 130–1, 137, 186, 264–77, 281–3
Australia 18, 20, 53, 65, 155, 159, 194, 220, 231

bacteriological (germ) warfare 213–14
beach-head 146–7
Bermuda conference 264, 266, 276, 282
Bevin, Ernest (U.K. Foreign Secretary 1945–51) 3
  illness 15, 47
  Formosa and 32–3, 56, 79
  Manchuria and 101
  relations with China 29, 31–2, 70, 81, 93, 100, 102, 146, 153

relations with India 37–8, 78, 80, 89
relations with the U.S. 12, 27, 29–35, 37–8, 41, 54–5, 61–2, 70–1, 79, 86, 88–9, 91, 93–5, 100–1, 135, 138–40, 143–5, 151–3, 160, 170, 176, 280
relations with the USSR 23–9, 35, 63–4
the United Nations and 82–5, 92, 95–6, 152
blockade 14, 39, 122, 204, 266–7, 269
  naval 151, 205–7, 271
bridgehead 47–8, 109–11, 118, 122, 150, 172
brigade groups 52, 53, 54, 90, 99, 238, 239
British Joint Services Mission (BJSM) 14, 192
buffer area 83, 95, 96, 262
Burma (Myanmar) 9, 149

cabinet defence committee (U.K. government) 52, 184, 193, 198
Cairo declaration 29, 33, 129, 155
Canada 53, 54, 155, 159, 194, 232
cease-fire 83, 109, 112, 113, 116, 118, 120–1, 123, 129, 138, 142, 145, 151, 153, 155, 157, 158, 171
Chiang Kai-shek (President of the Republic of China 1948–75) 10, 11, 15, 123, 124, 141, 147–8, 153, 174, 207, 269
China
  aggression 30, 37, 39, 40, 138–46, 151–9, 171, 207, 266–8,
  Chinese People's Government (CPG) 32, 100, 145, 157, 161
  communist army 18, 68, 80, 99, 271

Kuomintang 11, 12
nationalism 6, 11, 12, 30, 80, 110, 112, 114, 116, 123, 207
  see also China, Kuomintang
representation of Communist China in the United Nations 12, 26, 29–31, 33, 35, 37, 40, 129, 155, 164, 178
sanctions against 80, 124, 135–6, 139, 151, 154, 156, 158, 163, 166, 196
Churchill, Winston (U.K. Prime Minister 1951–55)
  atomic weapons 273–5, 282
  see also atomic weapons
  China and 205–7
  communism and 6, 208
  Formosa and 207
  General Clark's office and 215–16, 228
  influence on U.S. 207, 227–30, 232–5, 238–9, 269, 282
  napalm bomb and 211–13
  see also napalm
  return to power 204
  USSR and 236
civil war 2, 11, 21, 153, 238,
collective security 142, 144
committee of three 163–4
Commonwealth 8, 9, 18, 19, 31, 36, 38, 53, 55, 65, 112, 135–45 (passim), 148, 152–3, 158, 162–3, 166, 216, 231, 270–1, 276, 280
  Old Commonwealth 192–3, 275, 276
communist indoctrination 242, 243, 245, 246, 248–51
  grading of 246–7
Czechoslovakia 228, 230, 237

*Daily Worker, The* 213, 249
demilitarised zone 83–9, 92–3, 95–6, 233, 237

democracy 6, 7, 57, 58, 59, 65, 239, 250
deterrence 8, 57, 275

Eden, Anthony (U.K. Foreign Secretary 1951–55) 3, 204, 212
  Acheson, Dean and 204–6, 219–21
  armistice and 207–9, 266–7, 270
  Churchill, Winston and 204, 206, 208, 269, 276
  illness 227, 264
  President Eisenhower and 218–19, 271, 277
  return to power 204
  U.S. military policy and 204–6, 271–2, 275–7, 281–3
Eisenhower, Dwight D. (U.S. President 1953–61)
  administration 276, 281–3
  atomic weapons and 266, 269, 274, 282
  Eden, Anthony and 218–19, 264, 271, 276–7
  Churchill, Winston and 227, 233, 235, 272, 273, 276
  comparison with President Truman 4, 281
  Rhee, Syngman and 234, 238–9
escalation of war 54, 63–4, 70, 91, 98, 136–7, 184, 189, 196, 264–5, 267, 270–1, 275, 281
*see also* world war III
Ex-Service Movement for Peace 249–50

Formosa (Taiwan) 10, 26, 27, 51, 116, 118, 179
  cessation to communist China 11, 14–18, 25, 29–32, 34, 40, 55, 113, 123, 153, 178, 182, 187, 207
  importance to the U.S. 33, 35, 56, 67, 78–9, 104, 110, 112, 114, 119–20, 121, 123, 125, 147–50, 155, 158, 184
  opinion of the U.K. 123–4, 129, 263

Geneva Convention 208–10, 216, 242, 257
Germany 6, 110, 136, 197, 279, 280
'Great Bug Out', the 98
Greece 27, 155
guerrilla warfare 11, 49, 69, 70, 83, 141, 142

Hamhung 99, 109, 111
Hitler, Adolf 7, 270
Holland (Netherlands) 18, 145
hot pursuit 87, 127, 270, 280

imperialism 15, 16, 51, 66, 100, 112, 122, 123
Inchon 56, 59, 60, 67, 109, 111
Indo-China 6, 9, 16, 19, 27, 42, 113, 114, 142, 150, 207, 263, 270, 276, 282, 283
interrogation of British POWs 243, 245–7, 249–60
  amnesia 253
  drugs 256–8, 262, 264
  hypnosis 251, 255–6
  projection 258–60
  sleep deprivation 251–5
  suggestion 251–6
  *see also* communist indoctrination; repatriation
isolationism 140, 234, 280

Japan
  peace treaty 17, 26, 31, 113, 117
Joint Intelligence Committee (JIC) 62–3

Kim Il-Sung (Supreme Leader of North Korea 1948–94) 10, 78
  Invasion of South Korea 10–11

land forces 14, 17, 18, 20, 47–53, 68, 86, 100, 136, 180, 197, 211, 272, 280
  tanks 14, 15, 50, 52, 53, 143, 211, 263
league of nations 140, 161, 235
limited war 124, 128, 129, 135, 148

MacArthur, Douglas (Commander-in-Chief of the United Nations Command 1950–52) 17
  conflict with China 93, 97–8, 188, 190–1, 100–1, 115, 149–50, 177–8, 180–5
  criticism of 102–3, 109, 147, 173–6, 184–5, 193–5
  dismissal from military command 2, 182, 185–7, 190–1, 193, 198
  Formosa and 56
  headquarters 53–4
  management of forces in Korea 54, 56, 62, 67–8, 71, 76–8, 80–1, 88–91, 94–7, 100, 111, 126–7
  President Truman and 79
  public statements 55–6, 78, 126, 184–5, 169–70, 177, 187, 190
  U.K. opinions of 126, 178–80, 182, 279
Malaya 6, 9, 18, 19, 27, 32, 34, 49, 50, 69, 98, 114, 120, 149, 263
Manchuria 4, 10, 269
  airfields 86–7, 91–100, 114, 180, 183, 191, 266
  Chinese military in 82, 86, 88, 115, 121, 143, 146, 196–7
  frontier 56, 63, 70, 75, 79–80, 83–4, 86–7, 101, 104, 172, 181, 196–8, 270, 271
    see also Yalu River
  immunity of 86, 114
  U.K. opinions of 122, 127, 205, 265
  U.S. violations of 64–5, 76, 79, 84, 88, 97–8, 101, 103, 181, 264
Mao Zedong (Chairman of the Communist Party of China 1945–76) 11, 40, 72, 114
Marxism 6, 114, 122
MI5 246, 247, 249, 251, 252, 260
Middle East, the 8, 9, 15, 18, 49, 101, 207, 268

napalm 210–12
neutrality 138, 194
Neutral Nations Repatriation Commission 228, 232, 236–7
New Zealand 18, 20, 53, 155, 159, 231

Pakistan 9, 31, 65, 230
Panmunjom 204, 218, 219, 228, 231, 234–7
peace observation commission 163–4
Persia (Iran) 15, 18, 23, 27, 207, 279
Philippines 16, 17, 38, 111, 113, 117, 119, 120, 155, 177
Poland 228, 230, 237
Potsdam declaration 155
power by proxy 3
propaganda 21, 29, 39–41, 63, 68, 115, 211, 212, 213, 214, 218, 242–7, 264

prisoners of war 216–21, 231, 233, 242–48, 251–2, 255, 257, 260, 262,
proxy war 57, 110
Pusan 47, 111, 238
Pyongyang 67, 68, 75, 172

Quebec agreement 127–8

repatriation 209, 216, 219–220, 222, 228, 230–1, 238, 244
  'Big Switch' operation 243
  British Repatriated Prisoner of War Interrogation Unit (BRPWIU) 243, 245, 247, 251
  forced 209–10, 216–18, 232
  'Little Switch' operation 243
  voluntary 208, 210, 218, 220, 223, 233
Rhee, Syngman (South Korean President 1948–60) 10, 59, 102, 231–2, 234, 237–8
  deposing 238–9
Royal Air Force (RAF) 6, 14, 20, 76, 260
Royal Navy 6, 77, 252, 260

Siam (Thailand) 9, 38
Singapore 111, 252
Sinuiju 80, 87
settlement of Korean War 21, 23, 25–8, 36–9, 41, 60, 104, 129, 141–3, 152–7, 159, 163–6, 178, 190, 227, 236–7, 282–3
South Africa 53, 159, 194, 231
'special relationship' *see* Anglo/American solidarity
Stalin, Joseph (General Secretary of the Soviet Union 1922–52) 2, 6, 12
  death 227

influence on North Korea 10–11
relationship with China 11, 114, 122
relationship with India 36, 38–41
subversion 15, 141, 142
Suez crisis (1956) 1, 2, 282
surrender of North Korea 62, 77–9
Sweden 228, 237
Switzerland 228, 237

Tibet 80, 115
*Times, The* 175, 214
Tito, Josip Broz (President of Yugoslavia 1953–80) 115, 122, 207
truce commission 58, 196, 216, 227, 238, 266
Truman, Harry S. (U.S. President 1945–53)
  Acheson, Dean and 219 –20
  administration 2, 12, 51, 280, 281
  atomic bomb 4, 108, 125, 130
    *see also* atomic weapons
  Attlee, Clement and 108, 110, 114–17, 121–2, 124–5, 127, 141–3, 145, 160, 163, 281
  Churchill, Winston and 207
  communism and 3, 12, 114
  Formosa and 35, 124
    *see also* Formosa (Taiwan)
  MacArthur, Douglas and 55, 67, 78–9, 126, 182, 186
  Marshall Plan, the 117
  the press and 104

unification of Korea 10, 61, 62, 66, 69, 84, 97, 176, 262
United Nations
  charter 13, 21, 30, 35, 54, 61, 102, 135, 143, 154

Collective Measures Committee (CMC) 142, 161, 162
Command (UNC) 68, 70, 208, 209, 211, 212, 216, 228–38 (*passim*), 242, 269,
Joint Chiefs of Staff 14, 100, 183, 197, 217
General Assembly 21, 58, 61–2, 65, 66, 100, 119, 121, 135, 145, 152, 159, 161, 177, 218, 219, 222
Political Committee 65, 152, 220, 221
Security Council (UNSC) 11, 12, 13, 14, 15, 17, 19, 22, 23, 38, 61, 62, 71, 80–5 (*passim*), 94, 103, 118, 119
  communist China and 24, 29, 31, 36, 37, 39, 41, 85, 100
  USSR and 41, 60, 61, 94
six-power resolution 119–20
United States of America
  aggression 22–3, 33

USSR
  aggression 8, 15, 19, 31, 32, 37, 43, 227
  air force 98, 109
  change of leadership 227
  Soviet Bloc 144, 158, 161, 277

Vladivostok 63, 115

Wonsan 75, 80
world war II 1, 10, 14, 48, 123, 207, 270, 279
world war III 3, 12, 16, 20, 43, 85, 98–9, 100, 111, 137, 139, 189, 193, 195, 197, 200, 205, 207, 270, 276–7, 281–2

Yalu river (boundary) 57, 58, 79–81, 84, 86–8, 91, 95, 100, 172, 176, 184, 196, 198–9, 205–6, 228, 248, 266–7, 269, 271

EU authorised representative for GPSR:
Easy Access System Europe, Mustamäe tee 50,
10621 Tallinn, Estonia
gpsr.requests@easproject.com

www.ingramcontent.com/pod-product-compliance
Lightning Source LLC
Chambersburg PA
CBHW082105250426
43673CB00067B/1792